Science
and
Dissent
in
Post-Mao
China

Science
and
Dissent
in
Post-Mao
China

The Politics of Knowledge

H. LYMAN MILLER

University of Washington Press

Seattle and London

This publication was supported in part by the
Donald R. Ellegood International Publications Endowment.

Library of Congress Cataloging-in-Publication Data
Miller, H. Lyman.
  Science and dissent in post-Mao China: The politics of knowledge /
  H. Lyman Miller
        p.   cm.
  Includes bibliographical references and index.
  ISBN 0–295–97505–9 (alk. paper)
  ISBN 0–295–97532–6 (pbk.)
   1. Science—Social aspects—China. 2. Science—Political aspects—China. I. Title
Q175.52.C6M55   1996   95–24846
306.4′5′0951—dc20   CIP

To Avis, rarissima avis

Contents

Preface

It has often been observed that when we study foreign cultures, we look for people whom we believe to be like us. In the midst of the foreign we find the familiar. In the familiar we find what is universal, affirming the humanity in all of us, despite our differences. The process leading to the writing of this book was like that.

The idea for this book grew slowly out of a casual reading of an arcane Chinese academic journal. In 1980, out of curiosity about the obscure, I placed a subscription to the *Bulletin of Natural Dialectics* (Ziran bianzhengfa tongxun) after noticing an advertisement for it in the mainland Chinese daily newspaper for intellectuals, *Enlightenment Daily* (Guangming ribao). Expecting a fairly dry, jargon-filled publication carrying articles on such abstruse verities as the "law of the negation of the negation," I found instead a journal bristling with debate and contention over issues that riveted attention. There were attacks on Lysenko, Uri Geller, and Lenin. There were biographies praising Einstein, Bohr, Oppenheimer, Darwin, and Fang Lizhi as models of the scientific outlook on life. There were explorations of the implications of some of science's newest ideas, including aspects of quantum cosmology, chaos theory, and the origins of life. There were critical surveys of the contemporary theories of the philosophy and sociology of science, including the ideas of Thomas Kuhn, Paul Feyerabend, Robert Merton, and Larry Laudan.

Most of all, there were debates. There were debates over the relationship of mathematical truth to empirical truth, the philosophical meaning of the problem of quark confinement, the measurement problem in quantum mechanics, and the lessons of plate tectonics for innovation in science. There were debates over science and religion, science and history, and science and ethics. As Chinese scientists, philosophers, and historians of science attacked each other by name and with ill-concealed sarcasm, I waited eagerly for each new issue—only once every two months!—to arrive. Certainly, I thought, these were people I had to know more about.

What did these kinds of debates represent in the context of a still highly authoritarian communist political system? How could intellectual warfare on this scale go on openly within the confines of a political system in which all speech was politically relevant and in which all debate was potentially dangerous? What interests and institutions did the participants in these debates represent? Where did they come from, and how did they get where they were? In short, who were these people?

The answers turned out to be surprisingly relevant politically as the 1980s wore on. The *Bulletin of Natural Dialectics* was not only an arena of a breathtaking conflict of ideas in China's intellectual arena; it turned out to be also a seedbed of political agitation and, ultimately, dissidence. By the late 1980s the names of the intellectual antagonists I had followed since the beginning of the decade emerged as controversial figures in the political arena as well: Xu Liangying, Fang Lizhi, Jin Guantao, and others. I had found people espousing values and ideals that were recognizably those that I called my own.

This study draws heavily on articles carried in the *Bulletin of Natural Dialectics* and a small number of academic journals of similarly narrow focus, and sets the conclusions of that analysis in the broader context of changing political and social trends in the People's Republic of China in the 1980s based on a thorough reading of the PRC press. The validity of its conclusions rests predominantly, therefore, on the skill, or lack of it, with which this reading was done and, above all, on the assumptions made about the place of China's media in political processes. This study also draws on conversations, interviews, and correspondence with Chinese friends, scientists, and scholars familiar with the events described here. Among them, I would like to express my gratitude to Professors Fang Lizhi and Su Shaozhi and to Mr. Shen Tong for their agreeing to answer many of the questions I posed. I would also like to thank Professor Su for commenting on portions of this book and for providing me with manuscripts of two very helpful forthcoming articles. Regrettably, under the prevailing political circumstances in China, I cannot give many of the others who read and commented on parts of earlier versions of this book or answered questions related to it the proper credit they are due.

In seeking answers to the questions my reading of the *Bulletin of Natural Dialectics* provoked, I had help and encouragement from several colleagues and friends. Franz Michael supported the project from the beginning and, as always, provided challenging insights and inspiration. Mary Brown Bullock, Ralph Clough, John Edinger, Nina Halperin, Larry Owen, Robert Sutter, Richard Suttmeier, and Lynn White III all read an earlier version of the manuscript and made thoughtful comments on it and offered advice and encouragement. Clifford Edmunds, Joseph Fewsmith, Carol Hamrin, Terry Weidner, and I debated aspects of China's contemporary politics on a daily basis for years, and much of the political analysis that follows reflects the stimulation I received from their intelligence and insight, however much they may want to deny it. Scott Kennedy read and commented on a near-final draft and also pointed out recent articles by Gan Yang, Liu Qingfeng, and others in Jin Guantao's Hong Kong journal, *Twenty-first Century* (Ershiyi shiji). Professors Andrew Nathan of Columbia University and Ernest Henley of the University of Washington's Department of Physics provided comments as readers for the publisher that were of indispensable help in the manuscript's final revisions. Donald Ellegood and Lorri Hagman at the University of Washington Press have proven gracious and accommodating guides into the mysteries of publishing a book. To all of the above, I am deeply grateful.

Four others were particularly important. Richard Wich helped me gain the time and latitude to begin research, read and commented on the original manuscript, and supplied simultaneous encouragement and pressure to get it done. Tybel Litwin read the original version, offered extensive advice on how to rewrite it, and applied her brilliant critical and editorial skills to my prose, breaking it down from the quasi-Japanese syntax I instinctively use and saving me again and again from my own unfortunate turns of phrase. A. Doak Barnett read repeated drafts, served as a reader for the publisher, and supplied gracious and kind advice and encouragement throughout the work of completing the study. James H. Williams of the University of California at Berkeley and I have collaborated on complementary research for seven years, trading source materials and manuscripts, debating points of argument and issues of evidence, eating *jiaozi,* and commiserating over the loneliness of solitary work in a field of research that at times seemed irretrievably obscure. To all four, the usual "one divides into two" dictum applies: they deserve whatever credit this book earns; I own its faults and errors.

To Chapell and Rebecca Miller, I am grateful for their patient understanding about and interest in what in the world I have been up to over the last few years. Above all, I am grateful to Avis Boutell, whose unfailing courage in speaking the truth whenever she sees it amazes me at every turn.

Science
and
Dissent
in
Post-Mao
China

1/ *Introduction*
Science
and
Liberalism
in
Contemporary
China

The post-Mao years of reform in the People's Republic of China under the leadership of Deng Xiaoping (1978–present) saw the first public expressions of distinctly liberal political dissent by a small number of leading figures of China's scientific community. The scientific dissident best known outside China was the astrophysicist Fang Lizhi, whose standing in the international physics community made his liberal political views the focus of attention both inside China and abroad. But Fang was not a solitary voice of liberal politics among scientists nor the sole scientist among the broader spectrum of political dissidents who emerged in China in the late 1980s, before the demonstrations at Tiananmen Square. Though not as well known to foreign observers, several other scientists—such as Xu Liangying, Jin Guantao, and Li Xingmin—became critics of the post-Mao regime and were central to the emergence of dissent in China's science community.

Some of these scientists—mostly physicists and philosophers and historians of science—were once elite voices in the vanguard of Deng Xiaoping's reforms, but by the end of the 1980s they had become dissident critics of the Deng regime. Their path to dissent is explicable in terms of the political conflicts, social dislocations, and intellectual tensions brought about by the leadership's new ideological goals and policy approaches and by the response of the larger scientific community, and of Chinese society in general, to Deng's reforms. In part,

3

scientific dissent in China is intelligible in terms of the impact of the reforms on the social prestige, standing, and livelihood of scientists as a key group in politics and society.

More centrally, their dissent—and their liberalism in particular —was inspired by powerful antiauthoritarian norms and rationalist values, aroused both by new conflicts of authority with the communist regime and by a larger crisis of social and cultural identity that the Deng reforms provoked. The dissident scientists saw these norms and values as essential to the healthy conduct of science and to the future of Chinese society. And so, when they believed these norms and values to be threatened both within the scientific community and within society at large, they spoke out—sometimes, as both Fang Lizhi's and Xu Liang-ying's examples showed, with seemingly disproportionate force.

For scientists such as Fang and Xu, the antiauthoritarian norms of science translated easily into a classically liberal politics. The message these scientists carried into the larger political arena defended above all the sanctity and worth of individual autonomy and conscience above the claims of state and society. They advanced a pluralist politics rooted in appeals to reason. They called for all of the freedoms attendant to liberal politics—freedom of speech, assembly, the press, and so forth. Above all, they placed sovereignty squarely among China's citizenry, not in the state itself. The main conclusion of this book is that emergence of a renewed liberal voice in China's political arena in the 1980s was in significant part a natural extension of what some scientists believed to be the norms of healthy science into politics.

SCIENCE AND POLITICS:
SCIENTISM, TECHNOCRACY, AND LIBERALISM

In all contemporary societies, science as an intellectual and social enterprise has become a powerful political force.[1] One way in which science has had a significant political impact in modern China has been in its appropriation by intellectuals as a basis for comprehensive political ideologies. Because science has had spectacular success in explaining aspects of the natural world, it has laid claim to a uniquely reliable kind of knowledge and become a powerful source of ideas and values. Thus, science has acquired a sometimes intimidating prestige and authority, leading at times to attempts to extend its methods beyond its domain. This extension of science's theories and methods beyond the study of the natural world, for which they were developed, is called scientism.

The heyday of scientistic ideologies in China was the May Fourth period (1919–28), during which China's professional science community got its start and the collapse of the imperial state and Confucian ideology and the massive influx of Western ideas spawned competing visions of a reunified Chinese polity. Some of these visions were all-encompassing doctrines that took science as a core element of progress and national survival. One such scientistic ideology was Marxism-Leninism, a political doctrine that addressed Chinese concerns in several respects at once. It offered a critique of Western imperialism, at whose hands China had been repeatedly humiliated over the previous eighty years. It offered a revolutionary approach to social progress and national development that was apparently succeeding in Soviet Russia at a time when Western liberalism seemed to be failing in the West. And it offered a comprehensive philosophy that united both the human and natural worlds according to a single set of universally valid principles and laws that were consistent with science, satisfying a traditional cosmological impulse with a thoroughly modern totalism.

The scientistic claims of Marxism-Leninism were not the only appealing aspect that moved Chinese to support the Chinese Communist Party (CCP), and probably not the most persuasive element to most people. But such claims remained central to the Party's identity and legitimacy, both during the revolutionary years and after it came to power in 1949. In the post-Mao era Deng Xiaoping staked the legitimacy of his leadership and the ideological correctness of his reforms, in part, on his claim to have restored the "scientific" methods of Marxism-Leninism as the basis for the Party's doctrines and policies after years of calamitous error and deviation based on Mao Zedong's utopian fantasies. The pragmatic test of empirical "practice," Deng argued, guaranteed the success of the Party's policies and the future of socialist China because it restored Chinese Marxism-Leninism to its true methodological foundations, consistent with and, in fact, encompassing within itself the substance and methods of modern science. One way that science was important in the post-Mao era, therefore, was as the basis for an official scientism.

Science was important politically in post-Mao China in a second way. As the driving force behind technological enhancement of productivity and material abundance, science in the modern world has acquired an enormous command of the material, intellectual, and, ultimately, political resources of modern societies. Technocracy, it is often argued, has therefore been and will increasingly be an irresistible consequence of the scientific revolution in all modern and modernizing societies, including China.

As science's economic consequences multiply, the argument goes, professional scientific and technical elites acquire increasing social standing and political power. The necessities of administering an ever more complex society whose prosperity rests on the efficient management of an increasingly technology-dominated economy make scientific elites the natural and inevitable allies of state leadership and bureaucracy. As the skills and methods of these elites become essential to the advancement and management of not only science but also society itself, decisions are more and more shaped, if not decided altogether, by experts. As political issues increasingly must be resolved on grounds of technical expertise, scientists and technicians in the process become part of or displace altogether the political elites of their society. Though the political elite may be broadened by the incorporation of technical and managerial elites, and its decision-making processes may become more consultative, the consequences of such a technocratic transformation need not favor democratization. Insofar as political decisions are made on grounds of expertise rather than popular assent, the rationalization of decision-making and governing processes need not extend to the establishment and defense of political liberties. The more likely political evolution is, over the immediate term at least, toward a more consultative but still authoritarian politics of expertise, in which the authority of state and science are firmly interlocked. This appears clearly to have been the case in China under Deng Xiaoping, as the communist regime fostered collaboration with and co-optation of expert elites to promote systemic economic change and rapid growth while resisting democratizing change in favor of still authoritarian, technocratic politics.

Science has emerged as a political force in China in a third way— as a source of liberal political values—that in some circumstances is antithetical to both scientism and technocracy. As a way of knowing about the world, science—in all contemporary societies, China included—rests on a cluster of ideals, values, and norms, which often conflict with systems of belief and value held by other groups within the society in which a science community works. As clashes of ideals and values among scientists, political elites, and other social groups within the larger society, such conflicts are inherently political and, in the broadest sense of the term, ideological.

Science frequently means different things to different people. Though broadly unanimous with respect to the goals and methods of science, scientists themselves often understand in different ways the science they practice, what science requires, and what value it offers their surrounding society. They may disagree about the unity or diversity of the methods they employ, the relationship of their individual disciplines to the body of scientific disciplines in general, the interpretation of their discipline's prevailing theories, or the significance of their science for society in general. The mechanism for refereeing such disputes is inherently pluralist, not authoritarian. Opinion becomes scientific knowledge within the scientific community upon acceptance by the "invisible college" among credentialed scientists through the process of publicizing findings, conclusions, and new lines of argument in the community's journals, seminars, and meetings.

Those not directly engaged in the conduct of science frequently have strong beliefs about science and its significance. For some, the progress of science is linked inextricably to the progress of humanity itself. Those who expound such scientistic views believe that the ideals, theoretical conclusions, and technological consequences of science have brought, and promise yet to bring, enormous benefit to society, both in terms of material abundance and cultural value. For them, the scientific outlook and its presumed method offer models and programs for the improvement of society itself, from the clockwork scheme of the Laplacian universe of the eighteenth century to the organic models of nineteenth-century social Darwinism, to the effort of contemporary quantitative social scientists to adapt the format of mathematical proof and to emulate the notation of mathematical physics in the human sciences.

For others, science embodies the core utilitarian values of an exploitative modernizing enterprise whose benefits must be weighed against the destruction it has also seemed to bring. They believe that science has been a mixed blessing, both materially, in the catastrophic power of modern warfare and in the defilement of the environment, and spiritually, in the dehumanizing mechanisms of modern organization and production and in the ruthless obliteration of values that have traditionally given lives meaning.

For others still, science is a central component in the ultimately humanistic project of enhancing the meaning of human life, locating humanity's place in the larger natural world. For such people, the expansion of scientific knowledge is therefore a liberating enterprise, displacing ignorance and superstition with the enlightening force of critical reason.

Scientific communities are not internally monolithic, and there is no reason to expect that they will act uniformly in their relationships with other groups. This is especially true with respect to their relationships with political elites. Often people holding very different outlooks regarding science—scientists and nonscientists alike—coexist within a given society, though they may tolerate each other uneasily because the issues that divide them are fundamental, never hidden completely from view. When they do confront one another, the conflicts are often spectacular, sometimes revealing themselves as profound crises of cultural and social values and illuminating deep social rifts. Confrontations between rationalism and romanticism, between Enlightenment modernism and late industrial postmodernism, between theories of evolution or cosmology and traditional religious dogmas of special creation all are conflicts over the values of modern society in which science has played an important part.

Because such confrontations reflect the competing visions, ambitions, anxieties and fears, and frustrations of different social groups, they are at bottom ideological and political. Though conflicts within the scientific community are mediated through the pluralist mechanism of the "invisible college," no parallel mechanisms need exist in the larger social and political arena. So in such confrontations, participants may resort to public organizations and informal associations for the advocacy of their positions. They may also seek legal protection for the public expression of ideas. In short, conflicts over scientific ideas and, especially, over the relevance of the values and methods of science beyond itself contribute to the assertion of a public sphere of political discourse and the erection of the institutions of civil society.[2] Such pressures favor political pluralism and liberal politics and counter the totalizing tendencies of scientism and the authoritarian consequences of technocracy. This has been the case, this study argues, in post-Mao China.

Scientism in modern Chinese intellectual history has already received considerable scholarly attention. Several scholars have convincingly illuminated the scientistic elements in the ideas of a broad array of Chinese thinkers since the late nineteenth century, including not only the founding fathers of Chinese Marxism, but also traditional Confucian reformers, liberals, anarchists, and neotraditionalists. Many observers of contemporary China have also been quick to note the essentially scientistic basis of Deng Xiaoping's restoration of Party orthodoxy stressing "practice" as the final criterion of policy correctness.

The technocratic impact of science has also received considerable attention in the study of communist systems. In such studies, assessments of the precise nature and scope of the impact vary, but evaluations of the general direction of political change do not. As ruling communist elites shift from legitimacy based on their charismatic mission of recasting the class structure of their societies ("waging revolution") to legitimacy based on performance on behalf of the society as a whole ("socialist construction" and "developing the forces of production"), the influence of professional and expert elites rises correspondingly. The co-optation of scientists, technicians, and other professional experts by a ruling Communist Party (or, in other instances, even the displacement of Party cadres by such elites) has the liberalizing effect of diluting the totalitarian ambitions of revolutionary Marxism-Leninism in favor of more consultative, procedurally routinized approaches needed to administer the increasingly complex societies they rule.

Such studies disagree over the degree to which Party elites co-opt or are displaced by professional elites, the degree of consequent pluralization of the political system, and the degree to which the Party's original social mission is diluted. Most argue, nevertheless, that the process of postrevolutionary liberalization is likely to move the political system from an all-encompassing revolutionary totalitarianism toward some form of authoritarianism but to stop short of full-scale democratization. The routinization of authority along legal-rational lines, such arguments suggest, need not progress so far as to include enforced legal protections for public debate of political issues.[3]

The liberalizing impact of scientific ideas on social and cultural values, and so on politics, in communist societies, and especially in China, has received less attention. This neglect is natural in view of the difficulties in discerning alternative viewpoints on such sensitive issues in the constrained political discourse of the state-controlled media of communist systems. When conflicts and tensions over values and ideas reach a point of general crisis, however, pressures for their expression force them into view even within the state-dominated arenas of discourse. During such episodes, conflicts become visible with sufficient clarity to allow us to identify their protagonists, analyze their dynamics, and follow their evolution.

The post-Mao period of reform under the leadership of Deng Xiaoping was such a period of crisis. As other scholars have pointed out, the Chinese Communist Party under Deng abandoned the messianic social revolutionary mission that characterized communism under Mao in favor of a postrevolutionary emphasis on performance. After the watershed Third Plenum of the Eleventh Central Committee in December 1978, the Party staked its future firmly on its ability to promote economic development and prosperity. In step with this strategic shift in Party mission, the standing and influence of professional and technical elites has grown. Emphasizing the authority of organizational procedure and routine in Party and state policy and stressing administrative competence and expertise in cadre recruitment, Deng reshaped the Party along recognizably technocratic lines. Naturally enough, those whose outlooks and careers were invested in the previous revolutionary ethos strongly resisted these efforts, and many of the intra-Party conflicts of the Deng period are intelligible in terms of the tensions generated by this transition.[4]

Paralleling the fragmenting effects of the reforms on the Party's cadre elite, the Deng reforms had a divisive impact on China's science community. As in other societies, China's science community is not a monolith, and the Deng reforms brought to the surface and widened rifts among Chinese scientists and technicians that may have been submerged under the long years of Maoist suppression. As the reforms progressed in the 1980s they affected sectors of the scientific community differently, elevating some in social, material, and political standing and alienating others.

At the same time, Deng's limited critique of Maoism and his explicit acknowledgment that the capitalist world, including the Pacific Rim states on China's periphery, was in the midst of an accelerating scientific and technological revolution triggered a broader questioning of China's past and future under communist leadership. In this "crisis of confidence" (*xinren weiji*) in Chinese socialism, debates over issues of national identity and purpose blossomed into a spectacular and heated "culture fever" (*wenhua re*).

In a context of sweeping technocratic reforms that cut unevenly across China's scientific community in the 1980s, and in the midst of cultural crisis of general scope, many scientists saw an uncertain future for themselves and their country. At the beginning of the Deng reforms, science was heralded as the key element in China's progress out of Maoist obscurantism and toward a modern future, and scientific intellectuals were called the vanguard of this advance, but by the late 1980s many scientists found their social standing declining catastrophically and the rationalist foundations of science under attack. Ironically, therefore, one important, unanticipated effect of the Deng regime's technocratic reforms and the crisis of values it spawned was political activism and agitation by some scientists and, ultimately, scientific dissidence among a few. Significantly, this activism and dissidence were of a distinctly liberal political temper.

Science was important in the post-Mao era, therefore, not only as a basis for the Deng regime's official scientism and for its technocratic approach to modernization, but also an important source of liberal values. The liberal political views of the dissident scientists studied in this book were, perhaps, not typical of the majority of their peers in China's science community in the 1980s. Given the prevailing circumstances in China at that time, it is difficult for us to know what the predominating political viewpoint of Chinese scientists was in the 1980s. In view of the fragmenting effect of the Deng regime's science reforms on the science community, it seems likely that there was no single, truly representative view. Nor is it the argument of this study that a democratic political system is essential for the conduct of professional science. It is the contention of this study, however, that *some* Chinese scientists believed that to be the case, and that this belief was the impetus for their extraversion of the antiauthoritarian norms of science into public life and was the basis of their political liberalism.

The liberal values and ideals the scientist dissidents espoused, emphasizing civil liberties and the defense of individual rights and conscience, were consonant with what they believed to be the norms of their scientific profession. But they were also consonant with the values of liberal intellectuals from the social science disciplines and humanities, whose values and ideals derived from other directions. The 1980s spawned a sizable community of intellectuals from the social sciences and humanities who asserted a new-found critical distance from the communist state and who helped to establish a new, alternative public discourse (though often couched in Marxist-Leninist jargon) that transcended and even subverted the authoritative lines of the Communist Party. Many of these critical intellectuals from the social sciences and humanities espoused ideas at the heart of classical liberalism. On the basis of these ideas, the natural scientists studied here and the social sciences and humanities intellectuals found common ground. Together, they participated in and shaped the revival of a genuine political liberalism in China, a political philosophy that had taken root in the May Fourth era but had been crushed in the trials of war and revolution thereafter.

But there were many pathways to political liberalism in the 1980s, and the natural scientists arrived at theirs from different sources and along a different route than their peers in the social sciences and humanities. In some ways, the liberalism of the natural scientists focused more sharply on human rights and the integrity and worth of the individual conscience. This focus may make theirs a more enduring liberal critique in the evolution of contemporary Chinese politics. Locating the liberal scientists along the spectrum of critical and dissident intellectuals and isolating what made them unique and distinctive will help to overcome the presumptions of monolithic outlook with which dissent in post-Mao China is sometimes viewed.

1989: SCIENTIFIC DISSENT AND TIANANMEN

The thrust of the liberal scientists' political message and the broader associations they had established outside the scientific community may be seen in what are perhaps the most broadly familiar instances of their political activism. These are the series of open letters they authored or cosigned with prominent figures from other intellectual fields preceding the massive popular demonstrations in Beijing's Tiananmen Square and in other Chinese cities in the spring of 1989. Though the scientists' expressions of intellectual dissent were dwarfed by the sheer scale of hundreds of thousands of people demonstrating in the center of Beijing and other cities and by the drama of their brutal suppression, the open letters were significant both as a spark for the larger protests at Tiananmen and elsewhere and as a symptom of deep rifts among China's social, professional, and political elites.

The intellectual protests began on 6 January 1989 with an open letter to China's paramount leader Deng Xiaoping by Fang Lizhi, the astrophysicist who, since his expulsion from the Party in January 1987, had become the foremost international symbol of Chinese dissent— "China's Sakharov." Fang's open letter called on Deng to declare a general amnesty for political prisoners, including Wei Jingsheng, the first of the dissidents formally convicted as a result of the party's crushing of the 1978–79 Democracy Wall movement.[5]

Fang's letter was followed on 13 February by another open letter to the CCP Central Committee and the National People's Congress (NPC) Standing Committee. The letter, expressing support for Fang Lizhi's, was signed by thirty-three intellectuals, drawn mostly from China's literary and artistic circles, but also from the ranks of prominent social scientists. The latter included Su Shaozhi (former director of and then researcher at the Institute of Marxism-Leninism–Mao Zedong Thought under the Chinese Academy of Social Sciences [CASS]) and Wang Ruoshui (the philosopher who was removed from his position as deputy editor of the Party newspaper *People's Daily* [Renmin ribao] as a result of the 1983 criticism of "spiritual pollution").[6]

On 26 February—during U.S. president George Bush's visit to Beijing—a third open letter emerged, this time addressed to Zhao Ziyang, Wan Li, and Li Peng in their roles as foremost leaders over the CCP Central Committee, NPC Standing Committee, and State Council, respectively. Couched in respectful tones, this letter called on the Party and government to press ahead with political reforms that provide "realistic guarantees" of basic freedoms, to release all those undergoing "labor reform" for "ideological problems," to prevent the recurrence of "historical tragedies in which people have been punished for expressing views or publishing articles holding different political views," and to increase support for science and education and improve conditions for intellectuals. This letter was signed by forty-two intellectuals, including twenty-seven natural scientists, thirteen social scientists, and two writers.[7]

Finally, a last open letter emerged from a meeting on 14 March at Beijing's Qianmen Hotel, reportedly suppressed by the Public Security Bureau, called to launch a new independent journal, *The Thinker* (Sixiangjia). The letter was addressed to an impending session of the NPC and, according to Hong Kong media accounts, was sent to the editorial boards of *People's Daily* and *Enlightenment Daily* for publication. It was signed by forty-three intellectuals, including the controversial political scientist Yan Jiaqi and several other CASS figures, as well as *Enlightenment Daily* reporter Dai Qing.[8]

The last two open letters were posted on the campuses of Beijing University and other colleges in the capital on 8 and 24 March respectively.[9] Their signers had already achieved prominence as organizers of or participants in the various "democracy salons" (minzhu shalong) that sprang up to debate public issues over the preceding months, in reaction to a perceived crisis of reform.

The letters were also remarkable because they were the first expressions of open, organized intellectual dissidence against the CCP regime since protests during the Hundred Flowers movement of 1956–57. A closer look at the signers of the letters will make clear the difference between these manifestations of dissent and previous episodes of intellectual deviation and dissidence, including the protestations of the Hundred Flowers period.

The signers included several intellectuals whose earlier political attitudes and activities had already put them beyond—or at best on the margins of—political acceptability to the regime. Fang Lizhi and Wang Ruoshui, and in some measure Yan Jiaqi and Su Shaozhi, for example, had already been ostracized during the criticism of "spiritual pollution" in 1983 or of "bourgeois liberalization" in 1987. Several Chinese literary and artistic figures who had suffered similar treatment were also among the signers. The fact that these people were already beyond the pale detracts in no way from the courageousness of their act, but it helps to illuminate their willingness to endorse an open expression of dissent.

What was remarkable was the number of prominent natural and social scientists in good standing in the regime's intellectual establishment who joined the ranks of the outcast intellectuals in signing the letters. The open letter of 16 February, for example, included prominent CASS philosophers Zhang Dainian and Li Zehou and historians Pang Pu and Bao Zunxin. The signers of the 26 February letter included such elite figures as Xu Liangying, physicist, researcher at the Chinese Academy of Sciences (CAS) Institute of the History of Natural Science, and translator of Einstein's works into Chinese; Wang Ganchang, a senior physicist and major figure in the development of China's first nuclear weapons; Li Honglin, philosopher and president of the Fujian Academy of Social Sciences; Qian Linzhao, former vice president of the prestigious China Science and Technology University; and Ye Duzheng, climate scientist and retired vice president of the CAS. Several of them were members of the prestigious Academic Board of the CAS. More than half were members of the Chinese Communist Party.[10]

These people cannot be dismissed as isolated malcontents on the fringes of China's intellectual community. They were all members of the privileged professional and academic elite, with positions of power and influence at the top of China's scientific hierarchy. Most had been in the front ranks of Dengist reform. Li Honglin, for example, was one of the most forceful advocates of ideological and political change in the critical early years of reform in the late 1970s. Xu Liangying was a frontline spokesman in that period for restoration of China's scientific establishment after two decades of Maoist policies.

For some elite intellectuals the leap from tolerated diversity of opinion within authorized, official channels to expression of dissent in open, unauthorized forums was shorter than for others. Artists and writers have always found their occupations politically hazardous, given the Party's intense, unwavering scrutiny of their activities. Nor is it surprising that the signers included a number of social scientists, given the uncertain standing their disciplines have always had in communist political systems. Chinese social scientists had routinely taken part in ongoing political conflicts and policy debates over the preceding decade. Occasionally, some who took controversial positions had found themselves stranded as the perimeter of acceptable opinion narrowed in the closing stages of such debates and conflicts. So the participation of a few such outcast social scientists was a predictable consequence of the tight linkage between the social sciences and the up-and-down course of political life in China.

Even so, the number of social scientists involved was noteworthy. There had been only occasional instances during the Deng period in which social scientists found themselves stranded as victims of changes in the larger political and policy context. Social science dissent was more normally an intraestablishment affair, in which intellectuals who lost in a political debate were exiled for long periods from the political arena and sometimes, though by no means always, from the academic limelight.

Even discounting Fang Lizhi, the participation of natural scientists was a phenomenon of an altogether different order. Science was at the heart of the policies of the Deng period, and scientists were among their most important beneficiaries. This episode therefore prompts fundamental questions. What accounts for the participation not only of a Fang Lizhi but also of a significant number of elite natural scientists in open dissidence? Scientists and those involved in the interpretation of science—historians and philosophers of science—seemed to have little to gain in breaking with a regime that made the rapid modernization of science and technology a cornerstone of its entire reform. It is understandable that they would engage in debate over the direction of overall science and technology policy, in battles for allocation of state resources, and in competition for higher positions of power within the scientific and political bureaucracies. But what motivated their participation in open dissent over issues of political principle? What was the common ground they shared with the social scientists and the writers and artists who also signed the open letters? And, most fundamentally of all, why did they espouse political liberalism?

THE ROOTS OF SCIENTIFIC DISSIDENCE

The path of the elite scientists and scientific intellectuals was a tortuous one that tells much about the complex political dynamics and contradictory purposes of the reforms of the Deng Xiaoping years. Analysis of the place of science and the scientific community in the reforms, the roles scientists were called upon to play, and the conduct of science within the Chinese political system reveals that the scientific community has been neither a monolithic nor a politically neutral actor in the post-Mao period. In the divergent responses of scientists as a social group and in the force of scientific ideas and ideals in the political arena in China, science had a far more complex and powerful impact than is often appreciated.

This book follows the path of this small group of scientific intellectuals along their course toward open, liberal dissent through the reform years. It is not a study of Chinese science per se, nor is it an examination of the politics of science in China in the usual, broad sense, though some aspects of that topic will be addressed. It is a study of the response of a small group of influential scientific intellectuals—theoretical physicists, philosophers of science, and historians of science—to the shifting political circumstances, social fortunes, and cultural crisis of the years of Dengist reform. In addition to exploring the main theme concerning the linkage between science and liberalism, it reaches three specific, subsidiary conclusions about the causes and dynamics of the emergence of liberal scientific dissent and the Party's reaction to it.

First, *scientific dissidence was an unintended but nevertheless natural consequence of Dengist reform.* As the reforms unfolded in the late 1970s and 1980s, not all scientists remained enthusiastic about the utilitarian orientation of the policies of Deng Xiaoping, who sought to harness China's scientific community to the single-minded pursuit of rapid national development. Deng and the political leadership attacked the baleful effects of Maoist political intrusions into science, but the utilitarian orientation of their reforms ultimately justified continued Party domination over science and even Marxist-Leninist hegemony over the interpretation of science's theories and conclusions.

Most scientists saw themselves as the major beneficiaries of the reforms at the outset. Deng hailed science and technology as the decisive factors in modern economic production and national strength, and so heralded scientists as the key intellectual force in China's development and national destiny. Many scientists therefore enthusiastically supported and sought to shape the reform program. As the reforms proceeded, however, they affected the fortunes of scientists and technicians unevenly. Many scientists and technicians, mainly in the applied science and technical sectors, got ahead, while others, mainly in the theoretical and basic research sector, were left behind. The members of the latter group—who once were the rising stars of reform—saw their livelihoods and social standing declining as a result of the reforms' very success in reorienting China's science community.

Their disillusionment was compounded by the effects of the official critique of Mao Zedong that accompanied the reforms. While the critique was intended to enhance the legitimacy of the communist regime and restore confidence in its Marxist-Leninist foundations, it unleashed a broader critical examination of the entire system and its appropriateness in China. In the ensuing "culture fever" a host of diverse cultural and intellectual viewpoints arose that threatened to throw scientific rationalism out with the scientistic claims of Marxism. Disillusionment with and antagonism toward Marxism-Leninism threatened confidence in science itself. By the late 1980s the Dengist reforms had made some scientific intellectuals a stranded and alienated elite.

The second conclusion regarding the emergence of scientist dissidence is that *the dissidence of some scientists in 1989 was more than a reaction to the renewal of political intrusions into science and the social pressures they faced as a result of Dengist reform; it also reflected their projection of the ideals and norms of the scientific community outward into the larger political and social arena.* In that arena the scientists' appeals to these norms evoked powerful echoes of political traditions from China's May Fourth period linking science and democracy.

Despite the highly stratified nature of scientific communities, science professes an ethos or ideology that is inherently antiauthoritarian. In co-opting science and its ideals in service of the reforms, the Deng leadership opened the way for scientists to judge the regime itself according to those ideals. At the same time, the regime's legitimacy and authority was tied explicitly to its claim to a scientific methodology and body of principles proven in practice; hence the Party leadership could not but be extremely sensitive to changes in interpretation of science's findings about the natural world. Issues of scientific judgment seemingly remote from political concern had the potential to rapidly become controversies about the correctness of prevailing Marxist principles. Out of such controversies emerged clashes over who was competent to judge the validity of scientific arguments, over the relationship between science and Marxism, and, ultimately, over the relationship between knowledge and power. When viewed in the context of these debates and clashes, Party theoreticians and some members of China's scientific community more closely resembled communities in conflict—each with a body of ideals and expectations that at first overlapped but increasingly were at fundamental odds—than collaborators in China's modernization enterprise.

The economic and social plight of the scientific intellectuals involved in these debates only exacerbated their conflicts over the conclusions of science and the implications of those conclusions for Marxist-Leninist doctrine. The challenges to scientific rationalism emerging in the "culture fever" debates of the 1980s were further cause for alarm. All of these issues and concerns together resulted in a politicization of science in the reform period and impelled some scientists to press for fundamental reform in China's scientific and, ultimately, political system. A stranded and alienated elite was thus also a radicalized elite.

In the eyes of these liberal scientists, the establishment and maintenance of autonomy for the scientific community was the essential key to the prosperity of science, both for the sake of China's survival in a rapidly changing world and for the sake of science itself. In demanding civil protections for the autonomy of science, these scientists displayed an evangelical readiness to carry the norms and ideals of science into society and politics. Just as the scientific community operates according to antiauthoritarian norms of free debate, they believed, so science prospers in an external environment that similarly tolerates pluralism and dissent. Intellectual pluralism was intimately connected to political pluralism.

In calling for political guarantees against a recurrence of Party intrusions into science, for arenas of public debate in which science could be defended against antirationalist intellectual trends, and for freedom from the hegemonic associations of science with Marxism-Leninism, scientific liberals such as Fang Lizhi and Xu Liangying found common ground with the critical and humanistic intellectuals from the social sciences, literature, and the arts. All of them wanted autonomous institutions and spheres of legitimate discourse in which to debate political issues of common concern, both for the health of their intellectual and artistic communities and for the public good.

Insofar as intellectual and political pluralism were inextricably linked in the eyes of these intellectuals, the slogan linking "science and democracy" from the May Fourth era—a time of vigorous cultural redefinition amid major mass movements and protests—had concrete meaning in the context of the 1980s reforms. The liberal scientist dissidents were acutely aware of this May Fourth tradition. Some of them, in fact, were only a generation younger than the main protagonists of that era and directly inherited their concerns. Deng Xiaoping and the elder leaders of the reform period were products of the same cluster of generations, and they also recalled the May Fourth era vividly, though they interpreted its legacy differently.

The clashes over science between the Party and the dissident scientists of the 1980s replayed again the tensions between national salvation and individual enlightenment that scholars of the May Fourth era had confronted in the 1920s.[11] In their open letters of 1989 these scientists—and the social-science intellectuals, writers, and artists aligned with them—resurrected the May Fourth era effort to establish a critical role for intellectuals against the suffocating constraints of state and society, an effort that was smothered after the May Fourth period but never altogether forgotten. In the context of the post-Mao period—with the growing stature and authority of science, the questioning of the communist system and of China's long past unleashed by the Deng regime's critique of Maoist excesses, and the emergence of scientific dissidence—the May Fourth era slogan linking "science and democracy" turned out to be a virulently contagious one.

The third subsidiary conclusion is that *the demands of some scientists for intellectual pluralism and autonomy for science raised fundamental problems of legitimacy for the regime,* threatening to unravel the ideological foundations of both Deng's platform for reform and the rationale of the Marxist-Leninist state. When the scientists' demands for intellectual pluralism and autonomy were translated into political demands, scientist activism and dissidence became an intolerable threat and the regime acted to suppress it.

The Party faced a dilemma with regard to pressures from those in the scientific community who eventually emerged as dissidents. It had a high political stake in maintaining Marxism-Leninism's intellectual integrity and congruence with science, on the one hand, and in ensuring the productive participation of Chinese scientists in China's modernization, on the other. In denying a unified structure of knowledge under the hegemony of dialectical materialist philosophy, the scientists were rejecting not only the methodological relevance of Marxism's guiding role, but also the authority of the Party to interpret its own doctrines. According to the scientists' logic, if Marxism-Leninism was truly a science, as the Party insisted, it should be liable to criticism according to the norms and processes of science in general. The true priesthood holding exclusive authority to interpret the validity of Marxism-Leninism's conclusions—and so the arbiters of the state's legitimacy—was not the Party's own theoreticians, but rather the "invisible college" of the scientific community.

In facing this dilemma, the Party sought through much of the reform period to steer a middle course. It attempted to accommodate the conclusions of modern science by introducing major revisions in some of Marxism-Leninism's philosophical tenets, without surrendering the prerogatives of doctrinal interpretation to the scientists altogether. At the same time, it attempted to show that Marxism's most basic philosophical principles continued to provide the key to the correct interpretation of science, without laying itself open to renewed charges of political intrusion into the domain of science and provoking massive scientific disaffection from the regime's modernization priorities.

This middle course was extremely difficult to maintain. The twentieth century's scientific revolutions have wrought far-reaching revisions in scientific understanding. Marxism-Leninism was formulated originally on the basis of nineteenth-century science, and the Chinese version of it was updated not much beyond Lenin. So the chasm between philosophical doctrine and scientific theory was wide. Though the ideas on both sides may not have been ultimately irreconcilable, the clashing ideals of Party and science were, given the zealous commitment of some Chinese scientists to an ethos of science abused in previous decades of communist rule. As the limits of accommodation were reached, scientific dissent was one of the natural consequences, and Party suppression was another.

IMPLICATIONS

The conclusions of this book raise two broad implications. The first regards historical perspective. The main conclusion—that the scientific dissidents espoused a strong form of liberal political philosophy that grew out of the norms of their profession—differs from some previous interpretations of the views of scientific dissidents such as Fang Lizhi. Such interpretations have seen these dissidents as expressing essentially elitist, pseudodemocratic views that recapitulate the mediating political roles of intellectual elites in traditional China. According to such views, the scientific dissidents, like other contemporary Chinese intellectuals, have been unable to transcend the intimate symbiosis of knowledge and power, of culture and politics, that gave the traditional scholar-gentry political standing in China's imperial bureaucracy and social status in traditional society. According to such interpretations, the dissidents' contemporary reprise of traditional roles inhibited their acquiring critical distance and independence from the political authority they at once served and legitimated. Only when they were themselves directly oppressed by the communist state—in the late 1980s—did they begin to espouse the civil libertarian ideals of true democracy.[12]

This interpretation rests implicitly on a framework for understanding modern Chinese history that has long been conventional—the "stimulus and response" framework. By this approach, China's historical evolution proceeded mainly within its "great tradition" until the fateful encounter with Western military and commercial power in the nineteenth century. Thereafter, China "responded" to the Western "stimulus," modernizing in revolutionary ways that at the same time showed telltale traces of persisting underlying tradition.[13]

Impetus for this approach to China's past derived greatly from the need to understand the revolutionary present—especially the communist revolution of 1949. On the one hand, interpreters using this approach sought to understand why revolution occurred, and ultimately why it was necessary and even inevitable, given the pattern of the recent past. For example, the Taiping Rebellion of the 1850s, seen as a precursor of communist-led peasant rebels of the 1930s and 1940s, showed that antitraditional agrarian revolution was at hand. The reforms of the Tongzhi period (1862-75) showed that China's Confucian traditions could not accommodate the demands of modernization even under the most favorable conditions. The Nationalist regime's embrace of Confucian morality in the 1930s only demonstrated its reactionary, and so moribund, status.

On the other hand, interpreters also sought to explain the peculiarities of the communist regime in light of Chinese traditions. Party chairman Mao Zedong ruled China and connived at politics in a manner thought to resemble the great emperors of China's past, presiding from an unchallengeable position over a court of bureaucratic functionaries. Chinese communism—in particular, Mao Zedong Thought— diverged from Marxism-Leninism in crucial ways that harmonized with traditional cultural and intellectual values, and so amounted to Marxism in a Confucian mold. Intellectuals found in their mediating roles in communist politics a way to recoup the traditional linkage between knowledge and power that their predecessors lost when the imperial system collapsed in 1911 (or perhaps when the traditional examination system was abolished in 1905). From the perspective of this framework, liberalism failed to flourish in China because the social and cultural soil in which its seeds were sown was inhospitable and because its individualistic ideals were unsatisfying to intellectuals specifically and to a populace at large whose cultural values aligned along collectivist and authoritarian lines. The Chinese revolution, in sum, was no revolution at all.[14]

From this conventional historical perspective, the emergence of liberal dissent in post-Mao China seems a stark anomaly. This seems all the more so given the fact (to be discussed in detail later) that the liberalism of the science dissidents was homegrown and derived from the social experience of the scientists, without direct experience of liberalism in the West, in contrast to the imported liberalism of intellectuals of the May Fourth era such as Hu Shi (Hu Shih) and Ding Wenjiang (Ting Wen-chiang, V. K. Ting). What social and political evolution in China explains such a phenomenon, in an environment presumably still so hostile to it?

The liberalism of the scientist dissidents comports more easily with a more dynamic picture of China's long-term social history and the evolution of its political culture that has begun to emerge in Western scholarship in recent years.[15] In contrast to the "stimulus and response" framework, the underlying premise of this new, still-sketchy picture is that China has indeed undergone and is undergoing a true revolution. The roots of this revolution are in social and economic changes that began in the sixteenth century and accelerated through the unprecedented demographic explosion of the eighteenth century. By the nineteenth century these accumulating trends presented the imperial state with challenges of governance that no previous dynastic regime had had to face. In conjunction with the dilemmas of security and cultural confrontation presented by the West, these trends irretrievably altered the social foundations of imperial rule. New social elites saw their political futures no longer in the traditional imperial system but in establishing new forms of governance both locally and at the center. The recentralizing propensities of first the Nationalist and then the Communist governments in this century co-opted new forms of local state-building and elite participation that had accelerated since the 1860s. Both regimes, but especially the Communists, pressed central authority to new, unprecedented levels over a rapidly changing society composed of new groups and classes and espousing diverse ideals and ideologies.

From this longer perspective on the Chinese revolution, the emergence in the 1980s of liberal dissidence among some scientists reflected in part the assertion of autonomy by a significant—and by now solidly established—professional community after a difficult and halting start. Scientists were a new social group at the beginning of this century. They struggled to establish their community in the 1910s and 1920s in a society where traditional attitudes and values still presented powerful obstacles to the modernity in outlook congenial to science. And so in this insecure environment, science found a helpful ally in the scientism espoused by intellectuals of the day, most of whom had no background in science. Even some of the more clearly liberal among these pioneering scientists, such as Ding Wenjiang, espoused scientistic ideas themselves.

By the 1980s the social and political context had changed. China now had a solidly established scientific community, thanks in no small part to the priority that both the Nationalist and Communist regimes attached to science and technology, however much each regime skewed science's development to its own purposes. The place of science in China was far more secure, and so scientism was no longer a useful ally. Liberally inclined scientists such as Xu Liangying and Fang Lizhi, in fact, identified scientism with the inhumanities and extremist intrusions into science of the Maoist years.

In other societies in which scientific communities have taken firm root, moreover, scientism is the natural ally of technocracy and an instrumental view of the value of science; it is not usually the benefactor of political liberalism and the liberal view of science as worthwhile for its own sake.[16] In China in the 1980s, in step with this, some scientists, such as Xu and Fang, saw scientism aligned with the technocratic and instrumentalist bent of the Deng regime. In their eyes, scientism and technocracy, as manifested in the regime's policies and its ideological allies, depleted the proper context for healthy science. For them, liberalism was the natural and necessary political context both for science as an autonomous professional activity governed by its own internal norms and for the healthy political life of the society in which the community of scientists lived and worked.

The significance of this linkage by some contemporary scientists of healthy science to liberalism in the political arena is that it underscores that China has indeed been undergoing for a long time, and continues to undergo now, a modern revolution. This revolution, furthermore, is producing within Chinese society indigenous constituencies for unmistakably genuine liberal political ideas. Amid the tide of swirling political outlooks and sentiments in present-day, post-Marxist China, liberal ideas have taken firm root and grown naturally according to the internal social norms of at least one social community of major significance to the nation's future. This conclusion invites us to inquire whether many of China's contemporary political and social trends are better understood through a framework of evolving modernity rather than the framework of persisting tradition that is more frequently applied.

The second implication raised by the conclusions of this book is philosophical and generalizes from China's experience in the longer historical perspective just described. The material presented here underscores the ambiguous political import of scientific knowledge. On one hand, science's utility to society in fostering technology—the "external" orientation of science—abets technocracy and scientistic ideas and ideologies. Marxism-Leninism's vision of governance by "engineers of society"—experts who advance society's progress and prosperity by applying the laws of history and nature that their dialectical materialist philosophy illuminates—is only an extreme expression of a broader Western technocratic tradition in political philosophy. On the other hand, the pursuit of scientific knowledge "for its own sake"—the "internal" orientation of science among scientists—promotes antiauthoritarian norms among the "invisible college" of scientists that align most easily with the pluralist norms of liberal politics.

The tension between these contradictory impulses in the politics of scientific knowledge need not resolve itself in favor of either direction. Cursory reflection on the broad experience of other societies—including formerly communist states such as the Soviet Union—suggests that the tension is never finally resolved. (A thorough examination of this proposition would require a breadth of analysis well beyond the purposes of this book.) The pursuit of scientific knowledge, however purist the ideals of the scientist, inevitably engenders efforts to apply its findings and administrative policies and investment intended to promote their application. Indeed, the boundaries between pure or academic science on one hand and applied science, research and development, and technology on the other have become increasingly blurred and meaningless in contemporary times. Yet science lives by an internal, antiauthoritarian ethic and ultimately humanistic mission that sees value in understanding nature for its own sake. Maintaining that ethic is, in the minds of some scientists, essential to their calling. China's experience in the 1980s is one clear example of this dynamic tension.

THE APPROACH OF THIS BOOK

The succeeding chapters explore in detail the various political, social, and intellectual factors that led to the emergence of scientific dissidence in post-Mao China. Chapters 2 and 3 are contextual, intended to illuminate the political and professional contexts that spurred scientific dissent to emerge. Chapter 2 provides a broad analysis of the transformation of official Marxist-Leninist ideology and policy goals brought about by the reform leadership led by Deng Xiaoping since the late 1970s. It views this ideological and policy transformation as an effort to reintegrate a fractured Chinese political community on foundations that would facilitate rapid modernization for the sake of national survival and prosperity over the long term. It looks in general terms at the place accorded intellectual diversity and exploration in this new utilitarian ideological structure and in the regime's developmental priorities, and points to some places where the regime's principles and priorities and those of science contained the seeds of potential conflict.

Chapter 3 surveys the restoration and reform of China's natural science and social science establishment. It focuses on the Chinese Academy of Science and the Chinese Academy of Social Sciences as the leading and most prestigious scientific bodies in China and the institutional homes of many of the most prominent dissident scientists. It also analyzes how the broader economic and social crosscurrents set in motion by the Deng reforms—both efforts to reprofessionalize science and to bend the science community's work more directly in service to the technological needs of economic development—affected the science community. Among the unanticipated consequences of these reforms were the fragmentation of the science community and the creation of anxieties and uncertainties over declining livelihood, broken career paths, and shaken social standing that pushed some scientific intellectuals toward dissent.

Only in chapter 4 do the main protagonists of the book emerge. Here are traced some of the debates on questions of scientific theory and ideological doctrine that erupted during the reform decade. In these debates, scientists sought to establish new scientific disciplines and explore modern scientific theories that had been ignored or suppressed during the Mao period. Those sympathetic to the needs of the Party—the foremost of whom was the philosopher Zha Ruqiang—sought to accommodate these theories in a manner that upheld Marxism-Leninism's predominating position over all fields of knowledge. For others, among them Xu Liangying and Fang Lizhi, such monistic attempts to uphold Marxism-Leninism's "guiding role" perverted the conclusions of modern science and violated its inherently pluralistic structure.

The chapter focuses on two particularly heated disputes: one concerns the implications of modern scientific cosmology; the other involves the interpretation of quantum mechanics and its related discipline, fundamental particle physics. These two fields of physics—frequently thought of as the hardest of the hard sciences—generated heated controversy because they introduced drastic changes in our understanding of the most essential properties and entities in the natural world—matter, motion, time, and space. They therefore raised questions about the validity of concepts vitally central to Marxism-Leninism's philosophy, dialectical materialism.

Chapter 5 moves from the abstruse formulations of dialectical materialism and the abstract formalisms of general relativity and quantum mechanics to an analysis of the larger political significance of these debates over scientific and philosophical theory. Two of the debates' major protagonists—Fang Lizhi and, even more centrally, Xu Liangying—were also originators of two of the four open letters of early 1989. The chapter seeks to illuminate their path toward open political dissidence by locating them and those associated with them in China's scientific and intellectual community in terms of generation, personal experience, intellectual associations, institutional affiliation, and political orientation. Given their particular place in the intellectual community, the path from intellectual diversity to ideological deviation to political dissent turns out to have been surprisingly short.

Chapter 6 illuminates the emergence of scientific dissidence in post-Mao China from historical and comparative perspectives. Many of the social tensions and competing intellectual and political outlooks of the post-Mao period resonate with those felt and held by Chinese intellectuals since the May Fourth era, but with important differences in emphasis and orientation that tell much about the evolving social context, cultural trends, and political circumstances in each period and the years in between. Part of chapter 6 examines the views of the liberal scientists in light of these continuities and discontinuities.

In some ways scientific liberal dissent in the 1980s drew on a distinctly Chinese inheritance and context: the May Fourth era tradition linking science and democracy, and the divergence of Chinese communism from that in the Soviet Union. There are parallels evident in the Soviet experience, however, particularly in the pattern of Soviet scientific dissidence that emerged in the post-Stalin period. Both in the USSR and in China many of the most active scientific dissidents were physi-

cists. In both countries, scientific dissidents found themselves at odds
with others in their scientific community and found common purpose
with writers, historians, and social scientists. These contrasts and parallels reveal both the commonalities of purpose that communities of
scientists may share with the political elites of communist systems and
the tensions and conflicts of ideals and interests that may divide them.
A comparative examination contributes to our understanding of the
roles of scientific elites and the political significance of clashes between
scientific ideas and ideals in all societies.

This book relies on two main bodies of evidence. First, it draws
heavily on a very close reading of articles carried in a small number of
academic journals and in the larger mass-oriented press in China, and
attempts to set the conclusions of that analysis in the broader context
of changing political and social trends in China in the 1980s. Second,
it draws on interviews and correspondence with some of the protagonists of events recounted here (such as Fang Lizhi) and with Chinese
familiar with them, some of whom can be appropriately acknowledged
and others who, under the circumstances, unfortunately must remain
anonymous.

Each category of sources has its own strengths and inevitable
drawbacks. Close reading of the Chinese press and journals requires
analytical skills that can sometimes yield great insight if applied with
persistence, thoroughness, and judgment. It can also lead to ill-founded
conclusions. The reader may mistake individual shadings on issues for
shadows of genuine conflict or, more frequently, overlook chasms of divergent meaning in seemingly innocuous differences of viewpoint and
expression. Before China's opening to the West in the post-Mao period,
these reading skills were the main stock-in-trade of students of contemporary Chinese affairs, but now that we have access to other avenues
of information-gathering and analysis, they are no longer so. Likewise,
interviews and correspondence with the protagonists of a story supply
invaluable perspective on personal backgrounds and individual intentions and reactions that usually can only be inferred, sometimes at great
risk of error if at all, from a close reading of the public sources. But
interviews and correspondence can mislead as well as enrich. Personal
memories fade quickly, and even the most vivid recollections may be
inevitably distorted and reinterpreted in light of subsequent experience

and events. In the best of worlds, historians may find it possible to use multiple types of sources in concert, trying to use each to strengthen the conclusions and overcome the pitfalls of the others and so to arrive at a clearer picture of what happened and why. That is what has been attempted here.

2/ Official Ideology in Transition

Liberal dissidence emerged in China in the larger political context of the sweeping transformations of politics, policy, and ideology during the decade of reform initiated in 1978 by Deng Xiaoping, the Communist Party veteran who gradually emerged as the nation's most powerful leader. Departing radically from the political priorities of the preceding decades, Deng abandoned Mao Zedong's goals of revolutionary social transformation, shunning the political disasters Mao's tactics and policies had produced. In place of Mao's goals, Deng promoted China's rapid modernization and the reconstruction of national political life.

In so revising the goals of the Communist Party, Deng and his supporters among China's leadership purposefully reduced the reach of the still-authoritarian Party into society and redefined the place of various social and professional groups and of individuals in China's political community. These departures from Maoist totalitarianism produced tremendous changes not only in China's politics, but also in its social and economic life, some of them intended and anticipated and others not. The transformation of state-society relations gave scientists explicit encouragement to act as a professional community on behalf of China's modernization, but left unresolved tensions and ambiguities regarding authority, autonomy, and professionalism that set the stage for new conflicts of many scientists with the Party and for the turn of some of them toward liberal dissent later.

IDEOLOGY AS POINT OF DEPARTURE

In communist politics, changes in doctrinal formulation, phrasing, and emphasis in leadership statements and authoritative Party documents

encapsulate alterations in meaning and policy of frequently dispor-
tionate, even gigantic scale. The watershed shifts during the post-Mao
years in judgment of Mao Zedong's place in Party history and the relevance of his interpretations of Marxist-Leninist ideology—Mao Zedong
Thought—indicate the scale of the transformation Deng Xiaoping envisioned.

Summing up the basic lesson of the Chinese Communist Party's
efforts over the previous three decades to build a modern state according to Marxist-Leninist principles, at the Twelfth CCP Congress in
1982 Deng called on the Party to pay due regard to "Chinese realities."
"The mechanical copying and application of foreign experiences and
models will get us nowhere," he said, adding that "we have had many
lessons in this respect." "We must integrate the universal truth of Marxism with the concrete realities of China, blaze a path of our own, and
build a socialism with Chinese characteristics"—an imperative that he
called "the basic conclusion we have reached after reviewing our long
historical experience."[1]

Deng's comments showed how far the CCP had gone in the six
years since Mao Zedong's death in transforming the principles the
Party declared to be the guidelines shaping all its decisions and acts.
Only five years before, Mao's successor as Party chairman, Hua Guofeng, had staked his claim to leadership on inheriting and maintaining the continuity of Mao Zedong Thought. In a landmark article on
May Day, 1977, marking the publication of a new volume of Mao's
works, Hua declared that Mao had "inherited, defended, and developed Marxism-Leninism" against deviation at home and "safeguarded
Marxism-Leninism" against "revisionist" deviation within the international communist movement. Mao's theory of "continuing the revolution under the dictatorship of the proletariat"—the ideological framework justifying the Great Proletarian Cultural Revolution (1966–76)
—would remain his everlasting contribution to "the treasure-house of
Marxist-Leninist theory," Hua predicted, insisting that loyalty to Mao's
banner was the "guarantee for the victory of our revolutionary cause."[2]

By the time the Twelfth Party Congress convened in 1982, Deng
Xiaoping had stood Mao Zedong Thought on its head. Claiming to have
restored Mao's philosophy to its true essence, Deng had succeeded in
discrediting the ideas that Hua Guofeng had enshrined as Mao's eter-

nal contributions to Marxism-Leninism. Deng saw them instead as the erroneous convictions of an aged leader grown arrogant in his seclusion from China's practical realities and deluded by the vicious machinations of opportunistic cliques around him.

In Deng's view, Mao's enduring contribution was his adaptation of the abstract principles of Marxist theory to the concrete realities of China's changing situation. Mao was now only the first among several veteran leaders in the Party's revolutionary pantheon. His thought, once officially regarded as the reflection of his unique creative genius, was now considered the "crystallization" of the entire leadership's collective wisdom.

Substantively, the new Marxism–Leninism–Mao Zedong Thought elaborated by Deng incorporated a broad array of concepts and approaches that were said to suit the particular needs and circumstances of contemporary China and that framed different goals than those authorized by the Party's ideology in prior years. They also legitimized radically different policies in pursuing those goals—policies of "reform," previously a term with derogatory connotations. Taken together, these principles comprised what the Deng leadership called Marxism–Leninism–Mao Zedong Thought in China's contemporary context, "socialism with Chinese characteristics."

Deng Xiaoping's transformation of the CCP's authoritative ideological stance redefined the relationship of state to society. "Socialism with Chinese characteristics" incorporated a new criterion for the regime's legitimacy and put forward a new mission for the Party. It redrew the structure, lines of authority, and relationships among constituent social groups within China's political community under socialism. It redefined standards of citizenship, consciously limited the explicit reach of the state, and drew a new, highly significant distinction between the ideals driving members of the Party and the objectives motivating nonmembers.

These ideological changes affected all sectors of Chinese society profoundly. Many of the astonishing changes in social life that emerged in the post-Mao period, while not necessarily initiated by the regime directly, found license in Deng's recasting of the ideological grounds of regime legitimacy. The political and social consequences of Deng's ideological reform, in fact, were frequently ambiguous and unanticipated.

As various social and professional groups adjusted their relationships with the state in step with Deng's ideological transformation and according to their own goals and interests, conflicts and tensions over authority and interest emerged. Much of the political history of the Deng reforms is intelligible in terms of these conflicts and tensions between the state and various social groups in the 1980s.

China's scientific community was one such arena of conflict. Many of the political tensions running through the community in this period parallel stresses and strains within other social and professional groups, including workers and trade unions, journalists, and the literature and arts communities. As we will see, however, the impact of the Deng reforms on scientists was different in some ways, owing to the special authority claimed for scientific knowledge and to the critical importance the regime attached to science and technology for its own developmental purposes.

IMPETUS FOR CHANGE

Several factors contributed to the major transformation of official ideology that Deng Xiaoping brought about in the late 1970s. First, and most obvious, was the longstanding commitment of leaders such as Deng to a fundamentally different conception of how a socialist society should develop and of the attendant role of the Party. These views and policy preferences had been visible at the Eighth Party Congress in 1956 and surfaced again in the early 1960s when Deng, together with Liu Shaoqi, Chen Yun, and others, worked to rehabilitate China's economy from the economic disruption of the Great Leap Forward and the natural disasters of the "three bitter years" (1959–61). These views had been at the heart of the policy conflicts with Mao Zedong that culminated in the Cultural Revolution and Deng's purge; Party literature of that period described this as a "struggle between two lines." Deng's views and policy preferences also contributed in 1976 to his removal for a second time as a result of his efforts over the preceding three years to apply a similar approach to overturning the policies of the Cultural Revolution and dealing with its consequences.

Deng re-emerged in the post-Mao period, then, as a man with a clear sense of mission that had long, demonstrated political roots. That these views remained controversial after Mao's death, and at a time when Hua Guofeng had staked his claim to leadership of the Party on continuing the policies of Mao's last years, was clear in the very terms of Deng's rehabilitation in July 1977.

Domestic economic and political conditions lent impetus and urgency to Deng's purposes. China in 1976 faced a crisis of economic stagnation brought about by years of excessive centralization and bureaucracy, sagging productivity and product quality, and sluggish growth, along with a steady deterioration of the country's industrial infrastructure despite years of stress on capital accumulation and high state investment. Politically, the Cultural Revolution had dissolved the CCP into a fragmented body of contending hierarchies of factional coalitions, bound together out of a shared need to defend mutual interests and for protection in an environment shorn of commonly accepted rules and expectations for political conduct. The Party's ability to mobilize the populace to its cause through idealistic appeals had been blunted by the years of twists and turns in Party pronouncements and the Cultural Revolution's politics of terror, which had left a legacy of cynicism, uncertainty, and caution.

Beyond China's borders, the world was a significantly different place than it had been over the preceding two decades. China's own economic difficulties were mirrored to one degree or another in all of the other socialist countries, several of which attempted to reform centralized Stalinist institutional systems and practices. In 1976 such reforms were only sporadic and intermittent (and were in fact routinely excoriated by the Chinese media as "revisionist"). But by the mid-1980s Beijing saw reform as a wave sweeping the entire communist world, a trend that justified and lent impetus to China's own efforts in that direction.

Capitalism as well had changed in ways unanticipated by the prevailing orthodoxy. It not only had proven more resilient and durable in its heartland, Western Europe and the United States; it had also fueled economic revolutions on the Asian periphery. Japan's startling resurgence was the most obvious (and potentially threatening) manifestation, but the burgeoning economic growth and prosperity of the smaller "four little dragons"—South Korea and the three ethnically Chinese nations of Taiwan, Hong Kong, and Singapore—was no less impressive.

A final factor lending impetus to the transformation of Party ideology was what Deng recognized as a new scientific and technological
revolution underway in the world. While not a new theme in Chinese
communist discourse, this trend was now perceived as global in scope
and, because it was setting new criteria by which national strength
would be measured, revolutionary in its import. It lay at the heart of
the spectacular success of renewed capitalist growth in the post–World
War II period, particularly among China's Asian rivals. The failure of
China to meet the challenge it posed (and, as Chinese commentary in
recent years has observed, of the other communist countries to do so)
accounted in part for China's sagging economic fortunes and threatened
national security in the long term. "Modern science and technology are
now undergoing a great revolution," Deng declared at a landmark conference on science in 1978. "A whole range of new sciences and technolo-
gies"—including electronic computers, atomic energy, astronautics and
space science, polymer chemistry, and lasers—was revolutionizing production in the world, thanks to the application of basic natural-science
breakthroughs to tasks of production "on an unprecedented scale and
with unprecedented speed."[3] The necessity of catching up with this new
revolution in the advanced industrial world significantly shaped and
lent urgency to the reforms brought about by the Deng leadership.

In response to the challenge of rebuilding China's fractured political system in a rapidly changing international setting, Deng revised the
CCP's ideological platform along lines radically different from the one
advanced by Mao Zedong. To appreciate the scope and depth of Deng's
transformation of China's political system and its legitimating ideology,
it is useful to review what "socialism with Chinese characteristics" has
meant in the Deng period, both in contrast to Mao's ideological vision
and in terms of its essential components.

USING MAO TO OVERTURN MAO

The transformation of Party ideology over which Deng Xiaoping presided after Mao's death cast into disrepute ideas Mao had developed
on how a society—and particularly Chinese society—advances through
socialism toward communism and on the Party's role in that process.
Mao had enunciated these ideas with increasing directness through the

late 1950s and early 1960s in opposition to others in the CCP leadership who saw the Party's goals and tactics differently. Mao's convictions about these questions in the face of high-level leadership opposition, and the considerations of position and power that were inevitably entwined with them, had been central to his decision to launch the Cultural Revolution.

The cornerstone of Mao's theoretical views—which eventually he elaborated into his theory of "continuing the revolution under the dictatorship of the proletariat"—was the critical role of class struggle in the advance of socialist society toward communism. Mao's differences with others in the CCP leadership on this issue are detectable as far back as the spring of 1957, when Mao's statements began to diverge from the consensus line established at the Eighth Party Congress the previous fall.[4] By the early 1960s, Mao's views had sharpened considerably. Far from receding as socialist society develops, Mao argued, class struggle intensifies. The increasing class differentiation and social stratification that naturally accompany modernization enflame class tensions rather than dispelling them. In this intensifying struggle, even the Communist Party may become corrupted by residual bourgeois ideas and the debilitation of Party vigilance against corruption, privilege, and bureaucratism.

In Mao's view, this corruption of the Party and deterioration of its ability to lead the masses in class struggle as socialism advances could eventually bring about a "restoration of capitalism," since Party leaders would no longer represent the interests of the proletariat. Such a retrogression, Mao believed, had already taken place in the USSR. Mao believed that, to prevent China from "changing color" from "red" to "white," the masses would be justified in rising up anew to overthrow corrupted state and Party institutions and leaders. The masses would be guided by their own developing class instincts and, in the case of China, by the theoretical and tactical genius of Mao himself. These ideas, enshrined in the slogan revived from Mao's years at the Party's wartime headquarters at Yan'an in northwest China—"To rebel is justified"—emerged as the rationale for the Cultural Revolution.[5]

In step with this ideological construct that Mao developed, there emerged the package of principles and policy preferences associated with Mao's leadership that is often called "Maoism" by Western observers of China. For scientists and intellectuals, the most important of these were a preference for political "redness" over intellectual and professional expertise (which frequently translated into distrust of intellectuals and an acute anti-intellectualism) and an insistence on egalitarian approaches to status and compensation.

These principles and policy predilections were embraced after Mao's death by his successor, Hua Guofeng. A landmark joint editorial by *People's Daily, Red Flag,* and the military newspaper *Liberation Army Daily* (Jiefangjun bao) on 7 February 1977, endorsed by Hua, enjoined the Party to continue to take Mao's ideas as the ultimate authority for all decisions and actions, urging adherence to the "two whatevers"—that is, to uphold "whatever decisions Chairman Mao made" and to obey "whatever instructions Chairman Mao gave."[6] At the Party's Eleventh Congress the following August, Hua reaffirmed the continuing authority of Mao's ideas as the Party's authoritative line. Calling Mao Zedong "the greatest Marxist of our time," Hua recounted in detail in his political report the tenets of the theory of "continuing the revolution under the dictatorship of the proletariat," comparing it to Lenin's theoretical contributions and calling it "the most important achievement of Marxism of our time."[7]

It was these ideological principles and policy preferences that Deng Xiaoping, restored to the Party leadership on the eve of the Eleventh Party Congress, set out immediately to overturn. In his brief closing speech at the congress Deng appealed to a different Mao, calling on the Party to restore traditions and practices Mao had pioneered during Party's revolutionary years. In particular, and in contrast to Hua's strident recitation of Mao's theses on class struggle, Deng called on the Party to "revive and carry forward" the practices of "seeking truth from facts" and of "closely integrating theory with practice" that Mao had fostered in the Yan'an period.[8]

In reviving the Yan'an slogan "Seek truth from facts," Deng was using Mao to overturn Mao. In the same way that Mao had used the slogan against his internationalist opponents, led by Wang Ming, in the Yan'an rectification movement, criticizing them for advocating policies out of step with the realities the Party faced at the time, Deng was implying that the Party needed to return to principles and policies consistent with China's contemporary realities after years of misguided fantasy.

Sounding this slogan as their keynote over the next year, Deng and his political allies contested Hua Guofeng's attempt to secure his own position as Party chairman on a platform of continuity with Maoist ideological principles as the touchstone of legitimacy. Deng's campaign of de-Maoization culminated in the watershed conclusions of the 1978 Eleventh Central Committee's Third Plenum and the landmark resolution adopted at the 1981 Sixth Plenum on Mao and Party history since 1949. Deng's success in this campaign paved the way for the adoption of new ideological premises, on which the array of "reform" policies associated with his leadership of the Party were to be based.

One component of Deng's campaign was to attack the infallibility of Mao's judgment and the supremacy of his position in the leadership pantheon. In doing this, Deng did not seek to discredit Mao altogether. Mao had been both China's Lenin and its Stalin; therefore, de-Maoization led by Deng could not proceed as far as de-Stalinization had in the USSR under Khrushchev. Deng sought instead an assessment of Mao that balanced these sensitivities—one that acknowledged Mao's errors in the years after 1956 but that also took due account of his contributions to the Party's cause and goals.

Deng's attempt to restore balance to the Party's estimation of Mao's life and legacy was visible at first only indirectly, in allegorical articles in the press on leaders from China's traditional past. Beginning in the months after the Eleventh Party Congress, calls for more balanced reassessments of historical figures appeared in the CASS Institute of History journal *Historical Studies* (Lishi yanjiu), in *Enlightenment Daily*, and, by the spring of 1978, in *People's Daily* itself. The most provocative of these assessed the merits and faults of the great unifier of China's classical past, Qinshihuang (first emperor of the Qin dynasty, 221-206 B.C.E.), an unmistakable symbol for Mao. The success of these allegorical assaults on Mao's exalted position was clearly registered in the communiqué issued at the end of the Third Plenum in 1978. Calling Mao only "a great Marxist," the plenum pointed out that he "always adopted a scientific attitude of dividing one into two toward everyone, including himself." "It would not be Marxist to demand that a revolutionary leader be free of all shortcomings and errors," the communiqué went on, adding that such an approach "would not conform to Comrade Mao Zedong's consistent evaluation of himself."[9]

The communiqué did not explicitly enumerate Mao's errors,

though it was clear that the gravest was the Cultural Revolution itself. Instead, the plenum called on the Party to view the Cultural Revolution "historically," urging that "shortcomings and mistakes" in the Party's past "be summed up at an appropriate time."[10] Deng's progress in pressing for such a judgment was reflected a year later in the long speech delivered by Party elder Ye Jianying on the PRC's thirtieth National Day, when Ye revealed that the Party had begun the process of formally "summing up" its successes and failures since 1949. He offered a "preliminary assessment" in anticipation of a summary judgment, including the Party's first explicit authoritative condemnation of the Cultural Revolution. Based on an estimate of the Party's political situation that "ran counter to reality" and incorporating "erroneous" policies and tactics, the Cultural Revolution had been a "calamity for our people" and "the severest reversal of our socialist cause."[11]

A second component of Deng's effort to transform the Party's ideological principles was his attempt to overturn Mao Zedong Thought as the exclusive basis for policy legitimacy. The spearhead of this effort was the campaign in 1978 to "take practice as the sole criterion for testing truth." Launched with a provocative article on the front page of *Enlightenment Daily* in May and quickly endorsed by Deng himself in a major speech at a conference on army political work in June, this campaign sought to overturn what it described as the rigidly "dogmatic" approach to Mao's thought embodied in the "two whatevers."

The gist of Deng's argument was that Marxism–Leninism—and its embodiment in China, Mao Zedong Thought—is not a fixed body of rigid doctrine to be applied literally to all situations. It is instead a body of principles and methods that must be applied flexibly and developed creatively according to the degree to which they meet new realities. The "basic principles" of Marxism–Leninism–Mao Zedong Thought are unchanging and universal, but their application requires due attention to the realities of particular contexts, Deng's argument ran. Their truth derives not from the genius of great thinkers but from their effectiveness in practice. New circumstances require new solutions. "Seeking truth from facts, proceeding from reality, and integrating theory with practice"—not the "two whatevers"—were the essence of Mao's thought. The specific ideas Mao Zedong derived from the practice of his time should be retained where they conform to China's present realities;

where they do not, they should be discarded.[12] By the Third Plenum at the end of the year it was apparent that Deng had been successful. The plenum communiqué authoritatively put "a high evaluation" on the discussion of "taking practice as the sole criterion for testing truth," observing that it would have "far-reaching and historic significance" in encouraging the Party to overcome "ossified" and dogmatic ways of doing things.[13]

A third component of Deng's effort to transform Mao Zedong's ideological legacy was the effort to discredit Mao's thesis of "continuing the revolution under the dictatorship of the proletariat." The first steps in this avenue of attack were taken in 1978, as articles in the press began to question the role played by class struggle under socialism. As in other aspects of Deng's campaign to overturn Mao's ideological heritage, the Third Plenum was also a turning point on this issue. Restoring the agenda of the 1956 Eighth Congress, the plenum called on the Party to "shift the focus" of its work to "socialist modernization." Paraphrasing the language used by Liu Shaoqi at the 1956 congress and by Mao in his 1957 speech on "contradictions," the communiqué stated that although class struggle cannot be completely abandoned, "the large-scale turbulent class struggles of a mass character have in the main come to an end." Class struggle would continue, the communiqué went on, but it would now be secondary to the main task of modernization and would be waged within the structure of socialist law.[14]

With this core element of Mao's thesis overturned, the entire theory unraveled. Over the next two years, articles criticized as erroneous the slogan attributed to Mao "Take class struggle as the key link." References to the danger of "revisionism"—classical Marxist jargon for the deviation of calling into question the basic tenets of the doctrines of Marxism-Leninism, and especially of abandoning class struggle—gradually disappeared from the press, not only in domestic political discourse but also in Sino-Soviet polemics. With the discrediting of class struggle as the focus of the Party's work under socialism, it became possible for the first time to introduce the idea of "reform" as a positive concept in political discourse.

All of these components of Deng's campaign to transform Mao's legacy were incorporated into the 1981 resolution on Mao and Party history. Although it was a compromise document that reflected a broader consensus than simply the views of Deng Xiaoping and those allied with him, Deng's stamp was clear in its authoritative redefinition of Mao's place in the Party pantheon, his place in Party history, and the elements of his thought that would continue to have significance. Mao remained a "great Marxist and a great proletarian revolutionary strategist and theorist," but he was only "the most prominent" among "many outstanding leaders" in the Party's past. Mao Zedong Thought remained "a correct theory, a body of correct principles and a summary of experiences" confirmed in the practice of applying Marxism-Leninism to Chinese realities. Mao Zedong Thought was not, however, Mao's alone, but rather the "crystallization of the collective wisdom" of the Party, to which "many outstanding leaders" made important contributions. Mao had committed errors, but these were only "secondary." The worst of them, the Cultural Revolution, was an unmitigated "catastrophe" for the Party. The theory of "continuing the revolution under the dictatorship of the proletariat" that rationalized the Cultural Revolution "conformed neither to Marxism-Leninism nor to Chinese reality." The true components of Mao Zedong Thought were the methodological principles whose application Mao had pioneered in China. "Seeking truth from facts" in the concrete realities of his time, concentration of the interests and views of the broadest number of people possible through the "mass line," and defense of Chinese independence were the essence of Mao's thought, and would remain relevant to contemporary China.[15]

THE "CRISIS OF CONFIDENCE" IN CHINESE SOCIALISM

Deng's dismantling of Mao Zedong's ideological legacy opened the way for the bewildering array of policy initiatives and institutional reforms that changed China so radically after 1978. In launching the reforms the Deng leadership drew on some of the views and policy preferences that had brought them into conflict with Mao in the 1950s and 1960s. Many of the overarching principles guiding the reforms and several of the specific reform institutions and practices, not to mention the encompassing vision of how a socialist society should modernize, drew explicitly on approaches and precedents from that time.

But the Deng reforms were not simply a restoration of a long-deferred vision of socialist modernization. The Deng leadership had also to counter the impact on Party legitimacy of both the Cultural Revolution era and their own dismantling of the Maoist heritage. These doubts, disillusionment, and cynicism about Marxism-Leninism were openly acknowledged in Party pronouncements as a "crisis of confidence" in Chinese socialism. Fed by the disasters of the preceding two decades and the Party's own acknowledgment of tremendous errors during that time, this disillusionment hurt the Party's ability to recruit new members and to mobilize support for its policies and causes.

Exacerbating this crisis of legitimacy, the vacillations in reform policy and the evident leadership contention over the reforms in the Deng years heightened suspicions about the Party's commitment to reform over the long term. Each new Party attack on deviations from the path of correct reform—from the campaign against "spiritual pollution" in 1983 to the campaign against "bourgeois liberalization" in 1987—fueled doubt and cynicism about the Party's intentions and impaired its attempts to rebuild legitimacy, hampering its ability to guide the country's modernization.

The range of doubts brought into the open by the Party's public critique of its past errors can be judged from the efforts to dispel and rebut them in speeches by the Deng leadership and in commentary in the media. Characterization of China as a poor, backward country—part of Deng's effort to deflate the unrealistic and boastful claims of the Maoist approach—and comparisons of the PRC's economic progress with that of other Asian countries, for example, served to exacerbate doubts about the effectiveness of socialism as a strategy for modernization. In 1980 Deng himself took note of these doubts in a major speech, in which he observed that the twenty years of "leftist" deviation from the central task of modernization had prompted "some people, especially young people, to be skeptical about the socialist system, alleging that socialism is not as good as capitalism."[16]

Similarly, the press frequently took note of spreading cynicism and disillusionment among various groups. Young people, students in particular, were said to have become apathetic in responding to efforts to recruit them for Party youth organizations and to enlist their enthusiasm for the Party and its causes. The Communist Youth League journal *China's Youth* (Zhongguo qingnian) began a regular column, "The Meaning of Life," which invited young people to vent their despair and share their ideals.[17] Students were said to slight or boycott altogether classes on Marxism-Leninism, believing Marxism to have been proven erroneous by the events of the preceding decades and to be irrelevant to their future. Instead, they concentrated on classwork that they believed relevant to their careers. They became infatuated with Western literary and philosophical trends, such as Sartrean existentialism, that "peddled despair." A CCP Propaganda Department survey of student attitudes toward classes in Marxist theory in universities in Guangdong, Fujian, and Hunan, for example, described what it took to be a typical situation in such classes at South China Normal College. "While the teachers were talking in the classroom," the survey found, "the students occupied themselves with their own 'private plots of land,' studying foreign languages, doing homework, studying technical books, reading novels, writing letters, and so forth. . . . They failed to prepare lessons before class sessions, nor did they review them after class. . . . All they did was cram for the examinations."[18]

Intellectuals disillusioned by the Party's past errors saw other profound defects in Chinese Marxism. Both of the themes later excoriated in the 1983 campaign against "spiritual pollution"—the idea that "alienation" could exist in socialist society as well as under capitalism and that the Cultural Revolution had brought about such vicious excesses because Chinese communism had suppressed the rightful place of "humanist" ideals in Marxism—emerged in the context of the "crisis of confidence" in 1979. Perhaps the best-known manifestations, however, were in literature and film. Writers of the genre that came to be known as "literature of the wounded" (semifictional stories examining the personal tragedies of ordinary people in the Cultural Revolution) evolved into works that were later criticized for inviting disillusionment and despair. The most famous of such works, the army writer Bai Hua's script "Unrequited Love," was condemned in 1981.

Commentary in the press also acknowledged significant disillusionment within the ranks of the Party itself, stemming from the experience of the Cultural Revolution and from the Party's self-criticism. The scale of this disaffection is difficult to estimate, but it clearly spanned a broad range of reactions. Some members apparently abandoned their commitment to the Party altogether, believing that the goal of achieving communism was illusory. While a small number remained committed to the ideological principles of the Maoist period out of conviction, many more were unsympathetic to the new Dengist goals because they perceived their own political positions to be threatened. Others apparently grew cynical about declared goals but nevertheless clung ruthlessly to their positions out of sheer self-interest.

The growth of cynicism and disillusionment with the Party in the Deng period, both because of the Cultural Revolution and because of the Deng leadership's criticism of the mistakes and disasters of the Mao years, meant that the Party leadership had constantly to fight a two-front struggle. On the one hand, it had to continue to criticize the "leftist" mistakes of the previous years and to root out those entrenched in the party ranks who were still committed to the policies of that time. On the other hand, it had to constrain those on the "right" who were ready to use the Party's own self-criticism as a pretext to press for policies more liberal than the Party would tolerate or to reject Party leadership altogether. Party criticism of one side in the 1980s tended to embolden the other side, requiring renewed Party attacks. The result through the Deng years was an oscillating pattern of Party criticism campaigns as the Party leadership struggled to maintain the center ground.

Added to this dynamic, opinions within the leadership on the question of the Party's need to criticize its past mistakes and on how to deal with the consequences of this critique were predictably divided and contentious. Those within the leadership who, like Deng, advocated reform proceeded from a variety of motives and concerns that did not always coincide. The reforms themselves also had unanticipated consequences and side effects that became objects of dispute.

Significant differences emerged over several key questions, including some of the most basic issues: how far and how fast reform should proceed in the economic and social arenas; how explicitly the Party could criticize its past mistakes without threatening perceptions of its competence and right to rule and without demoralizing its own rank and file; how thoroughly rectification campaigns should root out members to be held accountable for the mistakes and excesses of the past; and how far institutional and administrative reform could go in disrupting the careers of those with vested interests in the political apparatus as it stood. As those in the leadership whose political futures were tied to resisting Deng's reforms were removed, these cumulative differences among the reformers in the leadership came to the fore.

Attitudes on other questions at the same time united those in the reform leadership, setting limits on how far such conflict and dispute went. Perhaps most fundamentally, all of the Party reform leaders shared the belief that, even though the Cultural Revolution was a catastrophe and similar episodes must be avoided in the future, such "leftist deviations" did not reflect inherent flaws in Marxism-Leninism itself. Instead, they reflected, first, the mistakes of inexperienced Party leaders in understanding the doctrine's principles and how to apply them correctly to China's realities and, second, their failure to recognize the "historical limitations" of the ideas of Marxism's progenitors.

In response to the "crisis of confidence" surfaced by the Party's open self-criticism, authoritative Party statements and press commentary stressed again and again the ability of the Party to set a new course that returned the Party to the true basic principles of Marxism-Leninism. The socialist system and the communist ideals it pursued were not shown to be incorrect by the experience of the Cultural Revolution; only the Party's understanding needed to be improved and deepened through study and practice, and the socialist system needed only adjustments, not systemic changes.

"SOCIALISM WITH CHINESE CHARACTERISTICS"

"Socialism with Chinese characteristics," a formulation that Deng introduced at the Twelfth Party Congress in September 1982, was built on consensus around the fundamental proposition that the key to overcoming the "deviations" of the past and to spurring China's modernization in the future was to apply Marxism-Leninism "creatively" in the contemporary Chinese context. In practice, this new formulation provided the ideological basis legitimizing the range of economic, social, institutional, and cultural reforms the Deng leadership had sought to implement since the watershed 1978 Third Plenum.

Until the Thirteenth Party Congress in October 1987, however, what constituted "socialism with Chinese characteristics" was not defined specifically and precisely. The enumeration of its components by Party general secretary Zhao Ziyang at the congress, moreover, really represented more a summary of the various ad hoc principles and after-the-fact rationales that the reformers elaborated to justify the specific policy departures they introduced over the previous decade, than a systematic explication of a consistent body of theoretical propositions and derived corollaries.

Reform leaders offered no apology for this. They were quite explicit, in fact, in stressing that they had no fixed blueprint for the future, asserting that much of what they were attempting was experimental and pathbreaking in departing from classical Marxist-Leninist models of how socialist society advances toward communism. They asserted that this readiness to make up theory as they went along was a strength, not a weakness, of true Marxism because it ensured theory's correspondence to reality. "It is a general trend in the contemporary era that Marxism needs further, extensive development," Zhao declared at the Party congress. The new realities of the present era "require that Marxists widen their vision, develop new concepts, and enter a new realm," he went on. He reaffirmed that "changing socialism from an idle dream into science" was "the great historical merit of Marx and Engels." But "it is only natural," he said, "that people will discard some theses which are utopian because they were formulated by our predecessors within the limits of their historical conditions" and "will reject dogmatic interpretations of Marxism and erroneous viewpoints imposed on it" in the course of "developing the theory of scientific socialism on the basis of new practice."[19]

Along with the reform leadership's conscious recognition that traditional approaches had failed and that new ones, free from the constraints of classical dogma, needed to be found, the extemporaneous nature of much of the content of "socialism with Chinese characteristics" also derived from the political context from which it emerged. There was abundant evidence of vigorous debate among the reformers since 1978 over many of the elements that Zhao came to list as aspects of "socialism with Chinese characteristics." Debate was evident both in theoretical discourse in the pages of the Party press and in disputes over their expression in concrete policy. Nevertheless, it is possible to distill the basic premises and principles subsumed under the formula, bearing in mind the political reality of significant differences among the reformers, in regard to both the validity of specific elements and the application of those they did agree on.[20]

First, *Marxism-Leninism is a flexible, practical doctrine whose content evolves in practice, not a fixed dogma of unchanging and inflexible principles that apply regardless of time and context.* This approach was already implicit in leadership statements and commentary associated with the campaign to "take practice as the sole criterion for testing truth" launched by Deng Xiaoping in 1978 to redefine Mao Zedong's ideological legacy. It reached its strongest and most dramatic expression in later comment arguing that Marxism is most of all a method, not a body of specific substantive concepts. According to these formulations, authoritatively codified in Zhao Ziyang's remarks to the Thirteenth Party Congress, Marxism is a methodology for analyzing inherent laws of human social evolution based on the specifics of the present, using the past only as a general guide. The understanding and perspectives that Marx, Engels, Lenin, Stalin, and Mao derived from their analysis of the society around them may have been correct for their specific times, but may no longer be valid for the circumstances China faces today. The CCP faces in the contemporary world circumstances that Marx and the other great Marxist theoreticians and tacticians could never have imagined, and therefore the Party must "develop" Marxism, seeking new solutions to those situations and problems. The Party should be guided by their approaches and methods of analysis, but not necessarily by their conclusions.

One corollary of this proposition is that because China's circumstances are unique, past "models" and "paths" to socialist development that have been tried in other countries cannot be imported wholesale. The solutions the Party seeks to address contemporary realities in the PRC and in its dealings with the world must be both new and distinctly Chinese. Reform leaders therefore emphasized repeatedly that the Stalinist approach that the Party adopted in the 1950s no longer worked in China, and the point of departure for many of the economic reforms was specifically to remedy defects inherent in that approach.

The experiences of other communist states, notably in Eastern

Europe but also in the USSR itself, to reform similar defects in the planned economies they built using the Stalinist model could be of positive "reference value" in China's search for a new Marxist course. Out of this common search for remedies to the defects of the traditional Soviet planning model all adopted in their founding years, there might be an evolving convergence of approaches, an emerging congruity of principles, and a commonality of experience that all could share. Ultimately, however, the reforms and approaches they adopt could be strictly applicable only to themselves because of the distinctive differences of their national circumstances and character. China's socialism, of course, would have "Chinese characteristics."

A second fundamental element of "socialism with Chinese characteristics" is that *the measure of Marxism's success in China is the pace and scope of China's development as a modern country overall, and the rise of the standard of living and the quality of life of China's people specifically.* Enunciation of this principle clearly at the 1978 Third Plenum laid the crucial ideological cornerstone for the entire program of reforms introduced by the Deng leadership thereafter. In enunciating it, the Deng leadership was consciously restoring the Party's "general task" laid down by Liu Shaoqi at the Eighth Party Congress in 1956 and was overturning the ideological starting point—waging class struggle—for the entire Maoist ideological structure. Achieving the new "general task" of socialist modernization and "improving the people's living standards on the basis of a rapid growth in production" would "require diverse changes in those aspects of the relations of production and the superstructure not in harmony with the growth of productive forces, and require change in all methods of management, actions, and thinking that stand in the way of such growth."[21]

Through the 1980s this principle was reiterated as the point of departure in all of the Party's major decisions on reform. In particular, it figured as the core premise in the Party's two key documents laying out the principles guiding adjustment of existing "relations of production" and the social "superstructure" to accord with the development of "productive forces"—the "decision" on economic reform ratified at the Third Plenum of the Twelfth Party Congress in 1984 and the "resolution" on building "socialist spiritual civilization" at the Sixth Plenum in 1986. The

1984 economic reform decision built on the 1978 Third Plenum formulations in defining reform in the economic structure authoritatively and precisely:

> The basic contradiction in socialist society remains that between the relations of production and the forces of production, between the superstructure and the economic base. Reform of China's economic structure means reforming, on the premise of adhering to the socialist system, a series of interrelated links and aspects of the relations of production and the superstructure that are not suited to the development of the forces of production. As a form of self-improvement and development of the socialist system, this reform is to be carried out under Party and government leadership in a planned way. It should serve to advance, and not to impair, social stability, expansion of production, improvement of the people's living standards and the growth of state revenue. The essential task of socialism is to develop the forces of production, create ever more social wealth, and meet the people's growing material and cultural needs.[22]

Similarly, the 1986 Sixth Plenum resolution sought to define reform in the social and cultural "superstructure" as aimed at promoting social attitudes and behavior and cultural and educational policies conducive to the overall goal of development.[23]

The obvious and direct utility of these first two components of "socialism with Chinese characteristics"—that Marxism is a flexible method and that the primary measure of success of Chinese socialism is the extent to which the country's development advances—was that in combination they authorized the spectacular economic, social, intellectual, and cultural changes introduced into China by the policy of "enlivening the economy domestically and opening to the outside world." On the basis of these propositions, it became legitimate to experiment with a wide range of economic practices and institutional innovations that were previously condemned as "revisionist," "capitalist," or otherwise politically unacceptable. It also opened the way to explore the suitability of the entire range of foreign—both Western and Soviet bloc—practices, institutions, and ideas and to import and implement them as long as they contributed to the overall goal of speeding China's modernization.

Abetting such experiments and explorations, and building on these twin components of "socialism with Chinese characteristics," was the recognition that China remained at a considerably less historically advanced stage of development than the Party had acknowledged before. On that basis, reform leaders argued that efforts in the past to introduce "advanced" economic, social, political, and cultural institutions and practices in keeping with a "higher stage" of socialist development did not conform to Chinese realities. In Marxist-Leninist discourse, such approaches are classically "leftist" by definition. Instead, China needed transitional institutions and practices that suited the country's level of development at an early stage of socialism. This recognition of China's relatively limited progress in socialist development had figured in policy debates since the earliest years of the reform and in authoritative Party documents since at least 1981, when it appeared in the resolution on Mao and Party history. Its strongest authoritative formulation and elaboration, however, was in Party general secretary Zhao Ziyang's report to the 1987 Thirteenth Party Congress, where it was advertised as a major plank in the reform platform.[24]

In terms of practical policy, this recognition of the still initial stage of the Party's efforts to build socialism in China meant toleration and even promotion of a secondary but still significant place for a variety of economic institutions and practices that were mixed or even capitalist in nature within the overall predominating framework of socialist ones. Markets, systems of contracted responsibility for production of various commodities and even for labor, small-scale private enterprise and ownership, and capitalist mechanisms of capital formation all could have a place, albeit transitional, within the evolving structure of still-predominant state planning and distribution systems. This hybrid form of socioeconomic activity was given a new name, "socialist commodity economy"—a term introduced authoritatively into the vocabulary of Chinese communist political economy by the 1984 Party decision on economic reform.

Also accompanying the assertion that overall national development is the standard by which to judge the success of socialism was a readiness to tolerate some measure of what the Party recognized as social inequality and economic exploitation. In the explosive area of wages and income standards, for example, the slogans "To get rich is glorious" and "Some people must become prosperous before others" licensed economic policies that permitted significant income disparities in both the countryside and the cities.

Deng and other reformers defended such tolerance as an inevitable outgrowth of the fact that economic development always proceeds unevenly. Some measure of competition is necessary to spur growth even under socialism, they said, arguing that such social and economic differences, constrained by the provisions of overall equity and justice of the socialist system, would never become as severe as they are in countries developing under capitalism and would disappear as the society advanced over the long run. In presenting such arguments, these reformers explicitly rejected the overriding concern of the Maoist approach—to preserve social and economic equality even at the expense of economic development—as a mistaken egalitarianism that in effect guaranteed poverty for everyone, both in the present and in the future.

In a talk that was subsequently praised as a major exposition on what constitutes "socialism with Chinese characteristics," for example, Deng Xiaoping stated that "[Maoist] pauperism is not socialism, still less communism." "The superiority of the socialist system," he added, "lies above all in its ability to increasingly develop the productive forces and to improve the people's material and cultural life." Progress toward these goals through reforms based on the "socialist principle of [']to each according to his work,['] " he predicted, "will not create an excessive gap in wealth" nor will "polarization" in society result.[25]

Constraining unbounded application of the first two broad propositions of "socialism with Chinese characteristics" is a third element of the formula. This is the insistence that *all departures in policy and practice must be consistent with the goal of contributing to China's "socialist modernization"*—usually enunciated as the call to "uphold the socialist road, the dictatorship of the proletariat, the leadership of the Chinese Communist Party, and Marxism–Leninism–Mao Zedong Thought." Throughout the 1980s this call was normally referred to as either the "four upholds" (*sige jianchi*) or the "four basic principles" (*sige jiben yuanze*).

The effect of this third element of "socialism with Chinese characteristics" in relation to the other two was to demarcate a middle ground of legitimate policy departures as the reformers waged their two-front political struggle against pressures from both the left and the right. The first two principles overturned the legitimacy of "leftist" attitudes associated with the values and policies prevailing under Mao and authorized exploration and adaptation of reformist ideas and practices that would accelerate China's development. The third principle set limits on how far such explorations and reforms could go toward liberalization.

Exactly what constituted socialism—and what institutions and practices are consistent with it, beyond the broad stipulations of the predominance of public ownership in the economy and adherence to the principle of "to each according to his work" in distribution—proved difficult to define to everyone's satisfaction. The "four basic principles" were first enunciated by Deng Xiaoping at a major Party conference on theoretical work in March 1979, as Beijing moved to crush the Democracy Wall movement.[26] Thereafter, they were stressed repeatedly when more conservative-minded leaders in Deng's reform camp—and sometimes Deng himself—felt a need to curb ideas and practices perceived to threaten the Party's legitimacy and authority from the political "right." This defense against the "right" balanced emphasis on the necessity of reform by more liberal-minded members of the reform camp to blunt criticism from the political "left." As a result, the breadth of this middle ground of legitimacy expanded and shrank through the 1980s in conjunction with prevailing political sensitivities and reactions to changes in society at large.

Predictably, there was persistent, heated debate among the reformers over where to draw the lines in economic policy demarcating what was acceptable in a "socialist commodity economy" and what was not. These disputes, in turn, were exacerbated by some of the reforms' economic and social side effects. Zhao Ziyang's highly authoritative summation at the Thirteenth Party Congress of the meaning and significance of the judgment that China would remain at "the initial stage of socialist development" for a "considerable" length of time was intended to quell such debates, seeking to strengthen the ideological basis for the reformers to defend steps that had been controversial in the past and to take new, more aggressive ones in the future. In explicitly authorizing several economic reforms that had previously been the focus of controversy because of their "capitalist" associations—such as money markets, the issuance of stocks and bonds, and labor service markets—Zhao stressed that these steps were in keeping with China's

present stage of development and would advance the socialist economy. He enjoined "comrades throughout the Party" to understand these
points "better" and to "acquire unity in their thought" about them.

Similarly, the effort to define exactly what ideas, beliefs, values,
and social behavior were consistent with Chinese socialism at its current stage also sparked severe disputes. As defined authoritatively in the
hotly contentious 1986 Party resolution on the issue, "socialist spiritual
civilization" consists of those ideas, values, and ethical behavior that
advance China's material progress. They include all aspects of foreign
science and culture as well as the "best" from China's historical and
cultural traditions, moral and civic behavior based on "socialist ethics"
("the love of the fatherland, the people, labor, science, and socialism"),
and democracy within a framework of law and institutional discipline.

Concretely and consistently specifying what these broad elements
of "socialist spiritual civilization" were was the subject of unending dispute. As the attacks on "spiritual pollution" in late 1983 and on "bourgeois liberalization" in 1981 and 1987 show, ideas considered to have
an acceptable place in academic debate could quickly become anathe-
mata. Aggressiveness in commercial activities could be celebrated at
one time as consistent with the reformist enjoinder to "blaze new trails"
for the sake of China's material advance and be scorned as "seeking
money in everything" at another. Emulation of Western artistic styles
and social fashions might be applauded by some as indicating that
China was ready to participate in advanced world culture, but be seen
in the eyes of others as disgraceful borrowing of "decadent" aspects of
foreign culture.

UNIFYING CHINA'S POLITICAL COMMUNITY

On balance, the three main components of "socialism with Chinese characteristics" represent an effort by Deng and the reformers to provide an
ideological framework that could reintegrate a Chinese political community fragmented by the experiences of the previous two decades of
economic and social change and political conflict and that would enable
it to modernize within a socialist framework. The scope of social interests that this Dengist conception recognized, and the role of the Party

and government in it, differ fundamentally from the political community envisioned by Mao Zedong in his later years.

In accommodating a broader degree of diversity in the forms and variety of legitimate economic activity, "socialism with Chinese characteristics" extended recognition and legitimacy to a broader array of interests and social associations within China's body politic. This recognition was apparent in theoretical terms early in the reform period, when authoritative statements and commentary in late 1980 changed the characterization of China's political system from a "dictatorship of the proletariat" to a "people's democratic dictatorship." The new characterization, which comported with the reformers' assessment that China still was at an "early" or "initial stage" of socialism, was intended to signify that the social base of China's political community was broader and more diverse than indicated in the classical formulation.

The legitimacy of these interests derived from the Party's recognition that separate spheres of human activity have unique, objective "laws" of development that the Party must respect in formulating effective policy. This recognition, which Tang Tsou has called the Party's "sociological postulate,"[27] was reflected in the reformers' efforts to bring about the Party's withdrawal from the total and direct intervention and management of virtually all arenas of economic and social activity that had prevailed under Mao.

The Maoist vision had also recognized the existence of diverse social interests and groups within China's body politic, as Mao's classic 1957 essay "On the Correct Handling of Contradictions among the People"—a text also accorded a central place in the Dengist canon—made plain in delineating "antagonistic" and "nonantagonistic" contradictions." The critical difference between the Maoist and Dengist conceptions is in their diverging assignments for the Communist Party and, by extension, the government. In Mao's view the emergence of divergent social interests as modernization advanced sparked the inevitable class conflict necessary to drive socialism ahead toward communism; the role of the Party (or, when the Party was itself infected, of those having the most advanced revolutionary consciousness) was to push these class conflicts forward in the interest of human progress.

While in the Maoist vision the Communist Party remained an agent of revolution, in the Dengist conception the Party is the primary agent of social conciliation and the overall manager of modernization. Its role is to mediate the social interests and conflicts that the process of modernization inevitably brings, and to contain them within bounds that ensure the progress of society steadily toward communism through development of the "forces of production." It referees such divergent interests and social conflicts directly through the impartial and universal application of socialist law; through the organizational discipline of its own members and their continued presence in all areas of social, economic, and cultural activity; and through various indirect "levers" at the disposal of the state. This redefinition of the Party's role underlay the entire range of organizational reforms of the Deng period, including the new criteria for Party recruitment emphasizing education and expertise, the institution of Party disciplinary codes and discipline inspection commissions, the separation of Party and government functions, and the elaboration of codes of socialist criminal and civil law.

Ideologically, what integrates the Dengist political community is the shared "patriotism" of all its participants, which commits them to the overall goal of China's modernization, and their acceptance that only socialism can harmonize the interests of all equitably and provide necessary direction toward the goal of modernization. In combining these two elements, "socialism with Chinese characteristics" was conceived as the ideological glue that binds the disparate groups together and allows the state to play its mediating role.

In practical terms, the Dengists' frequent emphasis on patriotism in conjunction with "socialism with Chinese characteritics" was aimed at helping the reform leadership rebuild confidence in communism as the true vehicle of Chinese patriotism and in the Chinese Communist Party as the true representative of Chinese nationalism in contemporary times. This effort sought both to overcome the disillusionment wrought by the Cultural Revolution and to recoup some of the ability that the regime had in its early years to mobilize nationalistic popular support for its goals and causes dissipated by the disasters of Party leadership of the late 1950s and 1960s.

The linkage of socialism to Chinese patriotism was argued forcefully, for example, in a long "contributing commentator article" published in People's Daily several weeks before the Party adopted its landmark resolution in 1981 on Mao and the Party's history. (The rarely used byline "contributing commentator article" [*teyue pinglunyuan*] signified an important commentary supplied by writers not on the newspaper's editorial board—usually from the staffs of high-level Party leaders. They differed from "commentator articles" [*benbao pinglunyuan*], which, like "editorials" [*shelun*], were written by the *People's Daily* editorial board and so carried the full authority of the paper. In the early Deng period contributing commentator articles seemed regularly to espouse viewpoints associated with Deng's reform group.) The experience of the Cultural Revolution, the article observed, had led people to "doubt that socialism can save China" and to lament (like the intellectual protagonist in Bai Hua's condemned "Unrequited Love") that "it is not that I do not love the motherland, but that the motherland does not love me." The article called such doubts "quite understandable" but nevertheless "erroneous." The Party's steps to correct its past mistakes demonstrated that it "shares the same destiny" with the masses of patriotic Chinese people, and the crimes of renegades such as Lin Biao and the Gang of Four should not be confused with the Party and the "socialist motherland." All "true revolutionaries," the article insisted, must "first be patriots"; all true patriots must "devote themselves to building and defending the motherland and to socialist modernization" and must support the Party, whose struggle remains "the most concentrated and glorious expression" of Chinese patriotism.[28]

The appeal to patriotism in support of the Party and its goals was also reflected in the Party's united-front approach to potential supporters of modernization. The most important and controversial step in this regard was an attempt, after several years' evolution and debate, to differentiate ideals that applied to Party members from those that applied to all "patriotic people" who supported the Party's goals. The distinction was spelled out in the 1986 resolution on "socialist spiritual civilization," which identified "building socialism with Chinese characteristics and making China a modern socialist country having a high degree of democracy and advanced culture and ideology" as the "common ideal" uniting all Chinese people at the current stage. The higher goal of "building a communist society" remained the "ultimate ideal" to which all Party members must aspire. That ideal, however, could not be forced on the masses of patriotic people and any attempt to do so would reflect "narrow-minded views on the question of uniting with all possible forces to build socialism" that had "seriously harmed" the Party's cause in the past. Only on the basis of the "common ideal" could it be possible "for Party members and non-Party people, Marxists and non-Marxists, atheists and believers, and citizens at home and those living abroad" to rally behind their common cause.

This delineation of separate ideals was a momentous change. To be sure, it was a natural complement to the watershed change of 1978—the shift of the focus of the Party's work from class warfare under socialism to socialist modernization. Nevertheless, it was significant in its own right because it made explicit the premises of social interest and allegiance on which the Dengist conception of China's political community was based. Most importantly, it marked a deliberate retreat of the state.

The Maoist conception was truly totalitarian in recognizing no preserve of private interest beyond the legitimate reach of the state and public concern, no boundary between state and society. Under the Dengist approach China's modernization was seen as requiring recognition and sanction of the interests and ambitions intrinsic to distinct social groups as the means of reintegrating Chinese society and mobilizing it behind the Party's modernization goals. Such recognition entailed acknowledgment of the existence of a legitimate private sphere beyond the routine reach of the Dengist state. Individuals were free to disbelieve the validity of Marxism-Leninism and to hold alternative political and intellectual viewpoints as long as they did not actively challenge the Communist Party's hegemony over the state. On the basis of such interests and beliefs, moreover, individuals could form associations and establish affiliations in a legitimate though not fully autonomous public sphere. This public sphere was circumscribed by the overriding priorities and concerns of modernizing China and built on the presumption of an underlying community of interests shared by all "patriotic" Chinese citizens among themselves and with the communist-dominated state. But within that perimeter there could be an authorized public discourse on affairs of the day. On this basis, the Dengist reformers not only tolerated but actively encouraged the astonishing proliferation of public organizations and associations—from the revived Chinese People's Political Consultative Conference and its attendant "democratic" parties, to professional societies, to religious sects and

churches, to hobby groups and benevolent foundations—that constituted an emergent civil society in the 1980s.

According to this approach, trade unions could no longer simply
serve as "transmission belts" mobilizing workers on behalf of the Party's
goals, but, as they were encouraged to do in 1980, could also represent
the particular interests of workers to the Party and state.[29] Religious
organizations could inspire believers and bind them into communities
that need not conflict with and in fact might abet the longterm developmental aims of the communist state. Professions could legitimately form
associations to advance their callings and monitor professional ideals
and norms productively on behalf of the state. What legitimated such
activities was the collective commitment to the modernization of China,
an agenda that the CCP itself would continue to dominate and guide.

On balance, characterization of the political system this Dengist
conception envisioned depends a great deal on the definitions used
in classification and on assessment of steps taken to implement it.[30]
Two fundamental characteristics nevertheless stand out. First, while
the Dengist conception abandoned Maoist totalitarian ambitions, it was
still authoritarian. The retreat of the state was intended not to weaken
it, but rather to strengthen it by encouraging a revived and collabo-
rative society. The routine political intrusions and attempted regimentation that the Maoist vision authorized by "putting politics in command" were gone, and the Dengist approach authorized new diversity
and some measure of autonomy in many spheres of economic, social,
and cultural activity. But it stopped well short of authorizing political pluralism. Social groups could organize legitimately and agitate for
their particular interests under the umbrella of the communist state
only as long as such agitation ultimately served the state's developmental goals. There was no provision for legitimate independent groups
or bodies to compete for political power on behalf of their particular
interests against the overriding developmental goals of the communist-
dominated state.

Second, the Dengist conception of China's political community
was highly utilitarian, and not liberal. The developmental goals that
both the state and society were presumed to share always took priority
over defense of individual liberties and the enhancement of individual

happiness and capacities. Individual pursuits and public associations served these higher collective goals, and only secondarily the satisfaction of particularistic ambitions such as "art for art's sake," religious enlightenment, or individual fulfillment.

THE PLACE OF SCIENCE IN "SOCIALISM WITH CHINESE CHARACTERISTICS"

Though intended to provide a comprehensive ideological framework that would unite China's political community on the road to modernization under CCP leadership, "socialism with Chinese characteristics" contained within itself the seeds of new tensions and conflicts of authority. The Dengist ideological revisions retained the "totalist" ambitions of Marxism-Leninism—its focus on totality, its claim to encompass and integrate all spheres of human experience and knowledge into a comprehensive, unified, and correct view of the world. The Party's toleration of diverse ideas and ideals among the various social groups under the socialist state in China's new political community did not mean that it had abandoned Marxism-Leninism's claim to validity as the single universal truth that integrated all human knowledge and guided the Party's exercise of power. There could be divergent ideas and ideals in society, but there could be only one ideology that integrated state and society into a whole.

The delineation of separate ideals opened the way, potentially at least, for conflicts of allegiance. In sanctioning the establishment of social, religious, and professional associations beyond direct management by the Party according to its ideals, the Party permitted the legitimate assertion within such groups of ideals, norms, and values that their respective members held distinctively. These norms and values needed not necessarily overlap completely with those of the state. If they mobilized such groups effectively behind the state's modernization goals, they were of positive value. But they might also spur such groups to assert agendas not compatible with the Party's. The regrowth of the norms of journalistic professionalism in the 1980s, for example, meant the emergence of a conflict between the Party's role for journalists as "the mouthpiece of the Party" and the professional norms of independent and objective reporting.[31] Similarly, if social, religious, and professional groups were free, as long as they were "patriotic" (manifested by their efforts in behalf of China's modern development), not to believe the ideals of socialism, then it was possible that some might come to see their patriotic mission in a different light. Patriotism and support for the Communist Party need not always be synonymous, and some groups might begin to see the Party's constraints on their autonomy as obstacles to fulfilling their patriotic ambitions.

These tensions and conflicts could emerge in any social or professional realm under the new political community that Deng Xiaoping's ideological revisions legitimized. They emerged with particular force among the community of China's scientists, however, and led to the emergence of dissent among a small but visible number by the end of the reforms' first decade. This stemmed directly from the peculiar social roles that scientists play in modern societies, especially those governed by Marxist–Leninist parties, as the authorized interpreters of a kind of knowledge with unique and universal claims to validity.

To the Dengist reformers, there was no apparent conflict between science and the Party, in either the theoretical or practical realm. Science, in fact, has occupied a crucially central place in the conception of "socialism with Chinese characteristics." The epistemological premise that Marxism is primarily a method of "seeking truth from facts" and that "practice is the criterion for testing truth," for example, is based on what one observer has called a "naive inductionist" and "faintly Baconian" view of the scientific method.[32] The old epistemological method of "practice—knowledge—again practice—again knowledge," which Mao outlined in his 1937 lecture "On Practice" and which was canonized into the body of Mao's works of enduring contemporary value by the 1981 Party resolution on history, is consciously akin to the commonsense view of science as progressing through the sequence of observation, hypothesis, experiment, observation, reformulated hypothesis, and so on. Adherence to this method, Deng and others have insisted, is what distinguishes Marxism-Leninism as a science. The method's value lay in its power both to enable the Party to formulate realistic and effective policies and to dispel ideas based on prejudice, fantasy, and superstition. For the Dengists, therefore, Marxism's "scientific" nature was thus essential both in their effort to set China back on the track of effective progress toward socialist modernization and in their critique of the "utopian fantasies" of Mao in his later years.

Similarly, as will be discussed at length in the next chapter, Deng and the reformers, in declaring that development of the "forces of production" is the primary task during China's socialist stage, argued that science and technology had emerged in the contemporary world as an important—and, by the late 1980s, *the* most important—"force of production" to be developed. As Deng himself made clear in his landmark speech at the 1978 national conference on science and as reform advocates emphasized tirelessly since, development of modern science and technology would be the "key" to China's overall modernization. Steps to promote such development were at the heart of the succession of long- and short-range plans the reformers formulated throughout the reform period.

Science also occupied a central role in the Dengist conception of collective values and attitudes at the core of "socialist spiritual civilization." "In today's world, science is increasingly becoming a revolutionary driving force of history" and "a main indicator of the level of progress a nation has attained," the 1986 Party resolution on "socialist spiritual civilization" observed. Therefore, education and scientific research require sustained development "because without them, not only can there be no socialist culture and ideology, but there can be no sustained economic growth."[33]

The central place science occupied in the entire conception of "socialism with Chinese characteristics" and in the program of reforms the Deng leadership promoted made it a particularly sensitive arena in which tensions and conflicts could arise. There have been several such tensions. First, exactly how and how far to "develop" Marxism's conclusions through application of its method to contemporary realities—especially in light of contemporary scientific theories—were not at all clear and turned out to be extremely contentious issues throughout the entire reform period. There quickly emerged a tension between the necessity of maintaining the "vitality" of Marxism by applying the "stand, viewpoints, and methods" (*lichang, guandian, he fangfa*) of Marxism to draw new conclusions in light of contemporary realities on one hand, and the need to continue to "uphold" the enduring and eternally valid "basic tenets" (*jiben yuanze*) of Marxism on the other. Emphasis on one half of the complementary demands of "developing" and "upholding" is, in fact, a reliable indicator of the relative conservatism or liberality of individual participants in Party debates.

CASS Institute of Philosophy director Xing Bensi, for example, advanced a relatively liberal view of the issue in a *People's Daily* article in 1980:

> Marxism, whose nature is revolutionary and critical, does not recognize any absolutes except that all things in the world are in absolute motion. This Marxist spirit is, of course, completely applicable to Marxism itself. The history of Marxism is a history of continuously substituting new conclusions for old ones and enriching Marxist principles with new practice. Only by developing Marxism and continuously enriching it with new practices can the truth of Marxism win people's trust.[34]

Similarly, Yu Guangyuan, a key figure in the formulation of virtually the entire front of economic, scientific, and technological reforms, argued consistently throughout the Deng period that the vast differences between the world in the time of Marx and Engels and that of the present day require the "creative" development of "concepts that do not exist in the classical Marxist works." In a 1985 speech marking the ninetieth anniversary of Engels's death, for example, Yu stated:

> We Marxists have never held that classical Marxist works (including those written by Marx and Engels, whom we are commemorating today) can solve all the questions China needs to solve today. . . . The conclusion can only be that we must actively develop Marxism. This idea is itself Marxist in nature. Classical Marxism was written for socialist revolution and is the science of socialist revolution. Now that China has entered onto the stage of socialist construction, it is in pressing need of a Marxist science of construction to give powerful guidance to China's reform.[35]

By contrast, those holding more conservative views on the issue usually acknowledged the need to develop Marxism but emphasized that there is a central core of conclusions and principles that must be upheld throughout such development. Former Party Politburo member

Hu Qiaomu adopted this approach in commenting on the publication of a second Chinese edition of the works of Lenin in 1984:

In building socialism with distinctively Chinese characteristics, of course, it is impossible to find the answers from the works of Marx and Lenin. However, we must always bear in mind the fundamental principles of Marxism-Leninism and study new situations and solve new problems in light of Marxism-Leninism's stand, viewpoints, and methods.[36]

Duan Ruofei, a frequent writer in the Party's theoretical journal *Red Flag* on major ideological issues, also stressed the continuity of Marxism's basic conclusions in taking direct issue with Yu Guangyuan's view on the need to distinguish the Marxist-Leninist science of revolution from the Marxist-Leninist science of socialist construction. Marxism is like "a big, tall tree," he said. "Its world outlook is the trunk of the tree, and the theoretical results gained from the study of the realities of both the periods of revolution and construction are the branches, leaves, and fruit on the trunk." Such a division of Marxism as Yu proposes, he suggested, is "inappropriate" because "the leaves and fruit are taken to be the entire tree, while the trunk disappears from sight." The result will be "confused ideas among some comrades" who think that "there is not much left in Marxism that is useful for a country in the socialist period" and who thus "lose sight of the role of the Marxist world outlook in guiding our structural reform."[37] Duan had earlier taken a similar view at a 1986 forum on theory work and "socialist spiritual civilization," acknowledging the necessity of developing Marxism, but only with renewed study of the theoretical achievements as a necessary prerequisite. Stressing the continuity between Marxists of the classical period and those of the present day, Duan said that "to us, all the past theories are 'streams,' not 'sources.' "[38]

For some, the demands of adapting Marxism to the contemporary world were so extreme as to constitute a "crisis," and so they called for extensive and radical revisions. Philosopher Li Keming argued in *People's Daily* in 1986, for example, that all three main components of Marxism-Leninism (dialectical materialist philosophy, political economy, and scientific socialism) were completely outstripped by developments in contemporary times and so needed to be replaced by "modern socialism." Modern science and the "new technological revolution" are "changing the whole face of the world and changing people's outlooks," so that Marxist philosophy needs to "reform its entire system and form." The evolution of modern capitalism in ways that proved the classical authors wrong made it necessary "to draw new conclusions about capitalism in the new period." The emergence of reform movements throughout the socialist world, moreover, showed that traditional ideas about socialist construction were "more and more outdated."[39]

Others argued that as a science, Marxism-Leninism should expect to make "breakthroughs" in its basic tenets as well as its secondary conclusions, paralleling the fundamental revisions that take place in scientific revolutions in other branches of science. Deng Weizhi, among others, asserted in 1986:

> Some principles that are "basic" today may not be so tomorrow. . . . Great developments in Marxism have frequently been attained by renovating and breaking away from such conclusions. Such breakthroughs will not detract from the glory of Marxism, nor will they affect its great status and role in human history. If we aim at making breakthroughs only in minor details, however, then it will be acceptable only to dogmatists.[40]

Philosopher of science Li Xingmin offered a similar view in an article in *Enlightenment Daily* early in 1988. "Any scientific theory has its own time and place," Li said. "Once it oversteps these bounds, even truth becomes falsehood. . . . The same is true for Marxist philosophy, which is neither universally applicable nor appropriate for all times."[41]

As it emerged within debate over specific issues, this need to "develop" Marxism led to conclusions that rapidly transgressed the boundaries of acceptable "upholding." The redefinition of the fundamental task of socialism as promoting the development of the "forces of production" raised in the minds of Marxist humanist philosophers such as Wang Ruoshui the question of production for what? For Wang, the answer was that the aim of socialist production—as is, in fact, the "starting point of Marxism" as a whole—is to fulfill the material and spiritual needs of humanity, a view that was bluntly rebuked in the 1983 attacks on "spiritual pollution."[42] Similarly, attempts to defend Marxism's "scientific" validity by emphasizing its methodological congruity with science—each testing theory in "practice"—led to the objection that Marxism-Leninism's "prediction" of communism has never been and cannot be tested in practice. Therefore it is not a "scientific prediction."[43] Yet another example stemmed from the Party's acknowledgment of China's relative backwardness after thirty years of socialism, its critique of "feudalism" as the source of the "leftist" deviations in its work in the 1957–76 period, and its discussions aimed at defining the current stage of China's socialist development. These characterizations probably unintentionally invited speculation about whether socialism was actually premature in China and whether it is justifiable that China has "skipped a historical stage" (i.e., missed the capitalist phase necessary to prepare the way for socialism).[44] The raising of these issues added to the intensity of the larger debate over how to "develop" while "upholding" Marxism.

A second source of potential tension and conflict with the Dengist conception of "socialism with Chinese characteristics" has been that lines of authority within the political and social structure it legitimated were not clearly demarcated. With respect to science, this tension was manifested in the problem of deciding who directs concrete work in specific fields of scientific research, paralleling the similar problem of delineating authority between Party officials and enterprise directors in the industrial arena. Determining who decides what research topics are worthwhile, what research problems deserve funding, who has the authority to evaluate the success or failure of scientific work, and who makes decisions about promoting others were issues in which researchers, institute directors, institute Party leaders, and State Council and high-level Party officials believed they had a say. It proved extremely difficult to work out solutions to these problems within an ideological framework that authorized the withdrawal of "politics" from concrete areas of activity but also was slow to extend overall autonomy and authority to those same areas. This tension was also manifested more abstractly in the problem of specifying who could legitimately interpret the significance and meaning of science's results, especially as they bore on the reinterpretation and revision of Marxism itself. In many ways, therefore, these tensions underscored a more general problem: "socialism with Chinese characteristics" did not effectively resolve a fundamental crisis of authority.

A third source of potential tension was that in transforming the mission of the Party from waging class struggle to promoting the development of the "forces of production," "socialism with Chinese characteristics" fundamentally changed the criteria for the CCP's legitimacy, which thereafter rested on the degree to which it was successful in spurring China's development and in distributing the gains of that development equitably according to some commonly accepted standard of fairness. Richard Lowenthal has identified such a transition to legitimacy based on performance as marking a communist system's entry into its "postrevolutionary phase," a new stage that brings with it a quite different array of pressures and demands.[45]

That the Party was acutely aware of the dilemma of dealing with raised expectations of itself among the populace at large was clear as early as 1981, when, in announcing a major program of economic retrenchment, it was forced to acknowledge that it had unduly raised popular expectations during the surge of reform in 1980.[46] More recently, a lengthy discussion of reform prospects by several "young and middle-aged theorists," published serially in People's Daily in late 1987, observed that the transition from "a warm-back and full-belly economy to a well-to-do economy" in China, as in other Third World countries, brought with it new social tensions and new demands on the political system. These pressures were manifested particularly in terms of rising expectations for "premature" consumption among many groups in Chinese society and in the need to deal with the sense of injustice that results from differential distribution of the benefits of development. In this new situation brought about by the reforms, "people always underestimate, intentionally or unintentionally, the level of their own incomes and overestimate that of others." This led, the article observed, to "a strange psychological effect: everyone feels that he has been at a disadvantage" because of the reforms. Reform, moreover, led to "drastic readjustment" in the various interests of different groups in society. Some of these were intentional, such as efforts to overturn the old egalitarian practice of "everyone eating from the same big pot"; others were unintended, such as corruption and speculation by taking advantage of the transition between planned and market economic structures. The inevitable "frictions and collisions between different interest groups," therefore, dictate new steps to open up channels of communication and legal mechanisms to reconcile and harmonize clashing interests among different groups in society. They also dictate new means to ensure state authority through the "powerful organizational abilities of the Party and government" to achieve social stability.[47]

As the next chapter will spell out in detail, scientific intellectuals were one such social group whose expectations were repeatedly raised and to whom the Party had difficulty in delivering benefits. On the one hand, scientific intellectuals were praised as conducting work critical to the success of the reforms. Their standing and remuneration should have risen accordingly, not only because they were unjustly treated during the Maoist decades but also because their role should increase in significance as societies modernize. On the other hand, the real effect of the reforms through the 1980s on some sectors of the scientific community was to lower both their overall social standing and rate of remuneration.

A fourth source of potential conflict within "socialism with Chinese characteristics" was its linkage of patriotism and socialism. In appealing to Chinese "patriotism" as a means to restore confidence in socialism and mobilize support for the Party's goals, the way was open, as suggested above, for criticism of the Party on nationalist grounds. Enunciation of the "common ideal" of all Chinese to modernize China, as distinct from the communist "ultimate ideal" that motivates only the Party and its sympathizers, gave rise to the possibility that the Party's shortcomings and failures might be judged from the standard of "patriotism." From such a perspective, the Party itself might be seen as an obstacle to China's future, and not its benefactor.

Called on by the Party to do science for the sake of the country, whether they believed in the ideals of Marxism-Leninism or not, some scientists came to see Party intervention in their work as impeding their conduct of patriotic duty and began to believe that to advance science in the interest of the country, they must in good conscience criticize the Party. From the Party's viewpoint, patriotic science very quickly became subversive science.

3 / China's Science Community under Reform

One of the great ironies of the Deng era has been that scientific dissidence arose in political opposition to a regime that from the beginning attached a high priority to science and technology, worked actively to rebuild China's civilian science community, and sought persistently to enhance the standing of scientists as a social group. These policies made many scientists outspoken supporters of the Dengist reforms at the outset. Gradually, however, the reforms revealed a conflict of ultimate goals between the regime and some scientists. In addition, successive changes in orientation, structure, and funding of the civilian science establishment brought new strains and problems not anticipated by the reform leadership.

These trends and pressures influenced the various segments of the scientific community differently. Especially among those in the "basic" sciences—those pursuing scientific knowledge for its own sake—a conflict of professional mission and identity with the regime's utilitarian goals for science emerged. Among some, the reforms were seen not as alleviating problems in the scientific community but as making things worse. By the late 1980s many scientists were deeply frustrated with the reforms, anxious over their jobs and futures, and alarmed at their declining standing in a rapidly changing society. A few, at least, felt a deepening alienation from a regime that they had previously supported, spurring them onto the path to political dissent.

THE CULTURAL REVOLUTION BACKGROUND

During the Cultural Revolution, China's natural and social science community suffered the same disruption and turmoil that affected other sectors. The Party Central Committee decision launching the Cultural Revolution in August 1966 identified the sciences as one of several intellectual fronts that required the establishment of a "proletarian" outlook and criticism of "typical reactionary bourgeois academic 'authorities'" who propagated "reactionary views." On that basis, the civilian science sector became the focus of bitter conflict. The Chinese Academy of Sciences was identified as a "bourgeois headquarters," senior academic scientists in numerous fields—natural and social—were criticized, publication of scientific journals ceased altogether, and research and teaching virtually ceased in many fields.

Science remained a focus of conflict through the early 1970s as a divided Party leadership struggled to establish policy priorities for China in the waning years of the Cultural Revolution. One group of leaders, clustered around Premier Zhou Enlai, sought to restore development-oriented priorities to the shattered civilian science establishment. Other leaders, centered on what was later called the Gang of Four, tried to preserve and extend the Maoist orientation in science that the Cultural Revolution had sought to impose.

In 1975 Deng Xiaoping, acting on behalf of an ailing Zhou Enlai, began steps to restore development-oriented priorities and practices to the civilian science sector. Deng's initiative followed the re-enunciation at the Fourth National People's Congress in January 1975 of the goal of building the Four Modernizations—in agriculture, industry, national defense, and science and technology—before the year 2000. In the following summer Deng commissioned compilation of a study on the status and needs of the Chinese Academy of Sciences by two of his closest supporters, Hu Yaobang and Hu Qiaomu. The resulting "outline report" became one of "three big poisonous weeds" criticized by the Gang of Four as Deng himself became the object of attack, leading to his purge for a second time in 1976.

Mao's death in September 1976 and the arrest of the Gang of Four in October made possible a resolution of this conflict over the direction of science. While China's new paramount leader, Hua Guofeng, and a rehabilitated Deng Xiaoping probably differed over the proper approach to rebuilding and modernizing Chinese science, both clearly agreed on the necessity to do so. Hua had, in fact, worked with Deng in his efforts to rebuild China's centralized science establishment in 1975.

Emerging from the close of the Cultural Revolution decade following Mao's death, therefore, was a succession of shifts and reorientations in overall science policy reflecting a common view of the central role science and technology play in economic modernization. An initial effort, under the leadership of Hua Guofeng, attempted to restore the centralized "big science" approach that had marked science policy before the Cultural Revolution. Thereafter, under Deng's leadership, followed reforms and readjustments designed to enhance coordination between the efforts to rebuild and modernize the Chinese science establishment and to promote economic modernization.

THE RELAUNCHING OF BIG SCIENCE: 1976–1979

The general orientation of science policy and the overall direction of efforts to rebuild China's science establishment in the first two years after Mao's death were intended to suit the direction and goals of economic development set down by the new post-Mao leadership under Hua Guofeng. This modernization approach continued the compromise model put forward by Zhou Enlai at the Fourth National People's Congress in January 1975. It emphasized Stalinist development through comprehensive centralized plans that focused on several large-scale projects and attainment of several key targets, administered by large bureaucratic hierarchies, while retaining Maoist mass-based practices and methods in some areas. Signaled by the publication in December 1976 of Mao's 1956 Politburo talk "On the Ten Great Relationships," this approach was enunciated in general terms at national conferences on agricultural and industrial work in late 1976 and early 1977. It was eventually embodied in a new "ten-year" plan (actually only eight years), sketched by Hua Guofeng at the Fifth NPC in February 1978 and scheduled to run through 1985. In his report on the plan to the NPC, Hua outlined a new science-development program that stressed simultaneously the restoration of basic research in such key fields as high-energy physics and molecular biology; rapid progress in such applied science and technology areas as electronics, space technology, and nuclear power; and continued mass-oriented efforts at popularization of technical methods, especially in agriculture.

This approach to scientific modernization was spelled out in more detail at a landmark national conference on science in March 1978, immediately after the close of the Fifth NPC. Both Hua Guofeng and Deng Xiaoping emphasized in their speeches the key role that development of modern science and technology would play in achievement of the other three "modernizations." The conference also examined a new eight-year plan for development of science, scheduled to run in parallel with the ten-year economic plan, until 1985. As described by Fang Yi, the CCP Politburo member who had assumed responsibility for execution of the regime's science policies, the plan incorporated the same balance of priorities that Hua described in his report to the NPC. It also specified eight new "pacesetting" high-technology fields where China would strive to catch up with advanced world levels before the turn of the century. Typical of the high-target emphasis of the overall approach to modernization under Hua's leadership, these fields included such applied science and technology development areas as computers, lasers, and genetic engineering, which were regarded as key sectors of the world's "new scientific and technological revolution." Also mandated were plans for rapid development in high-energy physics and for the construction of a world-class proton accelerator—efforts that reflected a concern less for immediate application in economic production than for achievement in a glamour field that would bring international recognition and prestige to Chinese science.[1]

The priorities and general programs enunciated in 1978 reflected intensive efforts undertaken over the preceding year. Many of the steps through that period bore Deng Xiaoping's stamp, whatever misgivings he may have had about the overall approach. In a talk at a forum of science and education officials in August 1977, Deng said he had "volunteered" to take charge of science and education work immediately after his rehabilitation in July of that year, a request the Central Committee had approved.[2] Many of the steps leading up to the 1978 science conference, as well as some of the themes Deng himself elaborated there, were thus the product of his own efforts and those of his close associates.

The goal of these efforts was the rapid restoration of China's science establishment and the bureaucracy that oversaw it, accomplished by improvements in the political and ideological atmosphere that would allow science to grow and flourish. In his August 1977 talk, for example, Deng endorsed restoration of the State Science and Technology Commission (which had been abolished during the Cultural Revolution) to "exercise unified supervision" over all civilian scientific work. This proposal was authoritatively endorsed by a meeting held to prepare for the national science conference and by a Central Committee circular the following September.[3] In the same talk Deng advocated overturning the "two assessments"—the Cultural Revolution allegations, authoritatively affirmed in 1971, that education (and by extension, science) during the seventeen years from 1949 to 1966 had been dominated by a "bourgeois black line" and that the outlook of the majority of intellectuals was "bourgeois." Authoritative endorsement of Deng's reversal of these "verdicts" was apparent in his keynote speech to the national conference on education convened in April 1978, immediately following the national science conference.

Also in his August 1977 talk, Deng advocated returning leadership of scientific research units to professionals rather than Party generalists. He called for a tripartite leadership system in which scientific professionals guide research, Party secretaries exercise overall leadership, and "logistics" experts ensure provision of the unit's resource needs. Deng's reiteration of this idea at the 1978 science conference registered its authoritative acceptance. In the 1977 talk, he also recommended a number of steps to improve the atmosphere for scientific research. He called for the release of scientific researchers from the demands of political study, allowing them to devote at least five-sixths of their work week to research. He also called for an atmosphere of open scientific debate that allows "the conscientious quest for truth and permits no deceit." And he urged promotion of academic exchanges and the expansion of academic publications to break down a prevailing tendency toward hoarding and "monopolization" of information. These steps, too, gained the stamp of authority when Deng reiterated them in his 1978 science conference speech.

Other complementary efforts were launched in 1977. Soon after the arrest of the Gang of Four in October 1976, scientific intellectuals and writing groups began what turned into a three-year campaign to criticize the impact of the Gang on science. According to these criticisms, the Gang of Four had not only disrupted China's scientific institutions and persecuted its scientific community, but also had propagated "obscurantist" views on scientific theory. At the same time, leading scientists such as Qian Xuesen (the expert in mechanics and systems engineering who is regarded as the father of China's space and missile program) and authoritative commentators wrote articles laying out the predominant themes in China's science policy during this period. They focused on the relative backwardness of China's stage of scientific development and the explosive pace of the worldwide scientific and technological revolution, the critical role of science in economic modernization, and the need to study and borrow from advanced foreign science and technology.[4]

Out of these discussions emerged two other major revisions in ideological principle that Deng Xiaoping personally enunciated at the 1978 science conference and that remained cornerstones in the foundation of China's science policies throughout the Deng era.[5] One was his landmark declaration that science and technology were to be counted in Marxist political economy as "forces of production," not elements of the "superstructure." The significance of this revision in principle was that science as a human activity no longer had a "class nature." As such, the ideas and theories of science were, in direct contradiction to the presumptions of Maoism, neither "bourgeois" nor "proletarian," nor were science and the material production that results from it thought to serve automatically the interests of any particular social class.

As "forces of production," in fact, science and the changes in technology that it fosters in all modern and modernizing societies were now recognized in China as increasingly important agents of human social progress. As science and technology unlock the laws of nature to human advantage, the resulting increased economic productivity and material abundance produce new demands on the "relations of production" and promote overall social advance toward successively higher stages. In so doing, modern science and technology hasten capitalism's inevitable march toward socialism; and socialism, because of its innate superiority in consciousness and planning, will advance even more rapidly toward communism. Though Deng sketched these latter conclusions only in general terms at the 1978 science conference, his remarks there became the locus classicus of the principles and presumptions that underlay the intense interest, attention, and urgency with which the world scientific and technological revolution was regarded throughout the entire reform period.

Stemming from this fundamental revision in principle on the nature of science was the second major departure that Deng enunciated at the 1978 science conference. This was the conclusion that, as persons involved in the promotion of fundamental "forces of production," scientists and intellectuals were "part of the working class itself." The importance of this change was that it removed the political stigma attached to intellectuals under the Maoist policies prevailing through the Cultural Revolution decade and invested them with a position of legitimate standing in the political community.

As leadership speeches, official statements, and authoritative commentary stated with increasing clarity and forcefulness throughout the subsequent reform period, the position and allegiance of intellectuals— and especially scientists—in that community was thought to be critical. In step with the increasing impact of science and technology on economic production, according to this line of thought, the importance of "mental labor" versus manual labor increases in all societies; and as economic production becomes increasingly complex and sophisticated, manual labor increasingly involves mental activity. Therefore the value of intellectuals, both as researchers and as teachers, increases as society develops under the impact of the new scientific and technological revolution. On this basis, as subsequent reformist commentary stressed in elaborate theoretical detail, intellectuals came to be regarded as the key social group in China's modernizing future. These views underlay the entire array of revised policies on the remuneration and status of intellectuals, education, Party and government cadre recruitment and evaluation criteria, and related questions.

READJUSTMENT AND REFORM OF SCIENCE POLICY: 1980–1984

The grand plans for scientific development put forward in the spring of 1978 were postponed within a year of their announcement and eventually set aside altogether. The initial impetus for this change was provided by the revisions in economic strategy and planning foreshadowed at the Eleventh Central Committee's Third Plenum in December 1978 and subsumed under the program of "readjustment and reform" announced in the spring of 1979. To these considerations of broader economic development strategy were added problems in science policy itself and in policy toward treatment of intellectuals. Over the next several years a new reformist strategy toward science emerged, designed to address at once problems of coordination between economic and science and technology policies, problems in the structure and orientation of the science establishment, and continuing difficulties faced by scientists with respect to their professional lives and livelihood.

On the economic policy front, the period of retrenchment and reform from 1979 to 1982 set in motion concerted central efforts to resolve evident imbalances among the various sectors of the economy and to address the chronic problems and unrealistic projections universally associated with the centralized planning approach embodied in the 1978 ten-year plan. Also launched in this period was a remarkable initiative, extending well beyond 1982, to formulate a new development strategy suited to China's particular strengths and weaknesses and emphasizing a much higher degree of coordination among the various economic, social, and scientific and technical components of development. Out of this process of development-strategy revision emerged the broad elements associated with "socialism with Chinese characteristics," as well as many of the distinctive approaches to reform of China's economic structure that became the hallmarks of the Dengist reform era.[6]

Successive national planning efforts reflected the goals enunciated by the strategists. The first of these was the effort in 1979–81 to revise and reorient along more realistic lines work already under way to formulate the Sixth Five-Year Plan (1981–85), eventually presented by Premier Zhao Ziyang to the annual session of the NPC in December 1981, and a projected but never-completed twenty-year plan, to run from 1981 to 2000. A second phase began in 1983 with the first steps toward the Seventh Five-Year Plan (1986–90), a draft of which was adopted in principle at the 1985 national Party conference, and a new fifteen-year plan for the period 1986–2000.

These broad attempts to find a new model of development and the concrete work of drafting more realistic national plans also generated a number of major studies on aspects of China's development prospects and problems. The most important was the *China in the Year 2000* study begun in 1981, studied by the leadership in preliminary form in 1983, and revised and published in 1985.[7]

These planning efforts and developmental studies sparked a proliferation of research bureaucracies and centers attached to different levels of the State Council presided over by Zhao Ziyang. The work of these research centers concentrated the efforts of China's leading economists and social science specialists, together with the work of lesser-known experts associated with them in already existing research facilities, such as the CASS.[8] The wide range of theoretical issues in Marxist political economy and the more concrete questions of economic strategy and policy debated in China's proliferating social science journals through this period are intelligible mainly in the framework provided by the larger, leadership-driven efforts at strategic planning and study.

As Carol Hamrin's work shows clearly, the succession of plans and studies produced through this period carry indications of compromise in emphasis and orientation that reflect the different preoccupations, preferences, and concerns of various senior Party leaders regarding scope and pace of the reforms, the nature and relative order of various reform steps, and the anticipated consequences of the reforms. The planning efforts and studies also manifested two other significant trends. First, they reflected a growing, conscious emphasis on the importance of coordination between economic, education, and science and technology development policies. This was apparent in the pattern of reform decisions announced through the 1980s. The case in point was the 1984 Central Committee "decision" on industrial economic reform and the parallel decisions in 1985 on science and education reform: the drafting of all three decisions was supervised by the same leading group, and originally they were to be adopted as a single document.[9] The interlocking of reform in all three sectors in 1984–85 was typical throughout the Deng years, and the wavelike surge and ebb of initiatives in economic reform that Hamrin describes coincides with similar ups and downs in science reforms both in the preceding 1981–83 period and afterward in 1987–88 and 1991.

The second major trend in the planning and developmental study processes inaugurated in this period was the emphasis placed on modern "scientific" approaches to planning and decision making. In planning, this entailed an increasing appreciation of the utility and value of modern techniques of forecasting and projection, including the use of computers and cybernetics, information theory, and other "cross sciences." Decision making now called for methods derived from systems theory, feasibility studies, and expert analyses. This new emphasis on "modern" and "scientific" methods stemmed not only from dissatisfaction with traditional piecemeal planning approaches. It also reflected the leadership's evident preoccupation and fascination with the world scientific and technological revolution and its economic, social, and political implications for the world as a whole—inspired in part by such grandiose development plans as the u.s. Strategic Defense Initiative research and the European Economic Community's Eureka program— and a heightened sense of urgency about the potential implications for China.

Both dissatisfaction with the previous planning procedures conducted by the conservative State Planning Commission bureaucracy and preoccupation with the implications for China of the global scientific and technological revolution account for the striking prominence— and even domination—of high-level science administrators and experts in many of the reform and long-term plan processes of this period. The ubiquitous presence of State Science and Technology Commission figures (such as Yu Guangyuan, Tong Dalin, and Wu Mingyu) and people from subordinate research bodies (such as Lin Zixin) in all of the larger reform-planning and study efforts was striking, especially in the early years.

With respect to science and technology specifically, both the shorter-term considerations of economic readjustment and longer-term trends in planning and study of the future course of economic reform dictated fundamental changes. In addition, problems intrinsic to science policy and to China's scientific establishment demanded revision. Beginning at the end of 1980, the leadership began to debate how to reform the orientation and structure of science in China in light of all these considerations. By the end of 1982, it began a series of experiments and steps that prepared the way for the landmark reforms introduced at a major science conference in 1985. These steps and reforms altered the foundations of China's science establishment and set in motion trends that deeply affected the conduct of science in the PRC.

The problems the reforms addressed were the classical defects associated with the essentially Stalinist approach to science that China had adopted from the Soviet Union in the 1950s. In many ways, these problems paralleled the rigidities in structure and imbalances in orientation that beset China's economic system. Critical evaluations in the 1980–81 PRC press of China's science and technology system complained about scientific research's lack of impact on economic development despite heavy investment in science. Because of barriers between the bureaucracies administering basic and applied science research units, and isolation of basic and applied research units from production enterprises, very little of the results of China's basic and applied research contributed to the improvement of production technology. This bureaucratic structure also fostered extreme departmentalization, ensuring a lack of cross-fertilization in research and an orientation in basic and applied research that had little relevance to the needs of the economic sector. The institutional and bureaucratic barriers also led to an enormous duplication of research across the span of the system.

The system froze younger and middle-aged researchers within units where aging senior scientists occupied the top positions, leaving them low prospects for promotion and little possibility of transfer to other units. Because research-project approval and funding within a particular unit was routinely extended to senior researchers whose scientific education and experience usually dated to the 1930s, 1940s, and 1950s, younger researchers who were trained according to more contemporary standards ended up as assistants and had little prospect of initiating projects of their own design. Funding of projects overall was parceled out among various units within a given research department or institute on an egalitarian basis, regardless of the relative costs and material needs of the particular project. The inevitable results were overfunding of some projects and underfunding of others. The call at the 1978 science conference for efforts to build research units at every level as part of the effort to diffuse science and technology innovation and results led to a blind proliferation of underfunded and essentially empty research centers. As a long investigative article in a Shanghai paper reported in 1981, "Some research centers are dubbed 'three no' centers (meaning no research subjects, no funds, and no personnel), some are known as 'three diminutive' centers (meaning one room, one seal, and one empty shelf), while others are styled 'three machine' centers (one mimeograph, one stapler, and one telephone)."[10]

The first steps to reform this system were discussed at a national conference on science and technological work convened in Beijing in December 1980. Though the conference was not publicized at the time, later references to it state that it "discussed and determined the general orientation [fangzhen]" of Chinese science and technology development. It specifically prescribed that economic, scientific and technological, and social development proceed in concert, with economic development the primary task. The significance of this overall principle, together with a number of "concrete measures" discussed at the conference, was further spelled out in the "Outline Report on the General Orientation of Scientific and Technological Development in Our Country," drafted by the State Science and Technology Commission and approved by the Party Central Committee and State Council on 16 April 1981.[11]

Though this document was not openly publicized at the time, its general thrust was foreshadowed in a *People's Daily* editorial on 7 April and was evident from comments on it by State Science and Technology Commission vice minister Tong Dalin at a press conference on 27 May. The text was eventually published in a major documentary collection for "internal (restricted) circulation" (*neibu*).[12] Tong said the new guidelines were intended to "correct the past situation in which economic and scientific development were planned in isolation from each other." The core of the new approach, the editorial stated, would be to ensure that development in science and technology "first and foremost promotes the development of the national economy." While acknowledging that there were grounds for believing that the purpose of science is to "explore the unknown," it stated that its primary purpose was to "increase the forces of production" in keeping with "national conditions" and developmental needs. The new orientation of science and technology called for by these guidelines was a radical departure from the system resumed in 1978, an approach the editorial rejected as based on "leftist thinking."

On the basis of this reorientation of science, the guidelines specified a number of policy departures. First, emphasis in science policy would shift to applied research and technology innovation and application. To accomplish this, institutional links between research units and production enterprises would be established through a variety of means, including consultancy services, contract systems, and outright mergers. Second, in line with the overall reorientation of economic priorities underway since 1979, both the civilian and military science sectors would begin to focus on application of technology to production of consumer goods. Third, also consistent with the general reorientation in overall economic policy, a more discriminating approach would be adopted on the importation of foreign technology.

Finally, and in line with the general retreat from the high-investment approach of the previous period, several expensive projects— including the glamour item of the 1978 plan, the proton accelerator, and the launching of telecommunications and meteorological satellites— would be postponed. These postponements, Tong explained, did not signal a "de-emphasis" in basic research. That sector of science would now have to proceed gradually within the framework and progress of the economic readjustment. The editorial stipulated further that the Chinese Academy of Sciences itself, the bastion of basic research, should begin to adopt a more differentiated approach to the priorities of basic, applied, and technological research.[13]

Concerted efforts to implement these new guidelines did not begin immediately. An authoritative *People's Daily* commentator article on 20 June 1981 implied that a coordinated central push to carry out the guidelines was not in the immediate offing, and urged that administrators and scientists not "just wait around for the reforms" but rather think about "what they could be doing right now" to begin the reforms themselves in their units. Several factors may have delayed implementation of the guidelines. First, there was the distraction of renewing impetus to the reforms in the economic structure, signaled by the establishment of the State Council's State Commission on Restructuring the Economic System (CRES) in the spring of 1982. Another distraction may have been created by preparations for the already-delayed Twelfth Party Congress, which finally opened in September 1982. The primary reason for the delay, however, may have been bureaucratic confusion and obstruction within the separate State Council institutional hierarchies responsible for the different economic and scientific sectors that were now supposed to be collaborating on a coordinated strategy.

When the central leadership was finally ready to move ahead with the guidelines in 1982, a number of steps were taken in rapid succession. First, at a State Science and Technology Commission meeting on 24 August 1982, Fang Yi reviewed favorably steps that had been taken by science and technology units on their own initiative. He revealed that the Commission had already selected a "first group of thirty-eight key problems" to be tackled in the effort to combine economic and scientific and technological development. He also revealed that the leadership was considering drafting a new fifteen-year plan for the national economy, to run from 1985 to 2000, which would focus on the "key role" of science and in which technology would "become more visible." [14]

Second, at a national science awards meeting on 24 October 1982, State Science and Technology Commission chief Fang Yi and Premier Zhao Ziyang strongly reaffirmed the significance of the 1981 guidelines and the correctness of their orientation. Building on Hu Yaobang's call at the Party congress the month before to quadruple national income by the year 2000, Zhao spelled out several new steps to spur the integrated growth of science and technology and the economy. These included a renewed effort to get economics advisers and science and technology experts together in coordinating national plans and formulating steps to spur applied and technological research. The latter included the establishment of technical development centers, the integration of scientific research units with production enterprises and technical consultant services, and the creation of contract responsibility systems for scientific and technological research.[15]

Third, a working meeting of the State Science and Technology Commission Party group in November 1982 discussed measures to implement the reorientation of science and technology toward economic work. In particular, it decided to begin work on the fifteen-year plan mentioned by Fang Yi in August, with preliminary drafting to be completed before the end of the year. The meeting seconded Zhao's call for collaboration between scientific and economic experts, and urged new steps to "reorganize" science and technology personnel and to "restructure the science and technology system."[16]

Fourth, in his report on the redrafted Sixth Five Year Plan (1981–85) at the annual NPC session on 30 November 1982, Zhao strongly underscored the significance of science and technology in China's economic future, endorsing the view of veteran economist Sun Yefang that growth would have to depend on technological transformation of the existing base, not on its extensive expansion. Without such a focus, he said, not only would the "quadrupling" goal prove unattainable, but the economic and technical gap between China and the developed countries "may even widen." He also reiterated many of the steps he had spelled out at the October science awards meeting and confirmed that the thirty-eight key problems specified by Fang in August for technical solution had been incorporated in the new five-year plan.[17]

Finally, in January 1983 the State Council announced formation of a new body to oversee coordination and implementation of these steps. The main tasks of the new body, called the State Council Science and Technology Leading Small Group, were to "unify organization and management" of science and technology, to "unify leadership" over formulation of long-term science and technology planning, and to study and coordinate policy decisions intended to facilitate technical transformation of the economy. The composition of the group lends credence to the conclusion that bureaucratic obstruction and confusion even at the State Council commission level was impeding science and technology reforms and overall integration of economic and science and technology planning. The chair was announced to be Zhao Ziyang, with State Science and Technology Commission minister Fang Yi and State Planning Commission minister Song Ping as his deputies. Named as members were: National Defense Science and Technology Industry Commission chief Chen Bin; Minister of Labor and Personnel Zhao Shouyi; Minister of Education He Dongchang; State Economic Commission vice minister Lu Dong; CAS vice president Yan Dongsheng; and Zhao Dongwan, vice minister of both the State Planning and State Science and Technology commissions.[18]

Immediately thereafter, Chinese media reported a meeting of the group to accelerate the organization of experts to begin formulating the long-term science and technology development plan. A follow-up work conference to accelerate planning of science and technology development and technical transformation of the economy opened in June 1983, which revealed that work had begun on drafting the Seventh Five-Year Plan (1986–90) and a "tentative plan" for economic development for 1991–2000.[19]

Over the following year, trial measures based on the broad reorientation of science policy began to be reported in PRC media. In May 1984, for example, Xinhua News Agency reported that State Council regulations designed to spur the "rational mobility" of scientific and technical personnel and promulgated for trial implementation in selected units in the latter half of 1983 would be implemented on a trial basis nationally.[20] In the same month, a *People's Daily* commentator article praised the successful trial implementation over the previous two years of a technical research-contract system in the Zhuzhou Municipal Electronics Institute in Hunan, which corrected defects of the old research system.[21] Zhao Dongwan, in his capacity as director of the General Office of the State Council Science and Technology Leading Small Group, went even farther. Praising the Zhuzhou approach as of "far-reaching significance" in the reform of the national science and technology system, Zhao revealed that the central authorities had decided to implement similar technical research contract systems nationwide within three to five years. He also said steps would be taken to introduce a new funding system for basic and applied research.[22]

Paralleling all of these broad efforts in the 1979–84 period to integrate economic and science and technology planning, to reorient national science and technology priorities, and to reform the science and technology system itself was a simultaneous central effort to improve the lot of intellectuals as a key social group.[23] These efforts included not only an attempt to break down traditional barriers to the transfer of scientists and technicians from one unit to another, explicit in the 1983 trial State Council regulations just described, but also an attempt to draw attention to and improve their living and working conditions and to make it easier for them to join the Party.

In late 1979 press commentary began to focus on the problems and difficulties of scientists and technicians, and intellectuals in general. *Enlightenment Daily*, for example, published in December 1979 the "abridged minutes" of a forum held jointly by the policy research offices of the State Science and Technology Commission and the CAS on how better to mobilize the "enthusiasm" of scientific intellectuals. The forum reportedly reviewed a number of problems routinely faced by such people, many of which were classically associated with the prevailing traditional science and technology system. For example, research units were universally dominated by older scientists who monopolized the funds and prerogatives of the unit. All of the members of a technical delegation that had recently gone abroad, the *Enlightenment Daily* report noted, were over sixty. Furthermore, senior people often had too many jobs. A senior scientist at the CAS Institute of Acoustics, for example, had twenty-eight different jobs. Nevertheless, such senior people usually lacked authority over areas such as personnel affairs, so that their ability to guide research was hamstrung. They also lacked respect among "leading cadres" responsible for work, who should have been consulting them for their technical expertise.[24]

Later press accounts cataloged a variety of other problems, focusing increasingly on the ranks of "middle-aged" intellectuals. Ren Zhongyi, then Party chief in Liaoning and a solid Deng supporter, observed in an *Enlightenment Daily* article that there remained a prejudice in the Party ranks against intellectuals, a belief that vulgar "uncouth" behavior and anti-intellectualism were badges of proletarian integrity.[25] A *People's Daily* contributing commentator article on 18 April 1980 observed that resistance in the Party ranks to resolving the problems of intellectuals sprang from a belief that "to rely on intellectuals is to weaken or give up Party leadership" and from the "fear that intellectuals may 'seize power from the Party.'" It also spotlighted problems in the living conditions of intellectuals.[26]

The central Party apparatus was apparently spurred into action after veteran Politburo Standing Committee member Chen Yun referred to the critical importance of middle-aged intellectuals (those educated in the 1950s and early 1960s) in his speech to the landmark Party central work conference in December 1980. Thereafter the Central Committee's Organization Department and the State Science and Technology Commission began their own investigation into the problems of intellectuals, the results of which they reported to the State Council and central Party apparatus in September 1981. A Central Committee circular, issued in January 1982, called on lower-level departments to "check up" on implementation of intellectuals policy. The dispatching of work teams from the Central Committee's departments of Organization, Propaganda, and United Front Work to the provinces followed in June 1982 to enforce this work.[27]

This "check-up" drive confirmed the worst of the stories in the press about intellectual treatment and conditions. The most disadvantaged were middle-aged intellectuals, a group said to number 5.7 million and identified in official statements and authoritative commentary as the critical "backbone" of China's developmental future. Salary levels of middle-aged teachers were found to be lower than standards established in 1956, and professors and instructors at colleges uniformly were paid at levels far below standard scale. Middle-aged intellectuals had living standards ranked among the lowest for urban social groups, and many were distracted by routine household chores. Significant health problems, traced to stress and overwork, were said to have created a "surprising" situation in which the death rate of middle-aged intellectuals was higher than that of the elderly.[28]

As a result, the central authorities began a concerted drive to improve conditions for middle-aged intellectuals. Over the next year a series of authoritative People's Daily editorials and commentator articles stressed the importance of changing the conditions this social group faced and enforcing implementation of appropriate Party policies at lower levels. The press underscored the concern for middle-aged intellectuals felt by central leaders, such as veteran marshal Nie Rongzhen, coauthor with Zhou Enlai of a more compassionate Party policy toward intellectuals in 1962. The premature death of two middle-aged scientists because of overwork and poor conditions was spotlighted in the press at the end of 1982, along with expressions of dismay from leaders such as Hu Qiaomu.[29]

Steps were also undertaken to overcome Party prejudice against intellectuals. Among the revisions incorporated in the new state constitution, adopted at the December 1982 NPC session, was the stipulation that intellectuals were a "main social force" of socialist China, alongside workers and peasants. Hu Yaobang dwelled on the critical importance of intellectuals in the Four Modernizations in his March 1983 speech marking the centenary of Marx's death. In May 1983 the Central Committee's Organization Department and Party Literature Research Office published a book of forty-five leadership speeches and Party documents on intellectuals policy from the 1977–83 period—thirty of which had not previously been publicized—to facilitate "clear understanding of the importance" of the issue. A circular issued by the Organization and Propaganda departments called on lower-level departments to organize systematic study of the book.[30]

There were also calls to improve the pay and living conditions of middle-aged intellectuals as an essential element of "basic capital construction," though continuing financial problems and deficits appear to have limited what central authorities were ready to do. Press commentary also stressed the importance of straightening out the titles, ranks, obligations, and responsibilities of various categories of intellectuals.[31]

THE CHINESE ACADEMY OF SCIENCES
AND THE EARLY REFORMS

In a long interview published in the Party's new theoretical journal *Seeking Truth* (Qiushi)—the successor to *Red Flag* (Hongqi)—in 1988, CAS president Zhou Guangzhao divided the post-Mao history of the Academy into two broad phases: a period of "restoration and learning" from 1977 to 1982, and one of "exploration, reform, and development" thereafter.[32] These time frames precisely parallel the restoration and subsequent reorientation that characterized the evolution of broader economic and science and technology policy.

In 1977–78 the speed and direction that Deng Xiaoping and Fang Yi brought to bear in overall science policy were evident in the resumption of activities in the Academy as well. Though founding CAS president Guo Moruo continued to preside as a figurehead until 1979, Fang was named a vice president in January 1977 and quickly began steps to restore order. At the Fifth National People's Congress in 1978, seven more vice presidents were appointed, including leading scientists of the pre–Cultural Revolution years.

That change was under way was evident when, in a speech to the 1978 science conference, newly appointed vice president Li Chang said that "hardcore elements of the Gang of Four's factional setup" in the Academy were still putting up "stubborn resistance," but that decisive progress had been made in "dragging out" such people thanks to the efforts of Fang and several "old comrades" entrusted by the Central Committee. He predicted that such "screening work" would be completed "soon."[33] Media accounts reported progress in the "reversal of verdicts" on scientists persecuted during the Cultural Revolution, and several prominent scientists and CAS writing groups wrote scathing attacks on the disruption the Gang and their adherents had inflicted on the Academy.[34]

Judging by press accounts, the effort to restore the Academy to its pre–Cultural Revolution standing also proceeded quickly. Before the Cultural Revolution, the CAS, as China's most prestigious and powerful basic research institution, included more than one hundred institutes and research centers. During the Cultural Revolution, this number shrank to less than forty (either through outright abolition or transfer of institutes out of the Academy's supervision), though by 1973, perhaps thanks to Zhou Enlai's and leading science adviser Zhou Peiyuan's efforts, the number had grown to fifty-three.[35] After 1977 the CAS rapidly regrouped former regional affiliates, revived several old institutes, ceded its former Philosophy and Social Sciences Division to the newly founded Chinese Academy of Social Sciences, and founded many new institutes. Despite losing the thirteen research institutes of the Philosophy and Social Sciences Division to the CASS, the CAS in this period of restoration and expansion grew by 1981 to include 117 institutes and research centers and a staff of seventy-five thousand, of whom thirty-six thousand were researchers and technicians.[36]

Efforts to restore order to the internal organization and management of the Academy proceeded according to the overall principle, put forward by Deng in his 1977 talk and again at the 1978 science conference, of placing supervision of scientific research in the hands of scientists instead of Party committee and core-group cadres. The intent of instituting this division of labor within the Academy was, by designating it as a preserve to be governed relatively autonomously by the scientific community's standards of professionalism, to prevent the politicization of scientific research.

In his science conference speech Deng had stated that Party committees in scientific research units could not "handle everything," but should concentrate instead on "ensuring the correct political orientation" of their units through their participation in overall planning. Institute directors and their deputies should be given "a free hand" over research; and while Party committees should be "acquainted" with ongoing work and "check up on it," they "should not attempt to take it over." "Such matters as the evaluation of scientific papers, the assessment of competence of professional personnel, the elaboration of plans for scientific research, and the evaluation of research results" should be entrusted to "the judgment of scientists and technicians." When scientists disagree on such matters, Deng said, Party officials must "encourage free discussion" according to the principles of "letting one hundred schools of thought contend."[37]

Successive steps to rebuild the CAS's internal structure reflected this provision for the coexistence of continued Party leadership in the Academy and professionalism in scientific research. In 1978 the Party Politburo and the State Council approved the restoration of the Academy's system of five academic departments that had governed and coordinated the work of the institutes before 1966 but had lapsed during the Cultural Revolution. A CAS conference in the summer of 1979 provided for selection of "the country's outstanding scientists" to become members of the departments' standing committees through a process of nomination, appraisal, election by secret ballot by the departments' members, and approval by the State Council.[38]

Rebuilding the management of the institutes proceeded according to the same general principles. Publicity given to the first batch of new institute directors and deputy directors in December 1977, in fact, underscored the division of labor even before Deng first enunciated it publicly at the 1978 science conference, and CAS vice president Li Chang, in his speech to the same conference, affirmed that the Academy would continue to adopt it.[39]

The crowning step in this effort was the restoration of the Academy's Scientific Council as its "highest policy-making body." Originally set up in the major CAS reorganization of 1955, the Council lapsed during the Cultural Revolution.[40] In early 1979 the State Council approved its restoration, and in July of that year the CAS began the process of adding new members to the 117 who had survived the Cultural Revolution. This process was completed in March 1981, when Xinhua News Agency announced that the State Council had approved the addition of 283 scientists to the body, bringing its total to four hundred.[41]

In May 1981 the reconstituted Scientific Council convened its fourth full session—and its first since 1960—amid great fanfare in the press and attention from Party leadership. Intended to mark the completion of the effort to rebuild the Academy, the session elected a new leadership and adopted a new constitution on an "experimental" basis. In his report on the work of the Academy, President Fang Yi announced his intention to step down, suggesting that "a scientist should take over the job and the present system of giving leaders lifetime tenure should be changed." In the subsequent elections at the Council session, physical chemist Lu Jiaxi replaced Fang as president and five vice presidents were named, only two of whom had held the post before the session. All but Hu Keshi, who had assisted Fang Yi in the Academy since 1977 and was appointed vice president in 1978, had scientific backgrounds. Under the provisions of the new constitution, all were limited to a two-year term, with the possibility of election to a single subsequent term.[42]

The structure laid out in the new CAS constitution formally named the Scientific Council the "supreme decisionmaking body" and stipulated that its membership be limited to scientists and that it meet every two years. Between sessions decisionmaking was to reside in the Presidium, elected by the Council during its full sessions for four-year terms and convened three or four times a year. Two-thirds of the membership of the Presidium were to be drawn from among members of the Scientific Council; only a remaining third were to come from "departments concerned" in the Party and the State Council. Following these procedures, the 1981 Council meeting elected a twenty-nine-member Presidium. Day-to-day management of the Academy was left in the hands of the president and vice presidents.[43]

These steps to restore the Academy and to emphasize supervision of scientific research by scientists marked the resumption of the Party's hybrid "technocratic" approach to science, used in the 1961–66 period, which R. P. Suttmeier has described as the "bureaucratic-professional model"—perhaps now with accent on its "professional" elements.[44] Nevertheless, the CAS was clearly not intended to become an autonomous scientific body. The Academy was now subject to direct supervision by the State Council and its State Science and Technology Commission, which provided its budget and guided the orientation of its work.

Establishment of this line of command was an important change, formalizing a trend toward depoliticization of the natural sciences begun in the mid-1950s but interrupted in the Cultural Revolution decade. In the early years of the PRC, the CAS fell under the Party's Propaganda and Education System (Xuanchuan Jiaoyu Xitong) and ultimately reported through the Party's Propaganda Department. By the late 1950s this line of authority began in practice to be revised, concurrent with the efforts of Nie Rongzhen and Chen Yi to formulate a long-term science plan. Although most of the CAS reported directly to Nie and Chen (and after 1958 to the State Science and Technology Commission), the change was apparently not formalized.[45] In the post-Mao period, the CAS was finally shifted to the Party's Administrative System (Xingzheng Xitong). The significance of this shift was enormous in curtailing the direct politicization of science as had occurred in the Mao era. The purpose of the shift, however, was to facilitate the Academy's reorientation toward the practical needs of the economic sector, and so constituted politicization of a different sort.

The Party's influence, exercised through a variety of means, remained pervasive in the Academy. First, the system of replicated Party committees and core groups down through successive structural levels that the CCP has always deployed in virtually all organizations in China remained intact in the Academy. As a result, a network of branch Party committees and core groups pyramided upward through the research institutes into the Academy's top-level Party committee, chaired after 1981 by CAS vice president Yan Dongsheng. From there, the Academy Party committee and core group reported directly to the Party committee of the State Science and Technology Commission. In 1981 that meant reporting to Fang Yi, who, as member of both the Secretariat and Politburo responsible for the Party's supervision of the science community, remained China's highest leader in science.[46]

Second, the shift toward scientist responsibility for scientific research was accompanied by a concerted drive to recruit scientists into the Party and to appoint Party scientists into the leadership of the Academy and its institutes. A May 1980 meeting of the entire CAS Party apparatus to "discuss upholding and improving Party leadership within the Academy" emphasized the need to "develop Party membership among scientists and technicians by gradually increasing the percentage of scientists and technicians in the Party committee of each institute to over 50 percent."[47] In November 1981 Qin Lisheng, deputy secretary of the CAS Party committee, said that the effort to recruit scientists was proceeding well and that "many" had applied for membership.[48] President Lu Jiaxi and at least three of the six Academy vice presidents elected in 1981—including Yan Dongsheng, who also was elected to the Central Committee at the Twelfth Party Congress in 1982—appear to have been such Party scientists. Of the remaining three, Hu Keshi was a Party member but not a scientist.

Within the Academy such Party scientists were called upon to up-hold both professional standards and Party discipline and allegiance. At a joint CAS-CASS meeting of Party committees in July 1983, Politburo member Hu Qiaomu reiterated what these expectations were. Party scientists, he said, must play "exemplary and leading roles in scientific research work." At the same time, they should "take the Marxist stand, courageously struggling against all erroneous and reactionary tendencies and ideological trends" by giving "scientific explanations and proof and convincing publicity."[49]

Third, Party influence extended into the Academy's Presidium. Aside from the president and the vice presidents, who were Party members, the Presidium included several other Party scientists among its twenty-nine members. Four, in fact, became members of the Party Central Committee in 1982, and a fifth became an alternate.

Last, Party influence was conveyed—albeit with different emphases—by Yu Guangyuan and Yu Wen, both of whom served on the CAS's Presidium. Historically, Yu Guangyuan was the key figure in Party supervision of both the natural and social science work of the Academy before the Cultural Revolution. From the mid-1950s down to the Cultural Revolution, the CAS's Party apparatus reported directly to the Science Office of the Party Propaganda Department.[50] This office was directed by Yu Guangyuan, who, in addition, was after 1958 a member of the Party Central Committee Science Small Group (Zhongyang Kexue Xiaozu) chaired by Nie Rongzhen. Beginning in 1956 as a deputy secretary of the State Planning Commission under Chen Yi, Yu was responsible in the State Council for direct supervision of the CAS's natural and social science planning. On top of all of these posts he had been a member of the Philosophy and Social Sciences Department Academic Committee since its formation in 1954 and a vice minister of the State Science and Technology Commission under Nie Rongzhen since the early 1960s.[51] At the 1981 CAS Science Council meeting, Yu was elected a member of the CAS Presidium. Throughout his career, he had been known as a promoter of professional norms in the science community and of relatively liberal interpretations of Marxism-Leninism. Consistent with these predilections, Yu was a consistent exponent of the need to "develop" Marxism in the 1980s.[52]

In political temperament, Yu Wen was Yu Guangyuan's opposite. In the early years of the PRC, he served in Xinjiang with Wang Zhen and Deng Liqun—men who emerged as key members of the conservative reform camp in the 1980s. From 1958 until the Cultural Revolution, he served as a deputy secretary-general of the CAS Secretariat, which in those years oversaw implementation of administrative and academic policy in the Academy. According to Chu-yuan Cheng, Secretariat officials were drawn from among the Academy's leading scientists after the body's formation in 1954, but after 1956 these posts were held by Party veterans to ensure Party control.[53] Yu Wen resumed his post as CAS deputy secretary-general in 1977, when Fang Yi took overall charge of the Academy, and became CAS secretary-general in 1978. He continued to hold this post until 1983, when he left to become executive deputy director of the Party Propaganda Department, then directed by Deng Liqun. He was elected to the CAS Presidium in 1981. His tenure in that post concurrent with his position in the Propaganda Department was thus intriguing evidence of the survival of the Academy's link to that Central Committee department from the pre–Cultural Revolution years.[54]

In light of such pervasive Party influence and control of the Academy, it is not surprising that there were indications that the effort to give scientists principal responsibility for such functions as evaluating the performance of other scientists and supervising research, free from the direct supervision of Party cadres and committees, was less than successful. An account of an October 1980 forum on CAS cadre work, for example, made it clear that non-Party scientists were routinely discriminated against in such matters as promotion, assignments, and privileges. "The consensus [of the forum] was that there should be no discrimination between Party members and non-Party persons, whether in giving academic degrees and ranks, in assigning academic jobs, or in choosing persons to make inspection tours abroad and to receive foreign guests. It will not do to depend exclusively on Communist Party members," the forum concluded.[55]

Even more telling was an account of the five-year delay in the appointment of a non-Party institute director and the obstruction of his work by institute Party committee leaders, publicized in 1984 as an example of persisting "leftist" obstruction of the Party's policy on intellectuals. The saga began in 1978 when Zheng Zemin, a non-Party member, was appointed deputy director of the CAS Institute of Mechanics upon the death of the previous deputy director. The Institute had had no director since before the Cultural Revolution, when its last director, Qian Xuesen, had been promoted to higher positions. Institute scientists reportedly greeted Zheng's appointment very favorably, since he had been trained by Qian personally in the United States.

Zheng began to put the Institute's work in order in 1978, but after a new Party committee secretary was appointed in May 1979, Zheng was "often confronted with problems" created by the secretary's "disruption" of his work. When the Academy leadership investigated the situation in 1980, the Party secretary insisted that there was no qualified candidate for the directorship and appealed to Zhou Peiyuan to assume the job. Zhou declined and the Party secretary was eventually overruled. Zheng was appointed executive deputy director and began "to exercise the functions of director." Nevertheless, the Party secretary continued to obstruct Zheng's efforts, burdening him with "routine and tedious administrative affairs" and preventing him from acting in his role as a scientist. This obstruction persisted even after the Party secretary was removed in the summer of 1981, because his former deputy took charge of the Party committee and continued to harass Zheng.

In April 1983 the CAS General Office informed the Institute Party committee of its intention to admit Zheng into the Party, but the committee objected because of problems in his background. These obstructions were not removed until the CAS's Party core group "took up the matter directly" and sent an investigation team to the Institute. Zheng was admitted into the Party in late 1983 and appointed director in February 1984.[56]

Aside from the Party's presence, the overarching structure of Party and State Council supervision over the Academy naturally ensured that the orientation of its work suited the demands set for it by the national leadership and followed the general contours of the evolution of science and economic policy. After the demise of the national science and economic plans put forward in 1978, the Academy shifted its focus away from the high-investment science targets set for it and began to revise its orientation, first in light of the needs of economic retrenchment in 1979 and then in light of reform based on the more tightly integrated economic and science planning policies begun in 1982. The reorientation of the early 1980s in particular set in motion trends that, with the major reforms of 1985, began to change the Academy's mission and self-identity decisively.

In his 1988 interview in *Seeking Truth*, CAS president Zhou Guangzhao recalled the reorientation of the Academy's work begun in 1982 as expressly designed to overcome the defects of its traditional structure, forcing it to address technological problems raised in China's economy and make the results of its research felt more directly there. The Academy, he said, was originally designed to meet the needs of "pure planned economy" and to concentrate resources and expertise on a few projects vital to the state—such as nuclear weapons development—at a time when China's access to world technology was blocked. Its structure was copied directly from the Soviet Academy of Sciences, and while that system had its merits, it no longer suited contemporary realities requiring a more extensive, decentralized approach. The system, Zhou said, also led inevitably to all the defects that plagued China's science and technology system, including redundant staffing, duplication of research and organizations, steadily increasing average ages of staff leadership, and poor efficiency.

The reorientation of the Academy's work toward better serving the needs of the economy, he recalled, "caused a strong reaction in the Academy and a massive debate on the relationship between economic development and science and technology." Some scientists believed that the state should provide sufficient funds to advance research to world levels, regardless of the level of overall development nationally. Zhou's own view, he said, was that science could "no longer be developed in the study, as it was in Newton's day." Citing the example of debate in the United States over funding the superconducting supercollider (ssc), he stressed that societies could not support science without regard to economic capacity and impact.[57]

Concrete steps to reorient the Academy's research toward serving the economy were announced almost immediately after Zhao Ziyang enunciated the overall approach to science at the awards ceremony in October 1982 and at the NPC session the following December. At an annual CAS work conference in late January and early February 1983, President Lu Jiaxi announced a series of reforms designed to upgrade Academy attention to applied science and technology research problems and to strengthen its direct ties to production enterprises. Lu also laid out plans for trial implementation of research responsibility systems and corresponding employment contract systems that would potentially improve remuneration to scientists and technicians through a system of floating wages. He also spelled out arrangements to contract out Academy applied science researchers as consultants and for them to be paid out of the profits of such services, and he stipulated that Academy researchers could earn extra income through spare-time services outside the Academy.[58] The annual CAS work conference in February 1984 favorably reviewed implementation of these steps in the intervening year and emphasized the importance of continuing them.[59]

The people most anxious about the import of this reorientation were undoubtedly those engaged in basic scientific research. Such researchers persistently voiced concern about the impact on research on fundamental scientific theory of both the economic readjustment policies of 1979 and the reforms after 1982, often calling on the state to establish a national science fund to support such work.[60] The 1984 CAS conference stressed the need to "continue to attach importance to basic research," indicating that the trial reforms introduced the previous year were already generating anxieties in that field.

THE CHINESE ACADEMY OF SOCIAL SCIENCES AND THE REFORMS

The import of the CAS reforms is underscored by the fate of the Academy's former Philosophy and Social Sciences Department, which split off in 1977 to form China's highest social sciences research body, the Chinese Academy of Social Sciences. The benign official explanation of this separation was that it was intended simply to help "develop social sciences in China." But the true reasons were far more political. The split moved the CAS's natural sciences divisions out of the propaganda and ideology system, under whose supervision it had worked previously, and, in keeping with the thrust of the science reform's emphasis, into the administrative system that coordinated the State Council's work. The split left the CAS's former Philosophy and Social Sciences Department still under the supervision of the Party Propaganda Department and the Party's propaganda and ideology system and effectively insulated the CAS from the politicization that perennially infested its former department.[61] An examination of the different functions each academy was called upon to perform in the Deng period helps to illuminate these purposes and underscores some similarities and differences in the impact of the 1980s reforms on each.

The splitting of the CASS from the CAS was authorized by Party chairman and PRC premier Hua Guofeng on 7 May 1977.[62] Hu Qiaomu was appointed the CASS's first president at the NPC in February 1978, and over the following several months the press mentioned at least four vice presidents: Zhou Yang, Huan Xiang, Deng Liqun, and the ubiquitous Yu Guangyuan.

As did the CAS, the CASS focused much of its attention in its first two years on rehabilitating China's social sciences establishment from the impact of the Cultural Revolution and in formulating national plans for social sciences research.[63] A Xinhua report published in People's Daily in July 1979 recalled that nearly half of the former CAS Philosophy and Social Sciences Department's 2,100 researchers had been the object of "special investigations" during the Four Clean-ups" (Siqing) movement of 1963–64 and in the early years of the Cultural Revolution as a result of the activities of the radicals Wang Li, Guan Feng, Qi Benyu, and Chi Qun, as directed by Kang Sheng, Chen Boda, and Yao Wenyuan. In the end, there were "little more than two hundred" researchers actively working in the Department.

A special CASS team was set up in 1977 to review these cases, and over the following year it completed reinvestigation of 1,012 cases from the Four Clean-ups and Cultural Revolution period, and another forty-five from the 1957 Anti-Rightist campaign. As a result more than eight hundred researchers in the various social sciences were cleared and rehabilitated. These included such major figures as former Higher Party School chief and philosopher Yang Xianzhen; economist Sun Yefang;

historians Liu Danian, Li Shu, Yin Da, Lo Ergang, and Gu Jiegang; archaeologist Xia Nai; *Dream of the Red Chamber* specialist Yu Pingbo; historian of philosophy Hou Wailu; and historian of science Xu Liang-ying.[64]

In 1978 the CASS embarked on efforts to draw up three- and eight-year plans (1978–80 and 1978–85) for the social sciences, in line with corresponding work on national economic and science plans for the same periods. These were begun at a CASS meeting in March 1978, im-mediately after the NPC, and discussed at a major CASS conference the following September.[65]

The growth of the CASS's institute structure was particularly rapid. Table 3.1 shows successive snapshots of the institutes housed under the CAS Philosophy and Social Sciences Department from 1950 to 1977 and under CASS since 1977. Some aspects of the spectacular expansion after 1977 are particularly noteworthy. First is the rapid pro-liferation of economics institutes. These were formed in two phases, in 1978 and 1982, by splitting off research divisions from the Institute of Economics.

Second is the growth of foreign studies institutes, beginning with the establishment of the South Asian Studies Institute in 1978 and fol-lowed by the establishment of institutes for every other region of the world in 1981. The 1983 CASS handbook states that the Institute of Latin American Studies, founded in 1961, was transferred to the Party Interna-tional Liaison Department in 1963. Similarly, according to the handbook, an Asian Studies Institute, founded in 1961, was also transferred to the International Liaison Department, where it was reorganized into sepa-rate institutes of Southeast Asian Studies and of West Asian and African Studies. Preparations were made in 1964 for the establishment in the CAS Philosophy and Social Sciences Department of an Institute of Soviet and East European Studies, but that institute was formally established in 1965, again under the International Liaison Department.[66] It would appear, then, that the effort to establish foreign area studies in the early 1960s became caught up in the increasingly politicized foreign policy debates of the period, and that at some time in the late 1970s a decision was made to transfer these institutes back to their original home.

A third noteworthy feature is the establishment within the CASS of the Institute of Marxism–Leninism–Mao Zedong Thought. According to

Table 3.1

EVOLUTION OF CASS INSTITUTE STRUCTURE, 1950–1988

Year	Number of Institutes	Institutes	
1950	3	Archaeology (1950) Linguistics (1950) Modern History (1950)	
1955	7	Archaeology Linguistics Modern History Literature (1953)	Economics (1953) History (1954) Philosophy (1955)
1960	10	Archaeology Linguistics Modern History Literature Economics History	Philosophy Minority Languages (1956) Law (1958) Nationalities (1958)
1962	11	Archaeology Linguistics Modern History Literature Economics History	Philosophy Nationalities (1962)[a] Law Asian Studies (1961) Latin American Studies (1961)
1966	13	Archaeology Linguistics Modern History Literature Economics History Philosophy	Law Nationalities World Economy (1964) Foreign Literature (1964) World History (1964) World Religions (1964)
1978	20	Archaeology Linguistics Modern History	Foreign Literature World History World Religions

Table 3.1
(*continued*)

Year	Number of Institutes	Institutes	
		Literature	Industrial Economics
		Economics	(1978)
		History	Agricultural Economics
		Philosophy	(1978)
		Law	Finance and Trade (1978)
		Nationalities	South Asian Studies
		World Economy	(1978)
		Information (1975)	Journalism (1978)
		World Politics (1978)	
1980	24	Archaeology	Information
		Linguistics	World Politics
		Modern History	Industrial Economics
		Literature	Agricultural Economics
		Economics	Finance and Trade
		History	South Asian Studies
		Philosophy	Journalism
		Law	Marxism–Leninism–Mao
		Nationalities	Zedong Thought (1979)
		World Economy	Sociology (1979)
		Foreign Literature	Minority Literature (1980)
		World History	Youth and Juvenile Affairs
		World Religions	(1980)
1982	32	Archaeology	South Asian Studies
		Linguistics	Journalism
		Modern History	Marxism–Leninism–Mao
		Literature	Zedong Thought
		Economics	Sociology
		History	Minority Literature
		Philosophy	Youth and Juvenile Affairs
		Law	American Studies (1981)
		Nationalities	West European Studies
		Foreign Literature	(1981)

Table 3.1

(*continued*)

Year	Number of Institutes	Institutes	
		World History	West Asian and African
		World Religions	Studies (1981)
		Information	Latin American Studies
		Industrial Economics	(1981)
		Agricultural Economics	Urban and Rural
		Finance and Trace	Construction (1982)
		World Economy and	Econometrics and
		Politics (1981)[b]	Technical Economics
		Soviet and East European	(1982)
		Studies (1981)	Political Science[c]
		Japan Studies (1981)	
1984:	34	Same as 1982, with the addition of: Chinese Character Usage (1984)	Taiwan Affairs (1984)

NOTE: This table lists the institutes housed in sample years under the CAS Philosophy and Social Sciences Department from 1950 to 1977 and under the CASS after 1977. The component institutes of the CASS did not change after 1984 through the early 1990s. The year each institute was founded is listed in parentheses.

SOURCES: For listings through 1982: Chinese Academy of Social Sciences, *Zhongguo Shehui Kexue Yuan*. For later listings: *Xinwen gongzuo shouce* Editorial Committee and Editorial Board, *Xinwen gongzuo shouce*, 324; and Xinhua, 8 October 1988 (trans. in FBIS-China, 12 October 1988, 51). It is worth noting that the numbers listed by Chinese media frequently differ from those listed here.

[a]In 1962 the Institute of Minority Languages merged with this institute.

[b]Formed through the merger of the Institutes of World Politics and World Economy.

[c]Preparatory section in place; formally established in 1985.

its former director, Su Shaozhi, the institute's roots go back to Yan'an's Marxism-Leninism Research Institute, of which Yu Guangyuan was a member. That institute was inevitably affected by the political conflicts of the 1950s and 1960s, and was reorganized several times and finally dissolved during the Cultural Revolution.[67] According to Su, the proposal to establish a new Institute of Marxism–Leninism–Mao Zedong Thought in the CASS came from Hu Qiaomu in the wake of the 1978 Third Plenum. Hu originally intended to serve as its director, in addition to his post as CASS president, but gave the post to Yu Guangyuan.

Under Yu's supervision, the Institute rapidly emerged as a hotbed of explorations and reinterpretations of Marxist theory, assuring its entanglement in controversy and larger political conflicts. Its abolition was debated in 1983, and in 1987 (in the wake of the campaign against "bourgeois liberalization") its transfer from the CASS to the Central Party School—to place it under stricter supervision—was proposed.[68]

Administratively, the internal structure of the CAS was simpler than that of the CASS. According to the 1983 CASS handbook, its highest governing body was the Academy Affairs Committee (Yuanwu Weiyuanhui), which in 1982 was composed of thirty-eight Academy officials, institute directors, and deputy directors. Like the Scientific Council of the CAS, this body had the authority to make decisions on "major tasks" concerning research, administration, and evaluation and promotion of personnel. The Committee also could nominate the CASS president and vice presidents, who were appointed for three-year terms. Day-to-day administration, according to the handbook, was in the hands of the CASS Secretariat, whose secretary-general and deputies served under a "permanent appointment system."[69]

The presence of the Party and its influence on substantive research work was undoubtedly even more pronounced in the CASS than in the CAS. The CASS had the same interlocking hierarchy of reduplicated Party committees and core groups that the CAS had. These pyramided upward to the CASS's academywide Party committee chaired by Mei Yi, who also served as the permanently appointed secretary-general. The interlocking of other CASS officials with high-level Party organs, however, was clearly stronger than in the case of the CAS.

This was most obvious in the tenure of Hu Qiaomu as CASS president from 1978 to 1982 and as honorary president thereafter. There also was a strong, continuing relationship with the Party Propaganda Department. In addition to Yu Guangyuan, who had supervised CAS social science work as director of the Propaganda Department Science Office and as deputy director of the department's Theory Office in the 1950s and 1960s, the CASS's first crop of vice presidents also included Zhou Yang and Deng Liqun. All three served until CASS leadership underwent a major readjustment in 1982, and Deng continued to be involved in CASS affairs thereafter in his role as Party Central Committee Secretariat member in charge of propaganda. (Hu Qiaomu had done the same, serving as Central Committee secretary in charge of propaganda during the last two years of his term as CASS president.) Throughout the CASS's history in the post-Mao period, Propaganda Department officials routinely appeared and gave keynote speeches at CASS meetings. They included Deng Liqun and his successor on the Secretariat after 1987, Rui Xingwen. In the late 1980s they also included the Politburo Standing Committee member presumed to be in charge of the Party's Ideology and Propaganda Leading Small Group—Hu Qili.

The strong continuing relationship of the CASS with the Propaganda Department underscores the significance of the CASS's separation from CAS, reflecting the altogether different standings of the social sciences and the natural sciences in post-Mao China. While the CAS was moved into an entirely different Party system, the CASS remained in the Propaganda and Education System, where it had always been.[70]

While the move of the CAS out from under formal Propaganda Department supervision was intended both to enhance the coordination of its work with economic reform and to prevent the politicization of the natural sciences as had occurred in Mao's time, social science reform under the CASS was conceived along entirely different lines. In the early days of the PRC, communist officials abolished several disciplines outright in the process of reorganizing China's science establishment. Disciplines such as sociology, political science, and economics were dismissed as "bourgeois sciences," fields whose content was dictated by the needs and purposes of the exploiting classes. In their place were established the Marxist disciplines of political economy and scientific socialism, which purportedly offered a more realistic analysis of state, society, and economy on a more "scientific" basis and from a "proletarian" perspective.

Even while the natural science divisions of the CAS began to report to Nei Rongzhen and Chen Yi after 1956, the Philosophy and Social Sciences Division continued to report to the Party Propaganda Department. The separation of the natural and social sciences divisions was internally reflected in the fact that each had its separate Party groups within the CAS.[71] This early evolution of the natural and social science divisions within the CAS, interrupted by the Cultural Revolution and the leadership tensions leading up to it, foreshadowed their formal split as separate academies in the post-Mao period.

Post-Mao depoliticization was far more limited in the social sciences than in the natural sciences. Deng's declaration in his 1978 science conference speech that science has no "class nature" clearly extended only to the natural sciences. There was consequently no effort to press for social scientists to evaluate the results of social science research in the CASS, corresponding to the well-publicized effort to make such a demarcation in the natural science work of the CAS. Instead, Party and CASS representatives routinely noted throughout the 1980s that social science work proceeds "under the guidance of Marxism." The 1983 CASS handbook included this proviso in its "brief introduction," whereas the 1985 CAS handbook made no such stipulation.[72]

Even in relatively liberal times during the Deng era, when Party and CASS officials stressed the need to separate political issues from academic ones and emphasized the importance of the Party's noninterference in the resolution of academic debates according to the "double hundred" principles—that is, the approach of "letting a hundred flowers bloom and a hundred schools of thought contend"—spokespeople in the social sciences indicated an approach different from that proposed for the natural sciences.[73]

In effect, during the Deng era the approach to the relationship of the social sciences to Marxism called for a division of labor. Each of the social science disciplines had a rightful place within its specific field of inquiry, together with unique methods and approaches. Marxism's broader standpoint and methods offered a higher level of generalization, guiding evaluation of each field's work, ensuring its proper orientation, and synthesizing its specific disciplinary truths into broader "laws" in the science of society. Hu Qiaomu implied this division of labor in remarks on the restoration of sociology in 1979. "The Marx-ist theory of historical materialism supplies within a broad scope a stand, principles, and methods for our research into social life, social phenomena, and social development," Hu said. "However," he added, "historical materialism cannot replace the various social sciences," since "each of the various specific social sciences has its own specialized methods of research.[74] Similarly, a long analysis in *People's Daily* in 1979 sought to demonstrate how the social sciences, which possess class character, can produce "truth" that transcends class.[75]

This division of labor allowed social science researchers consider-able flexibility in investigating social thought and behavior across the entire range of approaches to social science—Western, Soviet, East European, neo-Marxist, and so on—but within the confines of ultimate political acceptability and in pursuit of the broader goals of China's modernization.

The division of labor also served the purpose of integrating the CASS's work tightly into the ongoing political and policy processes of the Party and government. In this regard, the CASS was evidently envi-sioned to play a role different from that of the CAS right from the start. CASS philosophers, historians, and social scientists under Hu Qiaomu's supervision supplied many of the opening salvos in Deng Xiaoping's attacks on Hua Guofeng's leadership and in his effort to overturn Mao's ideological legacy. Similarly, CASS economists became deeply involved in the reorientation of China's economic priorities after 1979 and in de-veloping a new integrated approach to economic, social, and scientific and technical development thereafter. They staffed many of the pro-liferating research centers under the State Council and wrote papers and articles contributing to the larger planning process. Ma Hong's replacement of Hu Qiaomu as CASS president in August 1982 under-scored this priority and may have been designed to facilitate planning. CASS involvement gathered even more force later in the 1980s, espe-cially after Party Politburo member Wan Li enunciated a new "soft sci-ences" approach to policy formulation in August 1986.[76] A Xinhua News Agency report in 1987 observed, for example, that "the social sciences are now playing an increasingly important role in providing the gov-ernment with consultation for its policy-making" and that "now it has become routine for the State Council, China's highest administrative body, to consult with specialists in its decision making on key economic projects."[77]

PROFESSIONAL SOCIETIES
AND FOREIGN TRANSLATIONS

The rapid expansion of institutes in both the CAS and the CASS reflected the recognition by China's leadership and its scientific community of the explosion in scientific knowledge in recent decades and of the proliferation of the disciplines that give knowledge structure. Recognition of this growth was also reflected in the spectacular proliferation of professional associations in China after 1977. The Chinese Association of Science and Technology, the umbrella organization for professional societies in the sciences, resumed activities in 1977 after its suspension during the Cultural Revolution, and by its second national congress in 1980 President Zhou Peiyuan announced that the number of affiliated professional societies for separate scientific disciplines had grown to ninety-five. By 1982 the number had grown to 107, and when the Association's third national congress convened in 1986 there were 138 member scientific societies.[78]

Most remarkable of all was the gigantic effort beginning in the late 1970s to translate foreign books into Chinese. A survey of titles of published translations listed in the monthly journal *National Listing of New Books* (Quanguo xinshumu) from 1979 to 1988 shows an astonishingly aggressive effort to translate hundreds of books—including textbooks, scholarly monographs, and semipopular accounts—in virtually every field of human knowledge. The translations included not only books from the English-speaking world, but also Japanese, Soviet, and East European works.[79]

For example, in physics, the field examined in detail later in this book, there were Chinese translations of the leading American textbooks, including David Halliday and Robert Resnick's *Physics* (Chinese trans. 1980–81) and their abridgement *Fundamentals of Physics* (1980), Francis Sears and Mark Zemansky's *University Physics* (1979–80), at least some of the five-volume Berkeley Physics series (1980), the MIT physics series authored by A. P. French, and the immortal *Feynman Lec-*

tures on Physics (1980–81). Among contemporary standard treatments of specialized fields of physics, there were translations of the second edition of Herbert Goldstein's *Classical Mechanics* (1981), Paul Lorrain and Dale Corson's *Electromagnetic Fields and Waves* (1981), and Franz Mandl's *Statistical Physics* (1983).

In the field of quantum theory, many of the contemporary standard treatments of nonrelativistic quantum mechanics were translated, including those by Leonard Schiff (1982), Claude Cohen-Tannoudji et al. (1987), and Lev Landau and Evgenii Lifschitz (1982). There were also Chinese translations of the classic treatment by P. A. M. Dirac, *Principles of Quantum Mechanics* (1979); and *Quantum Theory* by David Bohm (1982). Translations of James Bjorken and Sydney Drell's *Relativistic Quantum Mechanics* and *Relativistic Quantum Fields* were published in 1984; Richard Feynman and A. R. Hibbs' *Quantum Mechanics and Path Integrals* and Claude Itzykson and Jean-Bernard Zuber's *Quantum Field Theory* appeared in 1986.

In the field of relativity and cosmology, the collection of original papers by Albert Einstein, Hermann Hendrik Weyl, H. A. Lorentz, and Hermann Minkowski—*The Principle of Relativity*—was translated in 1980. A translation of Steven Weinberg's classic treatise *General Relativity and Cosmology* was published in 1980 and his popular treatment of big-bang cosmology, *The First Three Minutes,* appeared the following year. Oddly, the mammoth account of the same topics by Charles Misner, Kip Thorne, and John Wheeler does not appear to have been translated, although Chinese scientists and philosophers are clearly acquainted with it, judging by the footnotes in their writings. Several popular expositions are also available in Chinese translation, including Carl Sagan's *Cosmos* (1984), Harry Shipman's *Black Holes, Quasars, and the Universe* (1983), and works by William Kaufmann and Isaac Asimov on black holes (1983 and 1987).

Among translations of books related to scientific disciplines emerging only in recent years were Ilya Prigogine's *From Being to Becoming* (1986) and *Order Out of Chaos* (1987), and Douglas Hofstadter's *Gödel, Escher, Bach—The Eternal Golden Braid* (1984). Philosophy and sociology of science attracted considerable interest; translations included Thomas Kuhn's *The Structure of Scientific Revolutions* (1980) and *The Essential Tension* (1981), Karl Popper's *Objective Knowledge* (1987), A. F.

Chalmer's *What Is This Thing Called Science* (1980), Werner Heisenberg's *Physics and Philosophy* (1981), studies by the sociologist of science Robert Merton, and Paul Feyerabend's *Against Method* (1988).

THE 1985 SCIENCE REFORMS

Building on the reorientation of science and technology policy in the early 1980s, the central leadership formally instituted a series of sweeping reforms into the PRC's science establishment in 1985. These reforms extended to virtually every research unit in the country the steps laid out in the 1980 guidelines, described above, and begun on an experimental basis after 1982. Over the following year and a half, these early reforms produced what the leadership called "gratifying results," but they also led to some unanticipated problems.

Impetus for the 1985 reforms came from several overlapping concerns, and there were clear indications in leadership statements that a new push in coordinated economic and science reform was in the offing as the result of the previous three years of debates and planning and in conjunction with the inauguration of the new five-year plan in 1986. The central theme of these and other statements reflected the evident conclusion by the majority of the leadership that the "new technological revolution" under way in the world presented China's development with both "a challenge and an opportunity." Persisting resistance and difficulties in Party policy toward intellectuals, who were thought to hold in their hands the key to China's coming to grips with the new technological revolution, also lent impetus to the reforms.

That coordinated economic and technical reforms were in the offing was clear in Zhao Ziyang's report to the May 1984 session of the NPC. Stressing keynote themes that emerged from the effort to define a new developmental strategy in the early 1980s and that became the framework for the subsequent reforms, Zhao declared that the key to China's future lay in formulating a strategy emphasizing "unified leadership, overall arrangements, coordinated organization, and close cooperation" in order to "concentrate forces for a breakthrough." Calling on state bodies at all levels to put science reform "on their agenda," he extended the leadership's endorsement to the trial reforms applied in the Zhuzhou model—a method of contracting research pioneered by an electronics institute in Zhuzhou, Hunan—as the proper orientation for the coming reforms. Zhao cited the model's proven value in ensuring that research is oriented toward the concrete technological problems of China's development, in breaking down institutional and regional barriers to rational personnel and technology flow, and in raising funds for research without relying on the state budget.[80]

Both before and after Zhao's remarks to the NPC, there was a push to dramatize the urgency of the reforms in light of accelerating changes in the world. In March 1984 the media reported the launching of a lecture series for two thousand officials in Party and state organizations, sponsored by the Party Organization Department, the State Science and Technology Commission, and the China Science and Technology Association. Focusing on "China's strategy for socialist construction against the backdrop of the new technological revolution and the revolution's development in light of the international situation," the series included among its lecturers CASS president Ma Hong, Institute of Contemporary International Relations director Huan Xiang, and leading scientist Qian Xuesen. Fang Yi stated in his opening address to the series, "We must seize the opportunity offered by the new worldwide technological revolution—only thus will it be possible for us to skip certain stages and quickly achieve our strategic objective by making use of new technological results." In May a seminar of five hundred administrators and economic and scientific specialists opened to deliberate "what China should do to meet the challenge of the 'new technological revolution.' "[81]

In June the Party Organization Department circulated remarks by Hu Yaobang and Zhao Ziyang on the need for "cadres nationwide" to study "the world's new technological revolution and our countermeasures."[82] In July a long analysis by Huan Xiang of the impact of the new technological revolution on global economic, social, and political trends and on what China needed to do to catch up was published in CASS's premier journal *Social Sciences in China* (Zhongguo shehui kexue) and reprinted in the rabidly reformist Shanghai newspaper *World Economic Herald* (Shijie jingji daobao). Huan warned that if China failed to act on Zhao's call to "meet the challenge of the new technological revolution head on," it would "fall far behind" the rapidly developing countries on the Pacific Rim and "become a 'colony' " of other countries developmentally.[83]

In October the Party's Third Plenum adopted the landmark "Decision on the Reform of the Economic Structure." The decision gave highly authoritative endorsement to a hotly controversial new ideological framework for legitimizing diverse forms and practices of economic activity—"socialist commodity economy"—and reiterated many of the themes of science reform that were flooding the media. In enumerating the various reasons that made economic structural reform "a pressing necessity," the decision pointed to the "new opportunities and new challenges" presented by the new technological revolution, stressing that "this means our economic structure must become better able to utilize the latest scientific and technological achievements, promoting scientific and technological advancement and generating new forces of production." [84]

All of this attention to the linkage of economic and science reform coincided with a renewed campaign to improve conditions for intellectuals. That campaign derived not only from a revived recognition of the importance of intellectuals in the coming reforms and of continuing problems in policy on intellectuals, despite the 1982–83 push, but also from an attempt to overcome the impact of the Party's aborted campaign against "spiritual pollution," launched by Deng Xiaoping at the Party's Second Plenum in October 1983.

In conjunction with this drive, the press once again spotlighted continuing difficulties faced routinely by scientists, technicians, and other intellectuals in a variety of areas. Intellectuals frequently found their applications to join the Party blocked by bureaucrats who believed that excessive recruitment of intellectuals would "disrupt the class orientation" of the Party, so that the emblem on the Party flag would be changed "from the hammer and sickle to spectacles and pen." Therefore they invented reasons to shelve intellectuals' applications by ordering ever wider checks into their family backgrounds and social contacts, and other such "tests." [85]

The press also publicized persisting problems of remuneration and livelihood. A *People's Daily* commentator article in June 1984 noted that the average income of a forty-year-old intellectual was less than that of a twenty-year-old apprentice laborer. An *Enlightenment Daily* editorial around the same time cataloged a broad range of problems, including poor housing, inadequate research facilities, and unusually high mortality rates. "We should also see," the editorial warned, "that because of the serious damage done in the field of education by the ten years of internal disorder, the temporary shortage of talented people will be conspicuous in the future, the employment of today's middle-aged intellectuals will be prolonged, and if prompt measures are not taken to protect them it will lead to some unimaginable results." [86]

A series of authoritative commentator articles and editorials in *People's Daily* outlined the urgency of resolving the prevailing "irrational distribution" of scientific personnel. One in March 1984 noted that even though there sometimes was nothing for scientists and technicians to do in their own provinces, many units—particularly those in "technologically backward provinces"—were continuing to put barriers in the way of experts seeking to transfer to more advanced areas, where there was high demand for them. Such hoarding of intellectuals as unit "property" by these "independent kingdoms" amounted to "backward thinking" or "more exactly, a policy of slow suicide" for China's development.[87]

The Party also sought to overcome scientific intellectuals' fears of political persecution stemming from the campaign against "spiritual pollution." On the eve of the campaign a well-known specialist on intellectuals policy in Shanghai recalled the impact of the 1981 criticism of "bourgeois liberalization" on the intellectual community. "They thought another Anti-Rightist campaign was coming," Shi Ping said, and so "they were scared and worried. . . . To avoid the risks of research into present-day issues, many people working in theoretical fields busied themselves with research on ancient history and foreign countries. The whole field of theoretical research was plunged into a state of demoralization." [88] The campaign against "spiritual pollution" obviously raised even greater fears.

Steps to blunt the impact of the campaign appeared almost immediately after it was launched and as it began to take off in a widening perimeter of attack.[89] By January 1984 reform themes began to be reasserted clearly. In February a commentator article in the relatively liberal Xinhua News Agency journal *Observation Post* (Liaowang) warned that although the effort to overcome "corrosion by bourgeois ideology" remained "an important measure," it was "entirely wrong to set eliminating spiritual pollution against the implementation of intellectuals policy." In August an *Enlightenment Daily* article spelled out how local

Party cadres had used the campaign against "spiritual pollution" to persecute scientists and technicians in their units in the name of eliminating "economic crimes." It described how in 1983 technical personnel at a Tianjin research center had concluded a contract to provide consulting services to a Shanxi coal mine in their spare time—an activity that had been specifically encouraged by the science reforms implemented in 1982–83. When the campaign against "spiritual pollution" began, however, the Party committee at the research center decided that such contracts were "conducive to spiritual pollution" and "encouraged people to look for money in everything." As a result the contract was "unilaterally torn up, the latter stages of design work were stopped, and the scientists and technicians were attacked." Such episodes, the article concluded, "exerted a negative influence" on economic reform and intellectuals policy.[90]

The central leadership took a number of steps to cope with these problems. In addition to the new stream of authoritative press commentary on problems faced by intellectuals, the media spotlighted the concerns of the top leadership on this score. Hu Yaobang was described as severely criticizing treatment of a medical researcher, Xiu Ruijian, who had turned down prominent positions in the West and returned to China after making "pioneering" breakthroughs in microcirculation research during her training there, only to meet continual obstacles and jealousies on the part of her research unit's leadership.[91]

As another step, the Party Organization, Propaganda, and United Front Work departments issued a joint circular in January 1984 calling for a new campaign to "check up" on implementation by Party units down to the district level of Party policy on intellectuals, paralleling the 1982 campaign and making this check-up work a specific item on the agenda of the just-launched three-year Party rectification campaign. But on the issue of remuneration and living conditions the Party acknowledged that it could do little immediately, given "the limited financial resources of the state."[92]

The new reforms of the science and technology establishment, formally enunciated on 13 March 1985 at the landmark national science conference, sought to solve all of these problems in development, science, and intellectuals policy with a series of sweeping changes in the conduct of science along lines already experimented with over the previous three years. The Party Central Committee's "Decision on Reform of the Science and Technology Management System" adopted at the conference spelled out a series of changes in scientific research funding, organizational structure, and technology diffusion that sought to stimulate and enforce the orientation of the science sector toward technological problems of national development, induce a free flow of scientific and technical talent into areas that economic development demanded, and resolve the persisting problems of intellectuals' remuneration and living conditions. The details and implications of this decision were elaborated in a major speech at the conference by Zhao Ziyang.[93]

In the area of funding, the decision called for a gradual takeover by production enterprises of applied research and technology development funding, eliminating it from the state budget within three to five years. Institutes and centers engaged in this type of research were to aim at becoming independent, supporting themselves through research technology development contracts or by merging with the enterprises outright. The state would continue to fund major research projects, supplemented by an effort to introduce public bidding and contracting on a trial basis in some areas. A system of science foundations would be developed to fund basic research by drawing money mainly from the state. Under this system, funds would be granted to projects deemed "most feasible" and most relevant to national priorities.

The decision called for steps to "commercialize" research and technology. In January 1985 the State Council had authorized institution of a "technology market," allowing transfer of technology "as a commodity." The decision extended this further, spelling out provisions for compensation regulated by supply and demand "without restriction by the state" and calling for patent laws and regulations to facilitate the diffusion of technological results by this means.

Structurally, the decision called for a major decentralization of research-institution decision making and for intensified institutional links with the economic sector. It encouraged direct links with enterprises through negotiated contracts, calling for the opening of state research facilities to researchers from the production sector, for the merger of state research centers with research departments in enterprises, and for the creation of self-supporting independent research institutes.

The decision also mandated major efforts to upgrade and modernize China's scientific infrastructure and interaction with the international scientific community. Specifically, it called for the automation of information systems, for accelerated exchanges of scientific information and import of foreign scientific books and journals, and for expanded participation of Chinese scientists in international conferences and exchanges.

The thrust of these reforms could be seen in the Chinese Academy of Sciences, which had already begun making changes as the 1985 science conference opened. The Academy's annual work conference, held in January 1985, put forward a series of steps that anticipated the funding and structural reforms elaborated in the March decision. The Academy further decentralized authority in decision making on research projects. It cut funding of research directly from the state budget in favor of a competitive contracting system, under which the Academy's institutes bid for project funding either from the state plan or from production enterprises as a way of stimulating their orientation toward the economic sector. The conference also encouraged institutes to establish their own technological development companies to promote their own research products.

Under the reforms, the Academy sanctioned the "free flow" of scientific personnel outward into production enterprises as a way of breaking the promotion bottleneck within Academy institutes. It also began in subsequent months to open up several of its basic research institutes and laboratories to outside researchers—both domestic and international—who financed their research by applying competitively to a new science fund.[94] The State Natural Science Fund was established in February 1986 to provide money for basic science research, paralleling the CAS's inauguration of its own fund for its work in this area.

Similar steps followed in the rest of the civilian science sector. In an interview during the March 1986 NPC session, State Councilor Song Jian summed up the first year of efforts to carry out the reforms, noting that the reforms were going "smoothly" and "without major deviation." Transactions had been "brisk" in the inaugural year of the national technology market, amounting to 2.3 billion yuan. The effort to encourage "horizontal" links between research units and production enterprises had produced a diversity of new forms of collaboration, and over the year more than three hundred local research centers had become independent in their funding. The reforms were promoting more rational flows of scientific talent: "Thousands upon thousands of scientific and technical personnel" had "left their ivory towers" to diffuse their expertise in the economic sector. Similar assessments had been offered by Fang Yi in December, who called the first year's steps "only the beginning."[95]

Despite confidence in the overall direction of the science reforms, official statements and press commentary through 1986 and in early 1987 indicated that the reforms were leading to some unanticipated problems and were not solving some of those they were designed to resolve. For instance, a long review in June 1986 of the science reforms observed that applied and technology-development research was increasingly reoriented toward technological problems in the economy. It added, however, that most of the results were directed toward low-technology products that brought quick returns and toward medium and small enterprises in the collective and private sectors rather than toward the large state enterprises.[96]

Another problem was that the transfer of scientific and technical personnel was still blocked, and when there was movement, it often was not in entirely helpful directions. Along with problems in the orientation of their production, small and medium enterprises in the collective and private sectors were drawing off too many researchers and technicians, creating a shortage of such personnel in the large state enterprises. Researchers were leaving their posts in the state sector, especially from interior provinces, without the permission of their units' leadership and without bothering to change their unit registrations; wage, rationing, and domicile arrangements; and even their Party affiliations. As a result, the State Council formulated new regulations intended to promote a more orderly transfer of personnel and to ensure the "stability" of the pool of researchers and technicians in key state enterprises. The revised funding procedures also created problems. In some applied and technology-development research centers, state support was cut faster than the centers' ability to obtain funding through contracts from production enterprises, leading to severe operating deficits. This in turn resulted in failure to fulfill the expected payment and bonuses to participating researchers, dampening enthusiasm for the reforms.[97]

In funding basic research, the new system was inadequate and led to underemployment of theoretical and some applied science specialists. In applied research institutes, those unable to gain funding for their projects through the contract system were frequently absorbed into institute staffs, leading to overstaffing and misuse of talent. In basic research institutes, especially in the Chinese Academy of Sciences, inadequate funding was seriously hindering research and stifling initiative. How to resolve these underemployment and unemployment problems without adversely affecting the country's long-term basic research interests was becoming increasingly problematic. Livelihood problems for many scientists, especially those in research departments of state sector enterprises and in the CAS, not only persisted but actually were getting worse. On the one hand, management in some institutes and enterprises continued to block transfer of personnel out of their units. On the other, inflation set off by the economic reforms and price decontrols of 1984 and 1985 was making already-impoverished intellectuals even poorer. This made moonlighting an increasing necessity for such scientists; the reforms explicitly sanctioned this practice, but enterprise and institute leaderships continued to resist it.[98]

According to one account, these problems were particularly acute in the CAS, where a "sense of crisis" gripped researchers. Many feared that the Academy was at a disadvantage in competition for funding from enterprises, believing that enterprises would adopt a "sectarian" approach to awarding contracts and choose not to "use fertile water to irrigate other people's fields." The reforms were accentuating the Academy's already-distorted ratio of older, middle-aged, and younger researchers by triggering an exodus of the better-trained younger people. Academy-developed technology was not faring well in the new technology markets, where buyers preferred equivalent foreign technology even though it was higher priced. And the downgrading of basic research meant that basic research publications were not adequately supported, making it even harder for CAS researchers to establish the priority of their work and gain recognition for it.[99]

On top of these problems associated with the reforms was the impact, both actual and feared, of a new political campaign. In reaction to an explosion of liberal intellectual views in the "little Hundred Flowers" of the summer of 1986 and student demonstrations the following fall, in

January 1987 the Party launched the campaign to criticize "bourgeois liberalization." One of the campaign's top three targets was China's best internationally known basic researcher, the astrophysicist Fang Lizhi. That month Fang was dismissed from his post as vice president of the prestigious Chinese Science and Technology University in Hefei and expelled from the Communist Party.[100]

ACCELERATING THE REFORMS: 1987–1988

The response to these problems generated by the 1985 reforms was further reforms. In 1987 the central leadership announced a new wave of measures intended to take the 1985 reforms even further, calling for an intensification of efforts to link research institutes and centers to production enterprises. This extension was reinforced in 1988 and was supplemented by a new emphasis on a few carefully selected high technology areas to be developed in conjunction with the accelerated development of the already economically more advanced coastal regions.

New State Science and Technology Commission guidelines, announced in February 1987, prescribed two new steps to resolve the various problems that had emerged. One step was to accelerate state research institutes' formation of "horizontal" linkages with production enterprises by further decentralizing decision making in such units. The guidelines called specifically for 10 percent of the five thousand state research units either to become independent centers, supporting themselves through contracts with enterprises, or to merge with such enterprises altogether by the end of the year. The focus of these linkages with the economic sector was to be on large- and medium-sized enterprises in particular, with the state offering a variety of tax breaks and continued financial support to facilitate the transition. By October State Science and Technology Commission chief Song Jian announced that the year's target was almost achieved, with 491 institutes and research centers having become independent.[101]

The other step was to encourage more researchers and technicians in state institutes and centers to resolve problems of underemployment, unemployment, and livelihood by transferring to research units in large and medium enterprises or by becoming involved in technical development and consultancy ventures and agencies of their own. Such decontrols of technical personnel in the state research sector, Song Jian declared in December 1987, would allow "caged tigers" to become "tigers in the mountains," bringing their talent and initiative to where it could best be utilized and at the same time providing the best context for improving their livelihood and working conditions.[102]

Zhao Ziyang and the science leadership also sought to reassure the scientific community about the scope and aims of the ongoing criticism of "bourgeois liberalization." Fang Yi and Qian Xuesen reiterated at a China Science and Technology Association session in late February that the Party's "double hundred" policy on academic debate and freedom remained in force and that "differences of view and understanding over academic problems of natural science" should never be "rashly labeled advocating bourgeois liberalization"—a reference to the intellectual conflicts discussed in the next chapter. In his work report to the annual NPC session on 25 March, Zhao Ziyang insisted that criticism of "bourgeois liberalization" would remain within strict boundaries and should not affect scientific research and debate.[103] Chinese media meanwhile sought to show Fang Lizhi, one of the three targets of the campaign, continuing his work as a prominent scientist undisturbed by the campaign.[104] During the summer months, the media gave prominent publicity to the leadership's invitation to several scientists to vacation with them at the seaside resort at Beidaihe in Hebei as evidence of their concern and support.[105]

By the end of 1987 it was clear that Zhao had succeeded in restoring momentum behind the coordinated economic and science and technology reform program. The Thirteenth CCP Congress in October identified science and technology reform as the key priority in economic reform, and the technocratic orientation of the new Party leadership installed at the congress seemed to reflect those priorities. Soon after the congress, the long-criticized May Fourth period slogan "Use science to save the nation" was "re-evaluated." Found to be essentially "patriotic," "progressive," and "consistent with Marxism," the slogan was revised to suit current needs, becoming "Use science to invigorate the nation."[106]

All of these trends gained further impetus in 1988 in conjunction with the leadership's adoption of Zhao Ziyang's proposed "coastal strategy" of economic development, enunciated in the spring of that year. At a national science and technology conference in March, Premier-designate Li Peng strongly endorsed the priority given science and technology development and reform as justified by world trends and called for a further acceleration of the science reforms. New steps in science reform would be required, he went on, focusing on the introduction of "competition and the market mechanism" through contracted management of science and technology units, "subjecting those organizations to the law of the survival of the fittest," and on further promotion of the technology market.[107]

Out of the March science conference emerged a new "decision" by the State Science and Technology Commission, publicized in August 1988, to concentrate resources on serving economic development in the coastal areas. The most prominent step was to be the formulation of a program—the Torch Plan—to spur rapid development of a few carefully selected areas of high technology that would be both competitive in international markets and applicable to China's technological needs. This development would be concentrated in designated zones, including Beijing and several coastal cities whose level of industrial and technological development was already advanced by Chinese standards. The decision to focus on a few specific high-technology areas, such commentary acknowledged explicitly, was inspired by the recommendation in Alvin Toffler's *The Third Wave* that developing countries not attempt to catch up with the developed nations in every field, but rather leapfrog to world levels by concentrating on those areas of high-technology development particularly suited to their resources and relative advantages.[108]

Steps had already been taken in this direction with the announcement in 1986 of plans to build a Chinese "Silicon Valley" in Caohejing, a suburb of Shanghai, where efforts to develop computer and fiber-optics industries would be concentrated. In 1987, in conjunction with efforts to induce scientists and technicians in the state research sector to explore work outside their institutes, Chinese media had highlighted the blossoming of "Electronics Street" in the Beijing suburb Zhongguang-cun, where researchers from the CAS and other state research centers had formed a number of joint electronics research and production companies. The Torch Plan envisioned similar development in key coastal areas, using a diversity of forms of organization, ownership, and financing that stressed close integration of production and high-technology development.[109]

In the Chinese Academy of Sciences, the emphases of these various reforms were already being felt in early 1987. Foreshadowed at a CAS work conference in September 1986 and laid out at the Academy's annual administrative conference in March 1987, a series of reforms was inaugurated based on what came to be called the "one academy, two systems" approach. Instituting a "twin-path management system," the Academy set up separate systems to govern basic research on the one hand and applied and technology-development research on the other. Under this system, institutes and personnel involved in the latter sector—roughly two thirds of the Academy's workforce—would seek funding and remuneration by integrating with production enterprises in the manner prescribed more generally for state research organizations in the February 1987 guidelines. They would open their laboratories and facilities to enterprise researchers, form horizontal links with production enterprises through contract and merger arrangements, and form companies and research and development ventures on their own authority. Supervision of these institutes would thus be shared increasingly with local enterprises and governments. Basic research institutes would also be opened up to researchers from both the domestic and international scientific communities. Their work and personnel—the remaining third of the CAS workforce—would continue to receive funding from the state, now supplemented by proceeds derived from the CAS institutes involved in the applied and technology-development research sectors.[110]

The impact of this reform was apparently immediate. According to a 1988 interview with Zhou Guangzhao (who, as newly appointed CAS director, oversaw inauguration and implementation of the reforms), fifty-one of the Academy's laboratories and basic research centers were opened up in the first year to researchers from the outside. Meanwhile, seven thousand scientists and technicians from the applied and technology-development wing of the Academy had formed nearly four hundred companies, which constituted "a relatively independent system of technological development, production, and marketing." As a result, funding for basic research increased dramatically for the year. The 1987 state budget for the Academy's basic research had amounted

to 680 million yuan, an increase over the previous year of 3.8 percent—
"far below the rate of inflation." To this amount, however, was added
another 330 million yuan from the Academy's marketing of its expertise
and research results.[111]

CHINA'S SCIENTIFIC INTELLECTUALS IN CRISIS

However much the science reforms of the 1980s may have achieved
their purposes in reorienting China's science establishment in directions promoting economic development, it is also clear that, in terms of
their impact on China's scientific community, they led to consequences
that were neither intended nor anticipated. By late 1988 and early 1989,
there were abundant indications that scientific intellectuals were facing
what they saw as a crisis, not only in terms of their livelihood, but also
of their standing in society.

The science reforms of the 1980s had been intended in part to resolve what the Party leadership recognized to be conditions of serious
hardship for China's intellectuals, a social group whose significance
they also believed would increase as the country modernized. In the
end these problems not only were not resolved for many scientists, but
got even worse, as successive rounds of inflation triggered by the economic reforms overtook whatever gains they managed to get. This was
especially true in the summer of 1988, when leaked Party plans for price
reform triggered a round of inflation that exceeded 30 percent in many
Chinese cities, with catastrophic consequences for those, such as CAS
basic scientists, tied to fixed state salaries. More generally among the
urban population, an "inversion of pay standards" had developed by
late 1988, whereby the average manual laborer in Beijing who had no
high school education was paid an average 25 yuan more per month
than a worker who had finished high school, and 34 yuan more than
the average college graduate.[112]

As a result, science was coming to be seen as a path with no future.
Increasingly, *Enlightenment Daily* observed in August 1988, young
people "would rather take the 'red path,' which means 'going in for government,' and the 'yellow path,' which means 'going in for business,'
than choose a career in scientific research, which is now regarded as a
'dark alley.'" Those who did enroll in graduate programs and join sci-

entific research institutes, the paper also noted, increasingly regarded such education and posts as "transfer stations with terminals in foreign countries."[113] Concluding that education was irrelevant, those already in graduate school programs were dropping out. Encouraged by the science reforms themselves and pressured by their deteriorating livelihood, other people with established careers in scientific research were leaving for the better opportunities and salaries in private and collective business ventures.[114]

Out of these circumstances arose a new contempt for intellectuals. Though they inherited a long cultural tradition that valued intellectual activity and though they had been held up by the Party at the beginning of the reform period as the key social group in China's reform and future, intellectuals increasingly found themselves the object of social ridicule. The decline in their social standing was reflected in such popular jingles as "Today all things have gone up in price except two—professors and trash."[115] A brief article in People's Daily in late March 1989, on the eve of the first demonstrations in Tiananmen Square, observed that this deterioration in social status, far more than all the problems of livelihood and working conditions, may be "the main reason many intellectuals are in a bad mood."[116]

In the Chinese Academy of Sciences the succession of reforms had radically changed the mission and work of the country's premier basic research institution. In seeking to reorient the Academy's work toward aiding China's overall economic development, however, the reforms also created strains and problems. The reorientation of research toward applied science and technology development had led to an exodus of researchers out of basic research, so that by late 1988 the CAS leadership had begun to take steps to "maintain a relatively stable workforce" in that sector. Those who remained tended to be well-entrenched veteran researchers whose training was increasingly dated, a problem exacerbated by difficulties in recruiting younger researchers. "China's contingent of scientific researchers will face a grave crisis in another five years" if these trends continue, Zhou Guangzhao cautioned in August 1988. Although funds for basic research had increased significantly under the "one academy, two systems" approach, Zhou warned, "funds allotted to some research institutes are barely enough to cover wages and utility fees."[117]

Judging by press commentary, comparable problems were even worse in the Chinese Academy of Social Sciences, even though social scientists increasingly were called on to guide reform by analyzing economic problems, identifying social tensions, and recommending steps to resolve them. The average age of senior researchers in the CASS was even higher than in the CAS.[118] Funding was also a serious problem. An April 1988 meeting at the CASS of thirty-eight provincial and municipal social science academy presidents concluded that the social sciences in China were at the "crisis" stage because of funding cuts.[119] Added to these pressures was the continuing fallout from the campaign to criticize "bourgeois liberalization," as several leading CASS researchers— including some institute heads, such as Su Shaozhi and Political Science Institute director Yan Jiaqi—remained the object of conservative leadership pressure long after the natural sciences had been excluded from the campaign. Both Su and Yan, in fact, stepped down from their positions and were replaced in a major turnover in the CASS's leadership in the fall of 1988.

In summary, the science reforms of the 1980s had a powerful, divisive impact on China's scientific intellectuals. Hailed at the beginning of the decade as the vanguard of China's modern future, by 1989 many felt that their own futures were uncertain and troubled. Anxiety and frustration were particularly high among those engaged in basic or theoretical science. The reform's utilitarian reorientation of Chinese science toward the requirements of economic development fractured the science community, leaving basic researchers stranded and isolated. Still tied to state salaries, their already low living standards were catastrophically diminished by inflation.

Even the much-heralded provision for scientific professionalism suffered. Scientists who left the secure but bureaucracy-dominated confines of state research institutes to work in the freewheeling collective and private economic sector could now work more independently in the new autonomous institutes and services the reforms stimulated. But many felt that in doing so they were setting aside the idealistic pursuit of scientific truth.[120] In the CAS the utilitarian purposes of the science reforms even eroded or negated altogether the provisions for autonomy and self-regulation set down in the 1981 CAS constitution. The provisions for election to CAS leadership positions heralded and used in the Academy that year were thereafter set aside in favor of a return to the traditional Party-controlled system of appointment and promotion. This change was brought about by the Party reform leadership itself and ultimately by Zhao Ziyang, who was dissatisfied with CAS resistance to the utilitarian emphases of the leadership's science reforms.[121] If the early science reforms stressed the "professional" features of the "bureaucratic-professional" approach to CAS management, the later reforms saw emphasis shift to the "bureaucratic" elements of the model.[122] By 1989 some theoretical scientists had become a seriously aggrieved and disaffected group.

4 / Theories
in
Conflict

The 1980s saw the eruption on China's intellectual scene of a series of heated debates over the relevance of Marxist theory to contemporary knowledge. Some of the sharpest debates were over modern scientific theories that had until the Deng years been censured and even banished from Chinese science. Although modern physical theories such as quantum mechanics, general relativity, and cosmology provided much of the substance of these debates on science and Marxist philosophy, the deeper issues in dispute concerned the autonomy of the scientific community in interpreting the theories of modern science. Some of the most prominent participants in these debates—Fang Lizhi and Xu Liangying among them—were also leading agitators in the scientific dissidence of early 1989. Their dissident activities were directly related to their identities and self-conceptions as scientists. The strength of these identities and the ferocity of emotions they could arouse were nowhere more apparent than in the 1986–89 debates on science and philosophy.

UPDATING AND UPHOLDING MARXIST THEORY

The Dengist insistence that Marxism is above all a method of scientifically analyzing the world and its processes meant that the vastly different circumstances of contemporary times required the "development" of Marxism in light of new realities. Over the decade from the Third Plenum in 1978 to the Tiananmen demonstrations in 1989, this authoritative revision of the premises of the Chinese Communist Party's ideology licensed an aggressive re-examination of Marxism-Leninism's doctrines in light of contemporary knowledge and experience. All but the most basic tenets were scrutinized. In some cases this scrutiny led to dramatic revisions in an effort to update Marxism-Leninism, to enhance its claim to be the single, comprehensive branch of science that

125

provides a unified view of the world, and to restore confidence in its ability to guide China's survival in the modern world.[1]

This re-examination extended to all three of Marxism's main components—political economy, scientific socialism, and dialectical materialist philosophy. In this broader effort, the principles of dialectical materialism as applied to the natural world—often called "the dialectics of nature" or "natural dialectics"—were also the object of aggressive re-examination, as Chinese scientists, philosophers, and Party theoreticians sought to reconcile the classical tenets of Marxist-Leninist philosophical analysis of nature with the findings of modern science. Like re-examination of Marxism's principles in other areas, the process of "developing" Marxism in natural dialectics was the source of intense debate.

The reasons why issues involved in the accommodation of Marxist-Leninist principles to the theories and findings of the modern natural sciences ignited some of the hottest sparks of intellectual conflict in Dengist China are straightforward. One reason was the scale of the adjustments that needed to be made in the body of natural dialectics' fundamental principles and derived conclusions in light of modern science. This gap resulted in part from the particular formulation of natural dialectics that was received in China from the Soviet Union in the early 1950s and from its relatively frozen state of development thereafter.

Essentially Marxism's philosophy of science, natural dialectics was mainly the product of Engels and Lenin.[2] While Marx is normally credited with developing the theory of the dialectical evolution of human society and its material base, Engels's greater interest in the natural sciences led him to formulate the dialectics of the natural world. These efforts are conventionally understood by Marxist-Leninists to be the result of a conscious division of labor between Marx and Engels, each contributing to a total, scientific vision of the world and humanity's place in it. (Some Marxists, especially Western Marxists, dispute the reality of this division of labor and see Engels as having imposed a totalistic dialectical materialism on an essentially humanistic Marx.)

Engels's work on natural dialectics is reflected mainly in *The Dialectics of Nature,* a book begun in the 1870s but never completed. Extant only as an outline and a set of notes, this work sought to incorporate the advances of nineteenth-century scientific theory into an organized materialist philosophy that would undergird the materialist analysis of political economy developed by Marx and Engels together. Thus Marx's *Capital* and Engels's *Dialectics of Nature*, as one recent standard Chinese textbook on natural dialectics asserts, are "two intimately related works."[3] Both men sought to dispel "idealistic" and "theological" notions about the natural and the social worlds of their day, putting forward comprehensive analyses that they believed were firmly grounded in science and objective philosophy.

Two of Lenin's writings were considered by later Marxist-Leninist theoreticians also to be seminal contributions to natural dialectics. One was his 1908 tract *Materialism and Empiriocriticism*, a polemic against "idealist" trends in philosophy that he found in the views of followers in the Russian Social Democratic Party of the Austrian physicist and philosopher Ernst Mach. The other was his *Philosophical Notebooks*, posthumously published jottings made in the 1914–15 period on philosophical issues that interested him. Lenin's contributions, especially in the *Philosophical Notebooks*, lay in introducing a measure of flexibility in understanding and applying the philosophical system developed by Engels— for example, in broadening the definition of the concept of matter. But Lenin did not significantly advance the level of science encompassed within natural dialectics much beyond the nineteenth-century ideas incorporated by Engels.

Through the early years of the Soviet Union, the revolutionary changes in twentieth-century science were frequently debated in Soviet academic and theoretical circles, especially as the Soviet state moved to consolidate its hold and rebuild the Russian scientific establishment in the late 1920s. A broad span of viewpoints was put forward in these debates, but by the early 1930s this spectrum of opinion had been collapsed into a narrower orthodoxy, coinciding with the consolidation of Stalin's leadership over the Communist Party of the Soviet Union (CPSU) and the Soviet science community. Thereafter, in the late 1940s, a particularly politicized array of interpretations of modern science was canonized in the natural dialectics formulated under Andrei Zhdanov, the Soviet Party secretary who presided over ideological affairs in the immediate postwar period. It was this latter body of hardened, Zhdanovite doctrines of natural dialectics that became the received wisdom in China.

Soviet interpretations of scientific theories began to evolve after the death of Stalin, leading to a new period of change, debate, and revision in the 1960s. In China, however, this liberalization was short-lived. While criticism of the Stalinist orthodoxy in natural dialectics began in China during the Hundred Flowers period, concurrently with the broader de-Stalinization underway throughout the communist world, the philosophical interpretation of the results of science became indirectly but inevitably caught up in the intensifying politics and polemics of the Sino-Soviet split and of China's domestic scene.

Mao's elaboration of what he saw as the true path of society's advance under socialism and his critique of Soviet domestic and foreign policies under Khrushchev rested ultimately on a defense of Stalin. On top of this, Mao had a strong personal interest in and curiosity about the fundamental questions of science and philosophy, and as Edward Friedman has observed, one did not lightly challenge the chairman on questions of theory.[4] During the Cultural Revolution, Mao's perspectives on scientific theory continued along the essentially Zhdanovite lines of the Stalin period, justifying the banishment of such theories as relativity, cosmology, and quantum mechanics as "idealist" fallacies serving the "reactionary" purposes of bourgeois society. The logic of this approach was that the superior prospects for theoretical development under socialism would make possible the eventual "replacement" of the "bourgeois" scientific disciplines by natural dialectics itself and the broader principles of dialectical materialism. It was this highly politicized yet peculiarly frozen body of natural dialectics doctrines that the post-Mao theorists sought to "develop."

Science, however, had moved considerably in the twentieth century. The twin revolutions of the early 1900s, relativity and quantum theory, were followed in the postwar period by revolutions of similar scale in such fields as molecular biology and genetics, computers and cybernetics, and systems theory. All of these scientific developments raised questions of the most fundamental nature, inspiring in all societies uncertainty and debate, not just in philosophy but also in other spheres of human life that these ideas touched.

Such controversies in China inevitably led to deeper questions about the underlying relationship between Marxism and science. These questions involved issues of particular sensitivity: Does Marxism "generalize" the conclusions of science into a body of broader philosophical principles? To what extent can such Marxist philosophical principles guide science toward new, more effective theories by shoring up science's epistemological foundations and by providing criteria to evaluate scientific theory and results? Ultimately, such questions as these involve issues of authority and legitimacy, as will be explored more fully in the next chapter. This chapter examines some of the theoretical controversies that provoked such issues.

THEORIES IN CONFLICT

As a distinct discipline, natural dialectics is a surviving manifestation of Stalinist views of the organization of knowledge and in the contemporary world is almost exclusively a Chinese phenomenon.[5] Its subject matter was the object of serious academic inquiry in the USSR and the Soviet bloc in the post-Stalin era, but such research was conducted there under the general rubric either of dialectical materialist philosophy or, since the 1960s, of *naukovedenie* (science of science), depending on the particular focus.[6] A separate and distinctly different tradition developed in Japan, where Engels's ideas were taken seriously by some as a way of analyzing the natural world after his *Dialectics of Nature* was translated into Japanese in 1929. It was within this tradition that Sakata Shoichi developed his ideas regarding applying dialectics to particle physics, an approach that fascinated Mao Zedong in the early 1960s.

As Chinese Marxism-Leninism's philosophy of science, natural dialectics is located at the intersection of Marxist theory and natural science. This cross-disciplinary focus is reflected concretely both in its institutional location and in the sponsorship of its publications. Chinese academic and Party institutions devoted to philosophy normally include research in natural dialectics. The CASS Institute of Philosophy, for example, has among its eleven divisions that of Natural Dialectics Research. Philosophy departments in major universities normally teach courses on natural dialectics, both as a standard component of a mandatory curriculum in dialectical materialism and as a substantive specialty. At the same time, reflecting natural dialectics' institutional straddle, the CAS Institute of the History of the Natural Sciences also does natural dialectics research.

With respect to publications, natural dialectics research normally appears not in the substantive journals of the various natural science disciplines, but instead in a small number of specialized publications and in journals and newspapers that devote attention to issues of philosophy and the philosophy and history of science. The three most important periodicals available for public subscription are the CASS Institute of Philosophy's *Studies in Philosophy* (Zhexue yanjiu); the *Bulletin of Natural Dialectics*, published by the CAS under the general editorship of (who else) Yu Guangyuan; and the more recently founded *Studies in Natural Dialectics* (Ziran bianzhengfa yanjiu). In addition, a small tabloid newspaper, entitled *Natural Dialectics News* (Ziran bianzhengfa bao), was published twice a month in the 1980s.

The *Bulletin of Natural Dialectics* was founded with the encouragement of Yu Guangyuan in 1956 by Xu Liangying, a physicist and historian of science, about whom much will be said later. It was published as an internally circulating journal until its suspension during the Cultural Revolution. It resumed publication in 1979 as an openly circulating journal under the nominal editorship of Yu and the executive editorship of Li Baoheng and then, after 1980, Fan Dainian. Fan, a physicist and a philosopher and historian of science, had coedited the journal with Xu Liangying in the 1950s; he became the sole editor after Xu was condemned as a "rightist" in 1958.

The *Bulletin of Natural Dialectics'* subtitle—"A Comprehensive Theoretical Journal of the Philosophy, History, and Sociology of Natural Science"—intimates a particularly broad conception of the scope of natural dialectics. This breadth is typical of the intellectual ambitions of the journal's editors and, frequently, its contributors in the 1980s. Throughout the decade the *Bulletin of Natural Dialectics* regularly published bold explorations of the frontiers of modern scientific disciplines and analyses of their implications for Marxist philosophy and natural dialectics, earning for the journal a reputation for intellectual boldness and liberality. In the debates on "developing" versus "upholding" in philosophy and science, the *Bulletin of Natural Dialectics* was the foremost arena of controversy. In 1983 it was branded by Qian Xuesen, a star Party scientist, as a propagator of "spiritual pollution" and it played a seminal role in sparking the spectacular debates on traditional Chinese culture and modernity that erupted in the mid-1980s.

It was in direct reaction to the *Bulletin of Natural Dialectics'* perceived liberality that *Studies in Natural Dialectics* was founded in 1985 under the sponsorship of the Chinese Natural Dialectics Research Society. The more conservative thrust of the new journal is reflected in its subtitle—"A Journal of Philosophy of Nature, Science, and Technology"—which conveys a narrower, more traditional focus. Despite the conservative purposes of the journal's founding, however, *Studies in Natural Dialectics* through the late 1980s published articles from the same broad range of contributors that the *Bulletin of Natural Dialectics* drew from, and so, as one observer noted, the difference in slant between the two journals was imperceptible most of the time.[7]

In addition to these specialized journals, significant and particularly controversial issues in natural dialectics in the Deng period were frequently treated in *Social Sciences in China* and in *Enlightenment Daily*. They were also discussed occasionally in the Central Party School journal *Theory Monthly* (Lilun yuekan) and in the broad range of philosophical and social sciences journals published at regional levels by provincial research institutes and universities. Natural dialectics issues were aired on occasion in *Red Flag* and *Seeking Truth*, as well as in *People's Daily*.

That such controversies spread out of the natural dialectics journals, which have extremely limited readerships, into the wider press is an indication of their significance.[8] These journals, in the order presented here, form an ascending hierarchy that facilitates analysis of controversies that appear in them. A rule of thumb in analyzing articles appearing in the Chinese open press is that the higher the rank of a press organ's sponsoring institution within the overall political system, the more politically significant it is. As applied to publications in the natural dialectics arena, this rule means that the farther up an article appears in the pyramid, the more sensitive it is politically. Moreover, as debate moves from lower, more specialized journals in the hierarchy upward into higher-level organs in the political arena, the norms of debate change. In the specialized philosophy and social sciences journals in the Deng years, when a concerted effort was made to depoliticize academic research, the Hundred Flowers ground rules normally applied. This meant that controversies in the pages of such journals were considered academic and, while still heated and potentially sensitive, they were less immediately significant in the political arena. Articles appearing in higher-level journals such as the CASS's frontline *Social Sciences in China* and the nationally circulating *Enlightenment Daily* had greater prominence and therefore potentially greater political relevance and sensitivity. These publications marked an important boundary between academic and political affairs. Debates that erupted into the pages of *Red Flag, Seeking Truth,* or *People's Daily* concerned issues that had acquired significance beyond the academic realm, becoming issues of direct political interest.

The media in which views of participants in a debate were published, in addition to the substance of those views, thus afford important clues to the larger political context of the controversy. At moments when the larger political atmosphere becomes charged, as during the 1983 campaign against "spiritual pollution" or the 1987 campaign against "bourgeois liberalization," the injection of political concerns into the academic arena is potentially greater and the lines of demarcation in this hierarchy blur. Alternatively, when the political atmosphere liberalizes and intellectuals see opportunities to inject themselves into leadership policy discussions, as during the 1986 Little Hundred Flowers period, the lines of demarcation also blur, as the airing of controversies in *People's Daily*, for example, signify ongoing policy debates relevant to the concerns of the Party leadership itself.

A survey of journals in the natural dialectics field through the post-Mao years reveals controversies over almost every aspect of modern science and Marxist philosophy. (When Chinese writers say "philosophy," they almost invariably mean "Marxist philosophy.") There were, for example, disputes over the implications of the Dengist postulate that "practice is the sole criterion for testing truth" for the impracticable "truths" of logic and, especially for the truths of the varieties of mathematical and symbolic logic developed in the West over the past century. There were controversies over Darwinian natural selection, molecular biology and the origins of life, and especially the ideas of sociobiology, whose emphasis on "selfish" preservation of individual genes as a motivation for altruism was attacked in *Red Flag* itself. The implications of information theory inspired disputes about the fundamental "categories" of Marxist philosophy, and the explorations of nonlinear dynamics in chaos theory generated controversies as well.

Interest in contemporary Western philosophy of science was also evident in these journals. There were explorations and debates about the implications of Thomas Kuhn's ideas on the genesis of "scientific revolutions." Imre Lakatos's theory of "research programs," and particularly his depiction of Marxism itself as a dying or at least invalid scientific research program, provoked controversy. For similar reasons, Karl Popper's views on falsifiability as the basis of scientific progress and the "anarchist" epistemological principle of "incommensurability" in the competing theories of Paul Feyerabend also provoked debate.

Two theories of modern natural science will be examined here in terms of the controversies they sparked in the 1980s with respect to Marxist natural dialectics. Quantum mechanics and big bang cosmology were the focus of particularly intense dispute in these years, partly due to the prestige of physics, the hardest of the hard sciences. This prestige, in fact, may have contributed to the central leadership's readiness to endorse construction in 1978 of a proton synchrotron—a particle accelerator that promised little in the way of directly applicable results in itself (aside from the technology required to build the machine in the first place), but which, it was hoped, would become a symbol of China's scientific modernity.

The other reason these two physical theories generated such debate in the effort to accommodate them within natural dialectics was that both address issues at the heart of dialectical materialist philosophy—matter, motion, space, and time. It would be difficult, in fact, to imagine scientific theories that at first glance seem more radically at odds with the presumptions of classical natural dialectics.

The heart of natural dialectics, as Chinese theoreticians argued the theory in the Deng era, are three universal laws and accompanying categories that are applied in constructing a unified picture of nature. The *law of the transformation of quantitative into qualitative change* asserts that change occurs in qualitative leaps as a result of accumulated quantitative change. The *law of the unity and contradiction of opposites* holds that all entities are a combination of oppositions, whose mutual interaction drives change within such entities and in the world as a whole. The *law of the negation of the negation* posits that each successive stage of development contains within itself the seed of its own destruction and replacement by a new stage that contains elements, on a higher plane, of the stage preceding it.

These laws are supplemented by a system of "categories"—the concepts and properties through which the laws are expressed. These include fundamental aspects of the world: matter (which includes energy), motion, consciousness, space, and time. They also include abstract characteristics of the world in change: cause and effect, universal and particular, whole and part, form and content, necessity and chance, and so forth. In the world, matter is primary and consciousness is secondary—that is, matter exists objectively in the world whether mind exists to perceive it or not, while consciousness cannot exist without matter. Through the operation of the laws of dialectics, matter in its various forms and characteristics undergoes constant change. Out of this interaction emerges the myriad phenomena of the world.

Within this general picture, some Chinese theorists in the 1980s sought to defend two particular interrelated propositions that were not necessary to a complete dialectical materialist view of the world but which Lenin himself believed essential. One was the assertion that space and time as basic "forms" of matter are infinite in extent. The other was that matter is "inexhaustible," usually interpreted by Chinese theoreticians to mean that each level of matter is "infinitely divisible" into a deeper level uniting mutually "contradictory" opposites. These two propositions were originally introduced as a means of banishing "theological" notions from science and philosophy about divine creation of the world: if the universe is infinite in extent and duration, there can be no place for a creating divinity to reside.

Both quantum mechanics and big bang cosmology incorporate concepts that present difficulties if this classical natural dialectics picture of the world is upheld rigidly. As the first nonclassical physical theory, quantum theory in particular has presented difficulties in interpretation for all philosophical systems—Marxist and non-Marxist alike. As Loren Graham has shown in his analysis of the theory's impact on the development of Soviet dialectical materialism, these difficulties are not insuperable if the concepts and terms of natural dialectics are interpreted loosely. The degree of liberality involved in such interpretations, however, presents the countervailing danger that the resulting philosophical system is so general that it loses analytical relevance to the world it seeks to explain.

Born out of a crisis in the classical physics of Newton and Maxwell at the turn of the century and formulated in the mid-1920s, quantum mechanics has provided an amazingly successful theory of the dynamics of physics at the atomic scale and below. At the same time, it has raised profound questions about the nature of physical reality and human knowledge of reality.[9] At the simplest, nonrelativistic level of quantum mechanics, information about the microworld (the atomic level and below) and its processes is derived from the mathematical manipulation of differential operators representing various "observables"—momentum, position, etc.—on an abstract "wavefunction," or alternatively on "state vectors" in a multidimensional "Hilbert space." The solutions of these wave equations provide a spectrum of probabilities for observing the particular quantities to be measured. That the predictions of quantum mechanics are only probabilities of particular future outcomes of a microworld process means that quantum mechanics is *indeterministic*. In contrast to classical physics, in which precise predictions can be made about future direction, momentum, and position of some particle from knowledge of these values for some previous time, quantum mechanics asserts that there are definite probabilities that such a particle can be literally anywhere. Immediately, therefore, classical and commonsense ideas about cause and effect come under suspicion.

This indeterminacy stems from quantum mechanics' incorporation of Heisenberg's "uncertainty principle," which says that simultaneous measurement of complementary pairs of variables—position and momentum, energy and time—is not possible because precision of one variable leads to correspondingly imprecise knowledge of the other. As a consequence, what particular property of a micro-object is perceived depends on what property is measured. Micro-objects display phenomena associated with particles when particle behavior is measured; they display phenomena associated with waves when wave behavior is measured. In contrast, at the level of classical physics—the everyday world—wave and particle behavior are mutually exclusive.

There are limits, therefore, to the precision with which the microworld can be known precisely. Its processes and relationships can be described in terms of perceptions of them, but knowledge of its objects and their properties *as they exist objectively* cannot be obtained. The observer and the act of observation are inextricably intertwined with perceivable reality in the quantum mechanical description of the world.

This conundrum is sometimes called the "measurement problem" in quantum theory.

This indeterminacy at the foundations of quantum mechanics has provoked and disturbed philosophically minded physicists everywhere. The conventional, though not universally accepted, view is the "Copenhagen interpretation" developed mainly by Niels Bohr. This view holds that the indeterminacy of quantum mechanics reflects the fundamental indeterminacy of reality itself—that statements about the properties of reality without reference to perception and measurement are without foundation and meaning. This approach, in the eyes of many classically minded scientists and philosophers, treads very close to philosophical idealism of one variety or another. For that reason the Copenhagen school has episodically been the object of criticism in the Soviet Union and other communist countries, including China.

A major effort to formulate an alternative interpretation, called the "hidden variables" school and promoted by Albert Einstein and his students, sought to show that quantum mechanics is an "incomplete" description of the microworld and to transcend the indeterminacy of quantum theory. The probablistic predictions of quantum mechanics, in this interpretation, emerge from the deterministic behavior of unknown variables "hidden" from our direct knowledge at a much deeper level. (A clear, often-cited analogy is the phenomenon of Brownian motion—the jiggling of small objects in a liquid as a result of their random bombardment by individual molecules of the liquid. Exact predictions about the motion of the objects could be made theoretically, but not practically, by calculating the effects of each of the millions of bombarding molecules; but accurate statistical predictions can be made that take overall account of the effects of millions of such collisions.)

The possibility of "hidden variables" interpretations of quantum theory has inspired experiments to try to validate one school of interpretation over the other, the most famous of which are the class of "thought experiments" based on a 1935 paper by Einstein, Boris Podolsky, and Nathan Rosen (thus the "EPR experiments") and the "Bell inequalities" or "Bell theorems," devised by CERN (Conseil Européen pour la Recherche Nucléaire) physicist John Bell in the mid-1960s. Experiments in the 1970s and early 1980s devised to test Bell's inequalities have effectively ruled out a whole class of "hidden variables" interpretations (the "local" theories) and preserved quantum theory's fundamental indeterminacy.

Whatever quantum mechanics means, it works remarkably well. On it and its relativistic versions, the quantum field theories, is based understanding of all the particles and forces of the atomic and subatomic world. These theories—the "gauge field theories" of quantum electrodynamics and quantum chromodynamics—successfully explain to an extraordinary degree of accuracy the interactions between the various classes of subatomic particles and three of the four fundamental forces of nature (electromagnetism and the "strong" and "weak" forces). These theories have shown the way to organize the burgeoning families of observed and predicted particles on the basis of "symmetries" and shared quantum numbers; they explain the multiplicity of intermediate-level particles out of a small family of six constituents, called quarks. Together with the leptons—another small family of six particles, including three types of electrons and neutrinos—the quarks are currently regarded as truly "fundamental particles." A "supersymmetric" quantum field theory uniting quarks and leptons may also eventually yield a picture that, with "super-gravity" modifications, unites all four of the known forces and particles and their interactions into a "grand unified theory of everything."

Turning from the very small to the very large, contemporary cosmology has also challenged concepts and interpretations of classical physics.[10] The sources of modern cosmological models are Einstein's theory of gravitation—the general theory of relativity—and the astronomical observations in the 1920s and 1960s. Einstein's "special theory of relativity," set forth in a revolutionary paper in 1905, reconciled fundamental inconsistencies between Newton's classical mechanics and Maxwell's electromagnetic theory by uniting the dimensions of space with time into a single "space-time" and by postulating that the speed of light is the same for all observers. The theory thus demolished classical notions of simultaneity and absolute space, showing that measurement of the time of an event and dynamics of an object depend on the reference frame of the observer.

The general theory of relativity went much farther, interpreting gravitation as the curvature of space-time by physical mass. The very geometry of space-time is thus linked to matter in it. As John Wheeler, one of the great theorists of general relativity, and his colleagues put it, "Matter tells space how to curve, and curved space tells matter how to move."[11] When applied to masses a little greater than three times the mass of the sun, general relativity predicts the existence of "singularities"—objects whose gravitational attraction is so powerful that even light itself cannot escape, so that great volumes of matter are crushed into a pointlike "black hole" in the fabric of space-time itself.

When applied to the structure of the overall universe, general relativity leads inevitably to the conclusion that the universe must be either expanding or contracting. The theory thus predicts that the matter and energy of the entire universe is emerging out of or collapsing into a singularity.

Observational confirmation that the universe is expanding was provided in the late 1920s by Edwin Hubble, an American astronomer who interpreted the "redshift" of light spectra from galaxies as indicating that they were moving away from Earth. Hubble's analysis showed further that the more distant the galaxy, the greater the redshift, meaning that those farther out are receding faster than those closer in. This led in the late 1940s to the theory that the present universe emerged from a primeval fireball in a "hot big bang," a theory that competed with rival "steady state" cosmological models until 1965. In that year, consensus swung decisively behind the big bang theory because of the discovery of a residue of radiation—the 3° Kelvin microwave background radiation—presumed to remain from the original big bang.

Since that time astrophysical research has elaborated the theory into a standard cosmological model that successfully accounts for the cosmological expansion inferred from galactic redshifts and the observed microwave background radiation, as well as a number of other observed features of the universe, such as the relative abundance of helium. According to this model, the universe began as the explosion of an initial cosmic singularity, in which the universe's matter—existing only as energy—had been confined in an unimaginably small and therefore unimaginably dense point. Because contemporary physics lacks a valid quantum theory of gravity, the dynamics of the first instant of expansion—the first 10^{-43} seconds, a period called the "Planck era"—is and may remain impenetrable to understanding. As the universe expanded beyond the Planck era and cooled, the four known forces of nature and the varieties of matter associated with them coalesced out, beginning the process of aggregation of the physical bodies we can observe in the universe today.

Two implications of big bang cosmology have proven controversial for Chinese theoreticians. First, the universe may prove to be finite in extent or, in relativistic terms, "finite but unbounded." The expansion of the universe is not the expansion of matter into an infinite space; it is the expansion of space-time itself. It is meaningless to ask what lies "beyond" the expanding universe, and there is no "edge" to the universe. Since the universe is expanding, it may also contract if the gravitational attraction from the mass of the universe is great enough to overcome the rate of its expansion. If that is the case, the universe is finite in extent and will not expand infinitely and forever.

Second, the universe appears to have had an origin, calculated backwards from the rate of expansion to be roughly ten to fifteen billion years ago. There is nothing meaningful that can be said about this original state or what set the present expansion in motion, but one speculative possibility is that the universe began as a "fluctuation" in the primal "false vacuum." This is just a short step away from the idea that the universe was literally "created out of nothing"—or, as Alan Guth, creator of the current "inflationary" modification of the standard model, says, the universe may prove to be "the ultimate free lunch."[12]

EARLY DISCUSSIONS, EXPLORATIONS, AND DEBATES

Discussions of the significance of quantum mechanics and cosmology in the first years of the Deng period criticized the banishment of these fields from Chinese science during the Cultural Revolution years and presented surveys of the theories and their various schools of interpretation. By the early 1980s significant differences in viewpoint began to emerge, as leading academics began to press for the "development" of natural dialectics in light of these and other modern scientific theories. These differences were aired at first without visible rancor or direct criticism of opposing views. But by the early 1980s positions appeared to harden, and larger questions about the relationship of science to Marxist philosophy were raised. Fang Lizhi played a leading role in disputes about cosmology, but he was not by any means the only prominent scientist or philosopher to take part.

Illustrative of the priorities of this early period, in January 1978 the first issue of the restored journal *Studies in Philosophy* carried a long rebuttal of attacks on cosmology appearing after 1973 in *Natural Dialectics Journal* (Ziran bianzhengfa zazhi), a periodical established in the early 1970s under sponsorship of the Gang of Four. Coauthored by Fang Lizhi and Yin Dengxiang, a natural dialectics researcher in the CASS Institute of Philosophy, the article defended cosmology against assertions that it was a "theology" that used "idealistic and a priori" philosophical approaches rather than a true science. Fang and Yin concluded that the best way to sort out various cosmological models was to allow science to resolve its own problems, free from outside intervention. Marxist philosophy, in their view, could play a "guiding role" in the process by helping to sort out disagreements within the professional cosmological community. Both in rebutting the views associated with the Gang of Four and in discussing cosmology's true agenda, Fang and Yin hewed to a conservative line on the issue of whether the universe is infinite or not, arguing that the universe studied by natural science is a finite part of the "infinite" universe studied by philosophy.[13]

The newly resumed journal *Bulletin of Natural Dialectics* subsequently began to carry articles exploring philosophical issues raised by modern cosmology and astrophysics. In November 1981, for example, it published an article on the development of the theory of black holes and its philosophical implications by Wang Guozheng, a graduate student at China Science and Technology University and presumably a protege of Fang Lizhi. After reviewing the particular modifications of the theory of black holes put forward by the British theoretical physicist Stephen Hawking, Wang drew attention to the possibility that a number of fundamental laws of physics—including that of cause and effect—may be violated in the extreme conditions presumed to exist in black holes. Noting that quantum mechanics had already weakened this law, Wang concluded with the speculation that cause and effect always had seemed so commonsensical that no one thought much about its ultimate validity. In view of the fact that many self-evident propositions had been overturned in the history of science, he observed, it is "worth thinking deeply whether the law of cause and effect faces a similar prospect."[14]

Quantum theory and the study of fundamental particles were treated in a similar vein. The inaugural issue of the *Bulletin of Natural Dialectics* carried a long account of a conference on the history of these fields, convened in October 1978 in Guizhou by the CAS and the journal's editorial board. After criticizing the approach to particle physics taken during the Cultural Revolution, the conference participants, according to the article, "made an initial attempt" to work out "how to use Marxist philosophy to guide basic-theory research" in the natural sciences. They concluded that in particle physics the key would be "to grasp comprehensively and accurately the philosophical idea of 'the infinite divisibility of matter'" as "the basic guiding idea" for future research in fundamental particle physics.

Foreshadowing themes raised in later debates, the account of the conference cited calls by Zhou Guangzhao and He Zuoxiu, both leading theoretical physicists at the CAS, and Chen Shi for caution and sophistication in applying this overarching principle. Raising the specific issue of "quark confinement" in this connection,[15] these physicists urged that the idea of the infinite divisibility of matter not be understood "in a mechanical manner" and in the same way at each successive level of matter. "Divisibility," they suggested, may be manifested differently at different levels. The conference concluded with a call for a "double hundred" approach to particle physics research, cautioning against calling any new, unconventional theory "idealist."[16]

The same issue of the *Bulletin of Natural Dialectics* also carried two articles by physicists taking different lines on how to apply the "infinite divisibility" principle of natural dialectics in particle physics. One examined what the authors, Zhu Hongyuan and Du Dongsheng, called the "challenge" of the psi particle. Zhu had been a participant in the development of the "straton model"—a theory expounded by Chinese physicists in the mid-1960s that posited, like the quark model, that the known fundamental particles could be understood as entities composed of more fundamental particles called "stratons" (quarks).[17] This model was inspired, Zhu recalled, by Mao Zedong's principle that "one divides into two" and by Engels's assertion of the infinite divisibility of matter.

The challenge of the discovery of the psi particle in 1974, Zhu and Du suggested, was that the effort to place it in the family of known particles required the addition of yet another "straton." As the number of quarks continues to grow, they said, there arises the possibility that they are not "fundamental" either and may be composed of even smaller constituent particles. If so, Engels's "infinite divisibility" principle and Lenin's specific prediction that even the electron would prove to be "inexhaustible" (that is, divisible) will be confirmed. From this perspective, Zhu and Du predicted that Chinese scientists, with dialectical materialism as their guide, would be in a better position than foreign scientists to make pathbreaking contributions in this field.[18]

A more cautious approach was recommended by CAS theoretical physicist He Zuoxiu in the next article in the same journal. As he had at the Guizhou conference, He urged a less literal application of the "infinite divisibility" principle. On the one hand, he rebutted the views of "some researchers" who believe that fields are continuous and therefore not "divisible," and so present a challenge to natural dialectics' formulation on the infinite divisibility of matter. On the other hand, he urged a figurative understanding of the concept of "divisibility" as diversity in the "forms" of matter, rather than just in the mechanical sense of cutting objects in half.[19]

While He urged flexible interpretation of the "infinite divisibility" principle, it was also clear that he was generally conservative in his views on how flexibly natural dialectics should be reinterpreted to accommodate the conclusions of modern physics. This conclusion may be inferred from an article that cited work by He defending "hidden variables" interpretations of quantum mechanics. Written by Shen Xiaofeng and a colleague at Beijing Normal University's Department of Philosophy, the article defended Einstein against charges by Cultural Revolution–era writers associated with the Gang of Four that he was an "idealist" who sold out to the Copenhagen school's interpretations of quantum theory. The article recounted how Einstein upheld a firmly "rationalist and materialist" viewpoint in his long debates with Niels Bohr, Werner Heisenberg, and others of the Copenhagen group, believing that a more complete, deterministic interpretation of quantum mechanics would emerge eventually. The article concluded by reviewing the efforts of Einstein's students to defend "hidden variables" interpretations of quantum mechanics and to criticize John von Neumann's completeness theorem (which rules out "hidden variables" theories on theoretical grounds and undergirds the Copenhagen interpretations). On the latter score, the article cited work by He Zuoxiu specifically.[20]

The remarks on "hidden variables" interpretations in Shen's article reflect the particular interest these theories received in China in the Deng period, especially among those relatively conservative-minded theorists who sought to accommodate quantum theory without having to bend the ideas of natural dialectics too far. Because "hidden variables" theories hold out the promise of an ultimately deterministic interpretation of quantum mechanics, they were seen as much more compatible with the deterministic premises of traditional natural dialectics than was the Copenhagen interpretation. This emerged clearly, for example, in another article by Shen and his colleagues in 1980, which reviewed five broad schools of interpretation of quantum mechanics, including the Copenhagen and "hidden variables" theories.[21]

Concurrent with these initial explorations of the fields of quantum mechanics and cosmology were efforts to rebuild natural dialectics as an organized discipline that could profitably "guide" scientific research. Some of the impetus for this rebuilding effort derived from the larger effort to move beyond criticism of Maoist-period abuse of the science community and to redirect scientific work toward contributing more effectively to China's modernization. This redirection of the science community's work paralleled the initial discussion of science reform and steps toward implementing it. Emphasis in this rebuilding effort was also on the need to "develop" natural dialectics aggressively, paralleling the Dengist stress on "developing" Marxism in general in light of contemporary realities. In shifting the focus of natural dialectics research from Gang of Four criticism and exploration of previously banished scientific fields to active revision of natural dialectics contents, the way was opened for more explicit debate. Divergent opinions over the relationship of science to Marxist philosophy—opinions that people had declined to express in the still-uncertain political atmosphere—now began to emerge in public arenas of academic discussion.

In step with the changing focus of natural dialectics research was an article in early 1980 observing that while there were some scientists who did try to study and apply natural dialectics, "the majority are still not much concerned or interested in it, and a minority are hostile toward it." The reason for this "apathy," the authors suggested, was that natural dialectics had become ossified and needed extensive revitalization by absorbing the issues and conclusions of contemporary science. In order to "guide" science, natural dialectics researchers had to avoid "brandishing sticks and issuing orders" to scientists and making themselves into "philosophical judges who pronounce judgment on the results of some branch of science and technology as idealism and metaphysics." Much of the content of classical natural dialectics had to be renovated, revised, and even discarded, the authors concluded. "Rejection of old conclusions in the face of new evidence is a commonplace in science that no one finds remarkable. . . . It ought to be that way in philosophy and social sciences, but this is a new issue for us."[22]

Also typical of the changing priorities of this time was the establishment of a national association for the discipline, the Chinese Natural Dialectics Research Society, along with many other professional societies for natural and social science disciplines. Drawing broadly from among China's theoretical scientists, philosophers and historians of science, and philosophers, the association met for the first time in the fall of 1981, electing Yu Guangyuan as its first president and accepting some 670 papers. In line with the shift in the orientation of science and technology policy under way at the time, one-third of the papers focused on how to make natural dialectics serve economic construction in addition to guiding scientific research. Discussions at the meeting reflected the desire to revitalize natural dialectics, and so focused on "old topics of continuing scholarly interest," including the problem of mathematical infinity, the divisibility of matter, the infinite extent of the universe, the transformation of matter, the nature of life, biological evolution, and the interpretation of quantum mechanics. There was also discussion of new issues, such as the philosophical problems of nonequilibrium thermodynamics, the relationship of brain and mind, artificial intelligence, the nature of information, and the methods of systems science.[23]

Encouragement of diversity and debate in the name of "developing" natural dialectics was also evident in the pages of Studies in Philosophy in 1982. A commentator article in the journal's April issue strongly underscored the need to revise the content of natural dialectics. The article denied that natural dialectics had become a "science of sciences" that "puts itself above all the specific sciences and encompasses them." Natural dialectics did, however, provide principles that, the article insisted, had repeatedly been proven since Marx, Engels, and Lenin developed them and that exceeded all other philosophical systems in terms of the richness and scientific nature of its content and in terms of its systematic completeness. Unfortunately, the article said, "the positive role of this dialectical materialist view of nature is usually not understood by most people (including some famous scientists) and is even denied outright by some people." A main reason for this, it said, was that natural dialectics researchers had yet to explicate these principles on the basis of "the newest results of modern science." It went on specifically to cite problems raised by the big bang model in cosmology (especially its conclusions that the universe is "finite but unbounded" and that the universe has a beginning) and by quantum mechanics and particle physics (quark theory in particular).[24]

Studies in Philosophy followed up in its June, July, and August issues by publishing a symposium of comments by leading scientists and philosophers on issues raised by the modern natural sciences for natural dialectics. Incipient debate and controversy, as well as an increasing readiness to examine what the proper relationship between science and Marxist philosophy should be, was apparent in the contributions to this symposium. For example, Fang Lizhi, who, in coauthoring his article with Yin Dengxiang, had in 1978 resigned himself to discussing cosmology solidly within the classical framework of natural dialectics, now conceded only declining relevance to philosophy. The "guidance" of philosophy in science, he asserted, would be manifested mainly in its "retreat" from areas taken up by science. He argued that philosophy's continuing contribution lay not in its ability to provide substantive answers, as was attempted by natural philosophy, but rather in its ability to clarify concepts through epistemological and methodological criticism. As an example, Fang cited the issue of whether the universe is finite or infinite, which he maintained was now properly the domain of science. Science could eventually resolve the issue, he predicted, since it rested on the correct notion, thanks to philosophy, that observations for part of the universe must hold true for the universe as a whole.[25]

In his comments in the same Studies in Philosophy series, Fang's former collaborator Yin Dengxiang took the opposite tack, asserting that developments in modern cosmology had strengthened rather than weakened four of natural dialectics' basic tenets. These were the "material unity of the universe," the "universality of motion in all matter" (a truth that even Einstein had resisted at first, leading him to tamper with his own relativistic field equations to produce a steady-state universe), "regularity" in the evolution of the universe, and the "infinite nature" of the universe. Upholding the view implicit in the 1978 article and directly contradicting Fang's contribution to the forum, Yin insisted that modern cosmology as a scientific discipline studies only the observable universe, which is finite, as opposed to the universe studied by philosophy, which is infinite. Yin dismissed the idea that science would ever resolve the question of whether the universe is infinite or finite, since science could settle questions only about what it could observe, which would always be finite. "Therefore, the validity of specific cosmological models will not in the slightest provide evidence of whether the entire universe is infinite or not." [26]

In the same series He Zuoxiu reiterated his confidence in the natural dialectics principle of matter's "infinite divisibility." He stated that more and more contemporary particle physicists were beginning to examine the possible existence of a level of matter deeper than quarks and leptons, and he specifically rebutted assertions that the problem of quark confinement disproved the "infinite divisibility" principle. While acknowledging that ultimately the principle may have to be abandoned, he insisted that it remained an "indispensable guiding concept" for particle physics. "If we have the materials of scientific experiment but lack a guiding concept," he concluded, "then it may be that in the face of this large body of materials we may listen but not hear, look but not see, and be unable to find a direction to follow in conducting scientific experiments." [27]

By contrast, Yang Changgui, a natural dialectics researcher from the Central China Engineering Institute, urged that the principles of natural dialectics be interpreted liberally. The "challenges" of modern science, Yang said, are not "setbacks" for Marxist philosophy but rather causes for its development. The problem of quark confinement did not disprove the principle that matter is infinitely divisible; it only demonstrated the "diversity" of the concept of "divisibility." The key to revitalizing natural dialectics, in Yang's view, lay in applying the appropriate sophistication in grasping the diversity of its principles' interpretation.

"As the natural sciences develop, it is entirely possible that specific viewpoints in the dialectical materialist view of nature will need revision and supplementing," he suggested. This had happened before, he continued, citing the example of the development of non-Euclidean geometry. This new conception of space "revealed the infinite nature of finite space and demonstrated that it is inappropriate to use the idea of unboundedness to prove the infinite nature of space and time," and so this approach had to be "revised and amended. . . . This was not a setback for dialectical materialism, but a manifestation of the forward development of dialectical materialism's view of matter."[28]

Once the door was open to debate in the name of "developing" natural dialectics, public positions sharpened visibly over the next three years. Fang Lizhi, who had previously stated his long-skeptical views of the lasting value of philosophy to physics with only a minimum of political decorum, spoke out with increasing bluntness, regularly citing examples from cosmology that demonstrated the inadequacies of natural dialectics and attacking the discipline as a bane to science. In 1984 he argued, for example, that physics may, after all, have a place for the notion of a "prime mover," since the development of a new model by Stephen Hawking provided for the possibility that the universe was "created out of nothing."[29] Cosmology is in "a fascinating period," Fang said. "A question that has always been considered a topic of metaphysics or theology—the creation of the universe—has now become a topic of physical science, for which the usual methods of physical science apply, namely the mutual corroboration of theory and observation." Alluding to the dismal prospects he saw for natural dialectics, Fang concluded that "what we can expect is that with the development of the physics of the creation of the universe, ancient creation myths, medieval church doctrines, and much still-current 'wild theorizing' will all become historical exhibits testifying to an earlier stage of human culture."[30]

Yin Dengxiang's opposing views on the correctness of natural dialectics' position on the infinite nature of the universe similarly sharpened. In *Enlightenment Daily* in the summer of 1985, he reviewed recent developments in cosmology—especially the new "inflationary model" proposed by the American physicist Alan Guth—to argue that modern cosmology was "overcoming mistaken conceptions, such as the theory that the universe is finite" and embracing the tenets of dialectical materialism. He also specifically took issue with the view put forward by Fang Lizhi (but without mentioning Fang's name) on the universe's "creation out of nothing." [31]

Also reflecting a conservative orientation, Beijing Normal University philosophers Shen Xiaofeng and He Xiangtao attempted to raise doubts about the central pieces of evidence for the big-bang model. They reviewed recent scientific research showing that the $3°K$ microwave background radiation may not have been so evenly distributed (isotropic) as originally thought and that quasistellar objects ("QSOS" or "quasars") may not be extragalactic after all. "We think that Engels's basic ideas are still extremely correct today," they concluded, predicting that any theory that violates the ideas that the universe is infinite and that matter is eternally in motion will inevitably be found faulty. [32]

Taken together, these articles indicate a clear trend of hardening viewpoints and sharpening debate in discussions of specific scientific issues and their relationship to natural dialectics following the call for its "development" in light of modern science. As sharp as the debate was becoming, it provided only the context for the real spark responsible for the explosive criticisms and countercriticisms that followed. That spark appears to have been supplied by the high-profile efforts of Zha Ruqiang to rebuild a new natural dialectics orthodoxy that could encompass all the modern natural sciences and "guide" scientific research.

ZHA RUQIANG'S RECONSTRUCTED
DIALECTICS OF NATURE

In his position in the late 1970s and early 1980s as chief of the Natural Dialectics Research Office in the CASS Institute of Philosophy, Zha Ruqiang frequently took the lead in discussing major issues of science and technology as they related to Marxist philosophy, and to Marxism-Leninism in general. Zha's efforts in this regard covered a diverse range of questions. In 1978, for example, he wrote an analysis of what he called the "third technological revolution"—the use of nuclear power, space technology, and electronic computers—and its economic, social, and political implications. Showing how this new technological revolution had brought about vast changes in the postwar capitalist world, he urged that science and technology's increasing importance as a "force of production" must be taken into account in the formulation of China's modernization strategy and policies.[33]

Returning to this topic in 1984, Zha published a long analysis of the historical relationship between revolutions in science, industry and technology, and society. He concluded that the world was in the midst of a "third industrial revolution" brought about by the scientific revolution (represented by quantum theory and relativity) and a con- sequent technological revolution (represented by nuclear power, space technology, and computer technology). In tracing the social and politi- cal implications for China and the rest of the world, Zha praised the efforts of "bourgeois scholars" such as Joseph Schumpeter, Daniel Bell, and Alvin Toffler for illuminating analyses of the impact of technology on economic production. But their analyses of the social impact of these developments, Zha concluded, "are at bottom inadequately scientific or even wishful dreaming due to their bourgeois perspective and historical idealist methodology."[34]

Similarly, in 1986 Zha published a detailed analysis of the social characteristics of "information society" as developed under various names by Western theorists, including Toffler. Zha dismissed assertions by such writers that a new "information society" would eventually replace both capitalist and socialist systems. He argued instead that "informationalization" would hasten socialist revolution in capitalist countries, while speeding the advance of the socialist countries toward communism. At the level of practical strategy, Zha recommended that China not attempt "advanced informationalization," but rather adopt a "catch-up" approach that would combine high technology and tradi- tional technology in a coordinated manner—an approach that Toffler himself recommended for developing countries.[35]

In addition to exploring broad themes of contemporary social evolution, Zha helped introduce and evaluate Western philosophies of science. Together with his colleague and successor in the Natural Dialec- tics Research Office, Qiu Renzong, he translated A. F. Chalmers's lucid text *What Is This Thing Called Science?* He also wrote a highly critical but comprehensive summary of the ideas of Karl Popper, Thomas Kuhn, and Imre Lakatos on explanations of change in scientific theory.[36] In the same vein, on the occasion of the centenary of Marx's death in 1983, Zha took issue with assertions by Western Marxists, various specialists in Marx studies, and "utilitarians" in the West—including György Lukács, Marcuse, Sartre, Maurice Merleau-Ponty, and Sidney Hook—that natural dialectics cannot be found in Marx but was the invention of Engels alone.[37]

Zha's most controversial project was his effort to modernize natural dialectics by demonstrating how the conclusions of the modern natural sciences had "enriched" its core principles. Zha outlined his ambitions in this regard in two major articles, in 1982 and 1985, both published in *Social Sciences in China*. Zha called for extensive revision of many of the classical concepts of natural dialectics, and these articles made him the leading "reformer" of this branch of Marxist philosophy in China. At the same time, his efforts were "conservative" to the extent that they sought to preserve the overall position of dialectical materialism at the apex of the hierarchy of scientific knowledge.

Zha's twenty-two page *Social Sciences in China* article in 1982, according to a footnote, was merely an "excerpt" from four lectures he had given at the Central Party School in 1980. Published in the July issue of the journal and entitled "The Four Great Achievements of Twentieth-Century Natural Science Have Enriched the Dialectical View of Nature," it elaborated conclusions Zha already had presented briefly the month before in a four-page contribution to *Studies in Philosophy*'s symposium on issues that the modern sciences had raised for natural dialectics.[38] Though ostensibly responding to Western Marxist attacks on the legitimacy of natural dialectics within Marxism, Zha was also clearly addressing assertions by Chinese intellectuals that the modern sciences had rendered natural dialectics erroneous and obsolete. This was particularly apparent in his dissent from the views of "some people"— a euphemism for targets of criticism in contemporary Chinese political and academic discourse—on the issues of the infinite divisibility of matter and the infinite extent of the universe.

The four "great achievements" Zha singled out were: the special and general theories of relativity; quantum mechanics and fundamental particle theory; the invention of the electronic computer and the accompanying development of cybernetics, systems theory, and information theory; and molecular biology and the discovery of nucleic acid as the basis of genetic inheritance. Relativity, Zha said, had scientifically proven philosophical propositions about the relationship of space and time and of matter and energy that Engels and Lenin put forward but could not prove, and had banished remaining "metaphysical" notions about absolute space and time residing in Newtonian physics. Fundamental particle research had further demonstrated the infinite divisibility of matter by revealing successively deeper levels, from atoms to nucleons to quarks and leptons, and had begun to address the possibility of levels beneath quarks. Quantum theory had given natural dialectics even more powerful validation, uncovering in the natural world a "fundamental contradiction" in the unity of oppositions of wave and particle and illuminating the scientific basis of the categories of necessity and chance through its statistical laws.

The computer had made human thought, "the most beautiful flower" in the "picture of dialectical development of the natural world," even "more beautiful." With the invention of the computer, Zha maintained, human thought had "taken a most basic form of matter [the electron] and in appropriate combinations produced a partial simulation of itself." By beginning to reveal the material basis of thought, the computer had delivered a powerful blow to idealism. Similarly, molecular biology was disproving various idealist fallacies by shedding light on the material basis of life itself.

In discussing these "enrichments" of natural dialectics theory, Zha vigorously defended the interrelated principles put forward by Engels and Lenin that matter is infinitely divisible and that the universe is infinite in extent. The fact that free quarks have never been observed, he said, did not prove that they do not exist, and so did not render the infinite divisibility principle suspect as "some people" believed. Engels's and Lenin's prediction of the divisibility of the atom had been proven, even though physicists of their day had believed that the fundamental level of matter had been found, and scientific research would continue to reveal successively deeper levels.

Noting that "some people" had objected that this prediction can never be proven empirically because it rests on the undemonstrable notion of infinity, Zha argued that at this point the "truth" of the principle requires the method of logical proof to supplement empirical proof. Thus: (1) according to the "law of the unity of opposites," all objects contain internal contradictions; (2) according to the principle that space is a "form" of matter's existence, each successively smaller level of matter still has extent, and therefore contains within it the distinction between part and whole; and (3) each level therefore has its own characteristics and properties, and therefore must have internal structure. In calling upon logical proof to supplement empirical proof, Zha implied that he was treading on controversial ground, noting defensively that the ultimate proof of logical assertions rests as always on their demonstration in empirical practice.

In an aside, Zha then extended this same logic to the principle that the universe is infinite. Each successively larger level of matter—the solar system, the galaxy, etc.—can never be proven empirically to be the final level of matter, because by definition observation is always confined to some finite region. Therefore no scientific cosmological model can ever prove that the universe is finite, and so criticisms by "some people" that the "finite but unbounded" models of modern cosmology have made Engels's ideas about the eternal and limitless nature of space and time outdated were without foundation. By the same token, proof of the universe's infinite extent must therefore rest on logical proof as a supplement.

Zha's other major contribution to updating natural dialectics was a major revision and new systematization of the theory's category system. Also published in the CASS's premier journal, the September 1985 article put forward a new system of forty major philosophical categories through which the laws of dialectics were reflected in the material world. These categories were themselves divided into five major groups according to their general characteristics. They reflected Zha's effort to incorporate modern scientific notions of systemic process and information theory alongside traditional concepts such as matter and motion. They also retained several traditional concepts from natural dialectics within his proposed category system, including a "law of infinite levels." Under this category Zha subsumed the notions of the infinite divisibility of matter and the infinite extent of the universe. Citing his own 1982 article, Zha reiterated his view that demonstration of this "law" rests on logical proof and called on science to test empirically predictions based on it.[39]

THE SCIENCE AND PHILOSOPHY DEBATES:
THE LITTLE HUNDRED FLOWERS PHASE

In 1986 Zha's two articles on natural dialectics became the focus of a heated debate about the relationship between philosophy—Marxist philosophy and Marxism in general—and science. This debate began amid the blossoming of a new period of licensed academic debate coincident with the thirtieth anniversary of the "double hundred" policy toward intellectuals and academic debate. The new "hundred flowers" episode had strong backing from the more liberal, reformist wing of the Deng leadership. This backing was signaled by authoritative statements by Politburo member Hu Qili and propaganda chief Zhu Houze to various gatherings of intellectuals and propaganda and cultural officials and by major articles by leading Party spokesmen in intellectual affairs, including reminiscences on the 1956–57 Hundred Flowers period by Lu Dingyi and Yu Guangyuan.[40]

The leadership's decision to use the anniversary of the Hundred Flowers movement to reinvigorate the intellectual arena coincided with new departures on other reform fronts. Most striking, discussion of political reform in the open media re-emerged for the first time since the 1980–82 period, following publicity for remarks by Deng Xiaoping on this question in March 1986 and republication shortly thereafter of his pathbreaking 1980 speech on the issue. Deng's own retirement from active participation in the leadership began to be mentioned in the media the following summer, suggesting that he was working to bring about a second major withdrawal of aged veteran revolutionaries from the Party's top leadership at the forthcoming Thirteenth CCP Congress scheduled for 1987, following the major turnover he had negotiated at the Party conference in 1985. Wan Li's long speech in August 1986, emphasizing the role of experts and the use of "soft science" approaches in modern leadership decision-making processes, was delivered in this context.

These trends in the central political arena lent an air of excitement and urgency to debates and discussions in other arenas. In inviting new academic debates, the leadership appears to have intended in particular to revive momentum behind the economic reforms stalled by the inflation and economic dislocations in late 1984 and early 1985, and to lend impetus to the various science reforms launched in the spring of 1985. As if to underscore the new breadth that the regime would tolerate and even encourage in academic debate, Chinese media spotlighted two disputes. One centered on the relevance of Western economic theory for China's economic reforms, sparked by an article in *Workers Daily* (Gongren ribao) by Nanjing University philosopher Song Longxiang writing under the pseudonym "Ma Ding." Yu Guangyuan personally defended the critical study of Western economic theory in service to the reforms, as urged by Song, against conservative critics who advocated the exclusive use of orthodox Marxist political economy.[41] The other dispute was over the application of Marxist criteria to the evaluation of literature; the antagonists were CASS Institute of Foreign Literature director Liu Zaifu and *Red Flag* writer Chen Yong.[42] This period of authorized academic freedom was brief, however, as the student demonstrations of autumn 1986 led to the fall of Party general secretary Hu Yaobang and the campaign against "bourgeois liberalization" in January 1987.

The first open attacks on Zha's effort to update natural dialectics came in two articles published in May 1986. The first, written by CAS Institute of the History of Natural Science graduate student Zhong Weiguang and published in the *Bulletin of Natural Dialectics*, was a scathing criticism of Zha's 1982 and 1985 articles from the viewpoint of the history of science and natural philosophy. Under the title "Is It Natural Dialectics or Is It Hegel's Natural Philosophy?" Zhong blasted Zha's effort to "create a grand system using the newest natural science terminology" as "a pedantic, arbitrary rehashing of Hegel's natural philosophy" that "does not accord with the principles and spirit of natural dialectics." In defending the notions of the infinite divisibility of matter and the infinite extent of the universe through logical rather than empirical proof, Zhong said, Zha was setting himself up as an "inquisitor" (*caipanguan*) who seeks to "control science and issue it commands."

Zhong recounted the "ossification" of natural philosophy into scholastic dogma during medieval times, following its birth and positive role in Greek science and its subsequent role as an obstacle to the development of modern science after the Renaissance. Its rigid category systems, in particular, hindered efforts by early scientists to "face the world as it is, not through pedantic terminology and conventions," Zhong said, crediting Galileo, Descartes, Newton, Hume, and Locke with fostering the skeptical outlook necessary for the emergence of modern science. Natural philosophy and its dogmatic category systems eventually receded almost everywhere in the West, giving way to a burgeoning science that was able to answer questions that had long been the domain of philosophy. Only in backward Germany, Zhong noted, did natural philosophy fail to retreat before science. Fostered by Kant and then Hegel, natural philosophy flourished, presenting great obstacles for Marx and contributing ultimately to the rise of fascism in twentieth-century Germany and, indirectly, in Japan.

Doubting that Marxism needs a system of natural science categories at all, Zhong recalled that during the Cultural Revolution "there were people who brandished cudgels in the name of natural dialectics and criticized various scientific theories," with the result that natural dialectics "does not have very much appeal among the young people of our country." Zhong observed that Marx himself had seen no need for a system of categories as constructed by Hegel, since it was completely contrary to his fundamental approach to all problems. "Whether we look at his younger years, his middle years, or his later years, whether we look at his views on philosophy, political economy, or scientific socialism, what he confronted was concrete problems and living facts," he said, declaring that Marx "had not a shred of pedantry nor any air of scholasticism in him." "What is hard to understand," Zhong concluded, "is why Comrade Zha Ruqiang has turned a deaf ear" to the views of Marx and Engels on this score.

If Marxism needs no system of natural science categories, Zhong went on, what is left of natural dialectics? Citing his mentor, the historian of science Xu Liangying, Zhong suggested that natural dialectics rests on three premises: that existence is objective and independent of human mind; that concrete problems require concrete methods of analysis; and that the investigation of problems requires a viewpoint of development and change. Consequently philosophy cannot "guide" science, but rather must follow science's lead. "What everyone needs is exploration of the meaning of science from the inside out, not from the outside in."

Zha's resort to logical proof, Zhong said, is the case in point. Citing Hume and Einstein, Zhong stated that logical proof cannot demonstrate anything about reality since it provides no means to assess the validity of its premises, a fact acknowledged by everyone from Marx to Mao. In resorting to logic to prove what he cannot prove empirically, Zha's approach is thus "scholastic." To counter the empirically based conclusion of modern cosmology that the universe is finite, Zhong went on, Zha should have adduced contrary empirical evidence. Instead he adduced empty philosophical principles that had no basis in science and that also had been used by people such as Lysenko to criticize genetics, relativity, and quantum mechanics. "The only outcome of using them," he said, "can be to benefit people like Lysenko, and what ends up damaged is Marxist theory."

In conclusion, Zhong emphasized that human knowledge advances by confronting the concrete realities of the world itself. "From Euclidean space to non-Euclidean space, from classical mechanics to relativity theory and quantum mechanics, science has increasingly required expert training, so much so that it has become difficult to accept its findings from the viewpoint of everyday practice," he said, noting that the ideas in Zha Ruqiang's articles were frequently mistaken because he attempted to explain problems of modern physics with concepts from everyday life. "No one has the right to talk about cosmology simply by looking at the stars and the sky at night," he concluded, cautioning that "those who believe they 'possess the truth' and do not want to 'seek truth' cannot play any positive role in the progress of science."[43]

The second criticism of Zha Ruqiang's articles on natural dialectics was coauthored by Zhong Weiguang, Liu Bing and Wen Zuoyue (of China Science and Technology University's graduate school), and Chen Hengliu and Xiong Wei (researchers at the CAS Institute of the History of Natural Science). Published in *Social Sciences in China*, the article dissected some sixteen instances in Zha's two articles in which his "understanding of scientific concepts is confused or even mistaken." The authors contended that Zha had demonstrated a flawed understanding of the Lorentz transformations in relativity theory, held "confused" ideas about Greek science, misunderstood special relativity's conclusions about the existence of the classical "ether" as a medium for the transmission of light, held erroneous notions about the role of symmetry in crystallography and in relativistic space-time, and failed to distinguish between quantum mechanics and quantum field theory in discussing wave-particle duality. On the basis of this dissection, the authors concluded that Zha Ruqiang "had not understood the scientific concepts he has used and had employed them arbitrarily to prove the various viewpoints he holds to erect a 'broad' theoretical system on that basis. . . . Regarding the reliability and correctness of a system built on this sort of basis, we cannot but have deep doubts."[44]

These scathing direct attacks on Zha's revisions of natural dialectics on scientific grounds by young researchers were followed by an indirect but no less sweeping criticism of Zha's work on philosophical grounds. The author of this criticism was Dong Guangbi, a researcher at the CAS Institute of the History of Science and secretary of the Chinese Natural Dialectics Research Society. A physicist by training, Dong had published work on major philosophical problems of modern physics, including a survey of experimental tests of "hidden variables" theories of quantum mechanics in 1984 and an article on the EPR experiments and the physical view of reality in the spring of 1986.[45] He was also engaged in extensive study of the views on philosophy and physics of Ernst Mach, the Austrian philosopher scientist whose followers had been the object of Lenin's criticism.

Dong's article, entitled "Just What Is Natural Dialectics?" and published in *Studies in Natural Dialectics* in July 1986, did not criticize Zha Ruqiang by name, but there could be little doubt whose views Dong had in mind. Dong reviewed the history of natural dialectics since Engels and concluded that two broad approaches of interpretation had emerged over what Engels had attempted to do. One saw Engels's efforts as intended to identify a specific set of laws applying to the natural world that are derived from the general philosophical laws governing all of reality in society and human thought as well as in nature; the other saw natural dialectics as an effort to generalize from the findings of the natural sciences to explicate the more general laws of nature, society, and thought as a whole.

Citing divergent approaches of Yu Guangyuan, Qian Xuesen, and Zha Ruqiang, Dong observed that since the 1950s there had existed no consensus over which approach natural dialectics work in China should take. Dong said he believed the second approach was correct, arguing that Engels himself had taken this route and had not attempted to establish a theoretical system of general laws that applied in the natural world corresponding to the universal laws of dialectical materialism. Attempts to erect some new system of general laws and categories in natural dialectics, he said, countered the proper role of philosophy in science. That role, he concluded, lay increasingly in formulating a Marxist science of thought that could clarify the concepts of science.[46]

Zha Ruqiang responded immediately and extensively, publishing three separate articles in August and September to rebut his critics.[47] The first, responding directly to Zhong Weiguang, appeared in the August issue of his own institute's journal, *Studies in Philosophy*, with a prefacing editor's note. The relationship of philosophy to science, the note said, is an "old problem" that had been revived because of the new content modern science had given to philosophy and because of the "highest level of categorical tools and methods of thought" that philosophy could supply science in its development.

Attempting to steer a middle road, the note said that "because of historical reasons," many philosophers had inadequate training in science and so were still groping along "the road of ascent from science to philosophy." Therefore it was "understandable and unavoidable" that some of their efforts to incorporate the results of science might be faulty. At the same time, many scientists had frequently failed to appreciate "the potential of philosophy, the proper relationship between philosophy and science, and the particular characteristics of philosophical thought," and so it was also "understandable" that some of their assertions about philosophy were faulty. The proper course, it concluded, was for philosophers and scientists to join together and each contribute to the progress of the other's enterprise.[48]

In his article, entitled "Is It Developing Natural Dialectics or Abolishing It?," Zha claimed to be astonished at the "crudity and arbitrariness" of Zhong's criticisms in "labeling" him a pedantic scholastic "inquisitor." While calling for "concrete analysis of concrete problems," Zha said, Zhong had really addressed only one or two issues among all that he had raised in his two articles. Zhong's negation of the value of Hegel's category system, Zha said, was ahistorical, metaphysical, and wrong. Marx had not rejected Hegel's system, as Zhong asserted, but had inverted it. Nor could one, he insisted, vaguely oppose category systems altogether since all human knowledge, including science, inevitably reflects reality through concepts of some order. His own effort to systematize natural dialectics was explicitly exploratory. On no account, he said, should such research become a new "forbidden zone."

Regarding the issues of the infinite divisibility of matter and the infinite extent of the universe, Zha objected that it was Zhong, not he, who was ready to draw firm conclusions about issues that remained open scientifically. Zha defended the specific logic he used on these issues as well, rebutting Zhong's charge that they lack scientific foundation. "Anyone with the slightest acquaintance with logic can see that these logical deductions are specific propositions deduced from general ones that are like axioms of a philosophical system, and so are like the drawing of conclusions from the premises of a system of natural science theory," Zha said. "Comrade Zhong Weiguang demands that I go from there to draw conclusions about scientific issues, but that would require me to commit the mistake of replacing science with philosophy," he observed. Finally, Zha took particular offense at Zhong's likening of his views on the relationship of philosophy and science to those of Lysenko, and pointed out four distinct ways in which Lysenko had confused science and philosophy while he had not.[49]

In a second article, in the September issue of *Social Sciences in China*, Zha rebutted the dissection of his understanding of scientific theories and concepts by Zhong and his four coauthors in the same journal. Zhong and the others had "distorted" his views and quoted them out of context, he said, and at the same time had "revealed their own deficiencies in scientific knowledge and mistakes in viewpoint." He then attempted a point-by-point refutation of the sixteen specific issues raised by Zhong and the others.[50]

Finally, in the September issue of the *Bulletin of Natural Dialectics*, Zha revealed what he took to be some of the personal background inspiring the attacks on his articles. Entitled "Putting on Hats and Fair Play," the article responded directly to Zhong Weiguang again and also to Xu Liangying, the CAS historian of science who, Zha claimed, had criticized him indirectly in an article in the same issue of the *Bulletin of Natural Dialectics* that had carried Zhong's attack. Noting that he had already responded to the substance of Zhong Weiguang's attacks elsewhere, Zha said he wanted this time specifically to address issues of proper academic debate that Zhong's and Xu's articles had prompted.

Xu Liangying's article, about which more will be said later, was a long defense of rational realism as the central premise in interpreting the history of science. In closing, Xu criticized two general trends he saw on the contemporary intellectual scene that he believed threatened this rationalist approach—one an antirational revival of Confucian traditions of philosophy, and the other an effort to build new philosophical systems based on revised categories and universal laws.[51] Though Xu had not mentioned him by name, Zha said, it was clear that he was the person to whom Xu was giving the mantle of "the prophet who had discovered the general laws of the universe." Since Xu had offered no concrete criticisms in doing so, however, Zha felt he was left with no way to respond. Xu's own article, however, demonstrated that Xu himself had deployed a category system in discussing rationalism in the history of science, and so, Zha hoped, Xu might demonstrate a little tolerance himself.

The crudity of Zhong's attack, Zha went on, blatantly violated the atmosphere of academic discussions, for which two things were necessary. One was avoidance of "putting on hats"—the use of political labels to delineate and polarize academic issues. Calling him "the inquisitor of science" had the opposite effect, dredging up all sorts of political and religious associations with medieval scholasticism, Stalin, and the Gang of Four. It was Zhong, Zha said, who was politicizing academic debate. Second, there had to be a common commitment to fair play— recognition that in leveling criticisms, critics should give their opponents a chance to respond. Zha recalled that Xu had himself launched the debate by proclaiming at a seminar in November 1985 that Zha's *Social Sciences in China* article contained at least a hundred mistakes. When Zha wrote Xu for an explanation, Xu had deferred, saying that he would detail his criticisms in print. After Zha read the attacks on his views by Zhong Weiguang, Liu Bing, and the others and learned that all were Xu's graduate students, he wrote Xu again to ask whether those articles reflected Xu's own views. Xu responded, according to Zha, that Zhong and the others had discussed the content of their articles with him, though he had not seen their final drafts. Xu also stated that he no longer planned to write his own refutation of Zha's views. "So, eight months after Comrade Xu Liangying openly criticized errors in my two articles," Zha stated, "I still don't know what he criticized me for, and

I also don't know which of the views in the articles his students wrote after talking with him are also his. As things are, I have been criticized but have no way to respond. Is this fair?"[52]

Following the publication of Zha's three articles, the dispute centered on his views expanded rapidly through the remainder of 1986. *Enlightenment Daily* announced on 20 October that it would begin a regular column devoted to the debate over the relationship between science and Marxist philosophy. In the inaugural column, the paper published a scathing criticism of Zha's response to Zhong Weiguang, entitled "Philosophy Must Defend Science" and coauthored by Dong Guangbi, Beijing Construction Engineering Institute researcher Han Zenglu, and Jin Wulun from Zha's own CASS Institute of Philosophy.[53]

Observing that many scientists objected to the idea that philosophy guides science, the article quoted a statement by a prominent "theoretical physicist," presumably Fang Lizhi: "I welcome philosophy serving as a tool; I loathe philosophy acting as a judge." Given the history of philosophy's abuse of science—specifically relativity theory, cybernetics, quantum mechanics, chemical resonance theory, Morganian genetics, psychology, and cosmology—in China, Dong and the other authors said, such sentiments were well founded. Science, they insisted, could recognize no authority except its own internal norms developed in its long struggle against "truths" imposed by philosophy according to "only what is in books" or "only what comes from above" or "only what comes from authority."

Dong and his coauthors recounted two broad historical traditions in philosophy's relationship to science. One was an Enlightenment tradition from Diderot through Kant (who examined the possibilities of empirical knowledge), Comte, and the logical positivists (who saw philosophy as increasingly based on the facts of science and saw philosophy's basic task as clarifying the language of science's propositions). The other was a Hegelian natural philosophy tradition, in which science supplied the footnotes in the effort to build grand category structures not on the basis of scientific fact, but by proceeding from philosophical "first principles"—"a big step backward" from the Enlightenment tradition. Marx and Engels, the article conceded, had "critically absorbed" Hegel's dialectics, but they had based everything on science, putting themselves squarely within Diderot's tradition. The impact of Hegel's natural philosophy tradition itself on science, however, was devastating, providing a lesson that "the philosophers of today have yet to absorb." "Philosophy does not have the qualifications to judge science; to the contrary, it should take the defense of science as its sacred mission," the article concluded.

Like Dong Guangbi, coauthor Jin Wulun was not a new participant in the debate with Zha Ruqiang. Only two weeks before the article in *Enlightenment Daily*, Jin had published in the same paper a scathing attack on Zha's views on the question of the infinite divisibility of matter. This was not a new subject for Jin, who had written about it twice in the preceding year and a half. In the December 1985 issue of *Studies in Philosophy* he had argued that the literal interpretation of the infinite divisibility of matter, according to which each level of "fundamental particle" would have to be a composite of smaller particles, was a survival of Hegelian metaphysical dialectics and so was incompatible with Engels's views. In January 1985 he had also criticized the idea from a different angle in the journal *Tianjin Social Sciences*.[54]

In his *Enlightenment Daily* article, published on 6 October 1986, Jin went considerably further, now arguing that the concept of the infinite divisibility of matter was no longer tenable in light of modern scientific findings. He noted that several observed phenomena, in addition to the often-cited problem of quark confinement, negate the idea.

First, he cited the phenomenon of pair annihilation, in which pairs of electrons and positrons (the electron's antiparticle, identical to the electron in all respects except for its positive electric charge) annihilate each other to produce photons (the "particles" of light). According to the principle of the infinite divisibility of matter, he said, this phenomenon should mean that photons are constituents of electrons. This, he objected, was obviously not so, and so the principle was wrong.

Similarly, Jin suggested, the process of beta decay, in which electrons are emitted from the atomic nucleus by means of the weak force, should mean, according to the principle, that electrons are constituents of the nucleus and of its constituent particles, protons and neutrons. This, again, was obviously not so. Finally, Jin objected that during the cosmological "Planck era" space-time had no meaning. Therefore, as a "form" for the existence of matter, it could not be "divisible." On the basis of these examples, Jin declared that the principle should be abandoned altogether in favor of new holistic approaches. "In recent years, new situations in theoretical physics, such as the EPR experiments to test for violations of Bell's inequalities, and new disciplines, such as systems theory and theory of dissipative structures, have all revealed the holistic nature of relationships between objects," and so underscore the need to move "from a belief in the simplicity of the world to a belief in its complexity."[55]

Fang Lizhi also rejoined the public criticism of Zha's effort to build a revised system of natural dialectics. In an article published in *Studies in Natural Dialectics* in September, Fang contrasted the recurring instances in which Marxist philosophy had abused science in China since 1949 with the forthright recognition of science's independent authority by its former persecutor the Catholic Church. Even today, Fang observed, some philosophers in China—clearly alluding to Zha—refused to do the same, and continued to "sit in judgment" over science, building "grandiose philosophical systems" that frame "general laws of the universe" with a facade of modern scientific terminology. The era of such grand systems reigning over science was "nearing an end," Fang predicted, suggesting that the new generations of Chinese scientists welcome philosophy only as "a useful tool, not a supreme authority."[56]

Though the articles by Dong Guangbi, Jin Wulun, Fang Lizhi, and Han Zenglu in the early fall of 1986 represented a powerful reprisal to Zha Ruqiang's defense of his natural dialectics system, his original critics in the public arena were not heard from at this point. The five younger researchers, Zhong Weiguang and the others, had planned to respond at length in the *Bulletin of Natural Dialectics*, but one of the journal's editors, He Zuorong, refused to publish their criticisms. He was supposedly sympathetic to their views, but faced heavy pressure from both Zha Ruqiang and his brother He Zuoxiu, a major contributor to the debate in its later stages. The five therefore had no immediate recourse.[57]

Zha responded directly to the article published in *Enlightenment Daily* on 20 October with an article of his own in the paper on 8 December. He brushed aside the criticism of his not giving a forthright response to Zhong Weiguang and for engaging in crude polemics, stating that they had given no real argumentation on that score.

Zha did take up Dong's criticism of his "Hegelian tendency" of arguing from philosophical first principles. Zha acknowledged that he continued to uphold the law of the unity of opposites, as did, he asserted, everyone in natural dialectics circles. The real issue was how to apply the law in the debate on the infinite divisibility of matter. The law, Zha stated, is the basis of the view that matter is infinitely divisible—the one is logically deduced from the other.

Zha stated that whether this deduction was correct depended solely on the scientific evidence for it; so far, he said, scientific practice had borne out the divisibility of "fundamental" particles. In this respect, the chain of deductive reasoning he was endorsing was not different from the role deductive thought had always played in scientific theorizing, and as an example he cited Einstein's deduction of special relativity from Maxwell's electrodynamics. Deductive reasoning, he said, had a rightful place because the relationship of philosophy to science was one of the general to the particular. It is altogether different from Hegel's reasoning from "idealist" principles that were not based on scientific fact and were never submitted to the test of scientific practice. In putting "labels" on him without concrete analysis, Zha concluded, it was not he, but Dong and the others who were guilty of "subjective methods."[58]

Thereafter, other philosophers and scientists joined the debate on the substantive issues that Zha had raised. In December *Studies in Philosophy*, the journal of Zha's own institute, carried two long articles implicitly critical of his views. One, written by Ai Ying, a political science researcher at a Shanghai pedagogical institute, called even more sharply for science's autonomy from philosophy than had earlier salvos in the public debate.[59] The other was a long review of the problem of the infinite extent of the universe by Wu Guosheng, Zha's colleague in the Institute of Philosophy.

Ai's article was prefaced by an editor's note expressing gratification that the original Zha Ruqiang–Zhong Weiguang exchange had spawned a prominent debate in the pages of several journals and papers. It also took the opportunity to reiterate some rules of academic debate that "though general, were not without usefulness." "What we need," it said, "is to develop debate between different schools of thought [xuepai] around different academic viewpoints, not the views of factions [menhu]." "Political and administrative interference" from the outside should be avoided, and neither side should resort to "announcements beforehand that the opposing side should be criticized."[60]

Wu Guosheng's article in the same issue of *Studies in Philosophy* was a long review of the history of the issue of the infinite extent of the universe. Wu's allegiances in the debates were already clear from a long article he had published in the *Bulletin of Natural Dialectics* the month before. That article, entitled "Fang Lizhi—The Kind of Scholar Our Republic Needs," recounted Fang's rise to prominence as an internationally known astrophysicist despite persecution through the Cultural Revolution, reviewed his views on cosmological issues, and praised him as a model of the philosophically minded scientist.[61]

In his *Studies in Philosophy* article Wu traced the emergence of two traditions of cosmology: a "natural philosophy" tradition emerging from the efforts of eighteenth- and nineteenth-century philosophers to incorporate the findings of the science of their day, and a modern scientific cosmology based on the findings of twentieth-century science. The two traditions clash, Wu observed, because they employ different methods and premises. The natural philosophy tradition's approach is speculative, intuitive, and conjectural; the scientific tradition is built on observation, and uses mathematics to systematize observational findings into theoretical models that yield predictions susceptible to observational confirmation.

The debate over whether the universe is infinite, Wu suggested, grew out of the natural philosophy tradition, and so contemporary efforts to accommodate the conclusions and findings of modern science to this older tradition were self-defeating. This was because those who attempted such accommodations (i.e., Zha Ruqiang) sought to respond to developments in contemporary science while preserving the original philosophical premises, an approach that actually "deepens the crack" between philosophy and science. Since scientific cosmology had begun to examine the question of the finite versus infinite nature of the universe on scientific grounds, it would be better, Wu suggested, for philosophers not to regard the issue as a "fundamental principle" and cede it to the scientists. A hundred years ago, he said, the founders of Marxism upheld the principle on the basis of scientific knowledge of that day and to banish "idealist" notions from science itself. To defend the theory "blindly" today, he said, could not defend materialism; only reliance on the spirit of science could do that.[62]

THE SCIENCE AND PHILOSOPHY DEBATES:
BOURGEOIS LIBERALIZATION

The onset of the campaign against "bourgeois liberalization" in January 1987 suspended the spectacular intellectual flowering of the previous nine months. In the larger political arena Fang Lizhi, a main participant in the debate over the relationship between science and philosophy, was one of the three leading intellectuals expelled from the Party and publicly criticized in the campaign. That criticism focused, however, not on his position in the science and philosophy debate, but rather on his views on politics—the role of Party committees in universities, the role of intellectuals in the political process, and so forth. A conscious and explicit effort was made, in fact, to separate Fang's political views, which the Party considered to be the object of legitimate attack, from his scientific views, which were viewed as "academic" questions.

Despite this delineation segregating political and academic issues, the "bourgeois liberalization" criticism cast a chill over the debate of the previous year on science and philosophy. Though the themes of the campaign were not explicitly injected into the debate, the views of the side more congenial to conservative Party orthodoxy—those of Zha Ruqiang—predominated in print in the first five months of 1987, to the virtual exclusion of the opposing viewpoint. The heightened political sensitivity of the debate was also signaled by the entry into the controversy of leading Party scientist He Zuoxiu, who published in both *Social Sciences in China* and *Red Flag*.[63]

Meanwhile, on the other side of the debate, Fan Dainian, a physicist and CAS historian of science sympathetic to Zha Ruqiang's critics, sought, in his position as executive editor of the *Bulletin of Natural Dialectics*, to end the science and philosophy debate in the journal in order to prevent criticism of Fang's views on cosmology. He Zuoxiu protested, calling for a special session of the journal's editorial board. At the meeting, despite Fan's resistance, He and Zha carried the day, and so the dispute continued in a one-sided fashion for several months.[64] The campaign also disrupted publication of a book of essays on the debate, to have been published in December 1986 under the editorship of Dong Guangbi and Liang Zhixue. The book was to have included a review of natural dialectics controversies since the 1950s by Xu Liangying,

Wu Guosheng's review of philosophical issues provoked by modern cosmology, Dong's essay "Just What Is Natural Dialectics?," reviews of research trends in the philosophy of science by Fan Dainian and Li Xingmin, and contributions from Han Zenglu and Liu Bing and the other younger researchers.[65]

The blunting impact of the onset of the criticism of "bourgeois liberalization" in January 1987 on the science and philosophy debates was immediately visible in the wider press and academic journals. On 19 January—the day of Fang Lizhi's expulsion from the CCP—*Enlightenment Daily* carried only brief excerpts of several draft articles that it said had been submitted for publication in its "Relationship between Science and Philosophy" column but which could not be published "because of the limitations of space." One excerpt was from an article by Wu Guosheng criticizing the view that Marxist philosophy "guides" science. "A great many of our philosophy workers have been eager to show that every advance in both the history of science and in the modern natural sciences themselves validates the principles of Marxist philosophy, and so assert that Marxist philosophy should play the greatest role in guiding science," he observed. The danger of this view, he said, was that "it encourages philosophers deficient in the rudiments of science to find fault and criticize the work of scientists."[66]

Despite the "limitations of space," the paper did publish, alongside the column of excerpts from submitted drafts, a long article rebutting the views on the relationship between science and philosophy of Dong Guangbi, Han Zenglu, and Jin Wulun as expressed in their 20 October article in the paper. Written by Zhong Xuefu, a researcher in the CAS Institute of Semiconductor Research, the article took issue both with the view of Dong and the others that the role of philosophy was to "defend" science and, without naming him, with Fang Lizhi's view that philosophy is a "tool" of physics. How, Zhong wondered, could philosophy possibly perform either role if it did not share with science common premises in method and epistemology? As such, philosophy therefore had its own scientific character.[67]

Thereafter, until May of 1987, the most prominent views in the major journals and newspapers were those of Zha Ruqiang and his supporters.[68] In this period Zha himself published four articles on the controversy. In January *Studies in Natural Dialectics* carried Zha's defense against assertions by "some comrades" that natural dialectics is a pseudodiscipline that should be abolished in favor of the philosophy of science. This would be inappropriate, he argued, since natural dialectics is an integral component of Marxism-Leninism and includes more than what is usually meant by "philosophy of science." Directly raising the totalist claims of Marxism in organizing and generalizing all knowledge, Zha emphasized that "the organically interlinked system of disciplines in natural dialectics" offers a framework for science and all knowledge superior to that available to Western scholars, who "generally deny the existence of philosophical laws, lack a unified view of the world (or 'ontology'), epistemology, or methodology, and lack a unified perspective in their view of nature and history." Because of this, he concluded, "they have difficulty in forming an organically interrelated disciplinary system out of all of the disciplines."[69]

On 2 March *Enlightenment Daily* carried a second rebuttal by Zha to that paper's 20 October article by Dong Guangbi, Han Zenglu, and Jin Wulun. Zha said he agreed with Dong and the others that philosophy must "defend science," but added that the issue was how exactly to carry this mission out. The critical distinction to make, he said, was between scientific truths that have been proven in experiment and scientific hypotheses that await verification. Since the latter frequently contain contradictory premises, they should not be defended blindly, but rather should depend on philosophy for clarification and analysis.

The lessons of past interference in science by philosophy raised by Dong should not be lost, Zha continued, but neither on that account should China's philosophers and scientists go to the opposite extreme of assuming there is no role whatsoever in science for philosophy. He concluded by citing the statements in the CCP's 1986 Sixth Plenum resolution on spiritual civilization opposing both adherence to Marxism as an ossified dogma and rejection of it because it is outdated. The views that philosophy can replace science and that philosophy has no role in guiding science are both wrong, he said. "The latter view may be said to be the penalty for the former; but it is still erroneous."[70]

In May *Social Sciences in China* published a long criticism by Zha of the views of Fang Lizhi on the possibility that the universe was "created out of nothing." These views had been expressed mainly in Fang's 1984 *Bulletin of Natural Dialectics* article, though Zha cited eleven other publications by Fang on cosmology in both *neibu* and public periodicals. Apparently recognizing that the article would appear in the midst of a full-blown campaign in national media criticizing Fang's political views, Zha stated in a note, dated 25 February and appended to the article, that he hoped his criticism would be taken in an "academic" vein. Zha explained that he had actually submitted the article the previous October and said that "now, as before, I regard the issues in this article to be academic questions concerning our respective views of nature and hope that Fang Lizhi will conduct academic discussions with me by reasoning things out."[71]

Also in May, Zha published in *Studies in Natural Dialectics* another article criticizing Fang, this one taking issue with the views Fang had expressed in his essay "Philosophy and Physics," published the previous October in *Studies in Natural Dialectics*, and with views attributed to Fang by Wu Guosheng in his adulatory biography of Fang in the same journal in November. In an appended note dated 4 February, Zha explained that his article had originally been part of the longer piece submitted to *Social Sciences in China* the previous fall, which that journal was now publishing. When the editorial board of *Social Sciences in China* recommended shortening the draft, he decided to make the part he took out into a separate article and incorporate the new materials in Wu's article. "As before," Zha said, "I regard the problems I raise in this article with Fang Lizhi to be academic problems," expressing hope that Fang would respond by "carrying out a reasoned debate with me."

In the article, Zha complained that since 1985 Fang had been accusing him of setting himself up as a philosophical "judge" over science, but as yet Fang had not refuted his ideas concretely. Actually, he said, he and Fang agreed on specific scientific issues and even on the relationship of science to philosophy in most respects; the real differences between them lay not in science but in philosophy and in the philosophical interpretation of the findings of science. These could not be considered intrusions of Marxist philosophy into science, he noted, since even Fang himself acknowledged that so far, the debate over whether the universe had a beginning was a philosophical problem, not a scientific one. In the face of such differences over problems of philosophy, Zha urged, the best way of proceeding was simply to allow philosophers and scientists to put forth their diverse opinions. "Comrade Fang Lizhi was himself harmed during the Gang of Four's heyday by crude interventions into science," Zha observed. "I hope," he concluded, "that he can understand the difference between normal debate and crude intervention, and will himself not use crude approaches to deal with different opinions."[72]

In the early months of 1987 Zha was joined in his criticisms by He Zuoxiu. He's views predictably coincided with Zha's. Because of his stature as a Party scientist and because *Red Flag* began to publish his views on the issues, his entry into the public controversy marked a significant intensification of the debate. As mentioned previously, he had intervened privately in the debate during the fall of 1986 by pressuring the *Bulletin of Natural Dialectics* not to publish rejoinders by the young researchers who had sparked the original public criticisms of Zha Ruqiang's views. His sympathies in the science and philosophy debate could be inferred from some of his earlier writings. For example, he had spoken out in the post-Mao period on the validity of the theory of matter's infinite divisibility as early as 1978 and had taken a personal interest in research that might weaken Copenhagen interpretations of quantum mechanics in favor of the "hidden variables" theories. In addition, in an article in *Red Flag* in 1984, he had defended the continuing relevance of Marxist philosophy in guiding science. In that article he indicated that he was engaged in research on problems concerning neutron mass that might shed light on whether the universe is finite.[73]

He Zuoxiu's main contribution in the spring of 1987 was a major critique, published in *Red Flag*, of attacks on the principle of the universe's infinite extent. An editor's note explained that the article had been written the previous December and "originally" published in the March issue of *Social Sciences in China; Red Flag*, however, was signed to press on 1 March, and so was actually available before the issue of the CASS journal. In the article, He did not attack Fang Lizhi by name, though it is clear from the various viewpoints on cosmology that he chose to rebut that he had Fang in mind. In defending the view that the universe is infinite, He particularly criticized the new model developed by Stephen Hawking, which Fang had taken up in 1984, and attacked the view that the inflationary cosmology model allows for the possibility that the universe was "created out of nothing."[74]

THE SCIENCE AND PHILOSOPHY DEBATES: RESUMPTION

The one-sided chill over the debate during the criticism of "bourgeois liberalization" was short-lived. By mid-March 1987 Zhao Ziyang was moving with Deng Xiaoping's backing to blunt the impact of the campaign on economic and scientific intellectuals. Looking ahead to the Thirteenth CCP Congress, which was to meet the following fall, Zhao worked to renew momentum behind the reforms, and the press began publishing commentary on controversial reform themes that the Party congress would endorse months later. Leading liberal intellectuals who were on the defensive in January now reasserted themselves and took the lead in sounding such themes. Foremost among these was Yu Guangyuan, whose article designating China's socialist development as only in its "initial stage" attracted enormous attention.[75]

In this context, by late spring and early summer the science and philosophy debate had resumed where it left off in January. Zha's critics re-emerged in print, now joined by several new participants, as the debate rapidly acquired new heat. Writing in the Harbin journal *Studies and Explorations* (Xuexi yu tansuo), for example, Wu Peng dismissed the notion of the universe's infinite extent as "purely the creation of human thought." Modern cosmology, he said, had "exposed several weak points that the fundamental tenets of dialectical materialism cannot tolerate, and so the time has come to replace them using the new cosmological theories."[76] In the May issue of *Social Sciences in China* Wen Xingwu, a natural dialectics researcher at Hebei University, criticized Zha Ruqiang's understanding of quantum mechanics as manifested in his 1982 article on natural dialectics. Wen contended that wave-particle duality could not be a "fundamental contradiction" of nature, as Zha maintained. Experiments involving the particles of the microworld could give us information only about the interactions of our macrolevel apparatus with objects of the microworld, not about microobjects as they exist independently, Wen said. Zha also misunderstood the abstract nature of the wave function of quantum mechanics—"It is a state vector in a Hilbert space and so is just a mathematical wave"—with particles as real objects, according to Wen. "We cannot set particles as real objects in three-dimensional space against mathematical abstractions to form a contradiction of natural reality."[77]

By the summer some of the stalwarts of the previous year's debate had returned to it. In July Wu Guosheng published a long review of the issue of the infinite divisibility of matter, taking issue with nearly everyone who had expressed himself on the question, including Jin Wulun, Wang Gancai, and Zha Ruqiang. His primary conclusion was that the principle of the infinite divisibility of matter was an "empty abstraction."[78]

Also in July, Jin Wulun renewed his attack, rebutting Zha Ruqiang's response in the 8 December 1986 *Enlightenment Daily* to his attack on the concept of matter's infinite divisibility in the 6 October issue of that paper. At the bottom of Jin's piece was the notation that "revisions" had been completed on 22 January 1987, suggesting that the article had been set aside as the campaign against "bourgeois liberalization" was beginning. In the article, Jin dissected Zha's use of the deductive method in demonstrating the logical validity of the concept of infinite divisibility; he argued that Zha's logic in fact had the reverse effect of calling into question the law of the unity of opposites—"perhaps not what Comrade Zha Ruqiang had in mind."

In conclusion, Jin took issue with Zha's assertion that the philosophical deduction that matter is infinitely divisible was only a "general conclusion" and that the specific conclusions of how atoms, quarks, and other particles are divisible internally could be arrived at only through "concrete study" by science. Such a predetermined framework made particle physics "like a set of Chinese boxes, with a big box enclosing a smaller box, and within this small box is enclosed an even smaller box, and so on." Such an approach was "a manifestation of mechanistic determinism" that saw no possibility of revolutionary change. "If we follow Comrade Zha Ruqiang's view," he concluded, "then such things as the 'point model,' one dimensional 'string models,' and multidimensional 'superstring theory' may not be taken up because they do not comport with Comrade Zha Ruqiang's theory of 'infinite divisibility.' "[79]

Among all of the contributions to the debate in the wake of the "bourgeois liberalization" period, however, the most significant was that of Xu Liangying. Xu, with Zha Ruqiang, was the true center of the dispute. Xu's students had ignited the public debate, and as his first and only contribution would show, he had been a key presence behind it since it began in 1986. In a long review of the dispute published in the *Bulletin of Natural Dialectics* in September, Xu finally responded to Zha Ruqiang's complaints that he had never taken up his criticisms of Zha fairly. Xu said that when he read Zha's criticisms of him in the same journal the year before, he decided not to "waste more ink" on the dispute since any reader "with the slightest scientific knowledge and independence of judgment" could reach his own conclusions. As a result, however, the debate had taken on a one-sided appearance, with Zha publishing articles in five or six journals and newspapers. Rebuttals to Zha's articles, he noted, had been rejected, and a long-planned collection of essays on the problem was suspended. *Studies in Philosophy* had published Zha's rebuttal of Zhong Weiguang with an editor's note that was clearly partial in the debate; and, he revealed, it had also refused to publish Zhong Weiguang's two draft responses to Zha's rebuttal. Similar predilections appeared to be governing editorial work at *Social Sciences in China* and even the *Bulletin of Natural Dialectics,* Xu said, and so Zha was already telling people that he had been "completely victorious" in the debate. This great victory, Xu said with irony, deserved a page in the history of Chinese science, particularly since it had occurred in the wake of celebrations of the thirtieth anniversary of the "double hundred" policy on academic debate.

Xu went on to recount the origins of the debate as he saw them. "Rumors" that he and Zha were "settling old scores" were untrue, he said. They had none to settle. Instead, the dispute involved differences over academic workstyle and how to handle basic issues in Marxist philosophy. Thus at a Chengdu conference on natural dialectics in 1979, he had objected to Zha's criticism of the conclusion of general relativity that the universe is "finite but unbounded" as a violation of Marxist philosophy. The issue of the finite versus infinite nature of the universe belonged to science, not philosophy, Xu recalled saying at the conference, arguing that the real violation of Marxist philosophy was to dismiss scientific conclusions on the basis of predetermined philosophical opinion. To express that idea, he had added a section in the conference's final communiqué on philosophy's influence (and presumably interference) in science in hopes of promoting philosophy's proper role as science's "rear guard."

Revealing a bitter past that was probably common among many who attempted to practice their sciences in authoritarian Marxist settings, Xu explained that the position he had taken at the Chengdu conference had been rooted in his own painful experiences. When he first began studying general relativity in 1939 and learned of its conclusion that the universe is finite but has no edge, he believed there was no contradiction with the tenets of Marxist philosophy. This attitude changed after the rise of Zhdanov and his deeply politicizing impact on the relationship between science and philosophy in the USSR in the late 1940s. For twenty-eight years thereafter—from 1948 to 1976—Xu attempted to hew to the hardened set of Zhdanovite natural dialectics tenets as they were implanted in China, writing articles attacking the finite-universe theory.

Through this twenty-eight-year period, Xu's views evolved gradually. A physicist by training, he had mixed politics and physics out of blind faith in Stalin and the USSR. Even though he did away with his "Stalin superstition" in 1956 and was expelled from the Party as a "rightist" in 1957, his belief in Mao Zedong remained unshaken. He emerged from the "miasma" of the Cultural Revolution and Mao's personality cult by the time of the campaign to "criticize Lin Biao and Confucius" in 1974, but the scales really dropped from his eyes only with the fall of the Gang of Four in 1976. What really opened his eyes and his mind was a remark—perhaps little remembered now—by Yu Guangyuan at a CAS conference in March 1978. "Marxism," Yu said, "is a science, and science allows people to study; it is not a law that commands people's obedience, and it is not a religion that calls upon people to worship it." These words, Xu said, he would never forget.

According to Xu, the present dispute began in November 1985 when Zha published his article on the categories of natural dialectics. Not only did Zha repeat the views he had presented in 1979, but he also suggested that what would be revised in the future was not philosophy's principles but rather science's hypotheses. These views naturally created a "big stir" among natural scientists, Xu continued, so the local natural-dialectics research society convened a seminar, inviting exponents on both sides of the issue. Disappointingly, Xu noted, Zha Ruqiang did not come, though "the person he criticized"—Fang Lizhi—did.

Xu acknowledged that at the seminar he had indeed claimed that

Zha's 1982 and 1985 articles contained a hundred errors, noting that he still believed this to be the case. He recalled that he had spent considerable effort together with two researchers—one an expert in computers and the other trained in biology—and had uncovered forty to fifty errors. He believed, moreover, that criticisms of particular views at an academic seminar, whether the proponents were present or not, was a normal feature of academic life. He added that in a letter he had informed Zha of this belief after Zha accused him of criticizing people "behind their backs."

Originally he had intended to write an article, as he had told Zha, but several "young comrades" had already taken up the debate, so he decided not to do so. His eyesight was bad, he complained, so that he could read small characters only with a magnifying glass; his researchers had wanted to save his eyesight by allowing him to "avoid reading things of no value." The five researchers accordingly published their criticism of Zha's views in an article in *Social Sciences in China*, which Zha rebutted, Xu observed, by claiming that his scientific knowledge was greater than theirs. The five wrote a response to Zha, but the journal refused to publish it, allowing Zha "to maintain his grand concept of himself forever."

After commenting on the difficulty of debating with people whose ignorance removed the possibility of a common language, Xu proceeded to offer Zha "the ABCs" on a couple of points on the "finite but unbounded" concept. Xu concluded that his main purpose in relating all of this in print was to urge Zha to emulate Engels in having a little humility and in not believing himself to be correct about everything. He had recounted his own mistakes over the preceding decades, Xu said, in order to encourage Zha not to go too far down the same road. He welcomed criticism of his own mistakes, he went on, but warned that those who attempt to "rely on force instead of knowledge and turn right and wrong upside down" will only be exposed in the end. "Paper tigers scare nobody," he stated.[80]

Through the summer of 1987, neither Zha Ruqiang nor He Zuoxiu published new comments on the debate, but by the fall, coincident with the publication of Xu Liangying's article, both re-emerged in print in full force. Between October 1987 and March 1988, He reasserted his high-profile presence in the debate, publishing four new comments on it. In October *Red Flag* carried a long "talk" under He's byline on the importance of philosophy's guiding role in science. Though he did not attack anyone by name, the targets of his criticisms were apparent in the distinctive views he chose to dispute. In particular, he singled out Fang Lizhi's view on the retreat of philosophy before science, Dong Guangbi's view that philosophy must "defend" science without "judging" it, and, to some extent, Zha Ruqiang's views on natural-philosophy category structures.[81]

He Zuoxiu also authored another defense on the validity of the fundamental tenets of natural dialectics, written in the Galilean "dialogue" format that he frequently used and published in two parts in the November and December 1987 issues of *Studies in Philosophy*, entitled "Matter, Motion, Space, and Time." This time He specifically footnoted views he sought to criticize, citing articles by Fang Lizhi and Wu Guosheng, among others.[82]

In the same month He also contributed another "dialogue," this one appearing in *Studies in Natural Dialectics* and criticizing Jin Wulun's attacks on the infinite divisibility of matter thesis in his 6 October 1986 *Enlightenment Daily* article. He characterized Jin's interpretation of the quark confinement problem as "strange logic." No one objects, He said, to citing the inverse variation with distance of the electromagnetic force as an example of the law of the unity of opposites. Yet, he went on, Jin seemed unable to recognize that the expression describing the strong force binding quarks into mesons and larger particles operated in formally the same way, though varying directly and not inversely with distance.[83]

In the March 1988 issue of the *Bulletin of Natural Dialectics,* He Zuoxiu also took issue with Xu Liangying's lecturing Zha Ruqiang on the "ABC's" of the concept "finite but unbounded." He's comments were preceded by an editor's note laying down new guidelines for continuation of the debate in that journal. The note expressed gratification that the debate between Zha and Zhong Weiguang originating in the journal in 1986 had spread to several other journals and that the debate had been conducted according to the "double hundred" policy and so had been beneficial to natural science research. Though the issues in the debate had become clear and readers could thereby form their own judgments about their merits, it continued, "some comrades" still thought some issues required further clarification. Therefore, in the interest of "saving space" and "deepening the discussion," the journal was stipulating new conditions for the debate to continue in its pages. Subsequently, it said, articles could not exceed two thousand characters in length or go beyond "academic" concerns. Further, both sides must "maintain academic demeanor, respect each other, and use serious and sincere wording; they must not use ridicule, sarcasm, and denunciatory language in engaging the opposing side. . . . Previously this journal did not pay sufficient attention in this regard, which is a shortcoming for which we should do self-criticism." The note also expressed the hope that "everyone hereafter will comply and monitor their conduct."

Under the constraints of this editor's note, He's article was a model of academic reticence, especially in contrast to the high visibility of his previous contributions to the debate. He had long wanted to avoid being drawn into the Zha-Xu debate, he said, but felt he could not help but respond after reading Xu's response to Zha. In particular, he felt no desire to involve himself in either Zha's or Xu's "category" systems arguments or to examine in detail how many mistakes Zha had made: Xu had said there were at least forty to fifty, his students claimed sixteen, and Zha had acknowledged only one, or perhaps none. Nor did he want to examine whether editor's notes in *Studies in Philosophy* were "genuinely Marxist" or "pseudo-Marxist."

Instead, all he desired was to point out to Xu that the "finite but unbounded" concept does not necessarily rule out the existence of a higher-dimensional space into which the "finite but unbounded" space is expanding. Inflationary cosmology was predicated on that possibility, he said, noting that there may be as many as 10^{50} or even 10^{2000} "metagalaxies."[84] "Such numbers are not worth treating in earnest," He concluded, "but at least this 'finite but unbounded' metagalaxy of ours may be 'supersedable,' allowing people to think about what's 'beyond' it."[85]

Zha Ruqiang also returned to the debate. In a short article in the September 1987 *Studies in Natural Dialectics*, he criticized Jin Wulun's October 1986 attack in *Enlightenment Daily* on the infinite divisibility thesis. Zha rebutted Jin on some of the same grounds used by He Zuoxiu, accusing Jin of using distorted "mechanistic" and "constituentist" approaches in understanding natural dialectics' tenets by way of disproving them.[86]

Zha Ruqiang's final broadside in the debate was a furious response to Xu Liangying's long remarks in September 1987. Appearing in the May 1988 issue of the *Bulletin of Natural Dialectics,* Zha's article was subject to the same guidelines announced in the editor's note preceding He Zuoxiu's article. Zha responded with outrage at the limitations placed on him, noting that while Xu had been allowed eight thousand characters to criticize him, he was confined to two thousand—treatment that was patently unfair. In the space allotted to him, Zha rebutted several of the specific points Xu had raised. The main thrust of his comments, however, was to accuse Xu of violating the very "spirit of science" and fair play over which Xu had called him to account. "My expectation of Comrade Xu Liangying is conduct of academic debate on the basis of equality and factualness!"[87]

THE SCIENCE AND PHILOSOPHY DEBATES:
CONCLUSION

Through the remainder of 1988 and the early months of 1989, the science and philosophy debates continued, though with less intensity and with a gradual shift in the cast of participants. Even across the great divide of the Tiananmen demonstrations and the oppressive political atmosphere that followed in China's intellectual life, the debate flickered and then revived, now refocused on the views of He Zuoxiu. Xu Liangying's painful recounting in the pages of the *Bulletin of Natural Dialectics* in the fall of 1987 remained his only published contribution specifically addressed to the debate. Increasingly thereafter, as the next chapter will demonstrate, his attention appears to have turned to broader political issues. Because of his activities preceding the Tiananmen demonstrations, from June 1989 through 1992 Xu was not permitted to publish his views on political or academic subjects. On the other side, Zha Ruqiang had intimated in his furious rejoinder to Xu in the *Bulletin of Natural Dialectics* in May 1988 his intention to write new comments on the debate, but none appeared before Zha's unexpected death in September 1990 at the age of 65.

Despite the departure of these two main antogonists, other participants in the debate did continue to comment on it. Jin Wulun, for example, responded to He Zuoxiu's criticisms of his views on the infinite divisibility thesis, attacking He's views from several angles in the May 1988 *Studies in Natural Dialectics*.[88] He's insistence on the continuing value of the infinite divisibility approach, Jin said, was misplaced from the perspective of the history of science. Thomas Kuhn's work had shown that major advances in science involved the overthrow of old research traditions in favor of new ones; thus new, comprehensive revolutions in particle physics would require major breakthroughs in the fundamental concepts, such as those of one- and ten-dimensional string theory. Similarly, the methods of particle physics could not be bound by any preconceived approach prescribed by philosophers and philosophically minded scientists wedded to the traditional dialectics of nature, but must emerge from the practice of science itself. Jin also drew together all of his arguments against the infinite divisibility theory over the previous two years into a book, published in November 1988, which traced the origins of the theory and laid out in detail the problems he believed contemporary science presented.[89] From the suppression of the Tiananmen demonstrations through 1992, Jin did not publish on the debate.

Wu Guosheng also continued to address the issues in the debate, both before and after Tiananmen. In November 1990 he wrote a long review of the history of cosmology that, given the prevailing hostile political atmosphere, was remarkably blunt in suggesting that the tenets of traditional natural dialectics were outdated. In tracing the course of cosmology from ancient times up to the contemporary period, Wu sought to show how contemporary scientific cosmology had finally begun to displace traditional cosmologies based on vastly different concepts and approaches. In doing so, scientific cosmology not only effectively described the true structure of the universe and explicated its phenomena; it also satisfied deep psychological needs, religious longings, and aesthetic ideals of humanity. Therefore it both "saves the appearances and saves the soul."

According to Wu, the emergence of scientific cosmological theories in early modern and contemporary times, however, threatened earlier dogmatic cosmological traditions. The harsh persecution that the heliocentric conception of Copernicus, Galileo, and Bruno received at the hands of religious authorities wedded to the traditional Aristotelian-Ptolemaic geocentric view "ought to have stood forever as a warning" that the succession of old cosmologies by new ones need not proceed peaceably, Wu observed. Unfortunately, the cosmological viewpoint of many philosophers in present-day China remained tied to the "ossified" infinite-universe conception, he continued, and so criticism of contemporary scientific cosmology's conclusions to the contrary was still considered a "combat task" on the philosophy front.

The question of whether the universe is infinite, Wu observed, could be approached on either scientific or philosophical grounds. Scientifically, it could be weighed according to the reasonableness of existing cosmological theory and in light of available observational evidence, such as efforts to infer the deceleration parameter q_o, which would indicate whether the universe has sufficient mass to slow and then reverse its presently observed expansion, and so indicate that the universe is finite in mass and extent. Scientific cosmology at present could not give a definitive answer to this question, he pointed out.

Insistence on the validity of the infinite-universe thesis in China's philosophy circles, Wu said, was based not on scientific grounds, but rather on considerations extraneous to science. Wu distilled objections in these circles to the conclusions of contemporary scientific cosmology to three basic lines of argument. First, some philosophers did not understand how space can be curved, or disputed that non-Euclidean geometry of space-time employed by general relativity describes the actual universe. Second, they disputed that the "universe" they mean is the "universe" meant by contemporary scientific cosmology. The universe in their minds is the "absolute universe" of all past, present, and future cosmologies. The natural sciences have no authority to address this ideal universe, since their observations are only partial, relative, and adequate to the current state of knowledge of the universe. This objection was essentially epistemological, Wu stated. Third was a kind of ontological argument—that because the real universe is beyond our direct knowledge or observation, what we know is only "our universe." The underlying premise of all three lines of argument, Wu said, was simply that the universe studied by scientific cosmology is not the actual universe, which scientific cosmology does not describe, has not been comprehended by science so far, and is forever beyond science's reach.

Wu concluded that attempting to refute such philosophical arguments using scientific argument was pointless, since philosophical questions could have only philosophical answers. The premise of the third, ontological line of argument, for example, was forever beyond the empirical reach of science; on such a premise one could just as easily assert the existence of God as the existence of matter or an infinite universe. Experience and practical reason had no way to address the absolute, Wu went on, which was why scientists had always honored Kant but spurned Hegel. Closing with a rather philosophically resigned judgment of his own discipline, Wu predicted that revolutions in philosophical concept would never be brought about by appeal to scientific fact or theory, or even logical proof, but only by "appeal to history."[90]

Other philosophers, scientists, and historians of science treated issues related to the debate. *Bulletin of Natural Dialectics* deputy editor Li Xingmin, for example, wrote frequently and provocatively on the need for science's autonomy from philosophy.[91] Li, Dong Guangbi, and Fan Dainian also criticized Lenin's misguided attacks on the idealist philosophical views of Ernst Mach, which they pointed out were important in paving the way for the revolutions in relativity theory and quantum mechanics.[92] Dong Guangbi put forward the beginnings of a "possible theory" of the nature of physical reality that proceeded from distinctions between empirical reality and perceptual knowledge on one hand and theoretical or mathematical reality and consciousness on the other, based on an extensive review of the EPR experiment and debates in Western philosophy of science over realism and positivism.[93]

By 1989, and especially in the post-Tiananmen period, the focus of the science and philosophy debates shifted away from the twin problems that dominated the controversy over the preceding three years—the issue of the infinite divisibility of matter and the infinite extent of the universe. A new problem emerged at the center of the dispute: the problem of "cognitive subjectivity"—that is, is objective knowledge of the world possible, or does all perception include subjective elements that inhibit acquiring objective knowledge? The heart of this dispute involved the "measurement problem" in quantum mechanics, an issue that had simmered in the background over the preceding years.

The main antagonist in the debate shifted, too. He Zuoxiu was by far the dominating figure after 1989. His high-profile approach to the measurement problem in quantum mechanics was two-pronged. First, he put forward what he regarded as a pathbreaking solution to the problem in a manner favorable to philosophical realism and the possibility of objective knowledge of reality.[94] At the same time, he wrote a sweeping criticism of subjectivist interpretations of the epistemological foundations of quantum theory that he believed had propagated unfounded idealist ideas in philosophy circles and more widely in the intellectual arena in China in the 1980s.[95] Confronting him in his defense of the continuing validity of natural dialectics' fundamental tenets were several philosophers and scientists who were either new to the science and philosophy debates or who had previously played only marginal roles in it.[96]

Although the central topic and the primary participants in the debates were new, the underlying issues, antagonists on both sides of the debate believed, were the same.[97] These were, as before, the questions of how much, if any, of the totalist system of Marxist philosophy could be retained in the face of modern science's revolutionary theories, and what role, if any, Marxist philosophy should play in the conduct of science and the interpretation of its theories.

5 / The Politics of Knowledge

The eruption of scientific dissent in the 1980s reflected in part the stresses, conflicts, disappointed expectations, and abused ideals described in the previous three chapters. The leading dissidents in the scientific community emerged from among the protagonists of the debates on science and philosophy and, in particular, from one side of the debates. The cluster of values and ideals that motivated their dissent can also be seen in the positions they adopted in the debates. This chapter traces the continuity in ideals and outlooks of those who became the leading dissidents of the late 1980s, as well as the continuity in the countervailing outlooks and values of those who opposed them. Viewed from that perspective, for some scientists the path from membership in the scientific vanguard of China's future to outcast dissidence was surprisingly short.

THE SEEDS OF ALIENATION

Impetus toward political agitation and dissent among scientists came from several converging sources by the late 1980s. First, the debates over scientific theories such as cosmology and quantum mechanics reflected a deeper conflict of authority. Though the debates started out as a clash over ideas and theories, they escalated almost immediately into disputes over the legitimate boundaries between intellectual disciplines and, from there, into conflicts over credentials, standing, and mission. At issue were the autonomy of China's scientific community and the conduct of science on one hand, and on the other the validity and jurisdiction of Marxist-Leninist philosophy and hence the fundamental legitimacy of the political system itself. The heat and apparent

183

bitterness of the debates derived from the participants' recognition that the underlying issues were fundamental and not easily reconciled.

This conflict of authority was engendered by the Dengist reforms and the central role that science was called upon to play in them. As described previously, Party reformers led by Deng Xiaoping had sought since 1977 to restore the legitimacy and authority of the CCP, in part by restoring the "scientific" basis of its policies under the slogans "Seek truth from facts" and "Take practice as the sole criterion for truth." Similarly, science and technology were seen as the centerpiece of China's economic modernization strategy and the key to its long-term survival in the modern world. Science was also recognized as the embodiment of the spirit of human progress, promoting values and ideals that epitomized modern culture and that lay at the heart of the Marxist-Leninist political enterprise. Science therefore was authoritatively enshrined as the cornerstone of the "socialist spiritual civilization" that the Deng leadership sought to inculcate.

In support of these political and developmental goals, the Deng leadership invited Chinese scientists to take on two missions. First, natural and social scientists were asked to criticize "superstition" wherever they saw it, both in the interest of overcoming the residual "feudalism" of China's premodern heritage and the "feudal leftist" legacy of the Maoist period and in the interest of establishing realistic policies for China's future. Second, they were encouraged to reprofessionalize China's scientific community.

Chinese scientists responded vigorously and enthusiastically to both invitations. The pages of the Party press and journals after 1977 resonated with a renewed critical spirit of science as prominent natural and social scientists took the lead in laying out the priorities and central themes of the Dengist reforms. Article after article attacked what were described as obscurantist, antiscientific, and dogmatic attitudes and policies of the previous two decades. These articles likened the Deng regime's outlook to a Chinese "renaissance," drawing explicit parallels between China's rebirth into the modern world during the May Fourth period and that in the 1980s under the CCP's new call to "liberate thought" for the sake of China's future. This Party theme was set out most explicitly by Zhou Yang, vice president of the CASS and deputy chief of the Party Propaganda Department. In a keynote speech in 1979 marking the sixtieth anniversary of the May Fourth movement, Zhou declared that the new movement inaugurated by Deng Xiaoping to "liberate thought" was the third such movement in China in the twentieth century. The first had been the May Fourth criticism of the superstitions of traditional Confucian culture, which aroused the awareness of the Chinese people of their modern predicament and paved the way for their embrace of Marxism-Leninism as the key to their future. The second had been Mao's 1942–43 Yan'an rectification campaign against dogmatism within the Chinese communist movement, "unifying" the Party's understanding of how the universal principles of Marxism-Leninism were to be applied to the particulars of Chinese realities. Deng Xiaoping's reform movement now confronted similar tasks, seeking to rouse China from two decades of Maoist superstition and obscurantism.[1]

The call by the Deng leadership to reinstill professionalism in the scientific community marked a fundamental reversal of the attempt during the Maoist period to deprofessionalize intellectual activity. Impressed by what he considered to be the usurpation of social and political power by new managerial, technical, and intellectual elites within the context of the socialist transformation under the First Five-Year Plan in the mid-1950s, Mao Zedong had sought to dilute the criteria of professionalism that demarcated scientists, engineers, factory managers, and intellectuals as distinct socioeconomic groups. Emphasizing political "redness" alongside expertise, Mao had replaced professional criteria with "mass"-oriented standards that were intended to dissolve the distinctive identities of those engaged in such work, diffusing their identities into the broader "masses" of society and ensuring their responsiveness to the authority of the Party.

The Dengist call for scientists to do the things they do uniquely as scientists paralleled efforts to reverse Maoist approaches and restore distinctive standards of professionalism among those engaged in other types of specialized socioeconomic activity. Efforts in other sectors included the re-elaboration of managerial and technical career tracks in industrial enterprises and the long-debated and finally realized restoration of ranks in the People's Liberation Army. On the same basis, the reformers reintroduced various ranks, titles, and academic degree systems that differentiated status within the scientific and technical community, and they encouraged appraisals and promotions within that status system in some measure according to the rational demands of the conduct of science.

In calling on scientists to criticize "superstition" and to restore professionalism to science, the Party leadership presumed a convergence of goals between themselves and the scientific intellectuals. Though the scientific community had won a limited but still considerable degree of autonomy in the new regime's policies, the presumption remained that scientists, out of a consensus of common purpose, would mobilize their energies and enthusiasms behind the goals of the state. Scientists' license to be scientists was still circumscribed by their continuing "patriotic" responsibility to serve the goals of China's modernization as defined by the Party in return for continuing state support for science.

This presumed harmony between scientific professionalism and responsiveness to state direction was apparent at the 1980 meeting revitalizing the Chinese Association of Science and Technology (CAST). Consistent with the antiprofessionalist direction of Maoist policies, CAST had been attacked as a bastion of elitism during the Cultural Revolution decade and was shut down. The 1980 meeting was its first national congress since 1960. As the umbrella organization for all professional scientific and technical societies in China, CAST was a natural forum in which to underscore the Deng regime's encouragement of science's critical spirit and scientific professionalism in service to China's socialist modernization. The meeting rewrote the association's constitution around these themes, and keynote speeches by CAST president Zhou Peiyuan and newly appointed Party general secretary Hu Yaobang emphasized them as well.

In his speech, Zhou Peiyuan declared that CAST was "the scientists' and technicians' own organization" dedicated to "representing the interests of the scientists and technicians in real earnest." The association, he said, must reinforce scientific standards within China's scientific and technical community, facilitate exchanges among scientists in various fields domestically and enhance their participation in the international scientific community, and promote popular awareness of science's achievements and support for its advancement. He also called on CAST and its member professional societies to serve as "links and bridges for scientists and technicians to establish close contacts with Party organizations," and he urged association members to be "good staff members and advisers for the Party and government in the science and technology field."[2]

Hu Yaobang's speech underscored the importance of science both as a decisive "force of production" in China's future and as an enterprise that fostered a previously lacking spirit of selfless, skeptical realism:

> Our Party hopes that science and technology circles will establish and carry forward a fine, scientific workstyle. Science is what it is simply because it can break down fetishes and superstitions and is bold in explorations and because it opposes following the beaten path and dares to destroy outmoded conventions and bad customs. Scientists are what they are simply because they possess a scientific spirit— the spirit of seeking truth from facts, the spirit of innovation, and the spirit of creation—and because they oppose indulging in exaggerations, using flashy words without substance, and sticking to the outmoded and preserving the outworn. Scientists keep on advancing simply because they are never satisfied with their own achievements, are capable of respecting other's achievements and conducting joint research and study with other scientists, and are skilled at unceasingly absorbing knowledge from the practice of the working masses as well as in absorbing nourishment from the advance of science and technology of foreign countries. Our Party hopes that science and technology circles of our country will painstakingly cultivate and propagate this good workstyle so that a hundred flowers will forever be in bloom and never wither in our garden of science.[3]

Despite the Dengist reformers' effort to harmonize these themes and priorities, they proved to be mutually contradictory in the minds of some Chinese scientists, as the debates on science and philosophy suggest. Inevitably, both the promotion of science's skeptical spirit and the restoration of scientific professionalism revitalized professional norms that universally epitomize science as a social activity. As ideals of expected behavior in the conduct of science, these norms constitute a professional ethos that is inherently and explicitly highly antiauthoritarian. The pioneering sociologist of science Robert Merton identified four such norms or "institutional imperatives" as the core of this scientific ethos: universalism, communism, disinterestedness, and organized or conditioned skepticism.

Universalism refers to the expectation that scientific knowledge and achievement must be judged solely on objective criteria without regard for status, claimed authority, or national boundary. Communism means that all scientific knowledge is the common property of the scientific community, and not the private possession of its originator or anyone else. This norm makes incumbent on the members of the scientific community the duties both to communicate their findings and to acknowledge their debts to the work of the community on which they drew. Disinterestedness refers to the expectation that scientists are motivated foremost by a deep curiosity about the world and its workings. On this basis, the scientific enterprise is worth pursuing for its own sake above all else, including whatever utilitarian purpose science's findings might serve technologically. Organized or conditioned skepticism means that there are no areas closed to skeptical scientific inquiry.[4]

To the extent that these norms inform the expectation of all who participate in a scientific community, science becomes an intensely public activity. Science, in the concise definition of John Ziman, is "public knowledge." Its ideas are tested not in the minds of individual scientists in the privacy of their offices and laboratories, but in the open arenas of scientific discourse—journals, seminars, and meetings of professional societies. These mechanisms of peer review establish an "invisible college" of all scientists, who (ideally) assess new scientific claims impersonally and skeptically without regard for status and authority.[5]

Merton's analysis of the norms of science has been criticized because it does not adequately explain or account for how much of science frequently works in practice. Scientific communities are not immune to external pressures, especially as the conduct of science in developed countries has become more dependent on large bureaucracies and heavy corporate and state funding. Within scientific communities individual scientists clearly vary in the degree to which they conduct themselves according to these professional ideals. Moreover, scientific communities are not egalitarian. They are highly stratified, a characteristic that arises out of the explicit hierarchy of credentials—degrees and titles—that differentiate standing within the community and out of the informal perceptions of status, contribution, and reward in the field.[6] But however much the norms described by Merton may be violated in letter or spirit in particular cases, they remain at the center of the values and ideals that bind the contemporary scientific community together, as a cursory survey of the commentary and letters pages of general science journals such as *Nature* and *Science* in the English-speaking world will readily show. This system of norms and values was exemplified in recent years both by the admiration shown and pride taken in physicist Richard Feynman's skeptical outspokenness in public hearings on the *Challenger* shuttle disaster and by the scientific community's open consternation at the manner in which claims of "cold fusion" were announced.[7]

Taken together, Merton's norms comprise an ideology distinctive to science—"ideology" defined in its broadest sense as a cluster of ideas that supply identity and purpose to a distinct social group. In the judgment of Merton and historians of science who have built on his work, the norms that he identified flourished first in a context of emergent political democracy arising out of the religious and social conflicts of seventeenth-century England. More generally, Merton believed, they prosper in similar democratic contexts. By the same token, he thought, the critical and antiauthoritarian bent of the norms of science mean that science encounters difficulty in authoritarian environments, whether religious or political.[8]

To some degree, the reprofessionalization of the scientific community encouraged by the Dengist reformers was consonant with these Mertonian norms. The restoration of meaningful degrees and titles, the provision for relatively autonomous governance of the CAS under its Scientific Council (temporary as it was), the promotion of "hundred flowers" approaches to "academic" questions (however fleeting), the resurrection and proliferation of professional journals, and the encouragement of international contacts and travel by scientists all comported with the conduct of science according to such norms. The regime's acceptance, however limited in practice, of these institutions and activities as normal and necessary features of science undoubtedly fed the evident enthusiasm of many in China's scientific community for the reforms in their early stages.

By at least some in the science community, the institutions and activities that were considered essential to the health of science in China were understood explicitly in terms of Merton's norms. With the restoration in 1979 of sociology as a legitimate discipline, and subsequently with the translation of Western works of sociology, discussions by Chinese philosophers and sociologists of science of Merton's norms began to appear regularly in academic journals, especially the *Bulletin of Natural Dialectics*.[9] These explorations into the Western sociology of science were part of a larger ongoing discussion examining the operation and institutions of scientific communities in general and of the deficiencies of China's scientific community in particular. By the mid-1980s there was active debate over the need for a separate discipline—a "science of science" (*kexuexue*), paralleling the surge of interest in similar questions and the establishment of *naukovedenie* in the USSR in the 1960s—that would combine the perspectives into questions of the sociology, philosophy, and history of science. In the process, references to universalism, communism (in Merton's sense), disinterestedness, and organized skepticism became commonplace terms in debates on science and its needs.

In this climate it was natural that, after the euphoria of the early years, scientists' dissatisfactions, frustrations, and conflicts with the reforms came to be understood as arising from violations of the norms of healthy science. This was clear in the debates on science and philosophy, expressed in terms of the divergent approaches taken toward the structure of knowledge, toward the structure of authority within the scientific community, and toward the scientific community's autonomy from external guidance.

Zha Ruqiang's attempt to modernize natural dialectics was consistent with the overall thrust of the Dengist reforms under "socialism with Chinese characteristics." Zha sought to accommodate the findings of the modern natural sciences within the framework of enduring fundamental truths of Marxism-Leninism, an effort that comported with and reinforced in the ideological sphere the overall attempt of the reformers to promote accelerated modernization under the enduring leadership of the CCP. With respect to the structure of knowledge, this meant preserving Marxist philosophy's traditional position at the apex of the recognized disciplines of human knowledge. In what might be called a monist structure of knowledge, Marxism incorporates the most general truths of the natural and social worlds: it claims totalist comprehensiveness as the true "theory of everything." Under the all-encompassing umbrella of Marxist philosophy, the specific natural and social science disciplines discover the particular versions of Marxism's general laws and truths within their respective fields. Marxism grows by generalizing the specific laws the sciences disclose in their systematic analysis of specific features of the world and its workings. Marxism in turn guides those disciplines in their search for new laws in their respective fields. In this manner, Marxist philosophy presides over the contention between the "hundred schools" of thought in the natural and social science disciplines, separating the "flowers" from the "weeds" and ensuring the orientation of science toward humanity's progress toward communism. From these premises about the structure of knowledge follows an implicit structure of authority that justifies the continued supervision of science by the Party.

Zha Ruqiang's critics, by contrast, called for a new structure of knowledge that, consistent with the norms of universalism and organized skepticism, emphasized intellectual pluralism and, accordingly, a new "pluralist" structure of authority that sanctioned the absolute independence of science from Party supervision. In seeking to dissociate science from Marxist philosophy, critics such as Xu Liangying, Dong Guangbi, Fang Lizhi, and Li Xingmin advocated the overthrow of Marxism's monistic hegemony over the disciplines of human knowledge. Marxist philosophy could no longer preside over and referee the debates between the "hundred schools" of thought; it was rather one of the hundred schools itself, open to the same skeptical scrutiny and falsification that applies to all other fields of systematic inquiry. In terms of the structure of authority, each discipline under the critics' conception is autonomous within a larger "academic democracy," free from the "guidance" of Marxist philosophy and free to judge its own goals and priorities and to evaluate its own successes and failures.

These assertions of autonomy within disciplines and of intellectual pluralism translated immediately into demands for autonomy and pluralism in other matters of concern to scientists, both individually and as members of a social group. Within the scientific community, for example, the insistence that only scientists have the credentials to interpret scientific results served to reinforce demands by scientists for control over membership in the scientific community and over issues central to the practical conduct of scientific research. Concrete questions were involved: Who had the authority to specify who is competent and who is not to evaluate the theories and experiments of science? Who had the authority to determine which scientists deserve recognition and which do not? And who was empowered to designate who decides on promotion, on assignment criteria, and on whose projects deserve funding and whose do not? Externally, with respect to the relationship between the scientific community and the regime, the conflict over autonomy and intellectual pluralism raised larger questions about what social and political context is necessary for science to flourish. Ironically, therefore, the regime's encouragement of scientific skepticism and professionalism for the sake of China's modernization and survival prompted the reawakening of a powerful antiauthoritarian scientific ethos within the liberalized but still authoritarian political context of Dengist China. Seen in this light, the emotional and ideological stakes in the science and philosophy debates were extremely high.

AN INSECURE SOCIAL CONTEXT FOR SCIENCE

The conflict of authority over science reflected in the science and philosophy debates played out in a larger social setting that some scientists found unsettling and even threatening. These social strains and tensions, stemming partly from the Deng regime's policies and partly from the rapid social changes of the 1980s, involved both the social standing of scientists and popular attitudes toward science. As previous chapters have argued, the regime's utilitarian attitude left little room for the pursuit of science for its own sake. Though the Party's statements cited science as a source of ideas and values for the "socialist spiritual civilization" it promoted, the overwhelmingly utilitarian thrust of its science policies led to the relative impoverishment of basic research. Unintentionally, the science reforms in the 1980s also brought about a dramatic decline in already austere living conditions for scientists still tied to the state sector, accompanied by a perceived deterioration in their social standing. The state's effort to force scientists out of state institutes and laboratories into technical jobs in industry meant for many a wrenching change in professional identity and self-image.

With respect to society and prevailing attitudes toward science, some scientists were distressed by the emergent popularity among young intellectuals of antirationalist ideas that flourished in the astonishing mid-1980s debates on the cultural roots of China's contemporary predicament. These debates—often called "culture fever"—were the outgrowth of what the Party itself called in the late 1970s the "crisis of confidence" in Chinese communism. Both the "crisis of confidence" and "culture fever" grew out of the disillusionment and alienation produced by the Cultural Revolution. As previously explained, the "crisis of confidence" referred to doubts and skepticism about the leadership of the CCP in the contemporary era. Thereafter, deeper reflections by writers and intellectuals on the Cultural Revolution sought explanations for the scale of the destructive emotions and utopian aspirations it unleashed in Chinese culture and, especially, political culture. These disturbing "feudal" patterns of political and social behavior were traced to the traditional political culture of the imperial era, and were discerned both in the outlook and actions of the Party's leaders and in the response of the Chinese people.

The Party's self-examination and reform platform abetted the intellectuals' reflections on politics and culture. As we have seen, Deng Xiaoping based his claim to leadership on a critique of Mao's last years and a return to what he said were the true principles of Mao's adaptation of communism to China. On that basis Deng overturned Hua Guofeng's claim to leadership, citing loyalty to the legacy of Mao's Cultural Revolution–era principles as the criterion. In so doing, Deng rejected Hua's explanations for the Party's errors of the Cultural Revolution period—the machinations of the "sham left but right right" cliques (Lin Biao and the Gang of Four) around Mao—and instead condemned the entire 1957–76 period as dominated by a profoundly destructive "leftist deviation" that infected the outlook of the entire Party. Applying prototypical class analysis to this political phenomenon, Deng and the Party reformers located the social roots of this "leftist deviation" in the preponderant numbers of peasants recruited into the Party during the 1930s and 1940s. The peasantry's "petty producer" outlook was reflected in "feudal autocratic" tendencies in the Party, and especially in

the personality cult around Mao. Based on this analysis, the Dengist reformers made criticism of "feudalism" in the Party's workstyle a staple
theme of political discourse in the early 1980s.[10]

At the same time, the reformers' "open" policies contributed to the
cultural critique of Chinese communism that emerged in the mid-1980s.
The contrast between China's stage of development and that of other
East Asian countries reinforced the criticism of the Party's leadership
over the previous three decades as encumbered with a tradition-bound
outlook. The tremendous influx of foreign ideas, spurred by the state's
own promotion of translations of foreign books useful to China's modernization, provided alternative theories and perspectives, mainly from
the West, that fueled "culture fever" in the mid-1980s. Various sects
of psychology—including those of Freud, Jung, Adler, and Rogers—
acquired an immediate vogue among students and young intellectuals, as did strands of contemporary continental philosophy expressed
in the works of Foucault, Heidegger, Lévi-Strauss, and Derrida. As in
the West, the indeterminacy introduced into scientific theory by quantum mechanics, chaos theory, and the theory of dissipative systems was
taken as indicating a larger indeterminacy in all human knowledge
and an irremediable uncertainty about the human condition in general.
Inevitably, China's intellectual youth had caught the dreaded disease
postmodernism.

The cultural critique drew on other trends among intellectuals.[11]
In literary circles the "literature of the wounded" of the late 1970s gave
way by the mid-1980s to writing that rejected the officially promoted
realism centered on mass society, focusing instead on the subjective
viewpoint of the individual. Infused in this literature were approaches
inspired by contemporary Western avant-garde, modernist, poststruc-
turalist, and postmodern trends. In historical circles China's imperial
past was re-examined for traits and patterns that would help explain
the nation's contemporary predicament. Impetus for this line of debate
came from a conference, held in Chengdu in October 1982 and sponsored by the editorial board of the *Bulletin of Natural Dialectics*, on the
reasons for the stagnation of Chinese science and its failure to spur
modernization in late imperial China.[12] The best-known product of this
historical debate was the 1987 television series *Heshang* (River elegy), a

searing attack on China's imperial political traditions and their legacy in contemporary political culture.[13]

The resulting "culture fever" produced a bewildering span of perspectives, explorations, and outlooks. Some—and this was the main theme of *Heshang*—called for a new cosmopolitan culture abandoning traditional roots and drawing heavily on foreign (especially Western) values and traits that would help China modernize and join the modern world. Some saw an undeveloped "enlightenment" in the late Ming period that had advanced values and ideals vaguely similar to those promoted in the European Enlightenment of the same period. Others saw humanistic elements in China's past that could mitigate the authoritarian excesses of the present. Yet others promoted a "new Confucianism" that, as other East Asian societies such as Taiwan and Singapore had shown, could provide an effective cultural basis for modernization. Still others reaffirmed the cultural iconoclasm of the May Fourth period and sought to rebuild China's culture on science and democracy, ideals that had been displaced since the 1920s.

In this swirling tide of ideas and intellectual fads were currents of antirationalism and romanticism that some scientists found disturbing. To scientists who held firm to the modernist ideals linking science and social progress, attacks on reason and appeals to Confucian traditions could only seem a retreat from the crisis that China faced in the contemporary world after thirty years of disaster.

Taken together, the conflict of authority over science, the decline of the livelihood and social standing of scientists, and the challenge to rationalism presented by "culture fever" presented China's science community, some scientists believed, with a powerful crisis of identity. At the beginning of the Deng decade they saw the Party leadership's commitment to reform as at last offering scientists an opportunity to secure a place for the free pursuit of science in service to society and for its own sake. By the end of the decade they saw the regime's utilitarian purposes and still authoritarian—if no longer totalitarian—methods as crushing that opportunity. At the beginning they saw themselves, with the Party's encouragement, as the vanguard of China's future. By the end the perceived decline in scientists' living standards and social prestige was making science a dead-end pursuit in the eyes of China's youth.

Scientists initially saw a chance to advance their society through rationalist enlightenment after decades of Maoist obscurantism and utopian fantasy, but by the end of the decade the society around them was turning to irrationalist intellectual outlooks, romantic aesthetic approaches, traditional Confucian values that had been discredited sixty years before, and superstitious practices such as *qigong* breathing exercises—all of which seemed unfriendly to science.

THE NATURAL DIALECTICS FAMILY IN PERSPECTIVE

The participants in the debates on science and philosophy responded to the larger crisis of national identity in ways that resonated with their views in the debates. The main antagonists in the debates can be sorted out, as shown in table 5.1, according to their generation and position on the relationship between Marxist philosophy and science—either affirming Marxism's guiding role (the monists) or rejecting it (the pluralists). This categorization will point up some significant continuities in outlook and shared experience that might not otherwise be apparent.

Generations 1 and 2, educated before 1949, are taken together as the prerevolutionary generations. Generations 3, 4, and 5, educated under the communist system, are grouped as the postrevolutionary generations. The lopsided representation of the postrevolutionary generations in the table reflects the fact that the monist side attracted no proponents among the people in those generations who participated in the debate in any regular or prominent way.

The participants from the two prerevolutionary generations have several experiences in common. All came from the Jiangsu-Shanghai-Zhejiang region of the lower Yangtze, the heartland of the nation's first professional science organization—the Science Society of China, from which much of the modern scientific enterprise in the early Republican era emerged.[14] They were educated mainly at three universities: Jiaotong, Zhejiang, and especially Qinghua. Those who attended Qinghua presumably have strong ties with a larger group of Qinghua graduates, including Song Jian (the Party science chief for much of the 1980s), who have predominated in China's contemporary science establishment.[15] Except for Zha Ruqiang, all majored in physics.

TABLE 5.1

THE NATURAL DIALECTICS FAMILY IN THE 1980S

Generation	Pluralists	Monists

1	Yu Guangyuan
	b. 1915
	Shanghai
	Qinghua University
	Physics
		Hu Qiaomu
		b. 1912
		Jiangsu
		Qinghua and Jiaotong
		  universities
		Physics
		Qian Xuesen
		b. 1911 Zhejiang
		Jiaotong University, MIT,
		  and California Institute
		  of Technology
		Physics

2	Xu Liangying b. 1920 Zhejiang Zhejiang University Physics Fan Dainian b. 1926 Zhejiang University Physics	Zha Ruqiang b. 1925, d. 1990 Jiangsu Qinghua University Foreign languages He Zuoxiu b. 1927 Jiaotong and Qinghua universities Physics
3	Fang Lizhi b. 1936 Beijing Beijing University Physics Dong Guangbi b. 1935 Beijing University Physics Jin Wulun b. 1937	

Table 5.1
(*continued*)

Generation	Pluralists	Monists
4	Li Xingmin	
	b. 1945	
	Shaanxi	
	Xibei University	
	Physics	
	Jin Guantao	
	b. 1947	
	Beijing University	
	Chemistry	
5	Wu Guosheng	
	b. 1964	
	Beijing University	
	Geophysics	

NOTE: This table sorts the major figures of the 1980s science and philosophy debates by generation and overall orientation. When known, date and province of birth, university attended, and field of study are listed.

The three postrevolutionary generations are a much more diverse group in terms of regional origin, but, with the exception of Li Xingmin and possibly Jin Wulun, all were educated at Beijing University after the communist revolution. All majored in physics or related disciplines.

The homogeneity in background of the prerevolutionary and post-revolutionary generations masks significant differences in outlook and personal ties and antagonisms. A survey of the leading figures in each generation will clearly show these differences between pluralists and monists in commitment and personal relationships. The following section discusses generations 1 through 4; because of insufficient information, generation 5 is not included.

The Prerevolutionary Generations

Generation 1. Among the first-generation figures, Yu Guangyuan and Hu Qiaomu show a striking parallelism in careers but a stark contrast in outlook and viewpoint. Both studied physics at Qinghua in the early 1930s.[16] Hu thereafter studied for a year at Zhejiang University—a link to the second-generation pluralists Xu Liangying and Fan Dainian. In 1935 both were involved as propagandists and organizers in the December Ninth movement against Japanese aggression in China. At Yan'an, both worked in the Party's propaganda and cadre reindoctrination apparatus, while Hu also served as secretary to Mao Zedong and Zhou Enlai. After 1949 both continued to figure prominently in propaganda, ideology, and intellectuals affairs. Hu was managing editor of *People's Daily;* Yu edited the Party journal *Study* (Xuexi). In the 1950s both served in the Party Propaganda Department, though at different times. Yu was heavily involved in the reorganization of the Chinese Academy of Sciences in the mid-1950s, becoming a member of the Standing Committee of the Philosophy and Social Sciences Department. With Hu Sheng and Wang Huide, Yu coauthored a long series of major articles on fundamental issues in Party strategy and policy regarding the "socialist transformation" of various sectors of China's economy and society. Hu Qiaomu wrote a landmark short history of the CCP stressing Mao Zedong's role and became a member of the Party Central Committee and an alternate member of the Party Secretariat in 1956.

Both were purged and persecuted during the Cultural Revolution. In 1975 they worked closely with Deng Xiaoping in his efforts to revise China's policies and priorities in step with Zhou Enlai's re-enunciation of the Four Modernizations at the Fourth National People's Congress.[17] Both served on the State Council's policy research staff and collaborated with Hu Yaobang in compiling the 1975 "Outline Report" on the CAS. After the fall of the Gang of Four in 1976 and Deng's second rehabilitation in 1977, they worked together to restore the CAS and establish the CASS. Hu Qiaomu was the CASS's first president; Yu became a vice president. Yu's involvement in the supervision of the natural sciences from his posts on the CAS's Scientific Council and on the newly established State Science and Technology Commission has been discussed. Also in the early years of the Deng reforms, both Yu and Hu played prominent roles in the reorientation of China's economic policies. Hu's landmark 1978 article on the necessity of observing rational economic laws in pursuing economic modernization spearheaded the revision of economic priorities at the 1978 Third Plenum. Yu meanwhile authored numerous articles on fundamental economic issues throughout the Deng years, including major articles in 1987 on the thesis that China remained in only the initial stage of socialism.

On the basis of career parallelism and their prominence in the Deng reform camp, Yu and Hu must have known each other very well in the 1980s. Nevertheless, it seems apparent that through that decade each proceeded from a different perspective on the central question of how to accommodate the tenets of Marxism-Leninism to contemporary realities. Judging by his articles and statements published in PRC media, Hu appeared to end up on the conservative side of the reform spectrum. He displayed a concern to maintain "purity" and preserve a core of "fundamental" Marxist-Leninist tenets, a predilection readily apparent in his long dissertation on the problems of humanism and alienation under socialism in the wake of the campaign against "spiritual pollution" in January 1984, and in other statements as well.[18]

Hu Qiaomu did not join the published debate on the relationship of science to philosophy, but his endorsement of Zha Ruqiang's monist views seems beyond doubt.[19] Hu and Zha may have known each other in the late 1940s and early 1950s when Zha was director of Beijing Daily's (Beijing ribao) Theory Department.[20] They certainly were acquainted during Hu's tenure as CASS president, a period when Zha headed the Institute of Philosophy's Natural Dialectics Research Office. In any case, Hu's antagonism toward Fang Lizhi's views was evident in his attack on an article on quantum cosmology that Fang published in the CAS journal Science (Kexue) in 1985. Hu's letter to the journal's editorial board called Fang's views an example of "objective idealism."[21]

Yu Guangyuan, in contrast, seems to have been considerably more liberal in his approach to harmonizing Marxism's classical tenets with contemporary realities and the conclusions of contemporary natural and social science. This liberality appears frequently to have gotten Yu into political difficulty. His views on "selfishness" and competition in economic life, for example, were attacked in 1987 during the campaign against "bourgeois liberalization," and his name was included in a list of intellectuals to be removed from the Party in addition to the three (Fang Lizhi, journalist Liu Binyan, and novelist Wang Ruowang) purged in January. In the end he was not removed, and was elected to the Central Advisory Commission at the Thirteenth CCP Congress later that year.[22]

Yu's liberalism of thought, in contrast to Hu Qiaomu's conservativism, may help to explain why Hu advanced into the top echelon of the Party leadership while Yu did not. Yu, in fact, has never been even an alternate member of the Central Committee.[23]

With regard to the issues at the center of the debates on the relationship between science and philosophy, Yu appeared to occupy a high middle ground. On the one hand, he did not in the 1980s call explicitly for discarding Marxist philosophy's "guiding role" in science and continued to uphold the integrity of natural dialectics as a discipline. He directed the editing of a new translation of Engels's classic *The Dialectics of Nature* and wrote a brief essay affirming its continuing value in the effort to revise natural dialectics by incorporating the findings of modern science.[24] He served as the president of the Chinese Natural Dialectics Research Society since its founding. Despite his long interest in the natural sciences and their philosophical implications, he did not actively join the published debates on science and philosophy. In all of the 1980s, in fact, he wrote very little on the modern natural sciences and their implications for Marxist philosophy, except for scathing attacks on the scientific credentials of parapsychology in 1982 and again in 1987, around the time a translation of a biography of the psychic spoon-bender Uri Geller was published in China.[25]

On the other hand, Yu was a powerful and outspoken advocate of "developing" Marxism in light of contemporary realities, as has been noted. Throughout the 1980s he served as chief editor, with Fan Dainian as his executive editor, of the *Bulletin of Natural Dialectics*, the CAS journal that inaugurated the attacks on Zha Ruqiang's ideas on natural dialectics and modern science. Twice in the reform decade Yu underscored the importance of a proper Party attitude toward science and the importance of intellectual pluralism. First, in 1980, the *Bulletin of Natural Dialectics* published his landmark speech at the 1956 Qingdao conference on genetics, where the impact of Lysenkoist doctrines imported from the USSR was first criticized in China in the midst of a major liberalization of the Party's policies on intellectuals. Then, in 1986, in launching the Little Hundred Flowers liberalization of that year, Yu published a major reminiscence on the Qingdao conference and on the importance of separating academic debate from politics.[26]

Yu's liberalism is also indicated by the outlook of his protégés. He tolerated, if not directly encouraged, the revisionist views of many of his students, some of whom went much farther than he in calling for the abandonment of some of Marxism's fundamental tenets. Yan Jiaqi, the CASS political scientist who fled China as a result of his involvement in the Tiananmen demonstrations in 1989, was a physics student at Chinese Science and Technology University in Beijing in the early 1960s before joining the CAS Philosophy and Social Sciences Department—under Yu's supervision—on the eve of the Cultural Revolution. Yu apparently encouraged Yan to take up problems in natural dialectics and the philosophy of science. In the late 1970s, Yu may also have encouraged Yan's move to political science, a field whose rehabilitation Yan supervised as head of the CASS Institute of Political Science in the 1980s.[27] Another of Yu's protégés, Su Shaozhi, who served as Yu's deputy in the CASS Institute of Marxism–Leninism–Mao Zedong Thought, was throughout the 1980s one of the most outspoken exponents of revising Marxism's basic tenets.

Yu's evident neutrality in the science and philosophy debates may reflect his longstanding relationships with participants on both sides and his desire not to take sides in a dispute that bitterly divided them.[28] Yu is the true founding father and patron of virtually the entire natural dialectics community in China, stemming from his supervision of both the natural and social sciences as head of the Propaganda Department's Science Office in the 1950s. One of Yu's subordinates in that office was He Zuoxiu. Yu knew Zha Ruqiang from the early 1950s; after Zha lost his Party membership in 1957 when his wife was condemned as a "rightist," Yu eventually got Zha appointed head of the Institute of Philosophy's Natural Dialectics Research Office. Yu also assisted Xu Liangying and Fan Dainian in founding the *neibu* predecessor of the *Bulletin of Natural Dialectics* in 1956.

Yu's ambivalence regarding the science and philosophy debates and the larger issues they entailed contrasts not only with the views of Hu Qiaomu, who did not publicly inject himself into the dispute, but also with the views of a third member of the elder generation of the natural dialectics community, Qian Xuesen. Though Qian shared many characteristics with the other members of the prerevolutionary generations, his career included some unique experiences.[29] For one thing, Qian had extensive foreign training as a scientist, having studied and taught at the Massachusetts Institute of Technology and the California Institute of Technology from 1935 until the early 1950s. Qian returned to China and began a long career as the father of China's missile and space programs. Aside from his expertise in classical mechanics, he was a leading authority in China on systems theory and authored at least two books on it, including one with Song Jian in the 1970s.

Politically in the 1980s, Qian was a leading Party scientist. Even before joining the Party in 1958—perhaps to demonstrate his absolute allegiance to the communist cause, despite his American training— Qian was an outspoken defender of the Party as the Hundred Flowers campaign of the spring of 1957 shifted into the Anti-Rightist campaign that summer.[30] Qian was first elected to the Party Central Committee in 1969 at the Ninth Congress, which consolidated the massive leadership changes of the Cultural Revolution, and he continued to hold seat on that body until the Thirteenth Congress in 1987.

Intellectually, Qian's views overlap with those of Yu Guangyuan in some areas but diverge sharply in others. Like Yu, Qian held that natural dialectics must keep pace with changes in scientific theory, some of which—including the indeterminism of quantum mechanics and chaos theory—made the science of Engels's day vastly outdated. He also urged that the scope of natural dialectics be broadened to include new content, including a "science of science" that focused on scientific methodology.[31] Qian shared Yu's rationalist convictions (as apparent in his attacks on parapsychology) and saw the resurgence of interest in Confucian values in the mid-1980s' "culture fever" as a step backward.[32]

In contrast to Yu, however, Qian was committed to a narrower Marxism-Leninism. While Yu declined to express himself on the issue, Qian declared flatly that science develops best when guided by Marxism, the most general system of human knowledge.[33] However deeply he believed that natural dialectics had to accommodate the findings of modern science, there were limits, in his view. In 1983 he criticized the *Bulletin of Natural Dialectics,* which Yu edited, as a purveyor of "spiritual pollution."[34] And while Yu's polymathic expertise in both the natural and social sciences implied an underlying scientism—a readiness to extend science and its methods beyond science itself, into all spheres of human activity—Qian was outspoken and explicit in his scientism. Through the 1980s, for example, he wrote repeatedly and extensively on the importance of putting policy-making in all arenas on a scientific basis through the application of systems theory. In this respect, Qian reflects a true technocratic outlook.

The ambiguity in Yu Guangyuan's views made him a centrist in the science debates of the 1980s, capable of bridging and encompassing the issues that divided many in the natural dialectics community he founded. Qian Xuesen, by contrast, was anything but ambiguous in his views, especially when it came to the ultimate authority of the Communist Party.

Generation 2. The central antagonists of the science and philosophy debates—Xu Liangying on one side and Zha Ruqiang and He Zuoxiu on the other—were all from the younger of the two prerevolutionary generations. In the opposing views and outlooks of these three, the contrasts that divide Yu Guangyuan from Hu Qiaomu and Qian Xuesen among the first generation are much sharper and are expressed explicitly and forcefully.

Xu Liangying's views in the science and philosophy debates, expressed in his single response to Zha Ruqiang in the fall of 1987, drew upon values and ideals that permeated all of his writings in the post-Mao period. He expressed an unyielding belief in intellectual pluralism in science; that democracy is the best political context for science; that the exercise of reason is the core element of both science and democracy; and that science, as the quest for truth about the world, is worth pursuing for its own sake as the centerpiece of human enlightenment, and not merely for the material benefits it provides through technology. These beliefs were held and expressed by all of the major figures among the postrevolutionary generations on the pluralist side of the science and philosophy debates. Hence Xu Liangying is an archetypical figure.

Though Xu enunciated these values and ideals with increasing clarity in the post-Mao years, he came to embrace them early in his life. The tortuous path of his career—his early commitment to physics, his decision to join the Communist Party in the Sino-Japanese War, and his experiences as a scientific intellectual in the troubled politics of the PRC's first three decades—tempered his convictions about science and the ideals he believed it encompassed. Against this background, his expectations for the Deng reforms and his subsequent disappointments took on a poignancy that makes his eventual political dissent intelligible.[35]

Xu Liangying came to science on the eve of the Sino-Japanese War, and his dual commitment to science and to the communist cause was shaped by the conditions and dilemmas the war created. Xu credits his life in science to Wang Ganchang, "the most revered teacher in my whole life," from whom he derived "the scientific spirit of probing the truth." His first encounter with Wang was in May 1937 when, as a middle school student, he attended a lecture in Hangzhou by the Danish pioneer of quantum theory, Niels Bohr, then touring China.[36] Bohr's lecture, on the theory of the nucleus, was delivered entirely in English, a language that Xu had studied—his science textbooks were written in English—but had never heard spoken. As a result, Xu recalled, "The only sentence I understood in the entire lecture was 'Hangzhou is a beautiful city.'" Nevertheless, Xu could understand Bohr's Chinese host, Wang Ganchang.

Xu's middle school was closed after Japanese forces landed on the north bank of Hangzhou Bay, and Xu began a year of independent study focused on books popularizing the discoveries of twentieth-century physics. Among these was Einstein's *The World as I See It,* from which Xu developed "a fanatical love [*kuangre de xi'ai*] for this mysterious and beautiful new realm." Thereupon Xu resolved to study physics at National Zhejiang University and passed a qualifying examination to get in. By this time, the faculty had moved several times as Japanese forces pressed southward. Xu finally managed to join the university in February 1939 in Yishan, Guangxi. There were nearly daily air raids by the Japanese, during which the entire faculty and student body sought shelter in caves in the banks of the Long River. It was during one such raid that Xu first met Wang Ganchang. Wang observed Xu in the cave reading G. P. Thomson's *The Atom* and, after learning which program Xu was enrolled in, encouraged Xu to seek him out. Thereafter, Xu began regularly auditing the seminar on modern physics taught by Wang and Su Xingbei. Su had studied theoretical physics, especially relativity, at the University of Edinburgh in Britain, and for a time had been Einstein's teaching assistant. It was presumably in this seminar and in classes with Su that Xu first studied general relativity and cosmology, interests that—together with his early fascination with Einstein—were to dominate his scientific life.

Xu recognized the powerful idealism that he invested in his commitment to one of the most difficult branches of theoretical physics. His entering class in the Physics Department had twenty-one students. By the beginning of the second year, the number was down to five, most of the remainder having transferred to the engineering school, where there were guarantees of a secure future. In physics, Xu observed, the only promise after graduation was "a life of monastic austerity." Nevertheless, Xu remained enthralled by the ideal of pursuing scientific truth. At the time, he said, Chiang Kai-shek was taking advantage of the effort to rally the country against Japan to "suppress democracy," propagating the slogan "Put the country above everything, put the military first!" Xu and his fellow students responded by hanging matching scrolls outside the doorway of the physics laboratory that stated, "Put science above everything, put physics first!"

Xu's commitment to the CCP was formed in this same period. In his travels to catch up with the university—by December 1939 it had moved again, from Yishan to Zunyi, Guizhou—Xu recalls seeing with his own eyes the hardships of the common people and the corruption of the Nationalists. In late 1939 Xu began reading books on Marxism-Leninism and communist tracts on the Chinese revolutionary movement. Though he appears to have seen much that was compatible in the pursuit of science and the ideals of Marxism, he recognized that he could not adequately serve both commitments simultaneously. Many of his recollections of the next several years express the frustrations, misgivings, and tensions involved in trying to fulfill his commitment to one at the expense of the other. In 1941, for example, Xu contemplated working with Wang, now formally his mentor, for several years on experiments in beta decay, hoping to prove the existence of the neutrino.[37] He reluctantly set this prospect aside, however, after the southern Anhui incident set off a round of "white terror" in Nationalist-dominated areas. In his "indignation" Xu resolved to return to Zhejiang, seek out the underground communist organization there, and participate in the armed resistance to the Japanese. Consequently, he wrote his departmental thesis only "cursorily"—disappointing Wang's expectations for him, he believed—in order to graduate. Thereafter, a colleague who was a member of the CCP talked him out of returning to Zhe-jiang. After a stint as a middle school teacher in Guilin, he returned to Zhejiang University, by then in Meitan, Guizhou, hoping to return to physics in collaboration with Wang. Even then, he recalled, he could not ignore his political ideals, and he became known as one of two communist organizers at the university.

Only in July 1946, as Zhejiang University finally moved back to Hangzhou, did Xu formally join the Communist Party. For the next two or three years, he taught as an assistant professor of physics as a cover for his underground CCP activities. The Department of Physics, he recalled, became the focus of communist activity at the university; a ceremonial photograph of the department's faculty and students in the summer of 1948, he observed, was a good representation of the univer-sity's underground Party organization. Not all in the department were members of or even completely sympathetic to the CCP, but all shielded those who were. During this time, the student democratic movement flourished in response to the larger political and social movements sup-ported by the Party and in the atmosphere established by university president Zhu Kezhen, a meteorologist and president of the leftwing National Association of Science Workers.[38]

With the communist victory and establishment of the PRC, Wang Ganchang, Zhu Kezhen, and Xu all moved to the Chinese Academy of Sciences in Beijing. Zhu became the first-ranking vice president of the Academy, and Wang helped establish the Institute of Modern Physics. By 1952 Xu was supervising "political inspection" of all of the Academy's publications and was editing, with Fan Dainian, a Zhe-jiang University physics classmate, the Academy's main journal *Scientia* (Kexue tongbao).

From this point on, Xu's dual commitment to science and the Communist Party went awry. In 1955 he was criticized as editor of *Scien-tia*, apparently for resisting extension of the Hu Feng campaign into the CAS.[39] An editorial in the September 1955 issue of the journal ac-knowledged that "among us scientific workers" the "harmful" belief has persisted that "counterrevolutionaries may be found in other ranks, but not in scientific research organs." This belief, it said, sprang from the fact that many science workers "had over a long time received a bourgeois education and are affected by the ideology and workstyle of individualism, liberalism, and sectarianism." The "defects" in outlook of these people, it went on, offer "counterrevolutionaries" the opportunity to "undermine the unity between Communist Party members and nonmembers, between scientific and technical personnel and administrative personnel."[40] Impetus for this attack on Xu and Fan Dainian, according to one account, came from criticism of *Scientia* by fellow Zhejiang University physics alumnus Hu Qiaomu, who distrusted the CAS and its orientation.[41]

As a result, Xu and Fan were removed as editors of *Scientia*. Over the next two years, as the regime debated a new science and technology policy, they collaborated on a small book defending the value of basic science and advocating a more open academic atmosphere as essential for the healthy development of science.[42] Also, on the proposal of Yu Guangyuan, they established and edited a new journal, the predecessor of the *Bulletin of Natural Dialectics*.[43] This work was interrupted in 1957, however, when both Xu and Fan were criticized in the Anti-Rightist campaign. Xu was labeled an "anti-Party antisocialist element," a "bourgeois rightist," and an "ultrarightist" and was forced to return to his hometown to work as a peasant to support himself and his mother. By this time Wang Ganchang had joined the joint Chinese-Soviet nuclear research team at the Soviet facility in Dubna, and Xu lost touch with him for nearly two decades. Over the years, Xu recalled, he reflected on the irony that had he stuck to physics research in collaboration with Wang, he might well have had an established and honored career working with Wang in the highly sensitive Chinese atomic and hydrogen bomb projects. Instead, he observed, his decision not to do so and to pursue political commitments made him a "class enemy" and a "target of the dictatorship."

Over the next twenty years Xu, as a condemned "rightist," could pursue scientific work only with difficulty and frustration. In 1962 he and Li Baoheng began work on a series of selected translations of Einstein's works, which they had nearly completed by 1965. The ensuing Cultural Revolution disrupted publication of this project, and Xu had to endure with frustration the use of his own translations by writing groups associated with Chen Boda and the Gang of Four to attack Einstein's theories as "idealist fallacies" serving the interests of the bourgeoisie.[44] The publication project, from which Xu derived a small stipend, resumed again in 1973, but was cut off as the campaign to criticize Lin Biao and Confucius began later that year. Through this time, according to Xu, Wang Ganchang helped support him, sending him 30 yuan a month under a pseudonym—an extremely dangerous thing to do, Xu believed, for someone involved in highly sensitive work in the defense and security sector.

Xu's fortunes changed only with the efforts of Deng Xiaoping and his political collaborators—presumably Yu Guangyuan, in particular—in the science arena. Xu apparently resumed work in the Chinese Academy of Sciences in 1977, when Deng, Fang Yi, Yu, and others began the effort to restore and expand it. His translations of Einstein's works were finally published in the late 1970s. In 1978 his political labels from the Anti-Rightist campaign were removed as a result of the wholesale exonerations that the Dengist reformers brought about. Through the 1980s Xu worked in the CAS's Institute of the History of the Natural Sciences.

By his own account, Xu's Marxist convictions were shaken by his experiences over the years after 1957. The Cultural Revolution and the last years of Mao Zedong's life, Xu recalled in his 1987 response to Zha Ruqiang, had caused the "scales to drop from his eyes" and shaken his faith in the leadership of Mao. He still was not ready to abandon his long-held political ideals, however. His Marxism now was tempered by the scientific ideals he had pursued for so long. These ideas were summed up, Xu recalled in his rejoinder to Zha, in Yu Guangyuan's declaration—at a CAS conference Xu attended in March 1977—that Marxism must operate according to the ground rules of science, and not the laws of the state or the dictates of religion. In this light, Xu probably saw the post-Mao changes brought about by Deng Xiaoping as at last offering the possibility of building a safe political environment for the pursuit of science within socialism.

Through the 1980s, therefore, Xu's writings resonated with the values and ideals that had inspired his life previously: unrelenting pursuit of truth in science for its own sake and belief in intellectual pluralism in science and in democracy as the best political context for science. Xu's bluntest defense of intellectual pluralism was published in *People's Daily* itself during the Little Hundred Flowers episode of 1986. Xu dismissed outright the contention "by some" that conflicts among scientific theories should proceed under the "guidance" of Marxism. He stated that "Marxism is a set of guiding principles for the country's political activities, not a conductor's baton for academic studies; it is a science, not a branch of theology that can dominate and lord it over science."[45]

Xu's insistence that political democracy is the essential context for the pursuit of science appeared over and over in his writings. In 1981, citing Einstein (as he frequently did), Xu underscored three "freedoms" necessary for science: freedom of speech, freedom for scientists to allocate their time and resources according to their own curiosity, and "inner freedom"—an intellectual readiness to think independently without constraint of political authority or social prejudice. Of these, Xu insisted, freedom of speech was the "most basic" and could be ensured only "under democratic institutions in which the people hold democratic rights." The foundation of academic democracy and so the prosperity of science, he concluded, was therefore political democracy.

Sounding themes he returned to repeatedly in the 1980s, Xu lamented the inadequacies of all of the communist countries in this respect. Though Lenin had predicted seventy years earlier that the capitalist world was entering its dying stage, "capitalism today, far from dying, has great vitality—so much so that we cannot have undue expectations of catching up with it." The West's advances in science and the "real content" of the democratic freedoms it developed enabled it to elevate the livelihood of its people and avoid the economic crises predicted by Marx and Lenin. Though the communist countries placed a high premium on developing science for the technological advances it promises, their inadequacies in building "genuine democracy" blunted their ability to modernize. Democracy, Xu concluded, is more than building "a democratic workstyle" and the "mass line," which are merely mobilization methods whereby progressive people "rule for the people," not institutions in which "the people rule themselves."[46]

Xu was even more blunt on this score in 1986. In a long analysis of rationalism as the core element of both science and democracy, he recounted the "cruelty and suppression" of science by "religion and politics," from the beginnings of modern science in the sixteenth century down to the twentieth century in Nazi Germany, the USSR, and China. "The lessons of historical experience," he concluded, "tell us: If a society can adopt a tolerant attitude toward diverse ideas, both permitting and nurturing them, if it allows academic circles to use free debate to understand the truth or falsehood of academic issues and does not exercise external interference (and especially political interference by thought police), science and culture will necessarily prosper; conversely, in a society that suppresses and controls academic freedom, science and culture will necessarily stagnate and wither."[47]

Xu wrote of two threats to science and, indirectly, democracy in China: the overwhelmingly utilitarian orientation of the Dengist reformers' science policies and the rise of antiscientific and antirationalist intellectual and cultural trends in the 1980s "culture fever." With regard to the former, Xu saw the prevailing focus on science as "a force of production," beginning with Deng Xiaoping's speech at the 1978 science conference, as leading to fracture of the scientific community. Deng's speech sparked a "science fever," in which technicians became regarded as "gods of wealth" in the push to rebuild China's economy around markets; meanwhile, basic research units whose work bore no immediate relationship to production faced increasingly straitened circumstances. These extremes, Xu concluded, arose from one-sided focus on science for its technological value and the state's failure to recognize science's role as a source of human knowledge and values in modern society. Science, Xu stated in 1989, is a system of objective knowledge, a method and spirit of seeking truth and creative renewal, that has inestimable value in human spiritual life. It is "the basis and most important component of modern civilization."

This one-sided appreciation of science, Xu continued, was characteristic of the socialist countries and was linked to their failure to provide the open political context necessary for science to flourish. While they have excelled at building enormous scientific establishments and providing vast material resources in support of science's contributions to technology, science's contributions to individual and social values and the political guarantees for the healthy conduct of science have been ignored. Consequently, science suffered "medieval persecutions" in the modern age:

In the 1930s and 40s, Nazi Germany fanatically purged so-called "Jewish science." In the 1940s and 50s, the Soviet Union liquidated Morganian genetics, criticized Einstein's theories of cosmology and relativity, and so forth. In the 1950s through the 1970s, China witnessed successive academic criticism campaigns and political movements. The reasons why the two great socialist countries would surprisingly follow in the footsteps of Nazi Germany, inflicting heart-rending stupidities on ourselves, were that politically there has been no democracy and that the people lack democratic civil consciousness.

Societies that support science for only its technological consequences and not its role in the values of social and political life, Xu concluded, could not provide the freedoms necessary to support scientific creativity and innovation. "In this respect, we have much to learn from the experience of the developed Western countries, where academic freedom is recognized as a necessary condition for human progress."[48]

Xu's concerns about emergent antiscientific trends appeared most stridently in his 1986 examination of rationalism in the history of science. Noting that the revolutions in physics of the twentieth century had contributed to a new and profound skepticism about the rationalist traditions of science among philosophers and even some scientists, Xu objected that such doubts were not from the mainstream. The contemporary scientific revolutions, he argued, did not require the overthrow of the rationalist tradition, but only the transformation of the basic concepts and frameworks of scientific theory. Science required a pluralism in discipline, but what bound all scientific disciplines together was their common commitment to the application of reason to experience. Without this core of rationalist premises, the disciplines of science would no longer constitute a scientific "community," but rather would devolve into the "isolated sects of a larger religion." Rejection of science's rationalist traditions was not a "revolution in science," as some claimed, but the destruction of science.

In defending the rationalist traditions of science in contemporary culture, Xu went on, by no means did he intend to defend all traditions. Quite the opposite: the scientific spirit was valuable because it sought to "break the bonds of the old" and "create the new":

It is worth noting that in the midst of the historical torrent of our country's rush toward modernization through reform and opening up, revering Confucius and propagating Confucian traditions have become a fad. Leaders of the May Fourth movement and Lu Xun have been condemned as criminals for cutting off China's cultural traditions. But what exactly are the Confucian traditions that such people take such great delight in talking about? They are nothing but traditions of feudal autocratic rule such as the "three bonds and five virtues" and the idea that "the people should be made to obey, not to know." They are nothing but blind, antiscientific superstitions, antidemocratic feudal privileges and policies of keeping the people ignorant, and antihumanistic, feudal, cannibalistic ethics. These chains have fettered the Chinese people for more than two thousand years, and it is hard to understand why we should continue to bind ourselves with these "national treasures."[49]

In summary, for Xu Liangying science operated according to rationalist ideals that it shared with the successful conduct of democracy. Science and democracy were mutually supportive: political democracy provided the open social context required for science's pursuit of the truth free from external pressure or constraint, and science supplied society with the ideals of rational inquiry and respect for the truth at all costs that made democracy feasible. Socialism in China had previously failed to address this essential symbiosis. And its utilitarian policies in the contemporary period and the antirationalist intellectual and cultural trends fostered by its previous misrule threatened science and democracy now.

As may be surmised from the science and philosophy debates, Xu's antagonists among the generation-2 members of Yu Guangyuan's natural dialectics family, Zha Ruqiang and He Zuoxiu, proceeded from different premises. Though both acknowledged the value of intellectual pluralism in science, that belief was circumscribed by their more fundamental commitment to a narrower Marxism-Leninism and its monistic hegemony over the structure of knowledge. While they shared Xu's hostility toward the antiscientific and antirationalist trends emerging from "culture fever," their views tended more toward cultural conservativism than the cultural cosmopolitanism that Xu espoused. Finally, He Zuoxiu in particular took Xu Liangying to task for his criticism of the regime's utilitarian science policies. In a 1991 polemic in the conservative ideological journal *Pursuit of Truth* (Zhenli de zhuiqiu), He specifically rebutted Xu's 1986 article on the rationalist foundations of science as improperly separating science as a system of knowledge from its natural complement in practice, technology, and thus negating science's primary role as a "force of production." Citing extensively from Marx, Engels, and Deng Xiaoping to the contrary, He concluded that Xu's divorce of science from its practical consequences was illogical and "unscientific."[50]

The Postrevolutionary Generations

Generation 3. Because of his public expulsion from the CCP in 1987 and the international notoriety he obtained both in his scientific career and from his political activities, Fang Lizhi is the best known of the scientists in the natural dialectics group. In the perspective of the previous discussion, however, it is clear that Fang's views on science and democracy were not unique. His views on the relationship of science to Marxism, on the political requirements for the healthy conduct of science, and on the rationalist and cosmopolitan cultural context in which science prospers were shared with people such as Xu Liangying of the generation that preceded him and with other scientific intellectuals younger than he. Since Fang has been studied extensively elsewhere, the following discussion will attempt only to underscore the congruities in values and outlook that he shared with others in the natural dialectics group.[51]

Fang's political attitudes, by his own words, grew directly out of the ideals he saw in the science he practiced.[52] His interest in cosmology was an accident of the Cultural Revolution. Sent down to work in the mines of Anhui after an initial period of confinement by the Red Guards, Fang managed to take only one book with him. This book, the Soviet physicist Lev Landau's The Classical Theory of Fields, pertained to Fang's specialization in electromagnetic theory, one of the two classical field theories. However, it also treated at length the other major classical field theory, Einstein's general theory of relativity. Reading this book several times through, Fang discovered modern cosmology, of which general relativity is the basis. But, as we have seen, cosmology was a banned field in Cultural Revolution China, and Fang's attempts to practice it after his rehabilitation in the early 1970s inevitably embroiled him in the polemics over science of that time. As Fang remarked many times in the late 1980s, the point of departure of his political views thus was cosmology.[53] Like Xu Liangying, with whom he became acquainted in 1980, Fang's early support for the Dengist reforms therefore stemmed from a deeper wish to build a larger social and political atmosphere conducive to science, and he was ready to criticize the Gang of Four and the legacy of Mao Zedong as antithetical to the ideals and values essential to science.

By the same token, Fang's travels in the West, and especially in Italy in 1979, impressed him positively in the reverse direction, arousing in him an awareness of the importance to science of a democratic political context and an open, pluralistic cultural environment. In a powerful essay entitled "A Hat, a Forbidden Zone, a Question," published in 1979, Fang summed up impressions of his two visits to Italy that year. The significant differences between China and Italy were not material, he believed, as much as they represented the enormous disparities between "cultural traditions and habits of mind." Thanks to the great battles between science and the Catholic Church fought by Copernicus, Galileo, and Bruno, Italy had established cultural values that promoted scientific inquiry. Persecutions of scientists had become "things of the past," so that now there was general acceptance that "freedom of thought is the friend of science and that any kind of deity, pseudodeity, or spokesman of deity is the mortal enemy of science." In contrast, judging by the events of the Cultural Revolution decade, China had yet to resolve the question of the proper criteria to evaluate science. "Doesn't this show," he asked, "that as far as science is concerned, the cultural gap is wider than the material gap?"[54]

Based on these experiences in China and abroad, Fang emerged in the 1980s as the most forceful and visible spokesman for the ideals he shared with Xu Liangying and others. Fang became increasingly outspoken as the thrust of the reforms shifted away from concerns that enlisted his support in the early years and instead emphasized utilitarian goals for science and a continuing "guiding role" for Marxism in science. As his international and domestic stature grew (he won a major astrophysics prize in 1985), and in the context of the Little Hundred Flowers period in 1986, Fang began to project his views of science and the political implications he drew from them outward into the larger political arena, attracting the attention of both the international media and domestic political authorities. In all of these speeches and writings, he set forth with great clarity and forcefulness the ideals he shared with Xu and the others: the link between the autonomy of science and intellectual pluralism on one hand and political democracy on the other; the value of science as a source of ideals and values; and the cosmopolitan cultural outlook that science both required and fostered.

At Zhejiang University—Xu Liangying's alma mater—in November 1985, for example, Fang stressed the "spiritual" benefits of science over its utilitarian technological ones: "Physics is more than a basis for technology; it is a cornerstone of modern thought."[55] In a speech to an August 1986 conference in Qingdao on Chinese and Western culture, Fang attacked several elements he saw in traditional Confucian culture as hostile to science. These included its focus on practical application instead of theoretical enlightenment ("speak of physics and one immediately thinks of household appliances"), its preference for ambiguity rather than precise analysis and evaluation, and its emphasis not on getting things right but on not getting something wrong. "In our present work of reform and reconstruction," he concluded, "we need to reflect upon the persistent defects of traditional Chinese culture from the scientific point of view."[56]

The connection between the freedom of science from political interference and the maintenance of political democracy pervades most of Fang's speeches and writings, but it appears perhaps nowhere more clearly and powerfully than in his September 1986 speech to a conference in Hefei on political reform. There he traced the contemporary prosperity of the West to the twin development in the European Renaissance and Enlightenment of modern science (by Copernicus, Galileo, and Newton) and of democratic political theory (by Locke and Rousseau). In contrast, China and the Soviet Union stagnated because their commitments to an ossified and isolationist orthodox Marxism froze the development of their science and suffocated the progress of their politics and societies.

Openness, freedom of expression, and pluralism, Fang stated, were the keys to both science and political democracy. Scientists in both the natural and social sciences must be open to all alternative ideas and independent of any authority, acting on their own consciences in their pursuit of the truth. In contrast, "because Marxism-Leninism has long tended to exclude all other points of view, new ideas or findings in the social sciences are often regarded as heresy." Such an approach lacks "even a rudimentary scientific attitude," encourages "pedantic, hide-bound interpretations of Marxism," and mindlessly relies on quotations from leaders in power for their authority. Like science, democracy rests on an openness and a skeptical attitude toward authority:

> We must start realizing that a government does not bestow favors on its citizens, but rather that the citizens maintain the government and consent to allowing certain people to lead on their behalf. We constantly hear about "extending democracy," but this is very mis-taken, because it suggests that democracy is something that can be "extended" from the top down. In a democracy, the power rests with each individual.

Ultimately, the goals of democracy (and science) are humanistic:

> We must respect the humanity of each individual. We are not going through the process of reforming our political system just so that we can treat people as obedient tools of the state, no differently than they were treated under feudalism. We are doing it in order to enhance their dignity, to empower them, and to give them the opportunity to freely develop their human potential.[57]

Given the directness and clarity of these views, it is not difficult to imagine how Fang rapidly acquired a following among the students he addressed publicly and frequently in the fall of 1986 and at the same time triggered the alarm of political authorities.

Generation 4. The experiences in the Cultural Revolution of Jin Guantao and Li Xingmin, a generation younger than Fang Lizhi, were quite different from Fang's, though their views on science and the politi-cal and social context it required are quite similar. Only Li participated directly in the science and philosophy debates of the 1980s, though both, as deputy editors of the *Bulletin of Natural Dialectics* under Yu Guang-yuan and Fan Dainian, were undoubtedly involved behind the scenes.

For Jin, the Cultural Revolution triggered a long period of philo-sophical reflection, emotional depression, and eventually rejection of philosophy, followed by a reaffirmed confidence in the hard sciences, which then inspired a vigorous effort to recast philosophy and the social sciences on models borrowed from the natural sciences.[58] On the eve of the Cultural Revolution in 1966, Jin was a chemistry student at Beijing University, and by his own account he buried himself in his science and English textbooks, earning a reputation among his peers as "a model white expert." As the Cultural Revolution began, he began to question everything, including his loyalty to family and society. Restudying the works of Marx for keys to understanding what was happening around him, he worked his way back to Hegel and rapidly acquired such prowess at deploying Hegelian dialectics in arguments with his fellow students that they began to call him "Jin Ge'er" (Jin [He]gel).

Over the next two years, Jin recognized that his explorations in Hegel were leading him in a circular path. Hegel's system, he found, "is like a dark grotto: one can go around in circles thinking one has gone a great distance, and so spend one's entire life within this circular system without recognizing it." Because of the collapse of his philosophical explorations in this period, Jin retreated into science. Though the political atmosphere was extremely hostile to serious study, there existed "an underground atmosphere for studying books." In particular, his own unit, the Beijing University arts team, provided him relative security. The team had become a haven for the "floaters faction"—freethinkers who by day painted portraits of Chairman Mao, but who also had a great deal of free time to read and debate ideas. There Jin began to read widely in contemporary science—books on Galois theory in algebra, Riemannian geometry (the mathematical basis of general relativity), and the measurement problem in quantum theory. He soon recognized that Hegel and Marx had been completely superseded by the advances of twentieth-century science.

Out of this recognition gradually emerged two conclusions in Jin's mind. First, he believed that scientific rationalism held the key to resolving the dilemmas of thought:

> I felt the light of scientific rationality slowly dawning in my mind, and as it grew stronger, I became conscious of a kind of method of thinking that was completely different from zealous speculations such as those of Hegel. For the first time I felt a formless power—the rationalism of

science—different from the enthusiasms of younger years, a kind of tranquil yet grave pursuit that filled my mind with a clear, constructive idea. I resolved that if dialectical philosophy really is scientific, then it must thoroughly reject Hegelian speculation and accept the demands of the scientific spirit on its theoretical framework.

At the same time, Jin felt a consequent "philosophical nihilism," in which he could find no basis for philosophy at all: "In my youth, philosophy was not only the truth of humankind, but also the grand summary of the social and natural sciences. Now this dream was pulverized. There was no philosophy nor was there any ism; there remained only a pile of problems." Having lost all confidence in philosophy, Jin resolved never again to read books by philosophers. Since philosophers' works typically "went on for thousands of words and yet deliberately turned the simple into the mysterious," he further resolved never to write anything longer than fifteen thousand characters.

Eventually, however, his fascination with philosophy revived. His own work beginning in 1974 as an instructor in the Chemistry Department of Zhengzhou University—"undergoing self-tempering by doing very ordinary work in the temple of science"—rekindled the idealism of his youth and provided a way out of his nihilism. Instead of seeking truths universal to humanity, he found a new sense of mission in explicating the evolving value systems of China's past in comparative perspective, hoping to find a new value system for China to live by. In 1978 he and Liu Qingfeng moved to Beijing, and Deng Xiaoping's movement to "liberate thought" further rekindled his sense of philosophical purpose. Now, he believed, he would attempt to reconcile the emphasis on process in dialectics with the indeterminacy of contemporary physics. Thereafter, in the early 1980s, Jin was exposed to the works of Western philosophers and sociologists of science Thomas Kuhn, Imre Lakatos, Karl Popper, Robert Merton, and Paul Feyerabend. He recalled that these writings appeared amid "a tide of antirationalist thought," which they abetted. Though he believed that a "countertide" of irrationalism was healthy in a context of predominating rationalism, Jin perceived that the opposite situation was emerging, a trend he found "dangerous." He therefore sought to counter this tide by synthesizing his previous explorations as the basis for a new rationalism that drew on the approaches of the natural sciences (and cybernetics and systems theory in particular) and extended them to understanding society.

In the 1980s Jin produced three works as part of this project: "Philosophy of Development" (1986), an effort to reconcile dialectical logic with the indeterminacy of modern science and mathematics; *Philosophy of the Whole* (1987), a methodological essay on unified versus pluralistic structures of knowledge of the world; and *Philosophy of Humanity* (1988), a study of the problem of objectivity in light of modern science.[59] In addition, in his *Crisis and Prosperity* (1984), which he wrote with Liu Qingfeng, he put forward the theory of "superstable" social structure, an attempt to use systems theory to explain the long-term stasis in China's traditional social and political structure. This appears to have developed from earlier work, also with Liu and historian of Chinese science Fan Hongye, on the causes of the stagnation of Chinese science. The essay on this subject by Jin and his coauthors in the *Bulletin of Natural Dialectics* appeared on the eve of the landmark Chengdu conference sponsored by the journal on this subject, which lent impetus to "culture fever," and was among the first to treat this issue in the post-Mao period.[60] Jin also edited the "Towards the Future" book series published in Chengdu, a highly influential effort to introduce modern ideas and trends of thought to young intellectual audiences, and he was an adviser to Su Xiaokang and the other writers of the television series *Heshang*.

Given this past, Jin fit easily into the larger natural dialectics group he joined in the late 1980s (he became a deputy editor of the *Bulletin of Natural Dialectics* in 1986 or early 1987), as did his attitudes on science and politics. At a forum on "socialist spiritual civilization" sponsored by *Red Flag* in the summer of 1986, for example, he argued that science and democracy were essential components of any such public culture. Science in particular, he said, emphasized three things of value: practice as the criterion of truth; creativity and toleration of diverse viewpoints; and "conditioned skepticism"—a reference to one of Merton's norms of science.[61]

Jin's contemporary among the natural dialectics pluralists, Li Xingmin, graduated from Northwest University in physics in 1969 and from the CAS's graduate school in 1981, joining the staff of the *Bulletin of Natural Dialectics* the same year.[62] Through the 1980s he wrote extensively on problems of contemporary philosophy of science, and especially on the philosophical significance of relativity theory and its progenitors, including Ernst Mach, Henri Poincare, and Albert Einstein. The latter interest was part of an effort to re-evaluate one of Lenin's two main contributions to natural dialectics, *Materialism and Empiriocriticism.*

Through the same period Li participated in the science and philosophy debates and wrote forcefully on the larger issues the debates raised. In January 1988, for example, he argued in *Enlightenment Daily* that if Marxism is to be considered a science, it must accept the inherently pluralistic structure of knowledge:

> A state or political party may choose to build itself on a school of thought and ascribe to it a supreme position. In the academic domain, however, no scientific theory has the privilege of being elevated above other scientific theories. In the past, we put Marxism on a pedestal. As a result, our self-imposed restrictions and parochial arrogance prevented us from studying other philosophies and schools of thought.... We must break free from our traditional unitary patterns of thought and adopt a pluralist way of thinking. Science is totally different from theology and autocratic politics. Such brutalities as burning Bruno at the stake and slashing Zhang Zhixin's throat will never happen in science; to the contrary, all scientific ideas, hypotheses, and statements may be freely put forward and will not be suppressed because of differences in understanding.

To preserve the sciences as an arena of open discourse, Li called for legislation to protect "genuine academic freedom."[63]

His most remarkable contribution to the debates on science and politics was an extensive analysis of the values of science and their relationship to political democracy, published in *Social Sciences in China* in 1990—after the suppression of the Tiananmen demonstrations. Li's dissection of the values of science drew explicitly on Robert Merton's norms of scientific communities and on the connection Merton saw between these norms and the larger democratic political and social context that is necessary for science to prosper. Within Merton's framework, Li set the entire array of concerns that his elder colleagues had expressed on the relationships among science, philosophy, and politics.

The norms of science that Merton described, Li argued, resonate with or are disrupted by the values of the society in which a scientific community is set. The norms of the scientific community, Li noted, are thus "not only interlinked with rational morality in human society but also provide an occasion for the healthy development of a democratic order into which it is integrated." By the same token, society's values may support or harm the scientific community's operation according to the norms Merton described. Though a utilitarian promotion of technology undoubtedly spurred the development of science in its early stages, "utilitarian approaches to science today—especially when taken to extremes—damage the proper orientation of science in onesidedly stressing utility as the basis of support, forcing scientists to abandon topics that are inherently worthwhile and so threatening science's continuity and stability."

Science, Li said, must therefore be a "relatively autonomous" subsystem of the larger social system. Scientific communities cannot function without guarantees of academic freedom that allow scientists to operate according to their own norms. For this reason, communities of scientists cannot ignore the larger society around them, and they must establish relationships with wider society that allow science to progress to the benefit of both. In this respect, the norms of science permeate not only the value judgments that scientists make about each other's work but also the relationships of scientists with the rest of society. Both to secure material support for pursuit of the scientific problems they choose to research and especially, as an "unshirkable task and sacred mission," to defend academic freedom, scientists must be active in society.

Because of this, and because science places the highest value on truth and the process of seeking it, Li continued, scientists display a passion for originality and independence of thought. The hallmark of these values is dissent:

> In the history of science, only when recognized and accepted ideas are publicly challenged in dissent (as, for example, Copernicus, Darwin,

and Einstein did) can there be progress. Dissent is the instrument of intellectual progress and is the inborn activity of scientists. Without dissent, there is no science, and without dissenters there are basically no scientists. Dissent, however, is not the object in itself. It is the standard of a deeper value—freedom—and, like originality, it is the standard of spiritual independence. If we say that originality and independence are the individual requirements for science's existence, then dissent and freedom are the public requirements for the existence of science.

From this analysis, Li drew the following conclusions about the connection of the values of science and human values in general:

> In summary, with respect to the scientific community [the problem of human values] is comparatively simple because it has a straightforward common purpose: to explore truth. What it must promote in the individual scientist is independence and what it must promote within itself is tolerance. From these basic premises—and they are themselves the foremost values—arise step by step a series of values: dissent, freedom of thought and speech, impartiality, honor, and human dignity and self-worth. These are the human values that science embodies, and people who espouse them promote both the development of science and the progress of society, and so cause these human values to be realized. Science and humanity are enriched and perfected in this interaction and tension.[64]

COMMUNITIES IN CONFLICT

The preceding survey across generations of major figures from both the monist and pluralist sides of the science and philosophy debates reveals continuities in outlook on a range of broader issues that divided the two sides. The positions taken reflected views on and attitudes toward more general issues concerning science, its relationship to the larger structure of knowledge, its relationship to political authority, and its place in society. Based on these continuities, the antagonists constituted separate communities, each bound together by common values and ideals that demarcated one group from the other, within the larger Chinese theoretical science community.

The monists remained committed to the totalist structure of knowledge under Marxist-Leninist hegemony that the Communist Party had imposed from the beginning and that continued to provide the ideological foundation of legitimacy for the Deng regime. They remained true believers in the Leninist conception of the Party's mission that Deng Xiaoping revived and in the structure of authority that conception required. They placed science within the larger context of the Party's goals and remained responsive to the Party leadership's concerns for science. In normal times, they defended the utilitarian orientation of the Party's science policies, believing that what was good for socialism was also good for science, and they reaffirmed the integrity of the Marxist-Leninist structure of knowledge by defending Marxism's "guiding role" in all fields of knowledge. In more politicized moments, they were ready to extend the Party's political goals into the academic arena, as shown by Qian Xuesen's 1983 attack on the *Bulletin of Natural Dialectics* as a purveyor of "spiritual pollution" and by the concerted attacks on the pluralists in the 1987 campaign against "bourgeois liberalization." Culturally, they tended toward the conservative end of the spectrum, in step with those in the Party leadership who saw the cosmopolitanism of such productions as *Heshang* as an expression of "national nihilism." Their backgrounds were similar. Most came from the Qinghua clique that dominated China's science administration establishment in the 1980s.

On the other side of the debate, the pluralists were committed to a very different set of ideals. They came either from Zhejiang University, in the heartland of the old Science Society of China (in the case of the prerevolutionary generation), or from Beijing University (in the case of the postrevolutionary generations). They denied the monolithic hierarchy of knowledge dominated by Marxism-Leninism that the Communist Party had traditionally imposed and that the monists sought to defend, rejecting any "guiding role" for Marxism in science. Instead, they sought a pluralist structure of knowledge that acknowledged the diversity of methods and conceptions that modern science employed and that diffused authority throughout science's disciplines. For them, the ideals of science superseded those of the Communist Party—insofar as the Party's Marxism claimed to be scientific, it had to answer to the norms that guide the conduct of science in all fields. These norms internal to science, moreover, required a particular political and social context externally—one that guaranteed open and unconstrained discourse in the scientific community. For the pluralists, the openness and internationalism of science also prompted a cultural cosmopolitanism, as the "all-around Westernizing" outlooks of Fang Lizhi and Jin Guantao attested. Science, as the impassioned pursuit of truth, was valuable above all for its own sake, and only secondarily for whatever technological benefits might accrue from scientific discovery.

As a group, the pluralists were thoroughly modernist in their outlook. For them, the norms and ideals were of direct benefit to society because they formed the basis of larger social values at the heart of the progress of the individual and society. The scientific community's norms of skepticism in the face of authority, toleration of diversity in viewpoint, independence of individual outlook, and freedom of expression fostered corresponding democratic traits in society and politics. Science's pursuit of truth through reason and observation promoted individual and social enlightenment by banishing prejudice and superstition. Conversely, they believed, the state's pursuit of utilitarian science policies and the emergence of antirationalist trends of thought threatened science and, ultimately, society and politics.

In their views on the linkage between science and democracy, the pluralists saw themselves as (and perhaps they in fact were) the true contemporary inheritors of the enlightenment tradition of the May Fourth era. Their writings constantly recalled the ideals of that period. Their defense of reason and social progress and their attacks on traditionalist appeals to Confucian values and on antirationalist intellectual trends were of a piece with the rationalist iconoclasm of that time. Both Wang Laidi (Xu Liangying's wife) and Liu Qingfeng (Jin Guantao's wife) were CASS historians of the May Fourth era.

Tellingly, the intensity of the commitment to Marxism of those in the pluralist group diminished with each successively younger generation, and all looked back for inspiration to the May Fourth era—ironically, the era that gave birth to the Communist Party. Xu Liangying wrestled disastrously with his dual commitments to science and to Marxism for much of his life. By the late 1980s, according to those familiar with him, his Marxism was heavily diluted and focused on Marx as a "humanist," presumably as interpreted from Marx's early writings. Fang Lizhi, according to many, was at best only marginally committed to Marxism up until the 1980s; thereafter, while acknowledging the value of some of its ideals of social responsibility, he rejected it altogether. The younger generations, according to some, retained no commitment to Marxism at all.[65]

From the long perspective of political sociology, the conflict between the monists and pluralists in the science and philosophy debates represented a conflict between two rival communities, each committed to different ideals and values. In each community, these ideals and values constituted a distinctive ideology that lent purpose and identity to it. The ideology of each community complemented or clashed with the goals and ideological purposes of the reform leadership dominated by Deng Xiaoping. The distinct ideology of each community shaped its response to the Dengist reforms in terms of the opportunities it saw to pursue its own goals and of the expectations it held out for the reforms. For the monists, the reforms offered an opportunity to revitalize Marxism after two decades of disastrous deviation, and so the degree of overlap in vision and purpose with the Party leadership was very high. In many ways their ideology was congruent with Deng's "socialism with Chinese characteristics."

The pluralists' ideology was built up from the antiauthoritarian norms of science. In the early years of the reform decade they believed that the reforms offered an opportunity at last to build a more democratic political context, within the framework of a more humanistic socialism, that would provide a secure place for the relatively autonomous pursuit of science. By the late 1980s they saw these hopes dispelled after repeated battles with their monist colleagues over Marxism's "guiding role" and after repeated violations by the state of science's autonomy—whether through utilitarian science policies or outright political campaigns. Increasingly, for some of the pluralists, optimism turned to alienation, and alienation fueled dissent.

On a personal level the conflicts of commitment, values, and beliefs between the rival communities inflamed often bitter antagonisms and suspicions, as illustrated by the charges and countercharges traded by Zha Ruqiang and Xu Liangying. The boundaries between the two communities cut across professional and institutional affiliations. The debates and conflicts did not simply pit scientists on one side against philosophers and Party theoreticians on the other, nor did they reflect one institution's members and agendas against another's. Instead CAS physicists and CASS philosophers could be found on both sides of the debates. Theoretical physicist He Zuoxiu joined CASS philosopher Zha Ruqiang against astrophysicist Fang Lizhi, CAS science historian Xu Liangying, and members of Zha's own Institute of Philosophy, Jin Wulun and Wu Guosheng.

Personal ties and animosities also played roles in these rival communities. Xu Liangying had strong personal ties with nearly everyone in the pluralist group. He had worked with Yu Guangyuan since at least the early 1950s. Xu met Fang Lizhi first in 1973, and grew closer in 1980 after both he and Fang's wife, Li Shuxian, had their "rightist" labels removed the year before.[66] Throughout the reform decade, Xu played a bridge role between younger scientists such as Fang and Yu Guangyuan, whom Fang never met.[67] Zhong Weiguang and the others who opened the public criticisms of Zha Ruqiang's views in the *Bulletin of Natural Dialectics* were students of Xu in the CAS graduate school. Wu Guosheng credited Xu with helping him write his portrait of Fang Lizhi, calling him "the kind of scholar the republic needs" in the *Bulletin of Natural Dialectics* in the fall of 1986.[68] Similarly, Xu was the object of Hu Qiaomu's antagonism since at least the Hu Feng campaign in 1955.[69] Xu and Zha Ruqiang had clashed in the early 1980s. In his attacks on Fang and debates with Xu in the mid-1980s, Zha had the active encouragement of Hu Qiaomu and Deng Liqun.[70] He Zuoxiu purportedly tried to block Fang Lizhi's appointment as vice president of Chinese Science and Technology University in 1983, leading to delays in the Party Secretariat's approval of Fang for the position. He Zuoxiu also may have opposed Fang's appointment to the Institute of Theoretical Physics after his dismissal from his university post in 1987.[71]

All of these personal allegiances and animosities colored the fundamental differences in intellectual ideals and ideological values that divided the scientists into separate communities. There were areas in which outlooks overlapped—both groups, for example, lamented the decline in living standard and social standing of intellectuals through the 1980s. Ultimately, however, each perceived the other side's beliefs about science, authority, and society as corrosive, competitive, and, in the final analysis, lethal to its own.

OPEN DISSENT

The dissident activities of scientists such as Fang Lizhi and Xu Liang-ying in the late 1980s are intelligible in light of the ideals, attitudes, and values described in the preceding discussion. The focus and content of their statements and writings makes sense from the perspective of their views on science and politics, and the pattern of their collaboration was already well established from their cooperation in the intellectual debates of the preceding years. Their dissidence may be understood as the outcome of their previous experiences and their expectations in the Deng reform period, catalyzed by the larger turn of political trends and change of social atmosphere of the late 1980s.

By the spring of 1987 Zhao Ziyang and Deng Xiaoping had managed to blunt the thrust of the campaign against "bourgeois liberalization" launched the previous January. High-level publicity to reform themes re-emerged, and the Thirteenth CCP Congress in October 1987 marked a momentary high tide of reform, as Zhao laid out new steps in both economic and political reform for the coming years. By the spring of 1988, however, this momentum was dissipating, and through the following summer trends in leadership politics moved again toward confrontation.

The issues around which this confrontation coalesced were economic. After mixed signals from Deng Xiaoping, Zhao and reformers associated with him began to work out plans for major steps toward price reform. As word of these planning discussions leaked, waves of panic buying swept Chinese cities in the summer months, driving inflation rates above 30 percent in many places. Conservative reformers led by Chen Yun used these dislocations in the economy to reassert control over the leadership agenda. After a series of informal meetings at the summer resort of Beidaihe and more formal Politburo and State Council meetings in August and September, Premier Li Peng, backed by Chen, unseated Zhao from leadership over the Party's Finance and Economic Work Small Leading Group, the key body in economic policy. Over the next two months Li spearheaded a new program of economic retrenchment, postponing new reforms for at least three years. The reversal in economic reform policy was the critical setback that paved the way for Zhao's political demise the following spring, in the context of the

Tiananmen demonstrations, and inaugurated the policy deadlock and decision-making paralysis that shaped the Party leadership's response to those protests.[72]

The vacillation of economic policy, the freezing of reform, and the perception of leadership paralysis further agitated an already restive urban population. Rumors of price reform raised the anxieties of urban groups tied to fixed state salaries and wages. Those whose fortunes were tied to the advance of reforms in the collective and private sectors, meanwhile, saw their futures in jeopardy with the stalling of reform. Intellectuals of all political stripes saw in the emerging political crisis the chance to press their particular agendas, and, under the relatively liberalized restraints on discussion prevailing at the time, they began to mobilize into groups to debate alternative political routes.

Students, who had chafed and protested annually over a broad range of concrete complaints and general anxieties, also began to mobilize. Through the fall and into the winter of 1988–89, "salons" sprang up among intellectuals and students on university campuses in the capital and elsewhere. Increasingly, these gatherings drew not only from the urban intellectual and student communities, but also from China's new entrepreneurial class and the quasi-independent think-tank researchers supported by them and, ironically, encouraged by the regime's own science reforms.[73] Opinions on the proper course for China ranged across the political spectrum, from a conservative "neoauthoritarianism," which saw the need for a firm authoritarian hand at the helm of state as it traversed the turbulent channels of economic and social change toward a later liberalized political order, to calls for radical democratizing reform. In this context of perceived national crisis, parallels with the May Fourth era seemed all the more striking and poignant, and the "science and democracy" message of scientific intellectuals such as Fang and Xu gained general currency.[74]

Fang Lizhi became increasingly prominent in these dissident activities and debates. After his removal from his university post and expulsion from the Party in January 1987, he had been assigned to work as a researcher at the Beijing Observatory. This need not have been a congenial home for his scientific work, insofar as the observatory director, Wang Shouguan, preferred the infinite universe viewpoint in the science and philosophy debates. Wang, however, had no interest in becoming embroiled in the politics of the debate.[75] Attempting to demarcate academic from political activities, the regime monitored and tried to suppress Fang's political activities, while underscoring that he was free to pursue his scientific work. For the next two years, including the period of his intensifying political involvement in 1988 and 1989, Fang adhered to a rigid work routine. In 1988 he was commended by the Beijing Observatory as the author of the most scientific papers of anyone on its staff over the year, and in February that year the CAS announced that he had received a promotion of two wage grades.[76] Meanwhile, the regime blocked his attempts to speak to student groups, using such administrative tactics as denying the required permits to meet and obstructionist measures such as locking the doors of the lecture hall in which he was scheduled to appear. Judging by the number of interviews he gave, Fang appeared throughout this period to have unobstructed access to the foreign press and international science community by telephone and in person in his Beijing apartment. He told the people he talked with, however, that he believed the Public Security Bureau was monitoring his telephone conversations.[77]

In a setting of rising student agitation in the spring of 1988, Fang did manage to elude the regime's obstruction, speaking at an unofficial celebration of the May Fourth anniversary on the Beijing University campus. Addressing more than five hundred students in the first of several "democracy salons" held on the campus over the following months, Fang called for freedom of expression, emphasized the need for a process of democratization if modernization were to succeed, and espoused persistence in the pursuit of democratic change. As he was leaving, he acceded to student requests that he inscribe the words "science and democracy" on a commemorative scroll.[78]

Fang's political activities increased. In an interview with the Hong Kong press during an August 1988 stopover in Hong Kong after a trip to Australia, he made critical remarks about leadership corruption, to which the regime responded by prohibiting further foreign travel. In the fall, he again managed to address a crowded lecture hall at Beijing University.[79]

On 6 January 1989 Fang publicized his open letter to Deng Xiaoping, appealing for a general amnesty for "political prisoners" such as Wei Jingsheng, the dissident arrested for his activities in the 1978–79

Democracy Wall movement.[80] He was blocked from attending a banquet at the u.s. embassy on 26 February during the stopover in Beijing of President George Bush.[81] And in these early months of 1989, Fang and Li Shuxian joined discussions among the various intellectual and entrepreneurial groups that debated their country's future.[82]

Xu Liangying's trajectory into dissidence directly paralleled Fang's and grew out of their collaborations in the science and philosophy debates. In June 1986, after Fang came under criticism for his views, Xu announced his readiness to launch a petition drive to defend Fang.[83] In late 1986 Xu, Fang, and the dissident journalist Liu Binyan planned to convene a seminar in early 1987 on the thirtieth anniversary of the Anti-Rightist campaign to review the harm it and other political movements had inflicted on intellectuals and on the Chinese people in general. These plans were quickly suppressed by the regime.[84]

As the campaign against "bourgeois liberalization" got under way in January 1987, excerpts from Xu's November 1986 *People's Daily* article on science and democracy were included in *neibu* study materials as an example of the view that Marxism was just one of the "one hundred schools of thought."[85] His name was also included on a list of intellectuals targeted for expulsion from the ccp as Party leadership conservatives moved to expand the purge begun in January with Fang Lizhi, Liu Binyan, and Wang Ruowang. In the end, although five were expelled in the fall of that year, Xu was not one of them.[86]

As the atmosphere of political crisis built in 1988, Xu's alienation appears to have turned increasingly to active dissent. In an interview in September 1988, Fang Lizhi recalled that Xu had expressed regret to him that the year before "he hadn't been kicked out of the Party with us [i.e., Fang, Wang Ruowang, and Liu Binyan]." "He was a true Marxist at the time, and he and I argued over this," Fang said, adding that "now he says it was all a dream."[87]

After Fang's open letter to Deng Xiaoping was publicized in January 1989, Xu joined Fang at a forum of intellectuals and entrepreneurs on 4 February at the Friendship Hotel in Beijing, at which Fang called on the regime to live up to the letter of the 1948 United Nations Universal Declaration on Human Rights. Xu seconded Fang's call. He also attacked advocacy of "neoauthoritarianism" by some intellectuals as reminiscent of intellectual efforts to defend the early Republican-period dictator Yuan Shikai and his efforts to establish a new Confucian dynasty centered on himself. Xu also saluted the participation of the entrepreneurs in the forum as fitting on the occasion of the two hundredth anniversary of the French Revolution, observing that the Third Estate had been the main force for democratic change in that era. Later in the spring, as the demonstrations were building in Tiananmen Square, Xu repeated many of the same ideas in an article in the quasi-independent Shanghai paper *World Economic Herald* (Shijie jingji daobao). He again attacked "neoauthoritarianism," rebutting the idea that "feudal autocracy" suited "Eastern characteristics," and he again called for a new "democratic enlightenment movement." "Thanks to the policy of opening up in recent years, speculators and novelty hunters have brought some counterfeit commodities from the dark corners of the free market abroad to serve as the theory of democracy in order to confuse young people, and so all sorts of strange ideas have been made to wear the 'hat' of democracy," he said. Democracy, he insisted, had four essential components: equality and inviolability of human rights; popular sovereignty; popular endorsement of government by means of elections; and supervision of officials by the people. It also required four conditions: freedom of speech and the press; rule by law and not by people; avoidance of concentration of power; and prohibition of military intervention in politics. "These points are the essentials of democracy; not a single one can be dispensed with."[88]

By early February Xu had already begun gathering signatures on the open letter publicized on 26 February, while President Bush was in Beijing. According to Xu, he had discussed the idea of a petition in mid-January with several former classmates and fellow underground Party organizers from his Zhejiang University days, including the CAS geographer Shi Yafeng, as a way of countering what they saw as ominous political trends. In particular, Xu recalled, the frequency of articles in the press about "neoauthoritarianism" escalated in January, a portent that "made us very angry," and so they sought to launch a "new democratic enlightenment movement." Xu then personally drafted the open letter, and he and several colleagues solicited signatures.[89]

The open letter drew heavily from among the Zhejiang University group—thirteen of the total of forty-two—in the science community and from Xu's friends in the social sciences. Of the total, twenty-three were from the CAS and four were from other science institutions, eight were from the CASS, five were social scientists from other units, and two—the poet Shao Yanxing and the writer Wu Zuguang—were from the literary community. More than half were members of the Communist Party.[90]

The open letter itself registered concerns that had preoccupied the pluralist community in the preceding years. It asserted that the effort to modernize China without an accompanying effort at democratization would inevitably fail: "World history and the present reality of China both tell us that democratization (including the rule of law) is the indispensable guarantee of economic reform and the whole modernization effort." As the foremost condition for democratization, Xu and the others called for guarantees of freedom of expression and freedom of the press: "As long as the people can speak out freely and differing opinions can be openly expressed, and leaders can be criticized without fear of attack or revenge, then the atmosphere in our country will be lively, uninhibited, and harmonious, and the citizens can fully exercise their democratic consciousness." In step with this, the regime should release "all young people who have been sentenced to prison or labor reform for ideological reasons." And citing the instance of a despondent former senior scientist who committed suicide, the signers lamented the disastrously declining livelihood of scientific intellectuals, urging the state to redress this crisis.[91]

These views were undoubtedly not universal among scientists, nor, probably, even among a majority of them. Many more likely shared the utilitarian outlook of colleagues such as Qian Xuesen and believed that they had a stake in the technocratic direction of many of the regime's administrative policies. The reforms had fractured the scientific community in China, in many ways isolating those in the basic or theoretical sector from those in the applied science and technical areas. Many saw their futures tied to the science reforms, and so may well have not appreciated the political troubles that Fang and Xu invited with their open letters and dissident activities. Many more were probably indifferent. Xu himself noted, in recounting the process of drafting his petition and gathering signatures, that scientists normally are not active in political affairs.

For Fang and Xu, the idealistic demands for democracy that

emerged from their conception of science made it possible for them to find common ground with social scientists and literary and artistic intellectuals voicing the same demands. Personal ties between the dissident scientists and social science intellectuals whose lineage also traced back to Yu Guangyuan—such as Su Shaozhi and Yan Jiaqi—came into play, to be sure. But the foundation of collaboration that the scientists, historians, social scientists, writers, and artists shared arose from a common humanistic conception of their respective disciplines as sources of ideals and values for the enlightenment of the individual and society, and from the parallel requirement of the free conduct of their professions.[92]

AFTER TIANANMEN

The crackdown on dissident intellectuals that followed the brutal suppression of the Tiananmen demonstrations on the night of 3–4 June 1989 reflected the regime's recognition of the threat their activities posed to its legitimacy. After the demonstrations in Tiananmen Square erupted in April and escalated through May, Fang Lizhi had avoided direct participation. The regime nevertheless decided to label him a principal architect of the protests, and on 11 June the Beijing Municipal Public Security Bureau issued a warrant for his arrest.[93] He sought and was granted refuge in the U.S. Embassy, and, after a year's stay in the compound, was permitted by Beijing to leave for the United States. Meanwhile, authoritative regime accounts of the Tiananmen demonstrations and their suppression and press commentary denounced Fang as a major conspirator in the protests.[94]

Like Fang, Xu Liangying appears to have avoided going to Tiananmen Square.[95] According to those familiar with his circumstances, he was never arrested after the crackdown. The authoritative official account by Beijing mayor Chen Xitong of the Tiananmen demonstrations and their suppression condemned Xu's "open letter." That it did not mention Xu's name or the name of any natural scientist who signed it, however, was a telling indication of the regime's dismay at the support Xu had gathered in the scientific community. Instead, it mentioned as the open letter's drafters only three of the social scientists who signed it—Li Honglin, Bao Zunxin, and Zhang Xianyang—and one social scientist who did not—Ge Yang. Jin Guantao, who did not sign Xu's open letter but who did sign the open letter signed by social scientists and historians publicized on 16 February was condemned by name in authoritative regime accounts of the demonstrations. Jin avoided arrest by fleeing to Hong Kong.

In the wake of Tiananmen, Xu's situation remained uncertain, and for more than two years he was not permitted to express his views publicly.[96] He finally re-emerged in print in late 1992 amid a relative political loosening and a new wave of economic reform dramatized by Deng Xiaoping's tour of South China the previous spring. Xu's views had visibly sharpened. In two blatantly provocative articles, he made plain his break with the Deng regime and his views on political and social trends in post-Tiananmen China. In one, a long article in the *Bulletin of Natural Dialectics* rebutting the view that May Fourth era scientists had espoused scientistic views, Xu drew parallels between the abuse of the term "scientism" and the misappropriation of the term "humanism." " 'Humanism,' " Xu said, "means upholding a humanitarian or humanist position—that is to say, respecting human dignity and integrity, respecting the basic rights of the individual, and promoting concern and love for humanity. . . . As for behavior that tramples human rights, suppresses dissent, and mercilessly slaughters people—even in the name of 'revolutionary humanism'—this can only be seen as a crime against humanism and humanity."[97]

The other article, appearing in the journal *The Future and Development* (Weilai yu fazhan), was a scathing attack on the eve of the Fourteenth CCP Congress on the "neoauthoritarian" idea that democratic reform could be put off while economic market reform moved ahead. Applauding the collapse of the USSR and the end of the Cold War as "a great victory for science, democracy, and reason," Xu called the entire development of socialism from the 1930s to the 1970s "a retrogression to medieval times." Xu recalled the hopes that he and other intellectuals had felt at the beginning of the Deng era—hopes that had been trampled. The events of June 1989, he said, had brought about a reversion to the practices of the Anti-Rightist campaign and the Cultural Revolution. "Criticisms and labels flew around, speeches and writings that featured a bit of independent thinking were all banned, while the nonsense and drivel uttered by liars, hoodlums, and prostitutes became treasured prizes to the powers that be, causing righteous people to sigh over the misfortunes of the Chinese nation." In this instance Xu had again crossed the line and the regime immediately suspended publication of *The Future and Development*.[98]

For several months after June 1989, press commentary attacked Yu Guangyuan, though not by name, as the intellectual patron of the pluralist project.[99] By the spring of 1990, however, Yu began to publish again in academic journals and, after Deng Xiaoping reasserted direction over the Party agenda in late 1990 and early 1991, Yu's views on economic reform issues re-emerged in the mass-circulation media.

Meanwhile, the Party sought to shore up its relationship with the scientific community, building on ties to those whose loyalty had remained unquestioned through the preceding crisis. In a show of praise that seems to have been intended also as an implicit condemnation of dissidents such as Fang Lizhi, Party leaders expressed their appreciation for the allegiance of scientists such as Qian Xuesen by celebrating Qian's winning of an international award for his scientific work. At the ceremony, on 3 August 1989, Qian underscored his own patriotism in returning to China after prolonged study in the United States, noting that he had seen at first hand the realities of so-called American "democracy" and "freedom." He praised the Communist Party's leadership of science, the success of which was evident in China's ability to build nuclear weapons and guided missiles despite the poverty of its resources. Perhaps in conscious counterpoint to Wu Guosheng's praise of Fang Lizhi as "the kind of scholar the Republic needs," *Enlightenment Daily* referred to Qian in an account of his accomplishments as "the true elite and backbone of the nation."[100]

For several months after June 1989 the leadership and press also took to task not only the political demands of the dissident intellectuals but also the underlying intellectual ideals that inspired them. In particular, press commentary attacked the idea of pluralism in science and reasserted the necessity of Marxism's "guiding role" over all intellectual inquiry.[101] Implicit in such commentary was the recognition that the Party could not afford to recognize intellectual pluralism without surrendering its own claim to legitimacy. With intellectual pluralism came plurality of authority. Were scientists allowed to take up the prerogatives of authoritative interpretation of Marxism, as long as it claimed to be a science, they would hold in their hands the right to extend legitimacy to or withhold it from the Party's exercise of power. Not surprisingly, the Party could not tolerate such a possibility.

6 / China's Scientific Dissidence in Perspective

Scientific dissent emerged in China in the 1980s as the response of a small number of scientists to the conflicts and social dislocations they experienced and to the disappointed ambitions and expectations they felt during the reforms that Deng Xiaoping brought about in the post-Mao period. Praised as a vanguard of China's future at the beginning of the reform period, scientists faced severe challenges to their sense of identity, mission, and well-being as the reforms proceeded through the 1980s. By the end of the decade, many saw their profession declining in social prestige, the autonomy they hoped to achieve threatened, and the society around them moving in directions they considered dangerous. Dissident political activism was the response of a small but politically significant number of them. This chapter examines their dissent in the post-Mao period from the longer perspective of China's modern history and in comparison with scientific dissidence in the Soviet Union.

LIBERALISM REVIVED

Scientific dissidents such as Xu Liangying and Fang Lizhi were important participants in the revival of a genuine political liberalism on China's political scene in the post-Mao period. The modernist orientation of their ideas and the heavy emphasis in their writings on the value of critical reason in social and political life, on the importance of law and institutional protections for political freedoms, and especially on the sanctity of individual conscience are hallmark themes of liberal political philosophy. The espousal of these ideals by Xu Liangying, Fang Lizhi, Li Xingmin, and others set these scientific intellectuals apart from their more conservative contemporaries, whether on the Marxist-Leninist left or the traditionalist right. It was the common ground they shared with dissident intellectuals from the humanities and the social sciences, such as political philosopher Li Honglin and legal theorist Yu Haocheng, who also espoused political liberalism.

The emergence of political liberalism among some scientific intellectuals in the 1980s derived from their view of their calling as scientists and of their social and political responsibilities. The interconnection between their professions as scientists and their lives as citizens was evident in their defense of rationalism in the intellectual arena and in politics. It was apparent also in their insistence on open academic debate, free from obscurantist external political intrusion, and on individual freedom of expression in public affairs. And it was expressed in the antiauthoritarianism of their attacks on Marxist-Leninist "guidance" of science, in both the Maoist past and the Dengist present, and on persisting Marxist-Leninist "feudalism" and re-emergent "new Confucian" traditions in contemporary public life.

These professional and political resonances grew out of the scientists' disillusionment with Marxism, in varying degrees, stemming from their individual experiences in the Anti-Rightist Campaign and the Cultural Revolution. Perhaps motivated in part by a guilty sense of complicity in the enormous disasters of that time, scientists such as Xu saw in the early Deng reforms the possibility of building in China a democratic context safe for the pursuit of science, according to the ideals they believed were common to science and democracy, still within the framework of an overarching but reformed socialism.[1] For them, the Deng reforms offered a last chance to pursue the ideals that had motivated their entire lives, despite the crushing setbacks of the communist regime under Mao. In pursuing these ideals anew, they looked consciously back to the May Fourth era as the inspiration for their liberalism.

The stages of the dissident scientists' agitational activities after 1976 reveal the constancy of their liberal commitment even as the tactics with which they pursued it evolved. In the early years of the Deng period, they asserted their ideals and ambitions openly, with the encouragement of Hu Yaobang and others associated with Deng, in an effort to condemn the brutalities, capricious abuse of power, and obscurantism of politics in the Maoist period. Perhaps the most vivid of these expositions of ideals was the fictional account of visits to the "courts" of religion, reason, and practice published in *Enlightenment Daily* in 1978—at the height of Deng Xiaoping's "practice" campaign—by Yan Jiaqi, the physicist turned philosopher of science turned political scientist who was tangentially a member of Yu Guangyuan's natural dialectics family. Contrasting the experiences of the religious inquisitions against Galileo and Bruno with the ideas of Rousseau, Voltaire, Diderot, and Montesquieu and invoking a parallel contrast between Cultural Revolution inquisitions and the "antifeudal" orientation Yan hoped would result from Deng's reforms, Yan's fictional account may serve as a manifesto of the scientific liberals' purposes.[2]

After this initial period of enunciating principles and attempting to shape the agenda of the reforms, dissident scientists sought to implement their ideals in their professional arena as their contribution to the overall reforms. In this effort they pressed for institutional and legal guarantees for open debate that they believed were essential to the conduct of science and that would contribute to the democratization of socialism, and thus ran afoul of the cross-purposes—of the broad coalition of those backing the reforms.[3] As it became clear to scientific liberals such as Xu Liangying that the orientation of both the political leadership and some of their colleagues in professional fields was abidingly utilitarian and Leninist in outlook, the rifts dividing them from those dominating the reform camp became increasingly unbridgeable. Though the 1986 Little Hundred Flowers relaxation offered a respite of hope, the ensuing purge of Fang Lizhi, Liu Binyan, and Wang Ruowang crushed these expectations. In hindsight, 1987 was a turning point for scientific liberals such as Xu. Their alienation steadily hardened, sending them down the path to dissidence on which Fang had embarked even earlier.

Ironically, the party leadership itself helped to create the conditions that led the scientific liberals from support of the reforms to political dissidence. The leadership's utilitarianism, the natural opposite of the liberals' focus on the value of individual conscience, was a major spur to their gradual alienation. More than that, the leadership authorized some measure of autonomous expression and organization in the scientific community, though circumscribed by a presumed identity of commitment to nation and socialism, to suit its own state-building and utilitarian purposes. Its invocation of science's critical spirit, its support for the reprofessionalization of the scientific community, and the decentralizing thrust of the science reforms—encouraging enterprises in all sectors to establish their own quasiautonomous research units—paved the way for the assertion of autonomy and open public discourse by the liberal dissidents and, by 1989, by others in urban society. These trends went well beyond what the leadership originally envisioned and, in the end, could tolerate.

As society asserted itself under the loosened constraints of the Dengist political community and sought new, more autonomous barriers against state power—a civil society in the making—the Party found itself as much reacting to trends and pressures in society as initiating and mobilizing social change. In the process, the presumed identity of commitment to nation and socialism splintered. In the eyes of the scientific liberals the Party appeared more an obstacle to social progress and national survival than the agent of these causes. The scientific liberals provided much of the rhetoric of the ensuing social dissent at Tiananmen Square, and, ironically, the regime's own propaganda emphasis on the urgency of China's needs in light of change underway in the contemporary world only intensified the message.[4]

MAY FOURTH ANTECEDENTS

The outlook, concerns, and experiences of scientific liberals in the Deng period evoke parallels and point up contrasts with those of scientists and other intellectuals who confronted similar dilemmas through much of the twentieth century. From a longer historical perspective, the intellectual debates in which the dissident scientists participated, the social tensions they felt, and the political stance they adopted in the 1980s appear as the latest episode in a longer story of the evolving relationship between knowledge and power, the changing role of intellectuals in contemporary society, and the place of science in a modernizing China. Examining these longer trends will help to underscore the significance of the events of the 1980s and illuminate their place in the longer span of modern history.

The May Fourth era, which takes its name from the demonstrations in 1919 protesting China's treatment at the Versailles Conference but which broadly signifies the period from the late 1910s through the early 1920s, was a key transitional period in modern Chinese history. Erupting in the wake of the collapse of the traditional imperial system and amid the frustrations and disappointments of early republican government, the intellectual flourishing and social turmoil of the May Fourth period occurred in what was perceived as a time of failed politics. These perceptions of domestic political weakness and disunity heightened fears for national survival in a rapidly changing international context dominated by an evolving constellation of great powers that had dealt China repeated humiliations over the previous eighty years. Though the pronouncements of the powers' statesmen after World War I frequently reflected a new liberalism in international politics, their actions just as often turned out to be truer to the power politics of the prewar era than to their liberal ideals, as the Chinese discovered at Versailles.

Meanwhile social changes in China that had undermined the foundations of the old imperial system accelerated, as new social groups and professions sought their place in an increasingly urbanizing society. One such group was intellectuals, who now emerged as a social group distinct from their gentry-literati predecessors. The abolition of the examination system in 1905 and the demise of the Qing dynasty in 1911 severed the traditional route to social prestige and political power linking knowledge, culture, and political service. With the resulting great divorce of culture and power, the new intelligentsia now made its living in the emerging legal, medical, and business professions, as administrators and experts in government bureaucracies, as educators in China's newly established universities and schools, as writers and journalists, and, increasingly, with the establishment of China's modern scientific community, as scientists and technicians.

These political and social changes created an atmosphere that combined nationalistic urgency and romantic idealism with intellectual uncertainty and ambiguity among intellectuals, who, in a context of failed politics, turned naturally to questions of culture and society.[5] At the core of their debates were issues of cultural and social identity. With the divorce of culture and politics, what were the proper role and responsibilities of intellectuals toward their society and the state? Should they work to establish and preserve the autonomy of knowledge and culture from political power, pursuing knowledge and art for their own sake and maintaining a critical distance from which to judge as outsiders the society and actions of the state around them? Or should they seek a new synthesis of culture and power, in which knowledge again served and informed power, of the kind that had linked the imperial state and traditional society for so long? In a postimperial era, what was the proper source of values? Could traditional values still provide an enduring basis for cultural and national identity in the midst of accelerating change? Or should traditional values be repudiated, because they inhibit progressive change, in favor of "modern" values, perhaps imported, that were presumed to promote it? In grasping these issues, May Fourth intellectuals set the stage for the emergence of a modern critical intelligentsia in China in the 1920s and 1930s.

In the course of these reflections, May Fourth intellectuals promoted an enormous flux of ideas, ideologies, and values, in which native traditions were re-evaluated and foreign ideas of all kinds attracted attention. Opinions on the contemporary relevance of various Confucian and other traditional schools of thought ranged from radical iconoclastic rejection by the New Culture Movement intellectuals, who sought to replace them with modern social and cultural outlooks and values that would abet China's overall modernization, to neoconservative attempts to accommodate traditional cultural values in a modern secular setting. Uncertainties about China's own traditions in a context of threatened national survival made a wide range of Western ideas and values appear relevant. Many rallied around "science and democracy," which were perceived to be the source of the West's international power and domestic prosperity. For others, however, the lessons of the Western experience, especially in light of the West's self-inflicted devastation during World War I, were not nearly so clear. For them, the cultural pessimism and intellectual skepticism that displaced the positivism and optimism predominating in prewar Europe tempered enthusiasm for the "progressive" Western ideas that impressed other Chinese intellectuals.

The attention given to a few spectacular debates in this period— such as that over "problems" and "isms" in 1919 between Hu Shi and Chen Duxiu (Ch'en Tu-hsiu) and the voluminous dispute over "science and metaphysics" in 1923 between Zhang Junmai (Chang Chün-mai,

Carson Chang), Ding Wenjiang, and others—has frequently left the impression that the differences among the leading intellectuals and those clustered around them over issues of politics and culture were clearcut and consistent. As Charlotte Furth and others have shown, however, the combinations and alignment of views on issues of culture, society, and politics seldom cut evenly along predictable lines.[6] Cultural radicals, such as New Culture Movement leader Hu Shi, were politically moderate, while cultural conservatives, such as members of the "national essence" (guocui) group, at the same time had supported anti-Qing revolution. Supporters of "total Westernization," such as Hu Shi, also found value in elements of China's traditional past that helped place it within a historically relativistic framework and so permitted China a future in the modern world. Conversely, scholars writing for the neotraditionalist journal Critical Review (Xueheng), founded in 1922, advocated not a narrow, reactionary embrace of traditional culture and exclusion of Western ideas but sought a new cultural synthesis of traditional values in a modernizing setting. Meanwhile, the most politically radical and culturally iconoclastic intellectuals, such as CCP founder Chen Duxiu, embraced universalistic theories that bore telltale traces of traditional cosmologies synthesizing politics and culture.

Intellectuals of the 1980s reflecting on the past looked back to the May Fourth era for inspiration and self-understanding because in their eyes that period had initiated many of the trends and dilemmas they encountered in their own lives. There were general similarities between the two periods. Despite the explicit optimism of the early Deng years, the implicit undertone was also a sense of failed politics. Bold leadership pronouncements on behalf of reform and "emancipating thought" rested on the recognition, explicitly acknowledged in the CCP's own self-criticism of 1981, that through the entire period from 1957 to 1976 Mao had led the Party down a tragically erroneous path that the reformers were now trying to correct. Despite the restorationist ambitions of the Party leadership, the catastrophe of the Cultural Revolution proved to many Chinese intellectuals that something far more fundamental was wrong with Chinese Marxism-Leninism than a "deviation" in leadership policies.

As during the May Fourth period, perceptions of the international context lent urgency to the intellectuals' reflections on China's contemporary predicament. The sense of danger was not immediate—perceptions of a Soviet threat to China declined through the Deng years—but general. The world had changed and was changing rapidly while China had taken a misguided detour. The regime itself sought to enlist patriotic support for its reforms by underscoring the broader recognition that a new scientific and technological revolution well underway in the world was revising the standards of national power and so the terms of national survival in international politics. For the same purposes, it also called attention to the economic success of China's Pacific Rim neighbors, a measure that probably provoked more critical reflection than anticipated.

Like the May Fourth era, the Deng years were a time of rapid social change brought about by the regime's revised economic policies. Not all of such changes were anticipated, but, as we have seen, some were consequences of a conscious retreat of the state from sectors of social life. Intellectuals, who were invited to lend their energies to the patriotic purposes of building a modern socialist China and so were granted greater autonomy over their own professions, were one social group who benefitted from this retreat, uneven as it was. As foreign ideas and intellectual trends flooded China and as Chinese scholars and students explored the world, the 1980s witnessed a flourishing of intellectual energy and activism unprecedented in PRC history.

In a context reminiscent of the May Fourth era, it is not surprising that Chinese intellectuals in the 1980s again turned to questions of culture. The Communist Party's own acknowledgment of its failed politics, the awareness that China was lagging behind even its smaller neighbors, and, most of all, reflections on personal experiences in the Cultural Revolution impelled intellectuals to look for explanations deeper in China's political culture and the social personality of the Chinese people. Mao Zedong's charismatic fanaticism and the coercive capacities of the regime aside, what explained why millions of Chinese were ready to follow his instructions to such zealous and savage extremes? How could the energies of millions of people be whipped into collective frenzies that suffocated and snuffed out the slightest expression of individual conscience? What complicity did intellectuals share in preparing the way for the Cultural Revolution in particular and, more generally, in China's troubled path in contemporary times?

These issues led quickly into deeper questions about history and modernity. Were the troubled lives of intellectuals for most of the twentieth century a reflection of their deviation from the "Chinese Enlightenment" themes of "science and democracy" expounded during the May Fourth years—ideals that had been subordinated to the goal of "national salvation"? Or was the entire "enlightenment" concept flawed from the start? Did its goals of social progress implicitly require a new synthesis of knowledge and power, reminiscent of the integration of culture and politics of traditional eras, that would inevitably corrupt the intellectuals' capacity for independent critical judgment and leave them vulnerable to the instrumental demands of an authoritarian state? How was it that the Chinese, whose traditional cultural brilliance was universally acknowledged, at the same time could vent such iconoclastic rage against their own civilization? Why had China, whose technological achievements had placed it in the forefront of the world up to the sixteenth century, not produced a scientific revolution comparable to that in the West? More generally, why had it had such terrible difficulties in catching up to the power and prestige of the West?

Though the "culture fever" of the mid-1980s was the most explicit expression of intellectuals' responses to these and similar questions, reflections on these issues were apparent in their writings and comments from the very beginning of the Deng years. The answers that intellectuals gave to such questions frequently clashed with one another. Over the reform decade, they expressed a complex span of viewpoints and opinions that Western observers have been slow to sort out and appreciate. Thickets of dense literatures that have sprouted up around particular subissues have made it hard to survey the controversies comprehensively and to locate their interconnections. As in the debates of the May Fourth era, the clustering of viewpoints and lines of argument in one controversy were not always clear guideposts to positions adopted in others. Participants in the debates spoke out from a wide span of scientific and humanistic disciplines, and frequently did so in journals outside their own field.

Nevertheless, as disparate in viewpoint as they were, almost all of the reflections and writings in the "culture fever" debates evinced a fundamentally humanistic orientation.[7] This was explicitly the case

with some, such as Wang Ruoshui, the philosopher who took humanism as the "starting point" for a reformed Marxism, and others who
participated in the debate on humanism and alienation under socialism
in the late 1970s and early 1980s. But a humanistic perspective was also
implicit in the elaboration of a subjectivist but still materialist critique
of modern Chinese thought by the aesthetician Li Zehou, the expositions on law and political reform by political philosopher Li Honglin
and legal specialist Yu Haocheng, and the expositions on "new Confucianism" by philosopher Tang Yijie and historian Pang Pu. A humanist
critique of authoritarian bureaucracy is pervasive in both the writings
of the Shanghai essayist Wang Ruowang and the investigative reportage
of journalist Liu Binyan. A humanist perspective informs the literary
criticism of Liu Zaifu (for much of the 1980s director of the CASS Institute of Foreign Literature) and the postmodernist attacks on the May
Fourth enlightenment movement by Gan Yang, who has adopted the
critical-theory perspective of the Frankfurt School and of continental
philosophers such as Foucault, Hans-Georg Gadamer, and Paul Ricoeur.
It is also apparent, as will be argued further below, in the criticism
by scientific liberals such as Fang Lizhi, Xu Liangying, Li Xingmin, Jin
Guantao, and others of the regime's science policies.

This broad humanistic critique of politics and culture included diverse strains. Li Zehou's subjective rationalism clashed with the romantic antirationalism of Gan Yang. Wang Ruoshui's humanistic Marxism,
stressing the writings of the younger, rather than the older, Marx, and Su
Shaozhi's cosmopolitan Marxism, drawing on broader strains of Eastern and West European Marxism as well as alternative Soviet Marxists,
was lost on the "new Confucians" and the younger liberal scientists.
Nevertheless, the experiences of the Cultural Revolution specifically
and, more broadly, the sense of a failed Chinese Communist politics,
which brutally crushed the humanity out of those it claimed to serve,
inspired a pervasive humanist critique that united all of these figures.

These intellectuals and others like them are significant in another
respect. The reference point from which they wrote and from which
they assessed their work and its relationship to society and especially
the state suggests a self-consciousness and an asserted independence
that verged on autonomy. This was evident from the very beginning of

the Deng reform era, but it became increasingly true through the 1980s, sufficiently so that it seems possible to see, as in the May Fourth period, an emerging critical intelligentsia.[8]

Certainly, all such intellectuals were still kept by the state. They drew salaries from the state institutions within which they worked and published in journals and newspapers that remained state-owned and state-operated. As employees in what Miklos Haraszti calls "the factories of culture," they were still inmates of the "velvet prison."[9] But as livelihoods of intellectuals declined as the Deng regime's economic reforms advanced, the prison was no longer as comfortable.

The quasiautonomous perspective of intellectuals such as these in the 1980s resulted from more than a decline in material circumstances, however. It resulted from more powerful motives and emotions derived from their past experience under the communist regime. In part, it derived from the vindication of their past viewpoints—by the Party's own acknowledgment that it had unjustly persecuted thousands of intellectuals over issues of conscience—and so from the consequent conviction that both their own principles and the future of the nation required them to speak the truth in the present. Perhaps for some, it also derived from guilt—from the recognition that in their idealism they either had actively contributed to the circumstances that led to the persecution they suffered and the disasters their nation endured or had stood idly by, failing to speak out when circumstances demanded it.

These motives—exoneration and guilt—were at the heart of what Liu Binyan called "another kind of loyalty," the readiness to speak the truth whatever the personal or political repercussions.[10] The degree of emphasis on exoneration versus guilt varied from intellectual to intellectual. But the force of the commitment to individual conscience, both as a matter of personal principle and in the larger public good, was the hallmark of all such intellectuals, however much they may still have seen themselves as genuine Marxists at the beginning of the Deng years.

This commitment led directly to the probing questions about culture and politics examined in the "culture fever" and associated debates in the 1980s. It inspired a new humanistic political discourse of criticism that frequently used Marxist frameworks and jargon but that was intrinsically subversive, examining concepts and affirming values far from those embodied in the Party's more limited critique of the past.

The commitment also motivated their collaboration in the reforms of the Deng regime and framed the critical perspective from which they assessed their participation. The regime's acknowledgment of the CCP past errors and its call at the 1978 Third Plenum to "liberate thought" to build a modern socialist China provided the opportunity for them to gain a fresh start both as patriots and as critical intellectuals. No longer were intellectuals simply explicators of the Party's line, loyally providing legitimacy to Party goals and decisions; increasingly they could extend or withhold legitimacy according to criteria intrinsic to their professional identities and individual principles. Liu Binyan is a clear example of an intellectual who predicated his role in the Deng reforms on such a critical and humanistic perspective. To Liu, the tension of choosing between the unquestioning loyalty demanded by the Party and his critical, independent conscience was apparent when he was purged as a rightist in early 1958. "Was it possible," he recalls thinking, "to be human and at the same time simply repeat what the Party said without using one's own judgment?" After his rehabilitation following Mao's death and after reflecting on the disaster of the Cultural Revolution—responsibility for which he laid in part on the failure of journalists, among other intellectuals, to speak out honestly—Liu reaffirmed that he could not simply be "an instrument, a tool" of the Party.[11]

Choices such as Liu's made intellectuals politically marginal figures in the reforms. They were marginal not in terms of importance, but in terms of where their loyalties lay. However much they were still Marxists, their commitment to individual conscience and humanistic orientation and their resulting critical stance put them at odds with powerful antagonists. They were at odds not only with Party leaders and bureaucrats whose persisting commitment to Party ideals and organizational discipline provided a different orientation, but also with those in the Party who were motivated by sheer self-interest and narrow personal ambition. The critical intellectuals thus operated at the margins of political legitimacy. Within the larger reform camp, they worked at the very perimeter of legitimacy, a position from which they could attempt to push outward the boundary of what was legitimate and what was not.

This marginality made the critical intellectuals controversial and their transition to open dissidence easy. When the circle of legitimacy shrank, many chose not to accommodate, their commitment to individual conscience and their sense of public good taking priority of loyalty over the Party and its goals for them. Through the 1980s the ranks of dissident intellectuals swelled, as critical intellectuals who were in the front ranks of reform in 1978 fell off or, in some cases, were pushed off the reform bandwagon. Wang Ruoshui was removed from his editorial post at *People's Daily* in the 1983 campaign against "spiritual pollution" for his defense of humanism and criticism of alienation under socialism, and he was eventually expelled from the Party in 1987. By contrast, the philosopher Ru Xin, who had written on behalf of similar views, recanted in the face of criticism and eventually was promoted to vice president of the CASS. Liu Binyan weathered repeated Party leadership displeasure with his investigative reporting on Party corruption until 1987, when he was purged at the same time that his patron, Hu Yaobang, was removed as Party general secretary. Ironically, in the context of the state's deliberate pullback from its previously deep reach into society and of accelerating access to foreign media, the loss of legitimate standing within the Party by such critical intellectuals appears only to have enhanced their stature in society and abroad.

SCIENCE AND SCIENTISM IN MODERN CHINA

Scientists were among the emergent critical intellectuals of the 1920s and the 1980s, and there are parallels and contrasts in the roles they played and perspectives they brought to bear in each period. First, scientists in both periods responded to the tensions and crises of their time in divergent ways, not as a monolithic bloc. They could be found on both sides of the debates on culture and politics in the May Fourth era. Ding Wenjiang's reply to Zhang Junmai's attacks on modern science as a source of values made him a leading figure in the 1923 "science and metaphysics" debate. But the same period saw Hu Xiansu (Hu Hsien-su), an American-trained botanist and cofounder of the Science Society of China, supporting the neoconservative views of the *Critical Review* group.[12] Similarly, among scientists of the 1980s, the views of Fang Lizhi and Xu Liangying on the political and cultural significance of modern science theory were rebutted adamantly by theoretical physicist He Zuoxiu, among others.

Second, the impetus for the political activism of scientists in each era was different. The scientists of the May Fourth period were the first generation of China's modern science community.[13] They acquired their scientific training abroad and returned to a China in which there were as yet only poorly established career paths for them. Their political activism, therefore, was in part directed toward establishing a modern science community in an inhospitable context: the warlord-dominated state was weak and ill-prepared to nurture a modern science establishment; culturally, traditional attitudes unfavorable to science still endured; and within society, the modern professions were only beginning to take root. The first generation of Chinese scientists, therefore, could not devote themselves foremost to the routines of professional scientists and instead had to become, in James Reardon-Anderson's characterization, "scientific propagandists, organizers, and entrepreneurs" who sought to institutionalize their profession in this uncongenial setting. These concerns shaped their political actions.[14] One example of such agitation were the manifestos that Hu Shi put forward in August 1920 and May 1922 calling for a return to republican government and for the defense of basic civil liberties as the necessary context for modern education, of which science was a central component. The latter manifesto, which Ding Wenjiang signed, presaged the short-lived liberal journal *Endeavor* (Nuli zhoubao), edited by Ding. As Charlotte Furth has pointed out, these manifestos were, in part, responses to the impoverishment of government support for schools by successive warlord administrations' diversion of money for military purposes, which provoked repeated demonstrations by students and professors.[15]

By the late 1920s and early 1930s, younger generations of Chinese scientists could hope to establish careers in a scientific community that was beginning to rest on more solid foundations. The newly founded Nationalist government in Nanjing had begun to resolve the uncertainties that the first generation of scientists faced and had thereby accelerated the professionalization of science in China. It supported an expanded system of research institutes—most significantly establishing the Academia Sinica in 1928—and it expanded and systematized universities. The Nationalist state itself took a direct role in guiding the overall work of the emergent science community through its National Research Council, which Ding Wenjiang helped to establish in 1935, and less directly through its National Research Commission, which pressed for the reorientation of most science toward economic development concerns. Meanwhile, the early efforts of pioneer scientists to establish the modern natural science disciplines in China, such as Ding Wen-jiang's efforts on behalf of geology, bore fruit in the first years of the Nationalist period (1927-49) with the elaboration of specialized professional societies. Though the expansion of career opportunities still could not match the numbers of scientists and technicians who were by then receiving training abroad and at home, increasingly the attention of China's scientists turned away from the political and cultural concerns that had engaged the founding generation of modern scientists and toward more narrowly focused professional concerns.[16]

The catalogue of problems, frustrations, and tensions that scientists confronted under the Nationalist regime reflected this narrower professional focus. The utilitarian needs of the government for science in national development and defense, especially as Japan loomed as a threat, placed demands on the science community that pitted its desire for autonomy over the orientation of its work against the state-decided needs of the nation for technology. Inevitably, these demands in turn triggered conflicts over state support for applied science versus the needs of basic science research. In the early years of the Nationalist regime, in Reardon-Anderson's judgment, a healthy balance emerged between the utilitarian demands of the government on science and the scientific community's desire for autonomy and control over its own agenda. But by the mid-1930s Japanese imperialism tilted the balance toward fulfilling state needs, a tilt that was pushed even farther after the Japanese invasion in 1937. Even so, after the chaos of the early years of the war, the relocation and revival of professional societies, universities, and publications in the Nationalist-held Southwest helped keep alive the professional ethos of the displaced science community during the war.[17]

Professional conflicts over the autonomy of the science community and the orientation of its work were also apparent in the early years of the PRC. By that time, however, new conflicts and tensions stemming from the communist regime's political and ideological intrusions into science added to the earlier ones. The most explicit complaints on these issues were expressed in the six-week outpouring of criticism of the Communist Party in May and early June 1957 known as the Hundred Flowers movement. These criticisms were permitted to emerge in a period in which the regime was revising its science policies in preparation for a new five-year economic plan and a proposed twelve-year science and technology plan. In keeping with this transition, the Communist Party had launched a new approach toward intellectuals, enunciated in a famous speech by Zhou Enlai in January 1956. Soon thereafter, in the early intimations of a de-Stalinizing thaw, the Party called for a new openness in intellectual affairs, authorized in a talk by Mao Zedong and a speech by Propaganda Department chief Lu Dingyi in May 1956 on "letting a hundred flowers bloom and a hundred schools contend." At the famous Qingdao conference on genetics, in August 1956, a general reappraisal of ideological constraints on scientific work was aired. The thrust of these steps was to reassess the validity and effects of the massive application of Soviet approaches to science that had been deployed during the First Five-Year Plan period (1953–57) in favor of more balanced policies that would benefit both science and economic development.[18]

In this context, in May 1957 scientists joined other intellectuals in public criticism of the Communist Party and its policies.[19] Scientists complained about poor working conditions and inadequate facilities, about the severe restrictions on career opportunities and mobility under the highly regimented Soviet-style bureaucratic approach to science organization that the regime had adopted, and about employment prospects for students in the sciences. They criticized the excessive emphasis in the regime's science policies on applied over basic science. They complained that nonscientists were often put in charge of scientific work and that scientists who had received their training in the West or who were not members of the Party were routinely discriminated against. They criticized Party control over universities and course curricula. They attacked not only the imposition of dubious Soviet-developed theories over specific scientific fields, such as Lysenkoism in genetics, but also the Party's assertion of Marxism's "guiding role" in science.

To those acquainted with this episode in CCP history and the history of science in modern China, the criticisms of the liberal scientist dissidents of the 1980s will seem familiar. Appropriately so, since most of the older dissident scientists played a role in the transitional science policies of 1956–57 or in the Hundred Flowers criticisms and suffered from the Party's Anti-Rightist campaign that closed the period. Yu Guangyuan, the patron of the natural dialectics community and exponent of liberalized approaches to scientific theory in the 1980s, was head of the Propaganda Department's Science Office in 1956 and a member of the committee drafting the twelve-year plan for science and technology. Yu delivered a keynote speech at the 1956 Qingdao conference.[20] Xu Liangying and his colleague from Zhejiang National University days, Fan Dainian, wrote a book on science policy support-ing the reorientation of science policies, pleading the case for greater state support for basic science research and for a more open intellec-tual atmosphere. For these views and for protesting the launching of the Anti-Rightist campaign, Xu and Fan were condemned as rightists them-selves.[21] Fang Lizhi, in 1957 a researcher at the CAS Institute of Modern Physics, as an alumnus joined the vigorous criticisms of regime science policies by Beijing University physics students.[22]

Beyond these personal links with the criticisms of the Hundred Flowers period, there are broader parallels. The complaints by the lib-eral scientists in the 1980s about declining living and working con-ditions and about the impact on basic science of the Dengist science reforms emphasizing the role of applied science in economic develop-ment are of a piece with tensions between China's science community and the state since the early years of the Nationalist government. From this longer perspective, such complaints are natural consequences of the professionalization of science in China and the institutionalization of science within a larger context of state power. They are also not ge-nerically different from the stresses, tensions, and frustrations expressed episodically in established science communities in other countries. Their re-emergence in post-Mao China is evidence of the tenacity of traditions of scientific professionalism in the face of two decades of the Maoist antiprofessional ethos.

The complaints about political and ideological intrusions into the scientific community in both the 1950s and the 1980s are different from those in earlier periods and follow from the particular nature of the Chinese communist regime. The totalist claims of Marxist-Leninist ideology, the organization of the regime along lines of "unified Party leadership," and the populist thrust of Mao's views on expertise clashed with the claims to authority of the scientific community over science and its interpretation and the community's claims to professional autonomy. The Nationalist regime shared none of these predispositions. Where there were ideological conflicts—such as over the pseudoscientific "vitalist" theories of the Chen brothers in the 1930s—such tensions served to encourage scientists to stay out of politics, reinforcing the professionalism of the science community and the autonomy of science within its own preserve.[23]

The complaints by scientists in the 1980s, in common with those of the 1950s, again illustrate the tenacity of scientific professionalism in China. Many of the criticisms in the Hundred Flowers period were made by scientists and intellectuals who had received their training under the Nationalist regime. Frequently, among the more prominent scientists, that training was gained abroad, especially in the United States and Great Britain. The criticisms also came from scientists who were not members of the CCP and who had, before the revolution, associated with the liberal third-force political parties of the civil-war era. Many such intellectuals, judging by Suzanne Pepper's analysis, had disliked the Nationalists' shortsighted, ineffective, and repressive policies and corruption, but also feared the perceptibly greater threat to civil liberties posed by the Communists, despite what they saw as greater prospects for political and social reform under the CCP. Consequently, such intellectuals held out, criticizing both parties and pressing for a coalition that would balance out the greater evils of either in favor of reform and civil liberty. Only on the very eve of the communist victory did such liberal intellectuals join the communist side, presumably hoping to work with the new regime on behalf of reform while blunting its repressive impulses.[24]

In this hope, in varying degrees, they must have been severely disappointed as the regimentation of political and social life in the "socialist transformation" policies of the new government and the constriction of intellectual life in the "thought reform" campaigns and massive Soviet influence of the early 1950s proceeded. To this extent, the outpouring of criticism by scientists in the spring of 1957 reflected a professionalism that was established under the previous regime and that frequently expressed the professional norms and traditions of the countries—especially the United States and Britain—in which they were trained.

In the 1980s this was far less the case. The complaints of scientists and intellectuals, those of older figures such as Xu Liangying aside, came from younger people—including scientists such as Fang Lizhi—who were trained entirely under the PRC and who, until the 1980s, had little or no direct experience with the professional traditions of scientific communities elsewhere. The consistency of some of the complaints by scientists and intellectuals in the 1980s with those as far back as the early years of the Nationalist regime is evidence of the strength of professional norms and traditions in China throughout this period, despite the severe tests and disruptions of the Maoist era.

Also striking is the predominance of physics and mathematics students in the political activism of both the Hundred Flowers period and the 1980s. According to one contemporary observer, the most radical critics at Beijing University in May 1957 were from the Department of Physics, of which Fang Lizhi is an alumnus. One such student, Tan Tianrong, founded the most prominent group of student critics, the Hundred Flowers Society, which translated and circulated among students the text of Khrushchev's secret speech criticizing Stalin at the Twentieth Congress of the Communist Party of the Soviet Union. Tan himself played a role in coordinating Beijing University's activities with those on other campuses in Beijing and Tianjin and became nationally known as a crack poster writer.[25] The predominance of physicists and physics students among the scientific dissidents of the 1980s has been remarked on previously.[26]

What has declined over the period since the May Fourth era is the spirit of scientism, and here there is a third and last point of comparison between the scientists and intellectuals of that period and those of the 1980s. Scientism is the presumption that the claims of science and its methods extend to all aspects of reality and that therefore science offers the only means to acquire true knowledge of reality. Because of the exclusivity of such claims, scientism (and its cousin positivism) carry with them monistic tendencies regarding the nature and structure of knowledge. Scholars of May Fourth intellectual history have argued that the leading intellectuals of the New Culture movement espoused scientistic views of one of two varieties.[27] One type, apparent in the views of geologist Ding Wenjiang and philosopher Hu Shi, was a methodological "empirical scientism," which stressed the scientific method as the only path to true knowledge about reality, in both nature and human affairs. The other type, evident in the views of anarchist and philologist Wu Zhihui and CCP-founder Chen Duxiu, was a cosmological "materialist scientism" that saw science (or what was believed to be science) as the basis of grand monistic worldviews that unified both the natural and social worlds.

The two varieties of scientism shared some features, but they had somewhat different roots and led in different directions politically.[28] Exponents of both shared an almost religious esteem for science as a corrosive to Chinese traditions that they regarded as backward and superstitious. In this respect—and in step with intellectual trends of that era in the West—Wu, Chen, Ding, and Hu, in criticizing Confucian traditions, all consciously drew on the positivist ideas and philosophies that pervaded Europe at the time. At the same time, scientistic views in China—especially the materialist variety—drew on a traditional cosmological impulse to establish a single, organic worldview that systematically unified the human and natural worlds according to a common set of laws or principles. From this perspective, as Charlotte Furth has argued, the transition from the last Confucian cosmologies—those of late nineteenth-century reformers, such as Kang Youwei and Tan Sitong—to the equally comprehensive cosmology of Chen Duxiu's Marxism was comparatively easy, because the cultural distance from one monistic worldview to the other was short, despite the latter's iconoclasm. Because of the totalism of this resulting cosmological philosophy, the call to political action was more powerful and the kinds of action necessary were more radical. By contrast, the empirical scientism of Hu Shi and Ding Wenjiang and its emphasis on science's method inspired a greater skepticism, and so inspired an experimentalist approach to problem-solving and a liberal pragmatism in politics. Nevertheless, Hu and Ding both sought and found roots in tradition—in the logical methods of Warring States period philosophers and early Qing Confucian empiricism—for their outlooks.

Neither of these varieties of scientism was present in the outlooks of the 1980s scientific liberals, perhaps with the exception of Jin Guantao. Xu Liangying, Fang Lizhi, Li Xingmin and the others, to be sure, relentlessly turned their science on what they regarded as Marxist superstition and obscurantism. In this spirit they often felt in their confrontations with Marxist theoreticians such as Zha Ruqiang a kinship with Western scientists who had struggled against Christian dogma. But in their attacks they stopped short of the full-fledged positivism at the heart of both varieties of May Fourth scientism. While they attached a prime value to reason in political affairs and in understanding society, they were careful to insist that rationalism is not the preserve of science alone, but is one of its cardinal elements. Their critique of culture and politics derived not from a scientistic impulse to extend the theories and methods of science into those realms—whose segregation from science they were, on the contrary, anxious to defend—but from their belief that some cultural values and political contexts facilitate science's autonomy, health, and progress, while others (specifically those of Marxism-Leninism as practiced in China) hinder them.

They appealed to a pluralism of epistemology, method, and values that requires tolerance, competition, and collaboration. Fang Lizhi, for example, frequently pointed to what he believed were differences in method between science and culture, but in the same breath he stressed their interconnections in the realm of underlying values. Art and physics, he said in 1988, seek common humanistic values but use different languages and approaches:

> Was Leonardo an artist? Or was he a scientist? It seems perhaps that he was neither, that both science and art were simply methods he employed in a more unified search for truth and beauty. With regard to what each one strives for and sets store by, science and art are in many ways indistinguishable. Art seeks beauty, and so does science. Art and science both advocate truth, and creation, and liberation from bondage; they esteem the works of nature and of humanity, and they also esteem that which transcends both nature and humanity.[29]

Religion and science cannot be mixed, he argued repeatedly, pointing to the long struggle in the West for the independence of science from the authority of Christianity. But religion, he has also suggested, shares important interconnections with science, and the two have coexisted productively in the West: "If one looks carefully at the construction of scientific theories, it is evident that collaboration and interaction among the various components of human civilization, including science and religion, are both necessary and important."[30]

The critical connection between science on one hand and culture, religion, and politics on the other is values they share. In a real sense, in Fang's view, cultural values transcend science. Culture and religion are important because they provide the intellectual outlook and posture generally and the predilections and assumptions specifically with which scientists begin. The most important of these to science, Fang stated repeatedly, is the presupposition that the natural world can be understood at all. The idea that the universe is intelligible, Fang suggested, is not a scientific idea but a cultural assumption, and one that was critical in the genesis of scientific attitudes in the West, but not developed in traditional China.[31] The crucial issues for Fang were thus which cultural values and outlooks and which political institutions and beliefs promote the autonomy of the scientific community and its work, and which do not.

Cautious as they were about the limits of science, still less did the liberal scientists such as Fang and Xu espouse the materialist variety of scientism, using the substance of science as the basis for grand organic theories linking human affairs and the natural world. While interested in quantum gravity and other problems at the heart of the quest for grand unification theories (sometimes called "theories of everything") in physics, for example, Fang explicitly ruled out the possibility of grand philosophical theories that subsume science and all other aspects of existence. The implication for him was that grand unification theories in physics are still just theories of physics, not theories of truly everything.

The closest that any of the liberal scientists discussed in this study come to a scientism of either variety may be found in Jin Guantao's explorations of the use of cybernetics and systems theory in analyzing China's traditional past and other questions. But Jin in the 1980s was also intent on exploring the subjective foundations of reason, and in this and in other respects, his scientism seems akin to the empirical rather than the materialist variety.

Xu Liangying, for his part, has explicitly rejected scientism. In a 1992 article in the Bulletin of Natural Dialectics building on the work of Western scholars such as Danny W. Y. Kwok and Charlotte Furth, he scathingly rebutted arguments that scientism had deformed the outlook of Chinese scientists since the May Fourth period.[32] Finding Kwok's definitions of two varieties of scientism confusing and vague,

Xu adopted the two alternative senses of "scientism" from *Webster's International Dictionary:* "the methods, mental attitude, doctrines, or modes of expression characteristic or held to be characteristic of scientists" and the view that "the methods of the natural sciences should be used in all areas of investigation, including philosophy, the humanities, and social sciences" so that "only such methods can fruitfully be used in the pursuit of knowledge." The first definition, Xu believed, was just the ordinary sense of what is called "the spirit of science" and so was unobjectionable. The second, he stated, was not commonly held in China's science community. "Because science demands that all theories and conclusions be tested in experience, each of the various sciences has its own particular objects of research, and so the methods applied and the knowledge gained cannot be unconditionally extended indefinitely." There are instances, Xu noted, where methods used in the natural sciences can be used in other areas, such as statistics in the social sciences and mathematics in economics, but such methods are not the sole property of the natural sciences.

As for the May Fourth period, Xu argued, influential scientists did advocate "using science to save the nation," but none advocated that "only science could save the nation." He added that Marxism may be scientistic theory, but almost no scientists turned to Marxism in the May Fourth period. The only exception, he said, was CCP cofounder Zhang Shenfu, but Zhang's Marxism was anything but orthodox, and in any case Zhang left the Party in 1925. Among May Fourth scientists whose "scientism" Kwok examines—Ding Wenjiang, Wang Xinggong, Tang Yue, and Ren Hongjun—none embraced Marxism. Only in the 1930s and 1940s, Xu recalled, did scientists turn to Marxism, and then only after accepting the CCP on political and patriotic grounds, not intellectual ones.[33]

Though liberal scientists such as Fang Lizhi and Xu Liangying did not espouse scientistic ideas, there were clear expressions of scientism on the Chinese intellectual scene in the 1980s. Perhaps the foremost of these were the reconstructed natural dialectics of Fang's and Xu's antagonist Zha Ruqiang and his supporters (such as He Zuoxiu), and the technocratic views of Qian Xuesen, typified by his efforts to extend systems theory, cybernetics, and information theory into leadership decision making. In particular, Zha's concerted attempt in the 1980s to recast natural dialectics on the basis of contemporary science reflected a full-fledged "materialist scientism" consistent with the monistic cosmology of traditional Marxism-Leninism it sought to shore up. Both Zha Ruqiang on one hand and Fang and Xu on the other denounced the obscurantist views toward science of the Maoist period, but their respective approaches to modern scientific theory were radically different beyond that point, as the science and philosophy debates show. There is a certain irony, therefore, in the reversal of positions in those debates as compared to the 1923 debates on science and metaphysics (though the comparison is not really apt, given the difference in public attention each debate received).[34] In the latter debates, Chen Duxiu, Hu Shi, and Ding Wenjiang all praised science as the centerpiece of modernity and a truly modern worldview, and they dismissed as "metaphysics" the skepticism of Zhang Junmai and others toward science as a source of values. In the mid-1980s Fang, Xu, and the other liberal scientists combatted the scientism of Zha Ruqiang. Criticizing his reconstructed Marxist-Leninist cosmology as "metaphysics," they insisted on the autonomy of science and defended a limited view of the range of science. (There is the further, curious irony that Hu Shi, in his relentless positivistic use of science against superstition and metaphysical speculation, defended the view that the universe must be infinite in extent.[35])

From the longer perspective of twentieth-century history, the divorce of science from scientism reflected in the altered stances in 1923 and the 1980s is a consequence of the institutionalization of professional science in modern China. As sociologist of science Joseph Ben-David has shown, scientific communities in the early stages of institutionalization in the still-traditional contexts of seventeenth-century England and eighteenth-century France sympathized and found common ground with secularizing scientistic movements among nonscientific intellectuals. Once established, however, the speculative excesses and imprecisions of the scientistic movements became a potential embarrassment and threat to the standing of the science communities, which therefore distanced themselves from scientism by retreating into a value-free or value-neutral posture.[36] The pattern of interaction in the May Fourth era, when natural scientists labored to establish their profession, followed by a steadily widening distancing thereafter—starting with the professionalization of science under the Nationalists, aggravated by the scientistic attacks on scientific professionalism under Mao, and then furthered by the promotion of scientific professionalism under Deng— suggests a similar course in twentieth-century China.

LIBERALISM IN PERSPECTIVE

Liberalism has had a difficult history in China. The ground for it to take root was prepared with the decline of the traditional late-imperial state in the eighteenth and nineteenth centuries.[37] Extraordinary demographic growth in the middle Qing period and the dramatic economic developments since the late Ming era that preceded and enabled such growth were accompanied by fundamental changes in society, especially in urban areas, and consequently in society's relationship with the state. Over the last century of Qing rule, social developments rapidly outgrew the ability of the state to keep pace. The reach of the state into local society, limited as it was even in earlier times, was further attenuated. In the opening space between the increasingly enfeebled imperial system and local society, new local elites asserted themselves, sharing and competing for power over affairs in the society around them and establishing a public sphere of discourse on the issues of local polity. From this perspective, the 1911 Revolution can be viewed as the outcome of a steady process of erosion of imperial authority by local and regional elites in a rapidly changing "early modern" society.

Meanwhile, a slow but steady process of state-building began in the post-Taiping period with the reconstruction and reform of the Tongzhi Restoration. While the central imperial authority withered, a pattern of reconstituting local government began that laid the foundations for the Nationalist regime's attempt after 1928 to reintegrate China with a much longer reach into local society. In turn, the recentralizing ambitions of the Nationalists—never fully realized for several reasons, including the Sino-Japanese War—were taken to unimagined extremes by the communist regime after 1949.

Political liberalism flared briefly in the interstice between the emergence of assertive local elites and an incipient public sphere on one hand and the process of state-building on the other, and in the tides of Western ideas that washed into the intellectual debates and political discourse of the first decades of this century. Its most vivid expression was

in the attempts of young intellectuals of the New Culture and enlightenment movements of the May Fourth period to recast China's political
culture along lines based on critical reason and individual conscience,
banishing what they perceived to have been the suffocating subordination of the individual to family and society by traditional Confucian
morality and superstition. As Vera Schwarcz's sensitive dissection of
this movement shows, the priorities these intellectuals attached to individual enlightenment (*qimeng*) were continually confronted with the
imperatives of national salvation (*jiuguo*)—China's survival in a hostile
international setting.[38]

   In the end, liberalism foundered. Political movements built on
subordination of the individual to the collective causes of national unity
and salvation—both Nationalist and Communist—commanded the allegiances of the day and smothered political causes based on the assertion and protection of individual rights and conscience. The conflicts
confronted by Xu Liangying, a generation younger than the liberal enlightenment intellectuals, vividly replayed this tension of competing
ideals—in his case those of "science and democracy" on one hand and
nationalist allegiance to the communist movement on the other—with
the same outcome.

   Like Xu Liangying, the liberal scientists younger than he—including Fang Lizhi and Li Xingmin—shared values and goals with their New
Culture movement predecessors. Neither group explicitly called itself
"liberal," but both shared commitments to the dignity of individual
conscience and so to the fundamental rights emphasized by classical
liberals (such as freedom of expression, assembly, and the press) and to
democratic politics. Both focused on the importance of changing their
surrounding political culture through education and free speech, raising
political awareness, and inculcating the critical attitudes necessary for
citizens to assert their rights. Both shared a preference for gradual,
piecemeal change addressing specific issues and problems rather than
comprehensive programs for radical change.

   But within these generally congruent commitments and preferences, there were significant differences in orientation and emphasis
whose origins and causes are not hard to discern.[39] Liberals in the 1920s
confronted a weak state, the legitimacy and eviscerated Republican ma-
chinery of which military strongmen vied to capture in a dangerous

international setting. The intellectuals of the period were transitional figures. Their professions and social identities were yet to be firmly established in a rapidly changing but still predominantly traditional society. Despite their modern, often Western, educations, they retained elements of the outlook of the traditional gentry elite from which most of them had sprung.

The liberals of the New Culture movement consequently espoused a liberalism whose ideals were diluted by pressures to respond patriotically to the urgency of national survival and whose focus was diffused by the political and social limitations of the period. Their defense of individualism centered less on intrusions of state power into the private preserves of individual rights, real as they were on occasion, than on social and cultural traditions that were perceived to weigh down an ignorant and unawakened populace. Their advocacy of individualism and their support for the prerogatives and institutions of liberal democracy were blunted by the centripetal obligations they felt to society and nation. They viewed democracy and enlightened citizens as useful for overall national strength and state-building in a context of weak republican politics and international security, not so much as the conditions best suited to pursuit of individual freedom and pursuit of happiness. The cosmopolitan cultural outlook of New Culture movement intellectuals such as Hu Shi lessened the appeal of their liberal political views among other social groups who shared a similar political agenda but whose nationalism and self-interest against the Western economic presence was offended by the intellectuals' call for "pan-Westernization."[40] While advancing their cause, the liberal intellectuals posited a particular role for themselves reminiscent of the elite role that the traditional Confucian orthodoxy assigned to the scholar officials.

The views and attitudes of Ding Wenjiang, the most famous scientist among the New Culture liberals, illustrate many of these tendencies. Ding's rebuttal of Zhang Junmai's attacks on science as a source of values in the 1923 science and metaphysics debate placed him solidly among the New Culture critics. So did his writing and editing for the liberal reformist journal *Endeavor* in 1923, and again in the equally liberal journal *Independent Critic* (Duli pinglun) in the 1930s. But throughout his professional career and involvement in politics, Ding showed a traditional preference for elitist leadership by intellectuals and a predilection for technocratic solutions over mass politics. He also was ready to sacrifice liberal ideals to the efficiencies of authoritarianism when, as in the 1930s after a trip to the USSR and in the face of the mounting Japanese threat to China, he perceived that a higher national good demanded it.[41]

The orientation and emphases of the political outlook of the liberal scientists of the 1980s were quite different, sharing few of the specific tendencies and stresses that colored the liberalism of the New Culture movement intellectuals. These divergences, again, derive from the enormous difference in social and political context they faced. In the 1980s the liberal scientists confronted a weakened and retreating but still ominously powerful state that retained the means, if it chose to use them, to blunt their attempts to publicize political views, to pulverize whatever organizational structures they tried to establish, and to overwhelm whatever public space they sought to defend. Socially, the scientists worked within a scientific community that now had deep, well-established roots in Chinese society and within a scientific profession that the regime itself had sought to shore up. The strength of the state, whose values they challenged, and the norms of the scientific community, on which they based their own liberal values, gave the outlook of the scientist liberals an unrelenting focus on the defense of individual rights and liberties against encroachment by the state that is different from that of 1920s liberalism.

The most abundant evidence of the emphases and orientation of the liberal scientists' views is in the extensive speeches, writings, and public comments of Fang Lizhi after 1986, but the same disposition is also evident in the writings of Xu Liangying, Li Xingmin, and the others. Fang's emphasis on human rights and individual liberty was the hallmark theme to which he returned again and again in his public statements. Such rights and liberties, he argued tirelessly, are not "bestowed" by the state—to ask the state to grant them betrays a "feudalistic" subservience to state power. They reside irrevocably in the individual citizen. Democracy, he insisted, is "built from the bottom up" on the basis of individuals possessing inherent rights of political viewpoint and action and inherent freedoms to realize their own potentials.[42]

Fang's defense of pluralism in science and in the structure of knowledge against scientistic monism extended directly into politics, where he repeatedly defended not only the inevitability but also the desirability of conflict and competition among individual viewpoints. Democracy in Fang's view is not valuable instrumentally, as a means of mobilizing a nation's people behind national causes, but as a mechanism for refereeing political differences. Taking blunt issue with the view of a National People's Congress delegate that unanimity and consensus— reflected in a People's Congress vote of 3,000 to 0—is better than the dissension registered in Western parliamentary votes of 51 to 49, Fang retorted that the delegate "knows nothing about democracy or politics in general":

> This viewpoint betrays utter ignorance of what democracy is about. Under democracy, groups of people from different nationalities and occupations and conditions of life come together to work out a balance between their diverse needs and interests. It is only when votes are not unanimous that the system is working! The vote in Western parliaments is indeed quite often 51 to 49, and this forces members to work cautiously and avoid mistakes. It also shows how much support or opposition there is for different measures, so that different sides can get together and negotiate a realistic balance. Votes of 3,000 to 0 suggest that everyone is happy, that an impossible ideal has been achieved.[43]

The state exists, Fang argued, not simply to spur the economic growth of the nation—the predominating theme of the Dengist reforms—but also to guarantee the rights of its citizens and promote their welfare and enlightenment through education. Xu Liangying also put this view forward with particular force in 1992 in a blatantly provocative and sarcastic article predicting that the upsurge of economic reform following Deng Xiaoping's tour of Shenzhen and Guangzhou would fail without steps to establish "political democracy." Xu scathingly criticized as misguided the blind enthusiasm for business and focus on economic growth that Deng's southern tour authorized and that were rationalized by reference to the dramatic economic progress of the "four little dragons" in East Asia under authoritarian political systems. Perhaps a more valid comparison, Xu suggested sarcastically, was with Hitler's Third Reich, which saw double-digit economic growth in the 1930s under Nazi "socialism."[44]

Nor did the pronouncements of Fang, Xu, and the others carry the elitist and technocratic undertones that colored the outlook of the May Fourth liberals. In deriding the mistreatment that intellectuals suffered under Mao, Fang used the argument widely discussed in China in the 1980s that work becomes increasingly intellectual as societies modernize, that workers must therefore acquire and use more mental skills than manual ones, and that intellectuals increasingly come to the forefront of social and material progress. But in doing so he cautioned strictly against constructing political hierarchies based on class, a mistaken approach of the Maoist past. Fang also lamented the obstacles to instilling democracy amid the ignorance and subservient attitudes found in rural China. But in the same breath he attacked "feudalistic" attitudes pervasive among intellectuals, ridiculing their unquestioning readiness to serve political authority and their uncritical mouthing of the official Party line.[45]

The divergent emphases and orientations, within an overall shared liberalism, between the New Culture movement intellectuals and the liberal scientists of the 1980s are understandable in terms of the political contexts they faced and the social conditions from which they emerged. But there remains another difference that is significant. Most of the intellectuals of the May Fourth era acquired their liberalism abroad, as a component of education in the United States, Britain, and elsewhere in the West, and imported it to a Chinese context not well suited for it to take root. None of the liberal scientists of the 1980s was educated abroad, nor did any travel outside China until the Deng years. Their liberalism grew directly out of the seemingly uncongenial soil of Chinese communism, as a response to conditions that made it difficult for science to prosper and contribute to wider society. In this respect, the pessimistic observation of Y. C. Wang that the professionalization of science under the Nationalist regime led scientists increasingly to stay out of the politics of their day and so may have diminished prospects for liberal democracy in China may be premature.[46]

THE LIBERAL SCIENTISTS
IN CONTEMPORARY PERSPECTIVE

Liberal scientists such as Xu Liangying and Fang Lizhi found common cause with other critical and dissident intellectuals who espoused a liberal political viewpoint, as linkages among those signing the open letters of January and February 1989 showed. The 16 February 1989 open letter, written in support of Fang Lizhi's letter to Deng Xiaoping calling for the release of political prisoners and signed by thirty-three literary and social science intellectuals, reflected the spectrum of divergent and sometimes clashing intellectual views that enlivened the mid-1980s debates on politics and culture. Among the signers were "new Confucians" Tang Yijie and Pang Pu, pathbreaking philosopher Li Zehou, and *Heshang* coauthor/producer Su Xiaokang. Also signing was Bao Zunxin, a CASS Institute of History researcher, editor of the eclectic journal of criticism *Reading Books* (Dushu), and collaborator with Jin Guantao in editing the "Toward the Future" book series. There also was Su Shaozhi, formerly Yu Guangyuan's deputy in establishing the CASS Institute of Marxism-Leninism and successor as Institute director until his removal as a casualty of the 1987 campaign against "bourgeois liberalization"; and Wang Ruoshui, the humanist philosopher purged as *People's Daily* editor in the 1983 campaign against "spiritual pollution." Joining them from the natural sciences establishment was Jin Guantao, assistant editor of the *Bulletin of Natural Dialectics*, editor of "Toward the Future," and collaborator in the production of *Heshang*.

The 26 February open letter, organized by Xu Liangying and drawn on CAS stationery, drew its forty-two signers mainly from the ranks of natural sciences but included telling crossovers from the social sciences. Joining the natural scientists were Yu Haocheng and Li Honglin, perhaps the foremost exponents—excepting Yan Jiaqi—of liberalizing legal and political philosophy of the post-Mao period. Historian Bao Zunxin, who had already signed the letter of the 16th, also signed Xu's letter. Xu Liangying asked Su Shaozhi to sign, but Su, having signed the letter of the 16th, declined, believing that multiple letters signed by the same individuals would defeat their common purposes.[47] His associate from the Institute of Marxism–Leninism–Mao Zedong Thought, Zhang Xianyang, did sign Xu's letter, however.

These collaborations in acts of public agitation built on a common liberalism—in very general terms, with some important differences in orientation and emphasis—in politics. In some cases, the liberalism that the scientist dissidents found in common with their colleagues in the humanities and social sciences drew on congruent attitudes toward specific political problems and on previous collaborations in the intellectual arena over the previous decade of reform. In other cases, their common liberalism in politics superseded significant differences in intellectual viewpoint.

The humanistic outlook of the liberal scientists, for example, converged with the humanism espoused by Party philosopher Wang Ruoshui since the beginning of the reform era, though it derived from somewhat different experiences and concerns. Wang Ruoshui's humanism emerged as the central component of his evolving critique of Party ideology over three decades of work in the Party's propaganda and ideology system.[48] It focused on and derived force from the tremendous mistakes in Party leadership under Mao—and especially the personality cult around Mao and the inhumane excesses and brutalities it led to in the Cultural Revolution. For Wang, humanism, especially as reflected in the earlier works of Marx as well as ideas from the French and German enlightenments, offered the best possibility of reconstructing a Marxism that would blunt the amoral determinism of the past. The humanistic orientation of Xu Liangying and Fang Lizhi undoubtedly also derived in part from their experience of and reflections on the brutalities of politics under Mao, but a more fundamental source was their understanding of the enterprise of science. As their writings repeatedly attested, however undeniably important science may be as a technological boon to society, it is essentially a humanistic undertaking because it illuminates humanity's place in the natural cosmos. In doing so, it underscores our species' uniqueness and so helps provide meaning and value to human life.[49]

The epistemological pluralism of the liberal scientists—their insistence on a pluralist structure of knowledge that set them apart from the monistic ambitions of Zha Ruqiang's and He Zuoxiu's defense of Marxist philosophy's "guiding role" in all fields of knowledge—had parallels among other critical and dissident intellectuals. Ironically, their views on the narrow question of the structure of knowledge verged closely on those of postmodernist philosophers such as Gan Yang. Gan derived his views from his reading of continental philosophers such as Gilles Deleuze, Michel Foucault, and Paul Ricoeur and of Anglo-American political philosophers such as Isaiah Berlin and John Rawls. For Gan, the pursuit of single, comprehensive systems of truth by intellectuals leads inevitably to a monism of values that tolerates only one standard of what is true, beautiful, or good to the exclusion of all approaches. When entangled in politics, such monistic claims lead to suppression of alternative paths to truth and value and to instrumentalist, utilitarian, technocratic authoritarianism aided by intellectuals who claim to speak for the common good. For this reason, Gan has been skeptical of the May Fourth linkage of "science and democracy," arguing that the complicity of intellectuals in the mistakes and inhumanities of CCP rule since the founding of the PRC stemmed from their uncritical acceptance of the implicit linkage of knowledge and power in this slogan. He has also been extremely critical both of liberal intellectuals—such as Li Zehou—who have put forward new philosophical syntheses and of the technocratic "neoauthoritarianism" espoused by some reform intellectuals of the late 1980s.[50] On this basis, Gan advocated a highly individualistic liberalism built on a pluralist approach to knowledge and values that the scientist liberals might accept, even if they clearly disagreed with his evaluation of the May Fourth spirit.

The political views of the liberal scientists also converged very closely with those of other liberal intellectuals, such as Li Honglin and Yu Haocheng, who signed Xu Liangying's open letter, and Yan Jiaqi, who signed neither the letter of the 16th nor Xu's. Li Honglin's liberalism figured constantly in his writings on political reform since the beginning of the Deng period, a forthrightness that repeatedly got him into political difficulty during moments when conservative Party influences were ascendant. Like those of other social scientists, Li's liberal political views appeared to derive from his reflections on the sources of the political disasters of the Mao era, whose recurrence he believed could be prevented through democratization and adherence to law. Li, along with Yu and Yan, thus spoke for a major strand of opinion in the Deng era calling for political reform on grounds of repairing a socialist system that was flawed at its institutional and procedural foundations and that provided no barrier to the tragic disasters of the past.[51] Throughout the 1980s this strand of liberal political reform opinion competed with and was frequently shunted aside by another political reform line, reflected in the administrative reforms undertaken by Zhao Ziyang, which held that the socialist political system was fundamentally sound, requiring only adjustments to accommodate and facilitate reforms in the economic system.

As much as Fang Lizhi and Xu Liangying agreed with the political views of Li and Yu, their liberalism, as with Wang Ruoshui's humanism, derived from a different source. Similarly, they shared much in common with Yan Jiaqi's liberal political views—which in some ways arose from parallel scientific backgrounds—but they differed from Yan in significant respects. Having studied mathematics and theoretical physics as an undergraduate at Chinese Science and Technology University and enrolled in 1964 as a graduate student studying natural dialectics with Yu Guangyuan in the CAS Institute of Philosophy, Yan was in some sense a wayward member of Yu's natural dialectics family. Yan emerged from the Cultural Revolution bent on studying, with Yu's blessing, political science. Probably with Yu's support, Yan became the founding director of the CASS Institute of Political Science, and from that position authored numerous articles advocating democratizing political reform.[52] In his advocacy of such reforms and fundamental human rights, Yan put forward views largely congruent with those of the liberal scientists he left behind in his move into the social sciences. But what he did not share with the liberal scientists was his strong scientism, manifested in his firm belief that science would emerge as the unifying ideology of the future. This was expressed clearly in his views on the range of the methods of science. All phenomena, natural and social, he declared, can be understood only through science's methods of discovering "the laws that govern them." All problems that humanity confronts can be addressed by its methods, he suggested, arguing that science is "the wellspring of human optimism."[53] Despite the congruence of the views of Fang Lizhi and Xu Liangying with those of Yan on liberal politics and on the social context that science promotes and also requires, one searches their writings in vain for statements displaying this degree of positivist optimism in science.

The views reflected in the open letters of January and February 1989 thus show a broad convergence on political issues built on perspectives on intellectual and moral issues that were sometimes similar and sometimes not. Liberal scientists such as Fang and Xu could find common political ground in the crisis of 1988–89 with "new Confucians" such as Tang Yijie and Pang Pu even though they disagreed profoundly on cultural grounds. They shared similar liberal political visions with Li Honglin and Yu Haocheng even though Li and Yu arrived at their liberalism along different routes. They could act in concert with social science intellectuals and philosophers on political issues even though they did not share the scientism of Yan Jiaqi or the residual totalism implicit in the views of Wang Ruoshui and Li Zehou. In some previous arenas and contexts, the views of each intellectual grouping had influenced the others. Jin Guantao's explorations of the "stagnation" in China's pattern of development historically had helped stimulate "culture fever" debates in the social sciences. Li Zehou's explorations of subjectivity had indirectly spurred debates on the subjective implications of quantum mechanics in the natural sciences arena. In other contexts they had taken issue with each other's viewpoint—as Xu had in attacking the resurgence of Confucian ideas earlier in the decade. There were thus many routes to liberal—or, in some instances, liberalizing—politics among the critical intellectuals in post-Mao China. The liberal scientists arrived at their political views along one such distinct path, which gave their liberalism a particular emphasis and, in some ways, a clarity and sharpness different from those arriving along other, equally distinctive routes.

Like all of their allies among the critical intellectuals, the liberal scientists, as suggested before, were marginal figures in the political arena of their day—marginal not in impact, but in terms of their location at the narrow margins between political legitimacy and dissent. For the critical intellectuals from the social sciences and humanities, this marginality was the natural consequence of working in academic fields that were still explicitly politicized. Despite the latitude authorized in establishing previously banished disciplines, the Deng regime never renounced the view that the social sciences still retained a class bias. Philosophy was still Marxist (proletarian) philosophy or else it was philosophy that served other (reactionary) class interests. Intellectuals working in such fields therefore could work to press outward the limits of what was legitimate only at the risk of sometimes finding themselves beyond the pale, in the realm of dissent and potential political disgrace, depending on the larger political climate in which they worked.

The marginality of the scientist liberals was different. The natural sciences were declared by Deng Xiaoping himself in 1978 to be devoid of class content, and so no ideological significance automatically attached to their work. Most of the liberal scientists came from theoretical physics and the history and philosophy of science, disciplines that are marginal in a different sense. Of all the fields of physics, cosmology—Fang's field—is one of the most marginal. Built up out of hypotheses resting on only a small, laboriously derived body of empirical evidence, it is a field that acquired scientific standing only in the middle decades of this century and that remains rich in theoretical speculation and poor in practical consequence. In a nation struggling to modernize and in the eyes of a regime that understood science in terms of technological applications, cosmology was a luxury. Similarly, philosophers and historians of science may be thought of as "metascientists," intellectuals who attempt to draw systematic conclusions about how science works and why. These disciplines, too, may have seemed marginal in significance.

But Fang the cosmologist and Xu the physicist and historian of science were not marginal figures among critical intellectuals. The marginality of their disciplines made them particularly sensitive to the norms and ideals of the scientific community, and in turn disposed toward their distinct pathway into politics in the public arena. Because of the marginality of their disciplines, their views may not have been typical of other groups in China's science community, although the degree of sympathy or antipathy other scientists felt toward their views would be extremely difficult to establish under the circumstances.

Once in the larger public arena, however, they were not marginal figures among the critical intellectuals from other disciplines. Their views carried the authority of hard science. Their congruent views on political affairs were attractive to social scientists who had also been reading translations of Popper's *The Open Society and Its Enemies*, Kuhn's *The Structure of Scientific Revolutions*, and other Western books of philosophy and history of science for new avenues of criticism in their own fields. Students eager to break out of the stultifying confines of text-

books still infused with Marxist-Leninist frameworks found the iconoclastic attacks of Fang Lizhi on Marxist platitudes in the name of science
electrifying.[54]

To the Deng regime, the liberal scientists' political views were
particularly threatening because of the hardness of their liberal critique and the authority they brought to bear as scientists. The scientists'
linkage of intellectual pluralism to political pluralism left the regime
the problem of discrediting their political views but not their science.
In dealing with critical intellectuals from fields other than the natural
sciences, the regime could discredit both, but it could not do so with
dissident scientists—at least not without intolerable cost to its assur-
ances of the apolitical nature of science itself. After his purge from the
Party in the criticism of "bourgeois liberalization" in 1987, Su Shaozhi was prevented from publishing altogether. By contrast, the regime
went to great lengths to publicize Fang Lizhi's continuing productivity
within his scientific specialty, even while it strove to suppress his views
on politics. By the same token, even after Su's access to avenues of publication in state-controlled domestic media was restored in 1988, once
the political winds shifted again, Fang's voice could be heard only on
narrow issues of science.[55]

THE RELEVANCE OF THE SOVIET EXPERIENCE

Though many early analyses of Chinese intellectual dissidence and
social change in the wake of the Tiananmen demonstrations have sought
parallels in the experiences of intellectuals and the evolution of civil
society before the 1989 revolutions in Eastern Europe, the emergence
of scientific dissent in the USSR is a more apt point of departure in the
case of the Chinese scientific dissidents. Here, the most relevant comparison is not with the concurrent era of Gorbachev's leadership in the
1980s, but rather with the Khrushchev and early Brezhnev periods in
the 1950s and 1960s, with the emergence of the "thaw generation" as a
force in Soviet political life. A cursory examination of the circumstances
surrounding Soviet scientific dissidence and a brief review of its place
in the spectrum of emergent Soviet dissent will reveal some striking
parallels and suggestive contrasts.

Many of the major political and ideological changes introduced under Khrushchev's leadership prefigured changes in the same areas by Deng Xiaoping in China after 1976. The defining political event of Khrushchev's period, of course, was the de-Stalinization campaign inaugurated by his secret speech delivered to the Twentieth CPSU Congress in February 1956, anticipating the critique of Mao Zedong's leadership launched by Deng Xiaoping two decades later. The ideological thrust of Khrushchev's denunciation of Stalin's errors—the exaggeration of class struggle, manifested in the great purges of the 1930s and late 1940s—prefigured Deng's criticism of Mao and the Cultural Revolution on the same grounds, encapsulated in the CCP's 1981 resolution on CCP history. On the basis of his critique of Stalin, Khrushchev decisively reoriented the focus of the CPSU's work from class struggle to "building socialism," a theme reflected in Soviet foreign policy in the approach of "peaceful coexistence" with the West and in domestic affairs with the designation of the CPSU as a "party of the whole people" and the USSR as a "state of the whole people." The incorporation of these revisions into the 1961 Party program, as Richard Lowenthal has observed, marked the USSR's entry into a "postrevolutionary phase." China entered the same stage at the watershed Third Plenum in 1978 when Deng Xiaoping made class warfare only a secondary priority of the Party, after "developing the forces of production" and socialist modernization.[56]

The implications of these political changes for Soviet science were far-reaching, as were the corresponding changes in China later. The designation of science and technology as a "force of production" was incorporated into the 1961 Party program, a characterization that Deng Xiaoping enunciated in China in his 1978 science conference speech. With this came the abandonment of Soviet "exceptionalism" in science—the attempt to establish a distinctly "Soviet" science that bore the class characteristics of socialism, altogether different from the "bourgeois science" of the West. This meant acknowledgment of the universalism of science. In turn, this recognition opened the way not only for the rehabilitation of Russian scientific achievements, whatever the political views of the particular scientist before the Bolshevik Revolution; it also permitted, in principle if not outright practice, collaboration with scientists working under differing social systems in the capitalist West.[57]

These changes in ideological formulation with respect to science accompanied a general relaxation in Party supervision of science, aimed at enhancing the technological impact of the Soviet science establishment. In March 1956, a month after the Twentieth CPSU Congress, direction of science was split off from the Secretariat's Propaganda Department and placed under a new Science and Culture Department (all-Union) and Sciences, Schools, and Culture Department of the Russian Soviet Federated Socialist Republic (RSFSR).[58] In 1961 the government agency supervising applied research was replaced by a more powerful State Committee for the Coordination of Scientific Research in order to plan research and development more efficiently in step with overall national priorities.[59] At the same time, the Academy of Sciences began a major devolution of applied science institutes out from under its wing and into new regional centers.[60] Under the prevailing production ethos of the Party and state under Khrushchev, as Stephen Fortescu has observed, the ideological values associated with "party spirit" (*partiinost'*) gave way to the production-driven demands of "collectiveness" (*kollektivnost'*).[61] The parallels with the reorientation of science in China in the Deng period are striking.

Though Khrushchev still supported Lysenko's views on genetics, the period saw a general retreat from the politicized approaches to scientific theory during the Zhdanov reign over ideology in the Stalin period. In Soviet debates on science and philosophy, the "epistemologists," those who argued that Soviet philosophy of science should concentrate on questions of method and cognition, steadily triumphed over the "ontologists," those who argued that Marxist philosophy offered the most general framework for scientific analysis of both society and nature.[62] Arguments for a natural dialectics discipline withered in the face of efforts to establish distinct philosophy of science and "science of science" disciplines. Soviet scientists worked to establish disciplines that had been neglected or prohibited outright under the Stalin regime.[63]

The political atmosphere and so the overall direction of Soviet science policies changed with the removal of Khrushchev in October 1964 and the ascendancy of the Brezhnev leadership coalition. The coup against Khrushchev finally ended Lysenko's influence in Soviet biology. But the technocratic orientation of the new leadership manifested itself in impatience with the poor direction of science and the science community's perceived continuing unresponsiveness to the technological needs of Soviet economic development, and with emerging dissident pressures for an even broader liberalization and extension of professional autonomy.

The subsequent reimposition of political controls over Soviet science seems to bear out David Joravsky's maxim that the primary focus of leadership concern for science was always on its relationship and contribution to economic productivity, and not on the compatibility of scientific theories with the tenets of Marxist philosophy. If a given scientific sector was perceived as collaborating productively in technological improvements in the economy, the leadership historically did not tolerate political intrusions into the scientific community by the Party's ideological apparatus; when the scientists were deemed uncooperative and deficient in the production arena, the way was open for political interference.[64]

The new leadership tried different strategies over the next few years to improve the responsiveness of the scientific community to the technological needs of Soviet economic development, first in the Kosygin reform period and then in the following period of Brezhnev's engagement of the issue. The expansion of professional autonomy tolerated under Khrushchev was eventually curtailed in the late 1960s.[65] Gradually the Party presence in scientific institutions increased, and the Twenty-Fourth CPSU Congress in 1971 gave primary Party organizations in research organs overall supervisory responsibility for work in their units. Though the leadership permitted no resurgence of attacks on the validity of specific scientific disciplines, as had occurred under Stalin and Zhdanov, the political attitudes of scientists were subject to increased scrutiny. By the late 1960s and early 1970s, the Party journal *Kommunist* was criticizing resurgent "bourgeois" attitudes among many scientists on issues of professionalism and increasingly "humanist" and "liberal" outlooks among them.[66]

Viewed as a whole, the Khrushchev and early Brezhnev periods contained clear parallels with subsequent events in China, but also differed in some ways from the pattern of changes in China after Mao's death. The Soviet scientific community remained relatively isolated internationally, not so much because of enduring ideological dictates in favor of Soviet exceptionalism in science, but because of prevailing East-West tensions that inhibited collaboration. In contrast, China's scientific community developed extensive contacts with the international science community in the Deng period because the international political environment favored such activities. Further, even before Stalin's death some areas of Soviet science had successfully defended themselves against or thrown off the politicized agenda of the Zhdanov period. An initial round of Zhdanovite attacks on the views on quantum mechanics of Academy of Sciences Institute of Physics researcher M. A. Markov in 1948, for example, was followed by a successful defense of conventional interpretations of the theory by scientists who used the tenets of Marxist philosophy to their own advantage.[67] In China the overthrow of Zhdanovite interpretations was wholly a post-Mao affair. Nevertheless, the broad Soviet-Chinese parallels seem clear enough, and the resulting pressures on scientists' professional and political lives were—in general, at least—similar.

The emergence and evolving orientation and tactics of Soviet scientific dissent are explicable within the broad trends in politics and science policy outlined above, and here, too, the parallels with China are suggestive. Some of the differences are also illuminating. Zhores Medvedev attributes the emergence of scientific dissidence specifically to Khrushchev's denunciation of Stalin in 1956, his efforts to establish the administration of justice according to law, and the ensuing liberalization in intellectual climate.[68] Early dissent appeared primarily among younger scientists who, aghast at the revelations of Stalin's terror, began to agitate for a broader criticism of Stalinism and for more extensive democratizing change. They criticized continuing ideological intrusions into science, such as Lysenko's influence in genetics, and as the Khrushchev liberalization proceeded, they pressed for the expansion of autonomy for the science community and the conduct of science according to professional norms. Scientists also called for greater say in the use of their work. Andrei Sakharov's dissidence arose in part over his persistent efforts to convince Khrushchev to prohibit atomic bomb testing in the atmosphere. They campaigned against instances of political and bureaucratic disregard for safeguards on technology, in response to the 1957 Chelyabinsk nuclear disaster and the 1960 moon rocket accident.[69]

Older, established scientists were slower to join their younger colleagues, since their stature in their fields and in the political establishment antedated Khrushchev. By the early 1960s, however, they began to support the younger scientific dissidents, who themselves had begun to participate in a broader, emerging democratic opposition movement. In their collaboration, the older scientists supplied money and secure facilities for their younger counterparts to organize contacts and publish *samizdat* (self-published) literature.[70] In many of the large regional academic centers, informal gatherings of scientists and other intellectuals began to meet to discuss broader issues of political life. Growing out of a private sphere of discourse in intellectuals' personal lives and relationships, according to Vladimir Shlapentokh, these "salons" provided forums "to be honest in public and to openly defend their liberal ideas."[71]

Many of these activities proceeded with official toleration or, in some instances, even encouragement through the Khrushchev years. Dissent moved rapidly beyond tolerated bounds, however, in the early Brezhnev period in response to indications of a rehabilitation of Stalin's image in 1964 and 1965 and especially to the opening of political trials of the dissident writers Andrei Sinyavsky and Yuli Daniel in February 1966. The trials were widely understood as signaling a return by Party leadership to the methods of Stalinism. Petition campaigns and protest letters emerged in reaction. Public demonstrations were organized, beginning with the December 1965 Pushkin Square protest. Dissident networks solidified into organizations promoting civil liberties.[72]

Scientific intellectuals played active and sometimes leading roles in these new activities, especially in the protest-letter and petition campaigns, and leading scientists who previously had adopted essentially apolitical outlooks became involved. Most shocking for the Party leadership was the participation of Andrei Sakharov and others of the most privileged scientific elite, whose status had seemed to make them unlikely supporters of the democratic opposition movement.[73] As these dissident activities blossomed into a full-fledged political opposition, which by 1967–68 was acquiring attention and contacts abroad, the regime took steps to suppress it. Through a variety of tactics, including arrest, dismissal from the Party and from official and professional posts, loss of security clearances, and prohibitions against publishing, the regime beat the movement down but did not manage to extinguish it altogether.[74]

Students of the Soviet political scene have discerned separate strands, each with distinctive orientations, in the broader dissident

movement that emerged in the USSR in the Khrushchev and early Brezhnev periods. Marshall Shatz, in his sensitive, historically minded account, has described three main strands of dissent. The first was a Marxist group, seeking a restoration of truly Leninist Marxism purged of the
excesses and deviations introduced by Stalin—a group that had close
ties with the Party leadership and whose views were not far from the
prevailing official outlook; this group was exemplified by the dissident
historian Roy Medvedev. The second, a Christian group drawing inspiration from religious (and especially Russian Orthodox) traditions,
was exemplified by Aleksandr Solzhenitsyn. Finally, a Western liberal
strand blended ideals of pluralist democracy with some abiding tenets
of socialism.[75] Vladimir Shlapentokh has described three slightly different strands of dissent. He identifies a "neo-Leninist" category more
or less equivalent to Shatz's Marxist group and a "liberal socialist"
group, which appears similar to Shatz's Western liberal strand. Shlapentokh does not include a Christian strand of dissent. He argues, in
fact, that a significant dissident movement focused on moralistic values
emerged only in the 1970s, concurrent with the resurgence of Russo-
phile and nationalistic dissident movements. He describes instead a
technocratic strand, focused on the elitist premise that professional experts should make the key decisions confronting Soviet society, and
cites Sakharov's *Progress, Coexistence, and Intellectual Freedom* as a representative exposition of this viewpoint. Scientists could be found among
both the technocratic and liberal strands, and technocratic and liberal
dissidents frequently collaborated in the 1960s; thus the two groups
blurred together. But they differed, Shlapentokh states, over what each
saw as essential for Soviet progress: "For liberals, democracy was the
necessary ingredient; for technocrats, science."[76]

A comparison of these groupings with the spectrum of intellectual
reactions in China to the Deng reforms, the critique of Mao Zedong and
his policies, and the "crisis of confidence" is suggestive. Interpreting
each of the categories of Soviet opinion liberally, equivalents of all can
be identified in post-Mao China: "neo-Leninists"—the Deng reformers
and their allies in intellectual circles who sought to purge Chinese communism of its Maoist deviations and to restore a genuine Mao Zedong
Thought; technocrats—scientists such as Qian Xuesen; traditionalists—
adherents of "new Confucianism" and other strands of cultural con-

servatism; and liberals of various stripe, including Xu Liangying, Fang Lizhi, Li Honglin, and Yu Haocheng. In contrast to the Soviet experience, however, the technocrats in China found common ground with the "neo-Leninist" reformers. They fought with the liberals over Marxist philosophy's relationship to science and, more fundamentally, over science's autonomy from Party authority.

The relevance of each country's historical legacy is also significant. Shatz depicts Soviet dissent in the 1950s and 1960s as the re-emergence of a long tradition, with roots as far back as the mid-eighteenth century, of efforts by the Russian intelligentsia to throw off the paternalistic patronage of autocratic tsarist rule. In the nineteenth century, intellectuals confronted a tension between the claims of reason on behalf of individual conscience on one hand and in service to the state on the other. The Bolshevik Revolution broke the tension decisively in favor of the latter. It was only with Khrushchev's denunciation of Stalin that intellectuals' doubts about and guilt over complicity in the Stalin period translated into rediscovery and reaffirmation of humanistic values on the sanctity of individual life and conscience.[77]

The impetus of this legacy toward liberalism suggestively parallels the tensions of the May Fourth era and the impact of the Cultural Revolution on intellectual conscience in China. But here again, there are important differences. In the Soviet Union, historical legacy was remote and abstract. The extermination of intellectuals in the Stalin purges of the 1930s meant that the prerevolutionary generations of scientific intellectuals were gone, and so dissidence in the 1960s was primarily an affair of postrevolutionary generations. In China the tensions of the 1920s and 1930s were still within living memory and the dissidence of the 1980s involved both pre- and post-revolutionary generations, as Xu Liangying's example illustrates.

SCIENCE AS A POLITICAL FORCE

The parallels and contrasts between scientific dissidence in the Soviet Union and China suggest a conclusion that is perhaps commonsensical but frequently appears at odds with common wisdom. Scientific communities are complex cultural subsystems of larger political and social systems. They are extremely sensitive to changes in political and social environment and to pressures that affect their internal processes. And so the factors that prompt scientists to become active politically outside their normal arenas of professional work are varied and complex. As political actors, scientific communities are not monolithic, and their impact is frequently complex. Technocracy and authoritarianism are one possible political consequence of the interaction of scientific communities with the society around them. Political liberalism, borne of values and ideals that are fundamentally humanistic and are antithetical to technocracy, is another.

In the Soviet and Chinese cases similar transitions in Party leadership and goals and in the agenda and direction in science policies created corresponding pressures on the science communities. Accordingly, the array of concerns that preoccupied dissenting scientists was similar. Professional norms and state abuse of them were the primary stimuli that galvanized scientists' participation in liberal dissident causes against political intrusions into science and on behalf of establishing a more democratic context for the conduct of science and for society as a whole. In articulating the linkage between these norms and larger political ideals, theoretical physicists played peculiarly important roles in scientific dissent.[78] Liberal scientists in the USSR found common ground with liberal intellectuals from the social sciences and humanities, as did their counterparts in China, because their perceptions of the requirements of their professions and their social responsibilities brought them to the same place. In other respects, the orientations and coalitions of groups of scientists worked out differently in each country, perhaps because of differences in the degree to which ideological or political intrusion into science was perceived as a continuing threat and because the relevance of historical memory and experience was more immediate in one case than in the other.

As in the USSR in the 1960s, the social and political significance of the scientific dissidents in China in the 1980s rests in their contributions to shaping discourse of public affairs beyond the controls of the communist state. In doing so, they helped to revive a tradition of political liberalism that had flickered four and five decades earlier and that had been suffocated in the trials of war and revolution thereafter. The variety of liberalism they espoused offered no finely worked out system of ideas and institutions for China's future. But it did offer an unusually clear focus on human rights and individual worth that derived from what they thought were the norms of their scientific profession.

It is possible that many of the liberal or liberalizing intellectuals who emerged in the Deng years will turn out to have been transitional figures, in much the same way that their liberal predecessors were in the May Fourth era. As China evolves toward a postcommunist future, the critical intellectuals' liberal views will not seem as relevant as they did in the Deng years. As powerful as it was in the early 1980s, for example, Wang Ruoshui's incisive critique of Marxism from a humanistic direction will no longer seem to address issues posed either by an authoritarian Chinese regime whose Marxist-Leninist commitment is even further diluted from what it was in 1993 (or has altogether evaporated) or by the dilemmas of postcommunist democratic politics of one kind or another. Because of the unusual clarity of its focus on individual rights and freedoms and because of its social roots in the norms of science, however, the liberalism of the scientists of the 1980s may not seem so foreign and irrelevant in new settings. And so it may turn out to possess a more enduring significance than the liberal critiques of Chinese communism that were put forward from other directions and whose relevance may ebb as China changes.

In the shorter term, the relevance of the liberal scientists' views is no less diminished. The crushing of dissent after June 1989 was the Communist Party's natural response to what it perceived as an intolerable challenge to its claims to legitimacy. As long as the communist regime continues to support the Chinese scientific profession as essential to the nation's future, however, the conditions that fed scientific dissidence in the 1980s will remain. As in the 1980s, some in the scientific community will continue to find inevitable connections between the ideals that motivate them as scientists and those that inspire their political lives.

Appendixes

MAJOR CHINESE COMMUNIST PARTY MEETINGS, 1976-1992

The Chinese Communist Party, like other ruling communist parties, ratifies authoritative decisions made by the Party leadership through the process of formal Party congresses and Central Committee meetings. Full-scale Party congresses, comprised of roughly two thousand delegates, meet every five years to review the work of the Party over the preceding five years, to lay out guidelines for work in the next five years, and to elect a new Central Committee to act in its stead in the intervening years. The Central Committee is composed of roughly two hundred members drawn from the most significant Party and state posts throughout the capital and the nation. It normally meets once or twice a year to ratify decisions deliberated through internal Party process and proposed by the Party leadership. A full Central Committee meeting is a "plenum."

TENTH CENTRAL COMMITTEE

Third Plenum	16–21 July 1977	Rehabilitation of Deng Xiaoping
Eleventh CCP Congress	12–18 Aug. 1977	Election of Eleventh Central Committee; political report by Hua Guofeng

ELEVENTH CENTRAL COMMITTEE

First Plenum	19 Aug. 1977	Appointment of new Politburo, top Party leadership
Second Plenum	18–23 Feb. 1978	Approval of Fifth NPC agenda
Third Plenum	18–22 Dec. 1978	Initial judgment of Mao Zedong; endorsement of Deng Xiaoping's ideological line
Fourth Plenum	25–28 Sept. 1979	Approval of Ye Jiangying's PRC 30th anniversary address
Fifth Plenum	23–29 Feb. 1980	Restoration of Secretariat; exoneration of Liu Shaoqi

285

Sixth Plenum	27–29 June 1981	Replacement by Hu Yaobang of Hua Guofeng as Party chairman; adoption of resolution on Mao and Party history.
Seventh Plenum	6 Aug. 1982	Adoption of Twelfth Congress agenda
Twelfth CCP Congress	1–11 Sept. 1982	Election of Twelfth Central Committee; political report by Hu Yaobang; Party constitution revised

TWELFTH CENTRAL COMMITTEE

First Plenum	12–13 Sept. 1982	Appointment of new Politburo, top Party leadership
Second Plenum	11–12 Oct. 1983	Launching of three-year Party rectification drive and of campaign against "spiritual pollution"
Third Plenum	20 Oct. 1984	Adoption of decision on industrial economic reform
Fourth Plenum	16 Sept. 1985	Approval of national Party conference agenda
National Party conference	18–23 Sept. 1985	Retirement of several veteran leaders; adoption of Seventh Five-Year Plan draft
Fifth Plenum	24 Sept. 1985	Adjustment of Politburo membership
Sixth Plenum	28 Sept. 1986	Adoption of resolution on "spiritual civilization"
Seventh Plenum	20 Oct. 1987	Approval of Thirteenth Congress agenda
Thirteenth CCP Congress	25 Oct.–1 Nov. 1987	Election of Thirteenth Central Committee; political report by Zhao Ziyang

THIRTEENTH CENTRAL COMMITTEE

First Plenum	2 Nov. 1987	Appointment of new Politburo, top leadership
Second Plenum	15–19 Mar. 1988	Report by Zhao Ziyang on Party work and reforms; approval of Eighth NPC arrangements
Third Plenum	26–30 Sept. 1988	Approval of scaling economic reforms back in favor of retrenchment
Fourth Plenum	23–24 June 1989	Approval of Zhao Ziyang's removal; appointment of Jiang Zemin as Party general secretary
Fifth Plenum	6–9 Nov. 1989	Approval of "39 Points" on economic retrenchment
Sixth Plenum	9–12 Mar. 1990	Decision on enhancing Party-people ties
Seventh Plenum	25–30 Dec. 1990	Approval of guidelines for Eighth Five-Year Plan
Eighth Plenum	25–29 Nov. 1991	Decision on agricultural reform
Ninth Plenum	5–9 Oct. 1992	Approval of Fourteenth CCP Congress agenda
Fourteenth CCP Congress	12–18 Oct. 1992	Election of Fourteenth Central Committee; political report by Jiang Zemin

MAJOR STATE MEETINGS, 1972–1992

The main institutions of the People's Republic of China are the parliamentary National People's Congress (NPC); its Standing Committee, presided over by a chairman; the presidency of the PRC; and the executive arm, the State Council, presided over by the premier. The NPC, composed of about three thousand delegates, meets every five years to review the work of the government, set forth guidelines for work in the coming five years, and elect a new Standing Committee. The NPC Standing Committee in its first session appoints the State Council.

The NPC meets in full session once a year, normally in the spring, to review the State Council's work over the previous year. The NPC Standing Committee meets several times a year to approve new legislation and conduct other state business. The CCP dominates the process of government through its system of "unified leadership." This includes concurrent appointment of top party leaders as top state leaders, membership of the most important state officials in the Party Central Committee, and guidance of state work through a system of Party committees and core groups within all state offices and organizations, including the CAS and CASS. Only the most important NPC sessions are listed here.

FIFTH NPC

First session	26 Feb–5 Mar 1978	Report by Hua Guofeng on government work; renewal of "big-plan" development
Second session	18 Jun–1 Jul 1979	Deferral of Hua Guofeng's "big-plan" approach in favor of eight-point readjustment plan
Third session	30 Aug–10 Sept 1980	Replacement of Hua Guofeng by Zhao Ziyang as premier
Fifth session	26 Nov–10 Dec 1982	Adoption of new PRC constitution; adoption of Sixth Five-Year Plan

SIXTH NPC

First session	6–21 June 1983	Appointment of new state leadership; report by Zhao Ziyang on work of government

SEVENTH NPC

First session	25 Mar–13 Apr 1988	Appointment of new state leadership, including Li Peng as premier; work report by Li Peng

MAIN CHINESE PRESS SOURCES

Bulletin of Natural Dialectics (Ziran bianzhengfa tongxun)

Specialized journal of the CAS, publishing articles on science studies, the intersection of science and philosophy, and especially Marxist-Leninist philosophy; strongly liberal outlook in the 1980s under editorship of Yu Guangyuan and Fan Dainian.

Social Sciences in China (Zhongguo shehui kexue)

Foremost journal of the CASS, and so the most prestigious social sciences journal in China; published bimonthly.

Enlightenment Daily (Guangming ribao)

Nationally circulating newspaper for intellectuals and united-front work. Ideas discussed are thought to be of interest to all intellectuals.

People's Daily (Renmin ribao)

Nationally circulating newspaper published in the name of the CCP Central Committee; the most important newspaper in China politically.

Red Flag (Hongqi)

The CCP's official political and theoretical journal; replaced in 1988 by *Seeking Truth* (Qiushi).

Seeking Truth (Qiushi)

See *Red Flag*.

Studies in Natural Dialectics (Ziran bianzhengfa yanjiu)

Founded in 1985 as the journal of the Chinese Natural Dialectics Research Society; publishes articles on the same spectrum of issues as the *Bulletin of Natural Dialectics*, but was intended to take a more conservative slant.

Studies in Philosophy (Zhexue yanjiu)

Specialized journal published by the CASS's Institute of Philosophy; the most important philosophy journal in China.

ABBREVIATIONS USED IN THE NOTES
AND BIBLIOGRAPHY

CAS	Chinese Academy of Sciences
CASS	Chinese Academy of Social Sciences
FBIS-China	Foreign Broadcast Service China Daily Report
JPRS	Joint Publications Research Service
Xinhua	Xinhua News Agency

Notes

1. INTRODUCTION

Sources included in the Selected Bibliography are listed here in abbreviated form.

1. The term "science" in this book is used narrowly to connote "reliable knowledge" about nature for its own sake and the effort and methods to produce such knowledge, corresponding to what is sometimes called "pure" or "academic" science, as opposed to the instrumentalist effort to apply such knowledge, often termed "applied" science, research and development, and technology. Within science communities in contemporary developed societies, of course, the distinction has become increasingly difficult to maintain. See Ziman, *An Introduction to Science Studies*, 1–11, 121–30.

2. Arguments asserting interconnections among science, scientism, and political pluralism are based on Robert Merton's pathbreaking argument about Puritanism and the establishment of the modern scientific role in seventeenth-century England. A clear, easily accessible account of the establishment of modern science in that period using Merton's analysis as a point of departure is Ben-David, *The Scientist's Role in Society*, chaps. 4 and 5. Debates on its validity are reviewed, together with comments by Merton himself, in I. Bernard Cohen, ed., *Puritanism and the Rise of Modern Science*.

3. General discussions of technocracy build on the insights of Max Weber on the role of bureaucracy in implementing legal-rational authority in modern societies. See in particular Weber's *Economy and Society*, vol. 1, 223–26, and the discussion of Weber's ideas in Bendix, *Max Weber*, 425–30. Representative views of technocracy and their implications for communist systems are surveyed in Baylis, *The Technical Intelligentsia and the East German Elite*, 1–20; and Lowenthal, "The Ruling Party in a Mature Society," 81–118. For a full-scale analysis of the Brezhnev period as a technocracy, see Hoffmann and Laird, *Technocratic Socialism*.

4. Studies of the changing composition of the political elite in the Deng period include Hong Yung Lee, *From Revolutionary Cadres to Party Technocrats in Socialist China;* and Cheng and White, "Elite Transformation and Modern Change in Mainland China and Taiwan," 1–35.

5. The text of Fang's letter is translated in Fang, *Bringing Down the Great Wall*, 242–43. "China's Sakharov" is something of a misnomer. Though their political views were similar, Fang did not work on projects of comparable importance and sensitivity to Andrei Sakharov's work on the Soviet hydrogen bomb, his stature in the Chinese science community was not comparable to Sakharov's in the Soviet science community, and he did not have access to the top Chinese leadership as Sakharov did to the Soviet Party leadership.

6. A translation of this letter is in Fang, *Bringing Down the Great Wall*, 305.

7. The text of the open letter is published, together with an interview with Xu Liangying (its principal organizer) and an article supplying biographic information on most of the signers by Fan Dainian (then executive editor of the Academy of Sciences journal *Bulletin of Natural Dialectics*) in the Hong Kong journal *Jiushi niandai* (The nineties), 1989, no. 4: 20, 21–23, and 26–28. A translation of the letter is in Fang, *Bringing Down the Great Wall*, 306–8.

8. The text of this leter is published, together with an interview with Dai Qing, in *Jiushi niandai*, 1989, no. 4: 24–25. See also the accounts of the Qianmen Hotel meeting and the petition in *South China Morning Post*, 15 and 17 March 1989 (trans. in Foreign Broadcast Information Service China Daily Report [hereafter FBIS-China], 15 March, 27–28, and 17 March, 14–15 respectively).

9. State Education Commission Ideology and Political Work Bureau, *Jingxin dongpo de wushiliu tian*, 11–12.

10. Xu Liangying interview and Fan Dainian article, *Jiushi niandai*, 1989, no. 4: 21–23 and 26–28, respectively.

11. See Schwarcz, *The Chinese Enlightenment*.

12. This is a main theme of the able survey of intellectuals' political attitudes in the post-Mao era by Merle Goldman, *Sowing the Seeds of Democracy in China*.

13. This is the explicit framework of the classic text John K. Fairbank, Edwin O. Reischauer, and Albert M. Craig, *East Asia: The Modern Transformation*, vol. 2 of *A History of East Asian Civilization* (Boston: Houghton Mifflin Company, 1965), especially pp. 3–10. For one evaluation of some of the strengths and weaknesses of this framework, see Paul A. Cohen, *Discovering History in China*.

14. This framework and general conclusion find interesting parallels in recent interpretations of China's modern history by Chinese intellectuals critical of the communist regime. Such interpretations emphasize the failure of China in the twentieth century to overcome "feudal" ideas and influences, which have corrupted the Communist Party and inhibited the flourishing of democratic ideas and behavior among the Chinese people and among the intellectuals themselves. This theme is implicit, for example, in the 1987 television series *Heshang*.

15. See, for example, Rankin, *Elite Activism and Political Transformation in China*; Rowe, *Hankow: Commerce and Society in a Chinese City, 1796–1889* and *Hankow: Conflict and Community in a Chinese City, 1796–1895*; Mann, *Local Merchants and the Chinese Bureaucracy, 1750–1950*; Bergere, *The Golden Age of the Chinese Bourgeoisie, 1911–1937*; and Strand, *Rickshaw Beijing*. In addition, the complementary reviews by Rowe, "Modern Chinese Social History in Comparative Perspective" and "Approaches to Modern Chinese Social History," are extremely useful, as is his provocative essay "The Public Sphere in Modern China."

16. Ziman, *An Introduction to Science Studies*, 183–93.

2. OFFICIAL IDEOLOGY IN TRANSITION

1. Deng Xiaoping, *Selected Works of Deng Xiaoping (1975–1982)*, 395.

2. *Renmin ribao* (People's daily), 1 May 1977, 1 (trans. in *Peking Review*, 6 May 1977, 15–27).

3. Deng Xiaoping, *Selected Works*, 103.

4. Useful, though not altogether congruent, accounts of Mao's attitude may be found in: MacFarquhar, *The Origins of the Cultural Revolution*, vol. 1: *Contradictions Among the People, 1956–1957*, 99–164; and Teiwes, "Establishment and Consolidation of the New Regime," 122–33. The seed of Mao's later view on class struggle is visible in his landmark essay "On the Correct Handling of Contradictions Among the People," in Mao Tse-tung (Mao Zedong), *Selected Works of Mao Tse-tung*, vol. 5, 395–96 and 409–10. This text is based on a speech Mao delivered at a Supreme State Conference on 27 February 1957, which was published belatedly, on 19 June 1957, in *People's Daily*, after Mao revised it. It should be compared with Liu Shaoqi's September 1957 "Political Report to the 8th National Congress of the CPC [CCP]", 37, 72–73, and 82. Authoritative Chinese public accounts in the post-

Mao period do not normally indicate that Mao disagreed with the Eighth Congress line, even though they do routinely state that the Party's "leftist" deviation over the entire 1957–76 period was due to his "erroneous" assessment of the circumstances and tasks dating back to that time or immediately thereafter. On the Eighth Congress, see, for example, CCP Central Committee Documents Research Office, *Guanyu jianguo yilai dang de ruogan lishi wenti de jueyi zhushiben*, 258–62; Hao and Duan, *Zhongguo Gongchandang liushinian* vol. 2, 467–77; and Liao, *Zhongguo Gongchandang de guanghui qishinian*, 258–60. A recent PRC account acknowledging that Mao disagreed with aspects of the Eighth Congress line is Shi Zhaoyu, "Mao Zedong yu Bada dui woguo shehui zhuyi zhuyao maodun lijie de yitong," 91–104.

5. The sharpening of Mao's views is apparent in his speech to the Eighth CCP Tenth Plenum, delivered on 24 September 1962, and in the famous "Nine Commentaries." Mao's Tenth Plenum speech has never been published in PRC media. A translation from documentary collections compiled and circulated by the Red Guards in the Cultural Revolution is in Schram, *Chairman Mao Talks to the People*, 188–96. The "Nine Commentaries" are the series of articles issued jointly in the name of the editorial boards of *People's Daily* and the party theoretical journal, *Red Flag* (Hongqi), between September 1963 and July 1964.

6. "Xuehao wenjian zhuazhu gang," [Study the documents well, grasp the key link], *Renmin ribao*, 7 February 1977, 1.

7. Hua Guofeng, report to the Eleventh CCP Congress, *Peking Review*, 26 August 1977, 24 and 39.

8. Deng Xiaoping, closing address at the Eleventh CCP Congress, *Peking Review*, 2 September 1977, 38–40. Deng's views on Mao and on the Party's continuing commitment to Mao's ideas were an issue in Deng's political rehabilitation. See his 24 May 1977 talk "The 'Two Whatevers' Do Not Accord with Marxism" and his speech to the Tenth CCP Third Plenum on 21 July 1977, in Deng Xiaoping, *Selected Works*, 51–52 and 55–60, respectively. The plenum communiqué sets out the terms of his rehabilitation. An unusually detailed public account of the steps leading to his rehabilitation is in Hao and Duan, *Zhongguo Gongchandang liushinian*, vol. 2, 670–73.

9. Communiqué of the Eleventh Central Committee Third Plenum, *Hongqi*, 1979, no. 1: 14–21 (trans. in *Peking Review*, 29 December 1978, 15).

10. Ibid., 13.

11. *Peking Review*, 5 October 1979, 7–31.

12. Contributing commentator, "Shijian shi jianyan zhenli de weiyi biaozhun" (Practice is the sole criterion for testing truth), *Guangming ribao* (Enlightenment daily), 11 May 1978, 1, 2; and Deng Xiaoping, *Selected Works*, 127–40.

13. Communiqué of the Eleventh Central Committee Third Plenum, op. cit., 15.

14. Ibid., 10–11.

15. "Resolution on Certain Questions in the History of Our Party Since the Founding of the PRC," adopted at the Eleventh CCP Central Committee's Sixth Plenum, 27 June 1981, in *Beijing Review*, 6 July 1981, 10–39.

16. Deng Xiaoping, *Selected Works*, 235.

17. The series ran for seven months in 1980, from May through December.

18. *Guangming ribao*, 3 November 1980 (trans. in FBIS-China, 14 November 1980, L2).

19. Zhao Ziyang, "Advance Along the Road of Socialism with Chinese Characteristics," work report to the Thirteenth CCP Congress, *Beijing Review*, 9–15 November 1987, xxiv–xxv.

20. Two earlier dissections of ideological change in the Deng period are Schram, *Ideology and Policy in China Since the Third Plenum, 1978–94*; and Tsou, "Back from the Brink of Revolutionary-'Feudal' Totalitarianism," in *The Cultural Revolution and Post-Mao Reforms*, 144–188.

21. Communiqué of the Eleventh Central Committee Third Plenum, 10–11.

22. "Decision of the Central Committee of the Communist Party of China on Reform of the Economic Structure," *Beijing Review*, 29 October 1984, v.

23. "Zhonggong Zhongyang guanyu shehuizhuyi jingshen wenming jianshe lingdao fangzhen dejueyi" (Resolution of the Central Committee of the Communist Party of China on the guiding principles for building a socialist society with an advanced culture and ideology), *Hongqi*, 1986, no. 19:2–9 (trans. in *Beijing Review*, 1987 October 6, I–II).

24. "Advance Along the Road of Socialism with Chinese Characteristics," Zhao Ziyang, iii–vi.

25. Deng Xiaoping, *Fundamental Issues in Present-Day China*, 53–58.

26. Deng Xiaoping, *Selected Works*, 166–91. Neither the speech nor the conference, which has since been cited as a key forum in the development

of the reform agenda in the wake of the Third Plenum, was publicized in PRC media at the time. On the conference, see Hao and Duan, *Zhongguo Gongchandang liushinian,* 693–95. Hu Yaobang's long speech at the conference's opening session is in the *neibu* (restricted circulation) documentary collection published by the government for nationwide internal study by party cadres after the Twelfth Congress (CCP Central Committee Documents Research Office, *Sanzhong Quanhui yilai zhongyao wenxian xuanbian,* vol. 1, 48–63). A useful analysis of the conference is Merle Goldman, "Hu Yaobang's Intellectual Network and the Theory Conference of 1979."

27. Tsou, "Back from the Brink of Revolutionary-'Feudal' Totalitarianism," in *The Cultural Revolution and Post-Mao Reforms,* 154–56.

28. "Aiguozhuyi shi jianshe shehuizhuyi de juda jingshen liliang" [Patriotism is a tremendous spiritual force for building socialism], *Renmin ribao,* 19 March 1981, 1 and 5 (trans. in FBIS-China, 19 March 1981, L12–22).

29. Ma Xingyuan, "The Independence of Trade Unions Must Be Recognized," *Gongren ribao* [Workers daily], 24 October 1980 (excerpted by the Xinhua News Agency in FBIS-China, 29 October 1980, L5–6). Ma stated that trade unions are "voluntary" organizations that must act "independently and responsibly" to carry out the "demands and aspirations" of the workers and defend their "democratic rights and material benefits." Recalling that the Party had usurped the proper functions of trade unions since the late 1950s, Ma said that the Party can guide trade unions but cannot substitute for them.

30. A survey of assessments by several authorities on China, for example, shows that all have agreed on the general direction of political evolution in the 1980s, but there remain important differences on exactly how to characterize it. Harry Harding concludes that "the reforms have greatly relaxed the degree of political control over Chinese society, without fundamentally altering the Leninist character of the Chinese political system" (*China's Second Revolution,* 174). Andrew Nathan suggests that "the reforms aimed to change China from a terror-based, totalitarian dictatorship to a 'mature' administered dictatorship of the post-Stalinist or East European type," in which "reinvigoration of the citizen's relationship with the state was only meant to contribute to a more consultative and predictable form of party dictatorship" (*Chinese Democracy,* 228). A. Doak Barnett argues that China's political system under Deng has evolved "from extreme totalitari-

anism toward liberalized authoritarianism," and while this evolution may proceed considerably farther, it is not likely to evolve into a "pluralist democracy" given China's historical authoritarian traditions and the difficulty of maintaining unity and stability in a society as large as China ("Ten Years After Mao," 52). Tang Tsou sees the Dengist reforms as a major retreat from the "revolutionary 'feudal' totalitarianism" of the Maoist period and the first real reversal since the May Fourth period of the state's steady penetration into Chinese society, though he predicts that this retreat will not likely go far toward political pluralism ("Back from the Brink of Revolutionary-'Feudal' Totalitarianism," in *The Cultural Revolution and Post-Mao Reforms*, 148–51).

31. Hu Yaobang, speech at a Party Secretariat meeting on 8 February 1985, published in *Renmin ribao*, 14 April 1985 (trans. in FBIS-China, 15 April 1985, K1–15).

32. Suttmeier, "Party Views of Science," 154.

33. "Resolution of the Central Committee of the Communist Party of China on the Guiding Principles for Building a Socialist Society with an Advanced Culture and Ideology," vi.

34. Xing, "Dui dangqian sixiang jiefang yundong de yixie kanfa," 5.

35. Yu Guangyuan speech marking the ninetieth anniversary of the death of Engels, *Renmin ribao*, overseas ed., 5 August 1985, 2 (trans. in FBIS-China, 12 August 1985, K17–18).

36. Hu Qiaomu remarks at a forum celebrating publication of the second Chinese edition of the collected works of Lenin, as reported by Xinhua, 24 September 1984 (trans. in FBIS-China, September 27, 1984, K4).

37. Duan Ruofei, "Makesizhuyi shi wanzheng de kexue shijieguan" [Marxism is a complete scientific worldview], *Hongqi*, 1987, no. 3: 10–16 (trans. slightly modified from Joint Publications Research Service [hereafter JPRS] *China Report: Red Flag*, 28 August 1986, 48–49).

38. Duan Ruofei, in *Hongqi*, 1986, no. 14: 29 and 40 (trans. in JPRS *China Report: Red Flag*, 10 April 1987, 15–23).

39. Li Keming, "Shidai dui Makesizhuyi zhexue de yaoqiu."

40. Deng Weizhi, "Makesizhuyi yanjiu de 'tupo.' "

41. Li Xingmin, "Huaiyi, pingquan, duoyuan".

42. A useful overview of Wang's views is Kelly, "The Emergence of Humanism," 159–82.

43. The raising of this issue is clear from the articles attacking it. See Ma Junqi, "Gongchanzhuyi zhidu de shijian jiqi dui gongchanzhuyi lilun de jianyan"; Chen Chengde and Guo Fengsheng, "Shijian—zhenli—kexue yujian"; Gu Yang, "Zhenli—biran—gongchanzhuyi xinnian"; and Zha, "Gongchanzhuyi yujian de zhenlixing he shijian biaozhun de weiyixing." Hu Yaobang also rebutted this view in his report to the Twelfth CCP Congress (*Beijing Review*, 13 September 1982, 22).

44. One such suggestion was taken up and extended beyond bounds acceptable to the Party in a Nanjing University social sciences journal article in the fall of 1980. The article asserted that the Party adopted a series of erroneous egalitarian policies in agricultural collectivization in the 1950s that were at odds with the prescriptions of Marxism-Leninism and that represented "agrarian socialism." These deviations, it said, stemmed from the Party's lack of a predominantly urban proletarian base and the attempt to build socialism in a "semifeudal" China that had not yet gone through the necessary stage of capitalism. Not surprisingly, the article attracted a storm of criticism—by Party Secretariat Policy Research Office chief Deng Liqun, among others—ending in a retraction and an apology by the journal's editors. The original article is Ying and Sun, "Guanyu shehuizhuyi gaizao houqi de jige lilun wenti." Among the critical responses, see: Deng Liqun, "Youth Is the Hope in Building Socialist Modernization," *Zhongguo qingnian bao* (China youth news), 7 May 1981, 1, 3 (trans. in *JPRS China Report: Political, Social, and Military*, 22 September 1981, 55); Xie Xin, "Kexue shehuizhuyi, haishi nongye shehuizhuyi?"; and Yan Ling, "Woguo nongye shehuizhuyi gaizao de biyaoxing, kenengxing jiqi shixian." *Nanjing Daxue xuebao*'s (Nanjing University journal) 1981, no. 4 issue carried both its editorial apology ("Xiqu jiaoxun, banhao xuebao" [Absorb the lesson, run the journal well], 1, and its own critical article by Zhong Ku ("Woguo nongye hezuohua shi kexue shehuizhuyi de huida shengli" [The cooperativization of agriculture in our country was a great victory of scientific socialism], 2–7).

45. Lowenthal, "The Ruling Party in a Mature Society" and "The Post-Revolutionary Phase in China and Russia." The significance of this shift in Party goals is also emphasized by Kenneth Jowitt, who sees the loss of the Party's social combat mission as ultimately "corrupting" its organizational ethos. See his "Soviet Neotraditionalism."

46. New Year's editorial, "Fulfill the Tremendous Task of Adjusting the National Economy on the Basis of Stability and Unity," *Renmin ribao*, 1 January 1981, 1 (trans. in FBIS-China, 2 January 1981, L6–10).

47. Luo, Zhu, and Cao, "Zhongguo gaige de lishi diwei."

3. CHINA'S SCIENCE COMMUNITY UNDER REFORM

1. The text of Deng's speech is in Deng, *Selected Works*, 101–16, and also in FBIS-China, 21 March 1978, E4–15; Hua's speech is in FBIS-China, 27 March 1978, E1–8; and Fang Yi's report is in FBIS-China, 29 March 1977, E1–22.

2. Deng Xiaoping, *Selected Works*, 61–72.

3. Xinhua, 22 and 23 September 1977 (trans. in FBIS-China, 23 September 1977, E1–7, and 27 September 1977, E1–9).

4. Qian Xuesen, "Science and Technology Must Catch Up with and Surpass Advanced World Levels before the End of the Century," *Hongqi*, 1977, no. 7 (excerpted and trans. in FBIS-China, 8 July 1977, E2–5).

5. Deng Xiaoping, *Selected Works*, 102–5.

6. The process of reformulating China's economic development strategy through this period, and the various planning and research studies that it generated, has been illuminated greatly by Carol Lee Hamrin in *China and the Challenge of the Future*.

7. Year 2000 Research Team, *Gongyuan 2000 nian de Zhongguo* [China in the year 2000] (Beijing: Keji Wenxian Chubanshe, 1984) (trans. in JPRS *China Economic Affairs* report, 6 March 1986).

8. In addition to Hamrin, *China and the Challenge of the Future,* see the studies on the role of economists in this process by Nina Halperin, "Scientific Decisionmaking." A brief description of the establishment and work of two of the most important of these centers in the State Council—the Economic Research Center under Xue Muqiao and the Technical Economics Research Center under Ma Hong—appears in Xie Jun, "Economic and Technical Experts Enter Zhongnanhai," *Guangming ribao*, 30 August 1981, 1 (trans. in FBIS-China, 10 September 1981, K16–17).

9. Hamrin, *China and the Challenge of the Future,* 96–100.

10. Xia Yulong and Liu Ji, "It Is Also Necessary to Eliminate Erroneous 'Leftist' Influence on the Science and Technology Front," *Jiefang ribao*,

2 June 1981 (trans. in FBIS-China, 11 June 1981, K8–12). On various other problems, see the commentator article in *Guangming ribao*, 15 January 1981 (trans. in FBIS-China, 6 February 1981, L12–15).

11. Yan Jian and Shi Yiwu, *Shiyijie Sanzhong Quanhui dao Shi'erjie Sanzhong Quanhui dashiji*, 36.

12. The text was published, together with a Central Committee and State Council transmittal notice, in CCP Central Committee Documents Research Office, *Sanzhong Quanhui yilai zhongyao wenxian xuanbian* [Selected important documents since the Third-Plenum], *neibu* ed., vol. 2, 759–76. A translation appears in the Taiwan journal *Issues and Studies*, vol. 18, no. 5: 84–101. See also the comments on it in Saich, *China's Science Policy in the 80s*, 18–19. Saich's study provides a succinct outline of the evolution of science and technology policy down to 1985. Other helpful secondary accounts of the science reforms of the early 1980s include Suttmeier, *Science, Technology, and China's Drive for Modernization;* idem, "Politics, Modernization, and Science in China"; and Saich, "Reform of China's Science and Technology Organizational System," 69–88. Editorial, "Further Clarify the Policy for the Development of Science and Technology," *Renmin ribao*, 7 April 1981, 1 and 4 (trans. in FBIS-China, 21 April 1981, K19–22).

13. Ibid. and Xinhua, 27 May 1981 (trans. in FBIS-China, 28 May 1981, K8).

14. Xinhua, 24 August 1982 (trans. in FBIS-China, 30 August 1982, K14–15).

15. Xinhua, 24 October 1982 (trans. in FBIS-China, 25 October 1982, K6–9).

16. Xinhua, 15 November 1982 (trans. in FBIS-China, 17 November 1982, K16–17).

17. Xinhua, 13 December 1982, (trans. in FBIS-China, 14 December 1982, K1–34).

18. Xinhua, 28 January 1983; and *Renmin ribao*, 28 January 1983, 1 (trans. in FBIS-China, 31 January 1983, K8–9).

19. Xinhua, 1 February and 3 June 1983 (trans. in FBIS-China, 9 February 1983, K17–19; and 7 June 1983, K28–29).

20. Xinhua, 3 May 1984 (trans. in FBIS-China, 8 May 1984, K8–9); and Xinhua commentator article, 3 May 1984 (trans. in FBIS-China, 7 May 1984, K13–14).

21. Commentator article, "The Key to Reforming the Scientific Re-

search System," *Renmin ribao,* 25 May 1984, 1 (trans. in FBIS-China, 15 June 1984, K15–17).

22. *Liaowang* (Observation post), 1984, no. 23 (June 4), 40 (trans. in FBIS-China, 3 July 1984, K12–14).

23. As will be plain from the discussion that follows, the term "intellectuals" in Party policy discourse in China encompasses a broad span of people—not only scientists and technicians, but also social scientists, scholars in the humanities, writers, and teachers.

24. "Correctly Recognize the Status and Role of Intellectuals in Building the Four Modernizations," *Guangming ribao,* 7 December 1979, 1 (trans. in JPRS *China Report: Political, Social, and Military Affairs,* [29 January 1980], 60–63).

25. Ren Zhongyi, "It Is Necessary to Regard the Broad Masses of Intellectuals as Part of the Working Class," *Guangming ribao,* 8 January 1980, 3 (trans. in JPRS *China Report: Political, Social, and Military Affairs,* [11 February 1980], 41–44).

26. Contributing commentator article, "A Marxist Policy toward Intellectuals," *Renmin ribao,* 18 April 1980, 2 (trans. in FBIS-China, 8 May 1980, L11–20).

27. Xu Minhe and Yang Ruimin, "The Party Central Committee Is Concerned about Middle-Aged Intellectuals," *Liaowang,* 1982, no. 7 (July 20) (trans. in JPRS *China Report: Political, Social, and Military Affairs,* [1982], 64–69).

28. Ibid.

29. Hu Qiaomu, "My Wishes after a Period of Painful Mourning," *Renmin ribao,* 29 November 1982 (trans. in FBIS-China, 30 November 1982, K22–25).

30. Xinhua, 15 May 1983 (trans. in FBIS-China, 16 May 1983, K12–13); and CCP Central Committee Organization Department and Documents Research Office, *Zhishifenzi wenti wenxian xuanbian,* preface.

31. Editorial, "Gradually Improve the Working and Living Conditions of Middle-Aged Intellectuals," *Guangming ribao,* 15 July 1982, 1 (trans. in FBIS-China, 22 July 1982, K9–10).

32. "Great Shock, Great Change, and Great Development—An Interview with Zhou Guangzhao, President of the Academy of Sciences of China," *Qiushi* (Seeking truth), 1988, no. 6 (September 16), 21–27 (trans. in JPRS *China Report: Red Flag,* no. 88-068 [31 October 1988], 18–25).

33. *Guangming ribao,* 2 April 1978, 2 (trans. in FBIS-China, 13 April 1978, E2–4).

34. Xinhua, 23 February 1978 (trans. in FBIS-China, 2 March 1978, G6–9); Xinhua, 20 March 1978 (trans. in FBIS-China, 20 March 1978, E18–20); and Xinhua, 9 October 1979 (trans. in FBIS-China, 11 October 1979, L12–14).

35. Saich, *China's Science Policy in the 80s,* 66 and 80 *n.25.*

36. Xinhua report on 1981 CAS Scientific Council session, 26 May 1981 (trans. in FBIS-China, 28 May 1981, K5–7).

37. Deng Xiaoping, *Selected Works,* 113–14.

38. *Guangming ribao,* 8 August 1979, 1 (trans. in JPRS *China Report: Political, Social, and Military Affairs* [9 October 1979], 51–52).

39. Xinhua, 24 December 1977 (trans. in FBIS-China, 27 December 1977, E13–14 [Deng]; and E3 [Li]).

40. Concise accounts of the organization and management of the Academy of Sciences before the Cultural Revolution are provided in Lindbeck, "The Organization and Development of Science"; and Chu-yuan Cheng, *Scientific and Engineering Manpower in Communist China, 1949–1963,* 16–25.

41. Xinhua, 29 March 1981 (trans. in FBIS-China, 31 March 1981, L21; and 1 April 1981, K13).

42. Xinhua, 19 May 1981 (trans. in FBIS-China, 20 May 1981, K6–7).

43. Xinhua, 18 May 1981 (trans. in FBIS-China, 20 May 1981, K4–5).

44. Suttmeier, *Research and Revolution,* 93–100 and 106–11; and also his "Science Policy Shifts, Organizational Change and China's Development," 220–25 and 230–35.

45. Interviews, 1990 and 1991.

46. Xinhua, 11 May 1981 (trans. in FBIS-China, 12 May 1981, K6).

47. Xinhua, 27 May 1980 (trans. in FBIS-China, 28 May 1980, L1).

48. Xinhua, 21 November 1981 (trans. in FBIS-China, 24 November 1981).

49. Xinhua, 5 July 1983 (trans. in FBIS-China, 6 July 1983, K29–30).

50. Chu-yuan Cheng, *Scientific and Engineering Manpower in Communist China, 1949–1963,* 16.

51. These details on Yu's posts are from his biographies appearing in Chinese Academy of Social Sciences Institute of Philosophy, ed., *Zhongguo zhexue nianjian 1983,* 343; and *Jingji ribao* (Economy daily) Editorial Board, *Zhongguo dangdai jingjixuejia zhuanlue,* 466.

52. Yu was supposedly liked by Party general secretary Hu Yaobang but distrusted as too liberal by Deng Xiaoping for these reasons. Interviews, 1990 and 1991. Su Shaozhi, however, recalls that Deng respected Yu's abilities. See Su Shaozhi, "Shekeyuan Maliesuo shinian zangsang."

53. Chu-yuan Cheng, *Scientific and Engineering Manpower in Communist China, 1949–1963*, 17.

54. Yu Wen was considered the true voice of party orthodoxy in the CAS. Interview, 1990.

55. Xinhua, 13 October 1980 (trans. in FBIS-China, 14 October 1980, L29).

56. Hong Tianguo and Chen Zujia, "An Appointment That Has Been Delayed for Five Years," *Renmin ribao*, 30 March 1984, 3 (trans. in FBIS-China, 6 April 1984, K2–5).

57. "Great Shock, Great Change, and Great Development—An Interview with Zhou Guangzhao, President of the Academy of Sciences of China," 18–20. Some Chinese scientists believed that the wholesale reorientation of the Academy's work toward the economy from this period forward amounted to "intervention in science by economics," as opposed to the Maoist period's "intervention in science by politics." Interviews, 1990 and 1991.

58. Xinhua, 3 February 1983; and Zhongguo Xinwenshe, 6 February 1983 (trans. in FBIS-China, 9 February 1983, K15–17).

59. Xinhua, 25 February 1984 (trans. in FBIS-China, 28 February 1984, K5).

60. Xinhua, 14 May 1981 (trans. in FBIS-China, 15 May 1981, K3).

61. Su Shaozhi, correspondence with the author, 15 July 1993; see also idem, "The Structure of the Chinese Academy of Social Sciences (CASS) and the Two Decisions to Abolish Its Marxism-Leninism Institute."

62. Chinese Academy of Social Sciences, "Mao zhuxi de jiaodao he guanhuai yongyuan guwu women qianjin," 2.

63. Su Shaozhi, "The Structure of the Chinese Academy of Social Sciences (CASS) and the Two Decisions to Abolish Its Marxism-Leninism Institute." Some details on the background, establishment, and early work of the CASS have also been published by a former researcher in CASS (and its CAS precursor) from 1966 to 1978: Zhou Xun, "Zhonggong shehui kexue yanjiu de xianzhuang ji qianjing."

64. Xinhua, in *Renmin ribao*, 14 July 1979, 1 (trans. in FBIS-China,

23 July 1979, L15–17). According to one Chinese observer, the two hundred Department members cited in the Xinhua report as still working actively in the mid-1970s included only those in good standing. Many more resumed work under lower standing. According to this observer, around four hundred of the 2,100 pre–Cultural Revolution members of the Department were too old to resume work. Most of the remaining 1,700 did do so, though under a political shadow, after returning to Beijing in 1972 from "re-education" at the May Seventh Cadre School in Henan. Interviews, 1990 and 1991.

65. Braybrooke, "Recent Developments in Chinese Social Science, 1977–79," 601 and 603; Xinhua, "Zhexue shehui kexue yao wei shixian Sige Xindaihua fuwu" [Philosophy and social sciences must serve the Four Modernizations], *Guangming ribao*, 4 November 1978, 1 (excerpts trans. in FBIS-China, 8 November 1978, E10–12). A major speech on the plan and ongoing CASS issues, delivered by Vice President Zhou Yang on 19 September, was published in *Zhexue yanjiu*, 1978, no. 10: 2–11.

66. Chinese Academy of Social Sciences, *Zhongguo Shehui Kexue Yuan*, 107–26.

67. Su Shaozhi, "Shekeyuan Maliesuo shinian zangsang." Zhou Xun (see note 63, above) erroneously links the CASS to the Institute of Marxism-Leninism (Makesi Liening Zhuyi Yanjiuyuan) under the CCP Central Committee before the Cultural Revolution, which was abolished by order of Kang Sheng and Chen Boda (Zhou Xun, "Zhonggong shehui kexue yanjiu de xianzhuang ji qianjing," 44). According to others familiar with the evolution of the CASS, the institute Zhou mentions was not the predecessor of the CASS institute, but was a body dominated by Chen Boda and abolished after his downfall in 1970. According to these observers, the CASS institute was founded by Yu Guangyuan when the social sciences academy was established to "develop Marxism in his own way" (interviews, 1990 and 1991).

68. Zhongguo Xinwenshe, 9 May 1988 (trans. in FBIS-China, 12 May 1988, 24–25); Su Shaozhi, "Shekeyuan Maliesuo shinian zangsang"; and idem, "The Structure of the Chinese Academy of Social Sciences (CASS) and the Two Decisions to Abolish Its Marxism-Leninism Institute." The observers cited in the previous note believe that the Institute ultimately was not moved because the Central Party School itself resisted and delayed it until the decision was finally overturned. Interviews, 1990 and 1991.

69. Chinese Academy of Social Sciences, *Zhongguo Shehui Kexue Yuan,* 2–3.

70. Su Shaozhi, "The Structure of the Chinese Academy of Social Sciences (CASS) and the Two Decisions to Abolish Its Marxism-Leninism Institute."

71. Interviews, 1990 and 1991.

72. Chinese Academy of Social Sciences, *Zhongguo Shehui Kexue Yuan,* 3; Chinese Academy of Sciences, *Zhongguo Kexue Yuan* [The Chinese Academy of Sciences] (Beijing: 1985) (trans. in JPRS-CR: Science and Technology 86-037 [9 September 1986], 1–2).

73. E.g., Hu Sheng, "Several Questions Concerning the Strengthening of the Study of Social Sciences," *Hongqi,* 1986, no. 9: 3–11 (trans. in JPRS *China Report: Red Flag,* 10 June 1986], 11).

74. Xinhua, *Renmin ribao,* 21 June 1979, 4.

75. Wu Jialun, "The Concepts Must Be Clear—Discussing Whether or Not Truth Has a Class Character," *Renmin ribao,* 7 August 1979, 3 (trans. in FBIS-China, 13 August 1979, L2–7).

76. Wan Li's "soft science" speech, delivered at a symposium on 31 July 1986, is translated in FBIS-China, 19 August 1986, K22–33.

77. Xinhua, 24 November 1987 (trans. in FBIS-China, 27 November 1987, 3).

78. Zhou Peiyuan report to the Second National Congress of the China Science and Technology Association, 15 March 1980 (trans. in FBIS-China, 26 March 1980, L10); *Xinwen gongzuo shouce* Editorial Committee and Editorial Board, *Xinwen gongzuo shouce,* 334; and Xinhua, 25 June 1986 (trans. in FBIS-China, 26 June 1986, K19–20).

79. *National Listing of New Books* includes basic publication data together with brief annotations indicating the books' contents. In the case of translations, the foreign authors' names are offered in Chinese transliteration. Chinese informants point out that many of the foreign books published for the general public in this period are translations that were previously published in limited *neibu* editions before the Cultural Revolution.

80. Zhao report to the Sixth NPC Second Session, 15 May 1984, *Beijing Review,* 1984, no. 24 (June 11), x.

81. Xinhua, 9 and 10 March 1984 (trans. in FBIS-China, 12 March 1984, K14–16); Xinhua, 9 May 1984 (trans. in FBIS-China, 10 May 1984, K15–16).

82. Xinhua, 24 June 1984 (trans. in FBIS-China, 25 June 1984, K17–18).

83. Huan Xiang, "Xinjishu geming yu woguo duice."

84. "Decision of the Central Committee of the Communist Party of China on Reform of the Economic Structure," adopted at the Twelfth Central Committee Third Plenum, 20 October 1984, *Beijing Review,* 29 October 1984, iv.

85. Commentator article, "Open the Party's Door to Outstanding Intellectuals," *Guangming ribao,* 20 November 1984, 1 (trans. in FBIS-China, 28 November 1984, K14–15).

86. Commentator article, "Give Intellectuals the Remuneration They Deserve," *Renmin ribao,* 26 June 1984, 1 (trans. in FBIS-China, 2 July 1984, K13–14); and the editorial "Improving the Working and Living Conditions of Middle-Aged Intellectuals Remains an Urgent Task," *Guangming ribao,* 3 July 1984, 1 (trans. in FBIS-China, 18 July 1984, K2–4).

87. Commentator article, "Break through Independent Kingdoms, 'Adopt' Boldly," *Renmin ribao,* 7 March 1984, 1 (trans. in FBIS-China, 9 March 1984, K3–4).

88. Shi Ping, "The Problem of Knowledge and Intellectuals," (Shanghai) *Shehui kexue* (Social Science), 1983, no. 4: 12–16 (trans. in JPRS *China Report: Political, Social, and Military Affairs,* 15 September 1983, 14).

89. Chinese informants state that because the CAS's line of supervision no longer went directly through the Party Propaganda Department headed by "spiritual pollution" campaign backer Deng Liqun, and instead went through the State Science and Technology Commission and Fang Yi, the Academy was successfully insulated against the campaign. Interview, 1991.

90. Commentator article, "Further Implement the Policies Toward Intellectuals in the Course of Party Rectification," *Liaowang,* 1984, no. 9 (February 27): 1 (trans. in FBIS-China, 22 March 1984, K2–4); and Wang Kang and Wang Tongxun, "Report on an Investigation into the So-called 'Economic Crimes' Committed by Several Scientists and Technicians," *Guangming ribao,* 1 August 1984 (trans. in FBIS-China, 8 August 1984, K2–4).

91. Xie Yining commentary, "It Is Gratifying to See that the Case of Xu Ruijian Has Been Satisfactorily Resolved," Zhongguo Xinwenshe, 29 February 1984 (trans. in FBIS-China, 1 March 1984, K11–12). According to informants, many Chinese scientists believed that Xiu Ruijian's work was not in

fact exceptional and that by spotlighting her work, Hu Yaobang succeeded only in demonstrating his own ignorance of science. Interview, 1990.

92. Xinhua, 24 January 1984 (trans. in FBIS-China, 25 January 1984, K12–13); and commentator article, "Give Intellectuals the Remuneration They Deserve," Renmin ribao, 26 June 1984, 1 (trans. in FBIS-China, 2 July 1984, K13–14).

93. "Decision," trans. in FBIS-China, 21 March 1985, K1–10; Zhao speech, delivered 6 March 1985, trans. in FBIS-China, 22 March 1985, K1–7.

94. China Daily, 8 January 1985, 1 (in FBIS-China, 9 January 1985, K26–27); and Yi Miao, "Opening Up in Order to Develop Faster—A Major Reform of the Chinese Academy of Sciences," Liaowang, 17 March 1986 (trans. in JPRS China Report: Science and Technology, 28 May 1986, 5–10).

95. Liaowang (overseas ed.), 1986, no. 16 (April 21): 6–7 (trans. in JPRS-CST no. 86-020 (28 May 1986), 14–18); Xinhua, 16 December 1985 (trans. in FBIS-China, 17 December 1985, K2–3).

96. Zhou Chengkui, "Revamping Science and Technology System."

97. Xinhua, 22 July 1986 (trans. in FBIS-China, 28 July 1986, K15–17); report and commentator article, Renmin ribao, 23 July 1986, 1 and 3 (trans. in FBIS-China, 30 July 1986, K22–26); and Ge, "Several Problems Encountered in the Reform of Research Institutes").

98. Zhou Chengkui, "Revamping Science and Technology System," 26–27; Ge Yuehua, "Several Problems Encountered in the Reform of Research Institutes," 36–40; and commentator article, "Thoughts Provoked by the Zhao Jianyun Case," Renmin ribao, 29 October 1986, 1 (trans. in FBIS-China, 6 November 1986, K8–9).

99. Fan Dainian, "Guanyu Zhongguo Kexueyuan fazhan zhanlue yanjiu de ruogan wenti de chubu tantao," 21–30.

100. On Fang's removal as vice president of Chinese Science and Technology University, see Xinhua, 12 January 1987 (trans. in FBIS-China, 12 January 1987, K11–12). On his expulsion from the CCP, see Xinhua, 19 January 1987 (trans. in FBIS-China, 20 January 1987, 01–2).

101. Xinhua, 3 and 7 February 1987 (trans. in FBIS-China, 4 February 1987, K15–16 and February 10, 1987, K10–11); and Xinhua, 14 October 1987 (trans. in FBIS-China, 15 October 1987, 16).

102. Xinhua, 3 February 1987 (trans. in FBIS-China, 4 February 1987, K15–16); and Xinhua, 14 and 23 December 1987 (trans. in FBIS-China, 15 December 1987, 15; and 28 December 1987, 27–28).

103. *China Daily,* 28 February 1987, 1 (in FBIS-China, 2 March 1987, K2–3); and Zhao Ziyang report to the Sixth NPC Fifth Session, 25 March 1987, *Beijing Review,* 1987, no. 16 (20 April): xvii.

104. Xinhua, 28 February 1987 (trans. in FBIS-China, 2 March 1987, K3); and Xinhua, 10 March 1987 (trans. in FBIS-China, 11 March 1987, K9); An Zhiguo, "Are Intellectuals Being Suppressed?" *Beijing Review,* 9 March 1987, 4, and Wei Liming interview with Zhou Guangzhou, " 'Double Hundred' Policy Remains Unchanged," 23 March 1987, 16.

105. Xinhua, 21, 25, and 26 July 1987 (trans. in FBIS-China, 22 July 1987, K1; and 28 July 1987, K1).

106. Contributing commentator article, "The Idea and Slogan of Using Science to Save the Nation Should Be Re-Evaluated," *Keji bao,* 15 November 1987 (as reprinted in *Renmin ribao,* overseas ed., 6 December 1987, 2, and trans. in FBIS-China, 8 December 1987, 17–18); and Bao Xin, "There Are Good Policies for Reinvigorating the Nation and the Opportunities Must Not Be Lost," *Liaowang,* overseas ed., 7 March 1988, 1 (trans. in FBIS-China, 16 March 1988, 26–27).

107. Li Peng speech, Xinhua, 12 March 1988 (trans. in FBIS-China, 18 March 1988, 10–12).

108. Xinhua, 25 August 1988 (trans. in FBIS-China, 29 August 1988, 36–37); and Du Yuejin, "China's Strategy for the Development of High Technology," *Liaowang,* overseas ed., 1988, no. 50 (December 12): 9–11 (trans. in FBIS-China, 21 December 1988, 33–36).

109. Zhongguo Xinwenshe, 31 March 1986 (trans. in FBIS-China, 4 April 1986, 03); Gu Mainan, Zhu Jigong, and Meng Xiangjie, "After Leaving the Research Institute: Things Seen and Heard on Zhongguancun's Electronics Street," *Liaowang,* 16 February 1987, 9–12, 17 (trans. in JPRS *China Report: Science and Technology,* [29 June 1987], 74–81); Zhongguo Xinwenshe, 6 May 1988 (trans. in FBIS-China, 19 May 1988, 35–36); Wei Liming, "Torch Plan Outlined," *Beijing Review,* 22–28 August 1988, 5.

110. Zhou Guangzhao, "The Chinese Academy of Sciences Advances in the Course of Reform," *Renmin ribao,* 28 March 1987, 4 (trans. in FBIS-China, 6 April 1987, K27–31); interview with Zhou Guangzhao, *Beijing Review,* 23 March 1987, 14–16; *Beijing Review,* 28 November–4 December 1988, 10; Yang Xiaobing, "One Academy, Two Systems," *Beijing Review,* 5–11 December 1988, 7.

111. "Science Academy Doubles Mission," *Beijing Review,* 28 Novem-

ber–4 December 1988, 10; Yang Xiaobing, "One Academy, Two Systems," *Beijing Review,* 5–11 December 1988: 7.

112. Xinhua, 15 October 1988, citing *China Daily,* 15 October 1988 (trans. in FBIS-China, 18 October 1988, 46).

113. Liu Lusha, "China's Contingent of Scientific Researchers Should Be Replenished Urgently," *Guangming ribao,* 3 August 1988, 1 and 4 (trans. in FBIS-China, 15 August 1988, 31–33).

114. Xinhua, 19 September 1988; interview with Zhou Guangzhao, Xinhua, 15 October 1988 (trans. in FBIS-China, 19 October 1988, 4); and Xinhua, 11 April 1989 (trans. in FBIS-China, 11 April 1989, 26).

115. Shu Zhan, "Give and Take," *Yangcheng wanbao,* 28 April 1988, 2 (trans. in FBIS-China, 10 May 1988, 16–17).

116. Mi Bao, "How to Treat Intellectuals," *Renmin ribao,* 31 March 1989 (trans. in FBIS-China, 7 April 1989, 29–30).

117. Xinhua, 9 November 1988 (trans. in JPRS-CST no. 88-023 [1988]: 25–26); and Liu Lusha, "China's Contingent of Scientific Researchers Should Be Replenished Urgently," 31–33.

118. Zheng Yefu, "The Problem of Aging Intellectuals Is Becoming Serious," *Shijie jingji daobao* (World economic herald), 12 September 1988, 13 (trans. in FBIS-China, 28 September 1988, 39).

119. Li Xinfeng and Min Jie, "Problems Facing China's Social Sciences," *Liaowang,* overseas ed., 9 May 1988 (trans. in FBIS-China, 19 May 1988, 29–31).

120. Suttmeier, "Reform, Modernization, and the Changing Constitution of Science in China," 1009.

121. Interview with Zhou Guangzhao, *Beijing Review,* 1987, no. 12 (23 March), 16; interview, 1990. Zhou Guangzhao's promotion to CAS president in 1987 was by leadership appointment, not election. Ironically, according to Chinese informants, Zhou turned out to be a much better administrator and defender of CAS's interests than was his predecessor, Lu Jiaxi.

122. These terms are drawn from the analysis in Suttmeier, *Research and Revolution: Science Policy and Societal Change in China,* 79–111; and idem, "Science Policy Shifts, Organizational Change and China's Development," 207–41.

4. THEORIES IN CONFLICT

1. A penetrating survey of some of these adjustments is Brugger and Kelly, *Chinese Marxism in the Post-Mao Era.*

2. Useful surveys of the development of natural dialectics, as "the dialectical materialist view of nature," include: Graham, *Science, Philosophy, and Human Behavior in the Soviet Union* 24–67; Scanlan, *Marxism in the USSR,* 57–142; Joravsky, *Soviet Marxism and Natural Science;* and Kolakowski, *Main Currents of Marxism,* vol. 1, 376–98; vol. 2, 447–58 and 461–66.

3. Chen Chengbin and Yao Sha, eds., *Ziran bianzhengfa yuanli,* 1.

4. Friedman, "Einstein and Mao," 57.

5. Scanlan, *Marxism in the USSR,* 43–45; Vucinich, *Empire of Knowledge,* 149–66, 179–82, 193–98, and 314–44; Joravsky, *Soviet Marxism and Natural Science,* 268–71; and Rabkin, "The Study of Science," 134–45. See also Dong, "Jiujing shenma shi ziran bianzhengfa?", 56–61; and Gong and Sun, "Ziran bianzhengfa de lishi fazhan he zhuyao neirong," 1–6.

6. Graham, *Science in Russia and the Soviet Union,* 151–55.

7. Interview, 1990.

8. Although the natural dialectics journal had a small reading audience, frequently the ideas debated in it gained a wider currency. Beijing University biology student and political activist Shen Tong does not recall reading journals such as *The Bulletin of Natural Dialectics,* nor was he aware of the debates on science and philosophy in which Fang Lizhi, Xu Liangying, Zha Ruqiang, and the others discussed hereafter were embroiled, although he had heard of some of the protagonists (interview, 1 July 1993). Su Shaozhi recalls reading *The Bulletin of Natural Dialectics* only "rarely." He was aware of the debates but did not follow them since he is "not a philosopher" and "did not understand them" (correspondence with author, 15 July 1993).

9. The basic ideas of quantum mechanics and the philosophical difficulties they present can be grasped through a number of recent books and articles, including Shimony, "Conceptual Foundations of Quantum Mechanics"; D'Espagnat, *Reality and the Physicist,* and his more technical *Conceptual Foundations of Quantum Mechanics;* Powers, *Philosophy and the New Physics;* and Jammer, *The Philosophy of Quantum Mechanics.* For elements of the theory itself, patient presentations for the mathematically reticent but not altogether shy include: Feynman et al., *Quantum Mechanics,* Vol. 3 of *The Feynman Lectures on Physics;* Park, *Introduction to the Quantum Theory;*

and Morrison, *Understanding Quantum Physics.* The chapter on the quantum theory of measurement in Bohm, *Quantum Theory,* 583–623, remains among the clearest and most sensitive to epistemological issues. On the physics of fundamental particles, there is Coughland and Dodd, *The Ideas of Particle Physics;* Perkins, *Introduction to High Energy Physics,* Griffiths, *Introduction to Elementary Particles;* and the essays by Close, Georgi, Taylor, and Salam in Davies, *The New Physics,* 396–424, 425–44, 458–80, and 481–91 respectively.

10. General introductions to big bang cosmology include Silk, *The Big Bang;* Zeilik et al., *Introductory Astronomy and Astrophysics,* 480–504; and the essays by Clifford Will and Stephen Hawking in Davies, *The New Physics,* 7–33 and 61–69, respectively. More technical is Ohanian, *Gravitation and Spacetime.* Parts of the grandaddy texts Weinberg, *Gravitation and Cosmology,* and Misner et al., *Gravitation,* will prove intelligible and exhilarating even to those to whom the language of tensors and modern differential geometry is foreign.

11. Misner et al., 5.

12. Alan Guth and Paul Steinhardt, "The Inflationary Universe," in Davies, *The New Physics,* 54.

13. Fang and Yin, "Weiraozhe xiandai yuzhouxue de yichang kexue yu jiakexue de lunzheng."

14. Wang Guozheng, "Heidong wuli de fazhan jiqi yiyi."

15. Although the existence of quarks, as constituents of other particles (such as protons and neutrons), seems evident on theoretical and indirect experimental grounds, no quark has yet been observed as an independent particle. Whether quarks exist independently, or only as entities "confined" within other particles (and if so, why), is still an open issue in physics. See Coughlan and Dodd, *The Ideas of Particle Physics,* 143–46.

16. "Xin de changshi."

17. Zhu's nationalism is evident in his use throughout the article of the term "straton" instead of "quark." It is also apparent in his preference for the name "psi" alone for the particle discovered in 1974. The particle is known in the international physics community by two alternative names— the "psi particle" and the "J particle," and frequently as the "J/psi particle." This is because it was discovered almost simultaneously in 1974 by two groups, one led by Burton Richter at Stanford's linear accelerator (which called it the "J particle") and the other by the Chinese-American physicist C. C. Ting at Brookhaven (which called it the "psi particle").

18. Zhu and Du, "J/psi weizi de tiaozhan."

19. He Zuoxiu, "Chang yeshi 'yi fen wei er' de."

20. Shen Xiaofeng and Chen Haoyuan, "Aiyinsitan yu Gebenhagen xuepai." On von Neumann's theorem, see Jammer, *The Philosophy of Quantum Mechanics*, 265–78.

21. He Xiangtao et al., "Liangzi lixue de jige xuepai."

22. Guan Shixu and Chen Changshu, "Kexue jishu de fazhan yaoqiu women zuo xie shenma?"

23. Dong, "Zhongguo Ziran Bianzhengfa Yanjiuhui shoujie xueshu nianhui gaikuang."

24. *Zhexue yanjiu* commentator article, "Jiji fazhan bianzheng weiwuzhuyi ziranguan de yanjiu."

25. Fang, "Cong 'wanwu yuanyu shui' dao 'shikong shi wuzhi zunzai de xingshi.' "

26. Yin, "Xiandai yuzhouxue fengfule bianzheng weiwuzhuyi de ziranguan."

27. He Zuoxiu, "Cengzi, qingzi yeshi buke qiongjin de."

28. Yang, "Bianzheng weiwuzhuyi de wuzhiguan yu ziran kexue de wuzhi guannian." Non-Euclidean geometry is the geometry of spaces in which the fifth of Euclid's five postulates, concerning parallel lines, is discarded. Einstein's general theory of relativity uses non-Euclidean geometry as developed by G. F. B. Riemann to describe the curvature of space-time.

29. A popularized description of this new model is provided by Hawking himself in his recent popular book *A Brief History of Time*, 136–41.

30. Fang, " 'Diyi tuidong' jinxitan." See also Fang's "Philosophical Problems of Modern Cosmology" (trans. in Williams, *The Expanding Universe of Fang Lizhi*, 55–64), which was published in 1985 but was actually delivered as a talk in 1978. I am grateful to Jim Williams for sharing with me his observations on the evolution of Fang's views of the relationship of science and philosophy through this period.

31. Yin, "Dabaozha yuzhouxue yu zhexue xiandaihua." The inflationary model was proposed to repair some difficulties the standard big bang model could not explain. It posits that the universe underwent a brief period of accelerated expansion—"inflation"—early in the big bang. Guth and collaborator Paul Steinhardt provide a clear and lively presentation of the theory's main points in Davies, *The New Physics*, 34–60. That account

is an updated version of an earlier popular account they had published in *Scientific American* in 1984, which was translated and published in *Kexue*, the Chinese edition of that magazine. Passages from that version are reproduced almost verbatim in Yin's article.

32. Shen Xiaofeng and He Xiangtao, "Yuzhou chidu de zaitupo." Quasars are starlike objects that exhibit very high redshifts, indicating that they are moving away from us at extremely high speeds and so are among the farthest objects observed in the universe. They have presented a conundrum to astrophysicists since their discovery in the early 1960s because of their brightness relative to other objects. Because of quasars' pointlike appearance and great distance from earth, this brightness means that they must radiate energy at prodigious rates—on a scale not easily explained by usual astrophysical processes. Quasars' energy production could be explained by familiar stellar processes if they were nearby and not extragalactic objects; that alternative, however, would mean abandoning the conventional Hubble correlation of redshifts with recessional velocity due to cosmic expansion and distance. See Zeilik et al., *Introductory Astronomy and Astrophysics*, 467–77.

33. Zha, "Kexue shi yuelai yuezhongyao de shengchanli."

34. Zha, "Shilun chanye geming."

35. Zha, "Shilun xinxi shehui."

36. Zha, "Jianping xifang 'kexue zhexue' zhong guanyu kexue renshi fazhan de jizhong xueshuo."

37. Zha, "Makesi he ziran bianzhengfa."

38. Zha, "Ershi shiji ziran kexue si dachengjiu fengfule bianzheng ziranguan"; and idem, "Ershi shiji ziran kexue de si dafaxian." An insightful overview of Zha Ruqiang's views on natural dialectics based on his 1982 article is Kelly, "Controversies over the Guiding Role of Philosophy Over Science."

39. Zha, "Ziranjie bianzhengfa fanchou tixi shexiang."

40. Hu Qili, May Day celebration speech, Xinhua, 30 April 1986 (trans. in FBIS-China, 2 May 1986, K2–10); Hu Qili, remarks to a Shanghai forum of intellectuals on 14 April 1986, *Liaowang*, overseas ed., 1986, no. 22 (2 June), 4–6 (trans. in FBIS-China, 4 June 1986, K1–2); Zhu Houze, "Several Points to Ponder About Ideological and Cultural Questions," *Renmin ribao*, 11 August 1986, 7 (trans. in FBIS-China, 28 August 1986, K8–13); Lu, " 'Baihua qifang,

baijia zhengming' de lishi huigu"; and Yu Guangyuan, "The thirtieth anniversary of the setting forth of the 'double hundred' policy," *Renmin ribao*, 16 May 1986 (trans. in FBIS-China, 2 June 1986, K1–8).

41. See Ma Ding, "Dangdai woguo jingjixue yanjiu de shi da zhuanbian"; interview with Ma Ding and comments by Yu Guangyuan, *Shijie jingji daobao*, 21 April 1986, 1 and 2 (trans. in FBIS-China, 9 May 1986, K1–2; and 12 May 1986, K8–10, respectively); and the appeal by *Gongren ribao* editor Xu Jingchun, *Shijie jingji daobao*, 12 May 1986, 6 (trans. in FBIS-China, 21 May 1986, K1–2).

42. The spark for this controversy was Chen Yong's article "On the Methodology of Study in Literature and the Arts," which criticized CASS Institute of Foreign Literatures director Liu Zaifu by name (*Hongqi*, 1986, no. 8: 21–32 [trans. in JPRS-CRF-86-011, 2 June 1986, 36–54]). Among the numerous comments the controversy sparked, see: interview with Liu Zaifu, *Ta kung pao*, 16 May 1986 (trans. in FBIS-China, 19 May 1986, W1–2); interview with Chen Yong, *Zhongguo Xinwenshe*, 15 June 1986 (trans. in FBIS-China, 17 June 1986, K4–6); *China Daily*, 18 July 1986 (trans. in FBIS-China, 18 July 1986, K11–12); and Liu Zaifu, "Breaking through and Deepening Literature in the New Period," *Renmin ribao*, 8 September 1986 (trans. in FBIS-China, 18 September 1986, K15–24).

43. Zhong Weiguang, "Shi ziran bianzhengfa, haishi Heige'ershi de ziran zhexue?"

44. Liu Bing et al., "Dui Zha Ruqiang tongzhi liangpian wenzhangzhong yixie ziran kexue wenti de shangque."

45. Dong, "Dingyu yinbian lilun jiqi shiyan jianyan de lishi he zhexue de taolun"; and idem, "EPR shiyan he wuli shizaiguan."

46. Dong, "Jiujing shenma shi ziran bianzhengfa?"

47. Fang Lizhi believed that Zha was encouraged by Hu Qiaomu and Deng Liqun. Correspondence with author, 3 July 1993.

48. *Zhezhue yanjiu* editor's note, 1986, no. 8: 57.

49. Zha, "Shi fazhan haishi quxiao ziran bianzhengfa?"

50. Zha, "Dui Liu Bing deng wu tongzhi 'shangque' de dabian."

51. Xu, "Lishi lixinglun de kexue shiguan chuyi."

52. Zha, "Kou maozi, fei'er polai."

53. Dong, Han, and Jin, "Zhexue yao wei kexue bianhu."

54. Jin Wulun, "Wuzhi kefenxing de liangzhong jianjie he weiguan keti de bianzhengfa"; and idem, "Xin wuzhi jiegouguan de dansheng." See

also Jin's discussion of Leibniz's theory of monads and its relevance to contemporary particle theory, "Laibunici de danzilun zhexue he dangdai weizi wulixue."

55. Jin Wulun, "Dui 'wuzhi wuxian kefen lun' de zairenshi."

56. Fang, "Zhexue he wuli."

57. Interview, 1990.

58. Zha, "Weiwuzhuyi de yunyong yanyifa he weixinzhuyi de 'cong yuanze chufa.'" See also the criticism on the same page by Wang Gancai, "Qingyi fouding 'wuzhi wuxian kefen' nan yi fu ren."

59. Ai, "Lun zhexue dui kexue de 'zhidao' zuoyong."

60. *Zhexue yanjiu* editor's note, 1986, no. 12: 21.

61. Wu Guosheng, "Fang Lizhi."

62. Wu Guosheng, "Bawo yuzhou de liangzhong guifan de zheng."

63. Fang Lizhi regarded He Zuoxiu as the equivalent of the KGB of ideology in science. Fang, correspondence with author, 3 July 1993.

64. Interview, 1990.

65. Wu Guosheng, "Bashi niandai ziran bianzhengfa jie zhenglun beiwanglu."

66. Wu Guosheng, "Zhexue nengfou zhidao kexue."

67. Zhong Xuefu, "Zhexue bushi 'xintiao' erhshi kexue." See also Zhong's criticism of Fang Lizhi, "Zhexue he wulixue guanxi de ruogan wenti."

68. The only exceptions were an attempt by Wu Guosheng to clarify some of the definitions and premises in the debate on whether the universe is infinite, the publication of which was probably decided on before the campaign against "bourgeois liberalization" (Wu Guosheng, "Yuzhou shi wuxian de ma?"), and a very brief summary, carried in the March 1987 issue of *Studies in Natural Dialectics,* of a longer critical analysis by Jin Wulun and Li Xi (originally published in the Shenyang journal *Social Science Quarterly* [Shehui kexue jikan] in early 1986) of contradictory aspects of the theory of the infinite divisibility of matter (Jin Wulun and Li Xi, "Wuzhi wuxian fenhua lun he xin de kexue shishi de maodun").

69. Zha, "Ziran bianzhengfa shi yige kexue tixi."

70. Zha, "Zhengque de bianhu he shishiqiushi de fansi."

71. Zha, "Ping 'Yuzhou shi yu wu.'"

72. Zha, "Ping 'Zhexue he wuli' ji qita."

73. He Zuoxiu, "Study Marxism, Apply It in Scientific Research,"

Hongqi, 1984, no. 14: 42–46 (trans. in JPRS *China Report: Red Flag,* 19 September 1984, 74–81).

74. He Zuoxiu, "You guan yuzhoulun de zhexue wenti." In the same period, He also defended the role of the Marxist philosopher in science (see his "Zhiyi ' "Yi fen wei er" zhiyi' ").

75. Yu Guangyuan, "Shehuizhuyi chuji jieduan de jingji."

76. Wu Peng, "Guanyu 'wuxian yuzhou' de xin tantao." Wu at the time was a researcher in the Society, Science, and Technology Institute of the Heilongjiang Provincial Academy of Social Sciences. See the response to Wu's article, "Lilun de daotui" by Jin Zhong.

77. Wen, " 'Bo wei er'xiangxing shi ziranjie de yige jiben maodun' ma?"

78. Wu Guosheng, "Wuzhi shi wuxian kefen de ma?"

79. Jin Wulun, "Yunyong yanyifa neng tuichu 'wuzhi jiegou wuxian kefen' ma?"

80. Xu, "Zhenglun cong he er lai?"

81. He Zuoxiu, "A Brief Talk on Some Questions Concerning the Guidance of Marxist Philosophy in Research in the Natural Sciences," *Hongqi,* 1987, no. 20: 28–36 (trans. in JPRS *China Report: Red Flag,* 4 February 1988, 25–33).

82. He Zuoxiu, "Wuzhi, yundong, shijian, kongjian."

83. He Zuoxiu, "Dui 'wuzhi wuxian kefen lun' de zai tantao."

84. "Metagalaxy," a term imported from Soviet debates on cosmology in the 1930s and 1940s, refers to the observable universe.

85. *Ziran bianzhengfa tongxun* editor's note, 1988, no. 2: 78; and He Zuoxiu, " 'Youxian er wubian' shifou jiu 'buke chaoyue.' "

86. Zha, "Wuzhi jiegou cengci wuxian lun de zaizhengshi."

87. Zha, "Kexue jingshen wei he wu."

88. Jin Wulun, " 'Wuzhi wuxian kefen lun' shi xingershangxue xinnian, bushi bianzhengfa."

89. Jin Wulun, *Wuzhi kefenxing xinlun.*

90. Wu Guosheng, "Yuzhoulun de lishi yu zhexue."

91. Li Xingmin, "Huaiyi, pingquan, duoyuan"; and idem, "Zai zhexue yu kexue zhi jian."

92. Summaries of papers by Fan Dainian, Dong Guangbi, and Li Xingmin at a conference on Mach's thought on science and philosophy, *Ziran bianzhengfa yanjiu,* 1989, no. 2: 70–72. Both Dong and Li had written exten-

sively on these questions: Dong, "Mahe de kexue zhexue yu Makesizhuyi"; Li Xingmin, "Luelun Mahe de 'siwei jingji' yuanli"; and idem, "Guanyu *Weiwuzhuyi he jingyan pipanzhuyi* diwuzhang de yixie sikao." For Liu Bing's parting shot, see "Dui ' "Youxian er wubian" shifou jiu "buke chaoyue"?' yiwen de zhiyi."

93. Dong, "EPR shiyan."

94. He Zuoxiu, "Liangzi lixuezhong de celiang guocheng shibushi bixu you 'zhuguan jieru'?" He's interpretation builds on work put forward in the West in the 1970s by Antonio Danieri, Angelo Loinger, and Giovanni Maria Prosperi which has been criticized by Wigner and others; see Jammer, *The Philosophy of Quantum Mechanics*, 491ff.

95. He Zuoxiu, "Xiandai wulixue neng wei 'renshi de zhutilun' tigong kexue jichu ma?"

96. Among the main contributions to the debate on "cognitive subjectivity" from both sides are: Wang Yubei, "Liangzi lixue de 'xingzhiguan' he 'shizaiguan' "; He Zuoxiu, "Why Does Jin Guantao Want to Negate the Objectivity of Objective Reality?—Commenting on His *Philosophy of Man*"], *Qiushi*, 1989, no. 23 (trans. in FBIS-China, 27 December 1989, 21–25); Wen, "Xiangduilun shikong lilun jiqi pingjia zaitantao"; He Zuoxiu, "Ping 'Liangzi lixue de "xingzhiguan" he "shizaiguan." ' " Liu Dixiu, "Jiu Feng Nuoyiman de celiang lilun yu He Zuoxiu xiansheng shangque"; Wen, "Xiangduilun shikong lilun zairenshi"; Gu Zuxue, "Shilun renshi zhutixing de sange cengci"; Liu Shuzi, "Xiandai wulixue yu renshi de zhutixing"; He Zuoxiu, "Fenqi zai nali"; He Zuoxiu, "EPR 'yangmiu' ji youguan de zhexue wenti"; Guan Hong, "Guanyu 'yueliang zai mei ren kan ta shi shifou cunzai?' de wenti"; Liu Shuzi, "Shiyong hongguan gainian lai miaoshu weiguan keti de bixuxing he juxianxing."

97. He Zuoxiu's remarks on the "three great debates" in physics and philosophy in recent years at the Second Physics and Philosophy Conference held in Beijing on 20–22 August 1990, as reported in *Ziran bianzhengfa tongxun*, 1991, no. 1, 77–78; and Wu Guosheng, "Bashi niandai ziran bianzhengfa jie zhenglun beiwanglu."

5. THE POLITICS OF KNOWLEDGE

1. Zhou Yang, "Three Great Movements to Liberate Thought," *Renmin ribao*, 7 May 1979, 2 and 4 (trans. in FBIS-China, 11 May 1979, L3–16).

Xinhua's account of the CASS meeting, presided over by Deng Liqun, is translated in FBIS-China, 3 May 1979, L2–3.

2. Zhou Peiyuan speech, Xinhua, 23 March 1980 (trans. in FBIS-China, 26 March 1980, L7–18).

3. Hu Yaobang speech, Xinhua, 24 March 1980 (trans. in FBIS-China, 27 March 1980, L18–25).

4. Merton, "The Normative Structure of Science" and "Science and the Social Order," in his *The Sociology of Science*, 254–266 and 267–278, respectively; Richards, *The Philosophy and Sociology of Science*, 102–4; Ziman, *Public Knowledge*, 84–90; Hagstrom, *The Scientific Community*; and Storer, *The Social System of Science*, 75–98.

5. Ziman, *Public Knowledge*, 116–17; and Popper, *The Open Society and Its Enemies*, 404.

6. See Hagstrom, *The Scientific Community*, which modifies Merton's scheme, and the discussion in Richards, *The Philosophy and Sociology of Science*, on the "sociology of scientific knowledge" school, 204ff. A landmark study in this line of analysis is Latour and Woolgar, *Laboratory Life*.

7. For Feynman's own account of his role in the *Challenger* inquiry, see Feynman, *"What Do You Care What Other People Think?"*, 113–237. On the "cold fusion" controversy, see Close, *Too Hot to Handle*.

8. This definition of "ideology" follows Berger and Luckmann, *The Social Construction of Reality*, 123–25.

9. Among numerous studies in Chinese journals, see, for example: Zhou Hua, "Shehui jiegouzhong de kexue"; Song, "Kexue gongtongti zai kexue huodongzhong de zuoyong"; Wu Zhong, "Houqi Modun de kexue gongtongti shehuixue"; idem, "Modun de poshi lunwen"; Liu Junjun, "Guanyu 'wuxing xueyuan'"; and Kong Xiang, "Manhaimu de zhishi shehuixue he Modun de kexue shehuixue pingjia."

10. Among numerous leadership speeches and authoritative Party documents and press commentaries that address this legacy of "feudalism," see Deng Xiaoping, "On the Reform of the System of Party and State Leadership," *Selected Works*, 317–22; contributing commentator article, "Correctly Understand the Role of the Individual in History," *Renmin ribao*, 4 July 1980, 2 and 5 (as trans. in FBIS-China, 7 July 1980, L1–11); and "Resolution of Certain Questions in the History of Our Party Since the Founding of the PRC," 25.

11. Two valuable discussions of the mid-1980s cultural critique are

Leo Ou-fan Lee's brilliant dissection of intellectual—and especially literary—trends, "The Crisis of Culture"; and Zi Zhongyun's illuminating survey, "The Relationship of Chinese Traditional Culture to the Modernization of China."

12. Zi Zhongyun cites this conference debate as the primary inspiration for the later debate in the "culture fever" years comparing the features of traditional Chinese versus Western culture in spurring successful modernization. For an account of the conference, see "Juyou zhongyao yiyi de tansuo."

13. For the Chinese script, see Su Xiaokang and Wang Luxiang, eds., *Heshang*; for an English translation and useful commentaries on the show's meaning and reception, see Bodman and Wang, trans., *Deathsong of the River.*

14. A fascinating analysis of the lower Yangtze origins of many of the founders of the Science Society of China is Buck, *American Science and Modern China*, chap. 5.

15. I am indebted to Professor Li Cheng for discussing with me his work on the Qinghua clique in Chinese science.

16. The details of Yu's and Hu's careers presented here are drawn from their biographies in Clark and Klein, *Biographic Dictionary of Chinese Communism*, 374–77 and 1021–23, respectively, in addition to the sources for Yu cited above, chap. 3, note 51.

17. Su Shaozhi, "Shekeyuan Maliesuo shinian zangsang."

18. Hu, "Guanyu rendaozhuyi he yihua wenti."

19. Fang Lizhi believes that Zha received direct encouragement from Hu Qiaomu. Correspondence with author, 3 July 1993.

20. A brief biography of Zha Ruqiang appears in Chinese Academy of Social Sciences Institute of Philosophy, ed., *Zhongguo zhexue nianjian 1984*, 367–68.

21. This was mentioned by Fang Lizhi in a talk in 1986, "A Natural Scientist Views the Reforms," in his *Bringing Down the Great Wall*, 126–27.

22. Shi Youxin, "It Is Impermissible to Negate Selflessness," *Hongqi*, 1987, no. 3 (February): 5–9, 10, 11 (trans. in JPRS *China Report: Red Flag*, 10 April 1987, 6–13); on Yu's inclusion on a purge list, see *Jing bao*, (The mirror) 1987, no. 7 (July): 28–32 (trans. in FBIS-China, 15 July 1987, K1–8). One interviewee familiar with this episode stated in 1990 that Hu Qiaomu was the main advocate of Yu's removal, but that Chen Yun, who believed that people such as Yu were important bridges between the Party and the

intellectual community, intervened on Yu's behalf. On the resumption of Yu's political difficulties at the end of 1988, see *Jiushi niandai*, 1989, no. 3 (March) (trans. in FBIS-China, 2 March 1989, 15–16).

23. One interviewee familiar with Yu said in 1990 that Deng Xiaoping did not like Yu because he was "too liberal." Su Shaozhi believes that Yu's forthright directness and outspoken truthfulness allowed the more devious Hu Qiaomu to discredit Yu in Deng's eyes. ("Shekeyuan Maliesuo shinian zangsang").

24. Yu Guangyuan, "Wei *Ziran bianzhengfa* xin yiben chuban jiang jijuhua." The new edition was published in 1984.

25. Yu Guangyuan, "Yao lingxue, haishi ziran bianzhengfa" and "PSI yu ta de bianzhong." That Yu was distant from the natural dialectics community in the 1980s is suggested by Fang Lizhi's comment that he never met Yu and thought of him primarily as an economist. Fang correspondence with author, 3 July 1993.

26. Yu Guangyuan, "Zai yijiuwuliunian Qingdao Yichuanxue Huishang de jianghua"; and "The thirtieth anniversary of the setting forth of the 'double hundred' policy," *Renmin ribao*, 16 May 1986, 5 (trans. in FBIS-China, 2 June 1986, K1–8). On the Qingdao conference, see Laurence Schneider, ed., "Lysenkoism in China."

27. Yan Jiaqi, *Wo de sixiang zizhuan*, 8.

28. Su Shaozhi recalls that Yu supported and followed work in natural dialectics, as evidenced by his new translation of Engels's *The Dialectics of Nature*, but he does not know why Yu did not intervene in the dispute between Zha Ruqiang, Fang Lizhi, and Xu Liangying. Yu's collaborator on the Engels translation was Fan Dainian. Interview, 1990.

29. These details on Qian Xuesen are drawn from his biography in *Zhongguo renming dacidian* Editorial Board, *Who's Who In China*, 546–47, and a biographical article on Qian published by Zhongguo Xinwenshe, 27 June 1986 (trans. in FBIS-China, 1 July 1986, K33–34).

30. Xinhua, 16 July 1957 (trans. in *Survey of the China Mainland Press*, no. 1594, 20 August 1957, 17).

31. Qian, "Ziran bianzhengfa yao yu kexue jishu tongbu fazhan."

32. Qian Xuesen and Sun Kaifei, "Establish a System of Ideology and Social Science," *Qiushi*, 1988, no. 9: 2–9 (trans. in JPRS-CAR-89-006 [17 January 1989], 1–8).

33. Qian, "Jichu kexue yanjiu yinggai jieshou Makesizhuyi zhexue de zhidao."

34. Interview, 1990.

35. The account of Xu Liangying's life that follows, except where indicated otherwise, draws from the brief account of his career given in Fan Dainian's analysis of the signers of the 1989 petition that Xu organized ("'Sishier ren gongkaixin' qianshuzhe jianjie") and from Xu's homage to his teacher and mentor for much of his life, the physicist Wang Ganchang ("Enshi Wang Ganchang xiansheng dui wo de qidi he aihu"). None of the interviews cited below was with Xu Liangying.

36. Details of Bohr's 1937 visit to China, as recalled by Wang Ganchang and others, are given in Yan Kangnian, "N. Bohr zai Zhongguo."

37. The neutrino, a particle of neutral electric charge and zero (or nearly zero) mass, was first postulated by Wolfgang Pauli in 1930 from principles of conservation of energy in the process of beta decay—the emission of electrons (beta particles) from the atomic nucleus. Neutrinos were first observed, confirming Pauli's prediction, only in 1956.

38. On Zhu Kezhen, see Boorman, ed., *Biographic Dictionary of Republican China*, vol. 1, 451–53.

39. Interview, 1990.

40. *Kexue tongbao* [Scientia] editorial, "Raise Vigilance, Eliminate All Hidden Counterrevolutionaries within the Ranks of Scientific Circles." For background on the extension of this campaign into the CAS, see Merle Goldman, *Literary Dissent in Communist China*, 151.

41. Interview, 1990.

42. Xu and Fan, *Science and Socialist Construction in China*.

43. Interview, 1990.

44. Xu and Qu, "Guanyu woguo Wenhua Dageming shiqi pipan Aiyinsitan he xiangduilun yundong de chubu kaocha."

45. Xu Liangying, "Political Democracy Is a Prerequisite to Academic Freedom," *Renmin ribao*, 6 November 1986, 3 (trans. in FBIS-China, 13 November 1986, K1–2).

46. Xu, "Shilun kexue he minzhu de shehui gongneng."

47. Xu, "Lishi lixinglun de kexue shiguan chuyi."

48. Xu, "Guanyu kexue jishu fazhan guilu de sikao."

49. Xu Liangying, "Lishi lixinglun de kexue shiguan chuyi."

50. He Zuoxiu, "A Rebuttal to the Statement 'It Is Unscientific to Say That Science Is a Force of Production,'" *Zhenli de zhuiqiu* [Pursuit of truth], 1991, no. 10: 6–8, 17 (trans. in JPRS: *China*, 26 February 1992, 1–3). See also a further attack on Xu's views on this score, though not naming him, by He, "The Great Significance of the Theory That Science Is the Primary Force of Production,'" *Qiushi*, 1992, no. 6: 11–17 (trans. in JPRS *China Report*, 16 July 1992, 11–17).

51. My own understanding of Fang's views and their evolution has benefited greatly from the work of James H. Williams, whose study of Fang promises to be definitive and who has graciously shared his views and insights with me. Williams's preliminary views of Fang are expressed in his article "Fang Lizhi's Expanding Universe" and in his introductory essays in Fang, *Bringing Down the Great Wall*, 43–49 and 85–91. Other presentations of Fang's views are: Schell, *Discos and Democracy*, 121–39, and his introduction to Fang, *Bringing Down the Great Wall*; Buckley, "Science as Politics and Politics as Science"; and Kraus, "The Lament of Astrophysicist Fang Lizhi."

52. Many of Fang's own political writings and speeches before his 1987 purge are available in Fang, *Minzhu bushi ciyu de*. English translations of many of his writings before and after 1987 are in the two collections edited and translated by James H. Williams, "The Expanding Universe of Fang Lizhi" and Fang, *Bringing Down the Great Wall*.

53. Wu Guosheng, "Fang Lizhi—The Kind of Scholar the Republic Needs," in Williams, "The Expanding Universe of Fang Lizhi," 92; and Schell, *Discos and Democracy*, 124.

54. Fang, "A Hat, A Forbidden Zone, A Question," in *Bringing Down the Great Wall*, 56–59.

55. Fang, "Thoughts on Reform," in *Bringing Down the Great Wall*, 95–125.

56. Fang Lizhi, "Reflecting on Traditional Chinese Culture from the Vantage Point of Natural Science," in Williams, "The Expanding Universe of Fang Lizhi," 65–74.

57. Fang, "On Political Reform," in *Bringing Down the Great Wall*, 135–56.

58. This discussion of Jin Guantao draws mainly from his own account, "Ershinian de zhuiqiu: Wo he zhexue" [A twenty-year pursuit: Philosophy and me], preface to his *Wo de zhexue tansuo*, 3–52 (see his "Wo shi zenmayang pandeng sixiang jieti de?" for an abridged version). A helpful

review of some of Jin's views is given in Brugger and Kelly, *Chinese Marxism in the Post-Mao Era*, 29–30, 61, and 69–79.

59. These treatises are collected in Jin Guantao, *Wo de zhexue tansuo*.

60. Jin Guantao, Fan Hongye, and Liu Qingfeng, "Lishishang de kexue jishu jiegou."

61. Jin Guantao, remarks at *Hongqi* forum, in *Hongqi*, 1986, no. 14 (trans. in JPRS *China Report: Red Flag*, 28 August 1986, 46–47).

62. There is a brief biography of Li Xingmin in *Guangming ribao*, 17 July 1989, 3.

63. Li Xingmin, "Huaiyi, pingquan, duoyuan." Zhang Zhixin was executed in 1975 because she spoke out against Maoist doctrines and stuck to tried-and-true Marxism-Leninism; the Deng regime has made her a model of unflinching allegiance to principle. Sheng Ping, ed., *Zhongguo Gongchandang lishi dacidian, 1921–1991*, 728.

64. Li Xingmin, "Guanyu kexue yu jiazhi de jige wenti."

65. Interviews, 1990 and 1991. Bill Brugger and David Kelly argue, with some cogency, that Jin Guantao, while disaffected from Leninist Marxism, remains an "ironic believer"—someone who has "believed through" his or her commitment to Marxism to a new, unstated commitment—in a group of "critical" and "humanist Marxists" (*Chinese Marxism in the Post-Mao Era*, 5 and 7).

66. Fang correspondence with author, 3 July 1993.

67. Ibid.

68. Fang Lizhi states that Wu's article was based on his Master of Science thesis at Beijing University and that Wu did not consult with him in writing it (ibid.).

69. Interviews, 1990 and 1991.

70. Fang correspondence with author, 3 July 1993.

71. Williams, "The Expanding Universe of Fang Lizhi," 8n17; Fang correspondence with author, 3 July 1993.

72. There is as yet no completely satisfying account of the leadership struggles of 1987–89, but helpful general accounts include Chu-yuan Cheng, *Behind the Tiananmen Massacre;* and Dittmer, "The Tiananmen Massacre."

73. On the rise of these groups and their social and political significance, see Bonnin and Chevrier, "The Intellectual and the State."

74. Among the flood of press attention to the relevance of the "science and demccracy" theme, see, for example, Wu Chunce and Shen Chong's

commentary on the relevance of the May Fourth slogan for the contemporary situation in *Liaowang*, 1988, no. 12 (2 May): 607 (trans. in FBIS-China, 18 May 1988, 25); Chen Chengde, "On the Synchronous Development of Science and Democratic Politics," *Guangming ribao*, 26 May 1988, 3 (trans. in FBIS-China, 16 June 1988, 29–32); Su Shaozhi and Wang Yizhou, "1989 nien zhishi women" [The year 1989 instructs us], *Zhongguo qingnian* (China youth), 1989, no. 1: 2–3; and Yan Jiaqi, "Jinri Zhongguo."

75. Zha Ruqiang (in "Ping 'Yuzhou shi yu wu,'" 65) cited Wang as supporting his perspective in the debates. Fang, however, states that Wang stayed out of the debate. Fang correspondence with author, 3 July 1993.

76. On Fang's work regimen, see Link, "The Thought and Spirit of Fang Lizhi," 104–5; and Fang, "My Life on May 21, 1987," in Fang, *Bringing Down the Great Wall*, 201. On his promotion, see Xinhua, 5 February 1988 (trans. in FBIS-China, 8 February 1988, 17). See also Zhongguo Xinwenshe, 4 February 1988 (trans. in FBIS-China, 9 February 1988, 19–21); and Li Chuna and Liu Yusheng, "Fang Lizhi's Academic Achievements," *Beijing Review*, 20 May 1988, 23–24.

77. On the regime's use of administrative tactics and Fang's belief that his telephone was tapped, see Link, "The Thought and Spirit of Fang Lizhi," 103. On his unobstructed telephone access to the outside, see Fang, "My Life on May 21, 1987," in Fang, *Bringing Down the Great Wall*, 200–206.

78. Lo Ping, "Storm Coming on the Mainland," *Zhengming*, no. 128 (June 1988): 6–9 (trans. in FBIS-China, 7 June 1988, 35–38); and *Ta kung pao*, 5 May 1988, 2 (trans. in FBIS-China, 5 May 1988, 19–20).

79. Link, "The Thought and Spirit of Fang Lizhi," 104.

80. Fang Lizhi recalls that the first open letter he wrote was in 1957, during the Hundred Flowers period. He states that the precedents in his mind for this kind of public agitation were Kang Youwei's seven open letters on China's future, issued over the decade preceding the Hundred Days Reform of 1898. He did not think of the parallel activities by Soviet scientists in the 1960s as immediate precedents, but he did recall the world peace movement supported by physicists such as Einstein and Robert Oppenheimer as underscoring for him when he was a student in the 1950s the importance of scientists' responsibility toward humanity (correspondence with the author, 3 July 1993). On his part, Su Shaozhi recalls the long tradition of Chinese intellectuals' remonstrance over public affairs through imperial times, and not protest activities such as those of Soviet dissidents

in the 1960s, as the immediate precedent for the open letters of January and February 1989 (correspondence with author, 15 July 1993).

81. Link, "The Thought and Spirit of Fang Lizhi," 101–2. See also the personal account by Fang Lizhi and Li Shuxian in *Zhongguo shibao* (China times), 28 February 1989, 3 (trans. in FBIS-China, 10 March 1989, 15–16).

82. See, for example, his remarks at a meeting of intellectuals and entrepreneurs at the Friendship Hotel in Beijing on 4 February 1989, as reported in *Zhengming*, no. 139 (1 May 1989): 22–23 (trans. in FBIS-China, 4 May 1989, 42–44).

83. Luo Ping, "The Inside Story of the Beidaihe Conference," *Zhengming*, no. 107 (September 1986): 6–10 (trans. in JPRS-CPS-86-79, 17 October 1986, 39–40).

84. Fang, "The End of Forgetting History," in Fang, *Bringing Down the Great Wall*, 271–72.

85. 1987 CCP classified document, "Some Materials Regarding Certain Theoretical Issues" (trans. in Tong, "Party Documents on Anti-Bourgeois Liberalization and Hu Yaobang's Resignation, 1987"). According to Yan Jiaqi, Xu—not Wang Ruowang—was to be expelled from the Party and made an object of the campaign against "bourgeois liberalization," along with Fang Lizhi and Liu Binyan, with whom Xu had been collaborating on the forum to recall the Anti-Rightist campaign. In a slip that his aides apparently did not question, Deng Xiaoping designated Wang instead of Xu Liangying (Yan Jiaqi, "The Nature of Chinese Authoritarianism," 13.)

86. Fang Lizhi, "Will China Disintegrate?," interview with Li Yi, in Fang, *Bringing Down the Great Wall*, 225.

87. Ibid., 230. In correspondence with the author, Fang confirms that Xu's Marxist convictions lapsed in this period but adds that he is unaware of the precise reasons.

88. *Zhengming*, no. 139 (1 May 1989): 22–23 (trans. in FBIS-China, 4 May 1989, 42–44). Xu, "Minzhu shi anding tuanjie de weiyi kekao baozheng" (trans. modified).

89. Interview with Xu Liangying, *Jiushi niandai* (The nineties), no. 231 (April 1989): 21–23 (trans. in JPRS *China Report*, 31 July 1992, 1–3. Fang Lizhi states that he was aware of Xu's efforts but not involved in them (correspondence with the author, 3 July 1993).

90. Interview with Xu Liangying, *Jiushi niandai*. See also Fan Dainian's analysis in ibid., 26–28 (trans. in JPRS *China Report*, 31 July 1992, 5–9). The

affiliation of those not identified by Fan can be found in a photocopy of the original handwritten open letter in the author's possession.

91. Text of the "Open Letter of 42," *Jiushi niandai*, no. 231 (April 1989): 22 (trans. in Fang, *Bringing Down the Great Wall*, 305–8).

92. Su Shaozhi, for example, knew Xu Liangying and was aware of his political views, but was not familiar with Xu's views on science and philosophy. Correspondence, 15 July 1993.

93. The text of the warrant is translated in Fang, *Bringing Down the Great Wall*, 317.

94. The most comprehensive authoritative account was Beijing mayor Chen Xitong's report to the National People's Congress Standing Committee session on 30 June 1989 (published in *Beijing Review*, 17–23 July 1989, i–xx). Among press attacks on Fang as a principal conspirator, see Zhao Qian, "Fang Lizhi, Zhang Xianyang and Their Like Have Long Proposed Creating 'Turmoil,'" *Renmin ribao*, 17 July 1989, 4 (trans. in FBIS-China, 20 July 1989, 20–21).

95. Shen Tong recalls that during the early weeks of the demonstrations, he and other student activists were eager for elder intellectuals to participate. By mid-May, however, most still remained on the sidelines, and though Shen understood their reasons for not joining, he believes that the students' previous eagerness turned to frustration. Interview, 1 July 1993.

96. Interview, 1991. Xu's name finally reappeared in print in late 1991. A *Bulletin of Natural Dialectics* account of the Third Young Natural Dialectics Researchers Conference records that he presented a paper at the session entitled "Thirty Years of Storms in Natural Dialectics in China," but recounted none of the substance of his remarks. This presentation appears to have been based on the article Xu contributed to the book on natural dialectics controversies that was suppressed in January 1987.

97. Xu, "Wei kexue zhengming."

98. Xu Liangying, "Reform Cannot Possibly Succeed without Political Democracy."

99. Li Huang, "What Sort of Things Do We Have Too Much of in Our Propaganda?," *Zhongguo jizhe* [China reporter], 1989, no. 7: 11–12 (trans. in FBIS-China, 29 August 1989, 18–21); and Xu Liqun, "How Did They Oppose the Four Cardinal Principles?" *Guangming ribao*, 22 July 1989, 3 (trans. in FBIS-China, 8 August 1989, 30–33).

100. Qian Xuesen speech, *Renmin ribao*, 8 August 1989, 4 (trans. in

FBIS-China, 11 August 1989, 24–26); *Guangming ribao,* 27 August 1989, as reported by Xinhua, 28 August 1989 (trans. in FBIS-China, 29 August 1989, 37).

101. Among various attacks on intellectual pluralism, see the speech by Li Ruihuan at a conference of propaganda departments on 20 July 1989, as reported by Xinhua, 20 July 1989 (trans. in FBIS-China, 21 July 1989, 7–10); and Xu Chengde, "Education in Marxist Theory Should Not Be Neglected—Refuting Several Erroneous Viewpoints of Bourgeois Liberalization," *Renmin ribao,* 12 July 1989, 5 (trans. in FBIS-China, 14 July 1989, 30–32).

6. CHINA'S SCIENTIFIC DISSIDENCE IN PERSPECTIVE

1. On the sense of guilt arising from feelings of responsibility for the Cultural Revolution, however indirect, see Thurston, *Enemies of the People,* 244ff.

2. Yan Jiaqi, "Zongjiao, lixing, shijian." For a fascinating account of how, expanding on an earlier effort to defend relativity theory, Yan came to write this article, see his *Wo de sixiang zizhuan,* 21–30.

3. See, for example, science czar Song Jian's comments in 1986 on efforts by the State Council to draw up legislation that would "give official status to scholarly societies and define their role as well as their relationship to the Communist Party, the government, and state-owned, collective, and individual enterprises" and protect them "against outside interference." That this legislation was a reponse to pressures from the science community was clear from reports on the session of the umbrella organization of scientific professional societies, CAST, then in session, which stated that the association had accepted the "views and demands" of scientists at the session that it "defend their legitimate rights" with respect to the Communist Party and government (Xinhua, 25 and 28 June 1986 [trans., respectively, in FBIS-China, 26 June 1986, K19–20; and 30 June 1986, K2–3]).

4. A powerful analysis of the rhetorical contribution of Fang Lizhi and scientific dissidents to the establishment of an arena of public discourse, paralleling the discussion here, is Buckley, "Science as Politics and Politics as Science," 18ff. On the emergence of an incipient civil society in China in the late 1980s, see Walder, "The Political Sociology of the Beijing Upheaval of 1989"; Strand, "Protest in Beijing: Civil Society and Public Sphere in China"; Perry and Fuller, "China's Long March to Democracy"; and Kelly and He, "Emergent Civil Society and the Intellectuals in China."

5. Insightful analyses of the May Fourth reflections on culture and politics are Charlotte Furth, "Intellectual Change"; *idem*, "Culture and Politics in Modern Chinese Conservatism"; and Grieder, *Intellectuals and the State in Modern China: A Narrative History*, 203–79.

6. Furth, "Culture and Politics in Modern Chinese Conservatism," 26; and *idem*, "May Fourth in History."

7. One of the most useful attempts to analyze the cluster of cultural issues in the 1980s debates is by Lin Tongqi, who depicts them broadly as a "humanist quest" ("A Search for China's Soul").

8. Others who have discussed the emergence of critical intellectuals in post-Mao China include Merle Goldman and Timothy Cheek, "Uncertain Change," 6–10; Kelly, "Chinese Intellectuals in the 1989 Democracy Movement"; Lin Tongqi, "A Search for China's Soul," 179; and Lin Min, "The Search for Modernity," 696. Timothy Cheek presents a somewhat more skeptical view in "From Priests to Professionals: Intellectuals and the State Under the CCP."

9. Haraszti, *The Velvet Prison: Artists Under State Socialism*.

10. Liu Binyan, *A Higher Kind of Loyalty*, 192–99.

11. Ibid., 96–97 and 160–94.

12. For this and other contrasting views of May Fourth era scientists, see Fan Hongye and Li Zhen, "Kexuejia dui Wu Si Xinwenhua yundong de gongxian."

13. On the establishment of the scientific profession in China, see Y. C. Wang, *Chinese Intellectuals and the West, 1872–1949*, 378–93; and Reardon-Anderson, *The Study of Change*.

14. Reardon-Anderson, *The Study of Change*, 79.

15. Furth, *Ting Wen-chiang*, 138. On the May 1922 manifesto, see Grieder, *Hu Shih and the Chinese Renaissance*, 189–99.

16. Reardon-Anderson, *The Study of Change*, 177–257. On the National Resource Commission, see also William C. Kirby, "Technocratic Organization and Technological Development in China."

17. Reardon-Anderson, *The Study of Change*, 293–318; *idem*, "Science in Wartime China."

18. On these developments, see MacFarquhar, *The Origins of the Cultural Revolution*, vol. 1, 33–35 and 51–56; Chu-yuan Cheng, *Scientific and Engineering Manpower in Communist China, 1949–1963*, 10–16 and 28–31; and Nie, *Inside the Red Star*, 659–75.

19. The following catalog of complaints is derived from the criticisms published during the period collected and translated in MacFarquhar, *The Hundred Flowers Campaign and the Chinese Intellectuals*.

20. Yu's speech is published in *Ziran bianzhengfa tongxun*, 1980, no. 5, 5–13. On Lysenkoism and the Qingdao conference, see Schneider, "Lysenkoism in China"; and idem, "Learning From Russia."

21. Xu and Fan, *Science and Socialist Construction in China*.

22. Williams, "Fang Lizhi's Expanding Universe," 460–61.

23. Reardon-Anderson, *The Study of Change*, 203–6.

24. Pepper, *Civil War in China*, 199–228.

25. Rene Goldman, "The Rectification Campaign at Peking University: May–June 1957."

26. Shen Tong, a student organizer in the 1989 Tiananmen demonstrations and himself a biology student at Beijing University from 1986 to 1989, remarked that no single discipline seemed to stand out among the science students active either in the fall of 1986 or in the activism of 1988–89, but then added that both of the graduate-student advisers to his Olympic Institute were in physics (interview, 1 July 1993). For his stirring account of his own organizing activities, see Shen Tong, *Almost a Revolution*.

27. Kwok, *Scientism in Chinese Thought, 1900–1950*, 3–30.

28. In addition to Kwok, *Scientism in Chinese Thought*, see Furth, *Ting Wen-chiang*, 13–16; and especially idem, "Intellectual Change."

29. Fang, "My Feelings About Art," in Fang, *Bringing Down the Great Wall*, 77–78. Cf. also his similar views in "Galileo and Milton: Physics and Poetry," *ibid.*, 74–75.

30. Fang, "A Note on the Interface between Science and Religion," in ibid., 37.

31. Ibid., 32–37.

32. Xu was responding to articles written by Gu Xin and, ironically, Liu Qingfeng, which argued that scientism had corrupted the May Fourth ideals of "science and democracy." His comments also drew on a reading of Danny W. Y. Kwok, *Scientism in Chinese Thought, 1900–1950* and Charlotte Furth's biography of Ding Wenjiang. See Gu Xin, "Weikexuezhuyi yu Zhongguo jinxiandai zhishifenzi"; and Liu Qingfeng, "Ershi shiji Zhongguo kexuezhuyi de liangci xingqi." See also the criticism by Huan Xuewen, "Jiu 'Ershi shiji Zhongguo kexuezhuyi de liangci xingqi' yu zuozhe shangque."

33. Xu Liangying, "Wei kexue zhengming." A similar perspective on

scientists of the May Fourth period is provided in Fan Hongye and Li Zhen, "Kexuejia dui Wu Si Xinwenhua yundong de gongxian."

34. On the 1923 debates, see Chow, *The May Fourth Movement*, 333–37; Kwok, *Scientism in Chinese Thought*, 135–60; Furth, *Ting Wen-chiang*, 94–135; and Grieder, *Intellectuals and the State in Modern China*, 256–60.

35. Furth, *Ting Wen-chiang*, 123–24.

36. Joseph Ben-David, *The Scientist's Role in Society: A Comparative Study*, 69–94.

37. The following interpretation of modern Chinese history draws on a new historiography that significantly revises the conventional picture of state and society relations in the late imperial period and after. For a list of landmark works in this new historiography, see chap. 1, note 15.

38. Schwarcz, *The Chinese Enlightenment*, 286–91.

39. The following draws on the discussion of New Culture movement liberalism in Grieder, *Intellectuals and the State in Modern China*, 241–53; Furth, *Ting Wen-chiang*, 1–16, 79, 92–93, 136–65; Chow, *The May Fourth Movement*, 216, 295–96, 358–61; Y. C. Wang, *Chinese Intellectuals and the West, 1872–1949*, 385–86, 393–402, 420–21; and Nathan, *Chinese Democracy*, 107–32.

40. Bergere, "The Chinese Bourgeoisie, 1911–1937," 777–87.

41. Furth, *Ting Wen-chiang*, 193–225.

42. Fang, *Bringing Down the Great Wall*, 145–46 and 166–67.

43. Ibid., 150–51; cf. also 128–29, 131, 133–34, and 146.

44. Ibid., 105–7; Xu Liangying, "Reform Cannot Possibly Succeed without Political Democracy."

45. Fang, *Bringing Down the Great Wall*, 109–12. The view here takes direct issue with that of Richard Kraus, who argues that Fang's statements on the increasingly important role of intellectuals amount to a traditional elitism, as do his comments on the obscurantism and subservience he finds in peasant society. This interpretation appears to be based on a serious misreading of Fang's comments. In citing Fang's comments on peasant attitudes, for example, Professor Kraus seems to have missed Fang's complaints, in the sentences that follow, of similar traits among his intellectual peers. See Kraus, "The Lament of Astrophysicist Fang Lizhi," 297–99, but compare the relevant and cited portion of Fang's speech at Tongji University on 16 November 1986 in Fang, *Minzhu bushi ciyu de*, 147. Fang has himself explicitly rebutted this characterization of his views, responding with typical sarcasm that such an interpretation would be true if opposition to the

dictatorship of the proletariat and advocacy of freedom of conduct and dissemination of scientific research, freedom of speech and publication, free elections, and multiparty politics could all be considered antidemocratic, elitist, and technocratic. Correspondence with the author, 3 July 1993.

46. Y. C. Wang, *Chinese Intellectuals and the West, 1872–1949*, 421.

47. Su Shaozhi, correspondence with author, 15 July 1993.

48. On Wang Ruoshui's humanistic Marxism, see Kelly, "The Emergence of Humanism."

49. This humanistic outlook is frequently expressed by scientists— especially in the theoretical sciences. See, for example, Feynman, *"What Do You Care What Other People Think?"*, 239–48.

50. Gan Yang's views on these issues are in his "Ziyou de linian" and "Yangchi 'minzhu yu kexue' dianding 'ziyou yu zhixu.'" More generally, see his two essays "Bashi niandai wenhua taolun de jige wenti" (Several problems in the discussions on culture in the 1980s) and "Cong 'lixing de pipan' dao 'wenhua de pipan'" (From "rational critique" to "cultural critique") in Gan, ed., *Zhongguo dangdai wenhua yishi*, 1–35 and 557–79, respectively.

51. Li Honglin's articles on political reform and intellectual politics from 1978 through 1985 are most conveniently available in his book *Lilun fengyun*. Yu Haocheng's views in the same period can be assessed in his collected essays, *Minzhi fazhi shehuizhuyi*.

52. Yan Jiaqi, *Wo de sixiang zizhuan*, 2–21 (trans. in Yan Jiaqi, *Toward a Democratic China*, 3–31).

53. Yan Jiaqi, "My Four Convictions Regarding Science," *Guangming ribao*, 10 May 1988 (trans. in Yan Jiaqi, *Toward a Democratic China*, 211–13).

54. Activist and biology student Shen Tong became aware of Fang Lizhi in his first semester at Beijing University in the fall of 1986 from Fang's articles in the press on democratization and university reforms. He recalls that he and his fellow students were dismayed at Fang's expulsion from the CCP in January 1987, which they first learned about from listening to Voice of America broadcasts in their study hall. Fang's purge, Shen has said, greatly deflated their estimation and expectations of Deng Xiaoping. Shen was not at all surprised that Fang re-emerged as an outspoken dissident thereafter. He and other students were encouraged in their own activities by Fang's January 1989 petition, and he had read Fang's article "China's Despair and China's Hope," published in the *New York Review of Books* (2 February 1989, 3–4). Fang's wife, Li Shuxian, had given him and Wang Dan a copy, which

they reprinted and circulated among Beijing University students. Shen also has said that although before 1989 he had not read any of Xu Liangying's writings, he knew of Xu and his open letter of February 26 and the open letter of February 16th, signed by thirty-three intellectuals, in support of Fang. Shen also had read works by Jin Guantao, including several books from the "Toward the Future" series Jin edited with Bao Zunxin. Interview, 1 July 1993.

55. Su's first article published after his purge in the fall of 1987 was his "The Two Historic Tasks of Reform," coauthored with his protege Wang Yizhou and published in *Renmin ribao* on 5 March 1988 (trans. in FBIS-China, 9 March 1988, 20–24). Note also the significance attached to the reappearance of Su in print, as a sign of a freer academic atmosphere, in the report by the official media: Zhongguo Xinwenshe, 3 March 1988 (trans. in FBI-China, 9 March 1988, 24–25); and Zhongguo Tongxunshe, 9 March 1988 (trans. in FBIS-China, 11 March 1988, 18).

56. Lowenthal, "The Post-Revolutionary Phase in China and Russia."

57. On these and other changes in the Soviet science community in this period, see Kneen, *Soviet Scientists and the State;* Fortescu, *The Communist Party and Soviet Science;* and Medvedev, *Soviet Science.*

58. Fainsod, *How Russia Is Ruled,* 201ff.; and Kneen, *Soviet Scientists and the State,* 64–67.

59. Medvedev, *Soviet Science,* 108–9; Parrott, *Politics and Technology in the Soviet Union,* 167–68; and Vucinich, *Empire of Knowledge,* 302–3.

60. Parrott, *Politics and Technology in the Soviet Union,* 167; Vucinich, *Empire of Knowledge,* 301–2.

61. Fortescu, *The Communist Party and Soviet Science,* 41–42.

62. Graham, *Science, Philosophy, and Human Behavior in the Soviet Union,* 22 and 59.

63. Vucinich, *Empire of Knowledge,* 257–74.

64. This is a main argument of Joravsky's masterful study of Lysenkoism, *The Lysenko Affair.* It is also repeated succinctly in his review essay "Bosses and Scientists." Also on the Lysenko episode, see Graham, *Science in Russia and the Soviet Union,* 123–34.

65. On shifts in science and technology policy, see Kneen, *Soviet Scientists and The State,* 83–84; Medvedev, *Soviet Science,* 106 and 132–34; and especially Parrot, *Politics and Technology in the Soviet Union,* 219–28 and 278–91.

66. Kneen, *Soviet Scientists and the State*, 82–86.

67. On the Markov-Kedrov affair, see Graham, *Science, Philosophy, and Human Behavior in the Soviet Union*, 15–17 and 325–29; Graham, *Science and Philosophy in the Soviet Union*, 75–81; Hahn, *Postwar Soviet Politics*, 78–84.

68. Medvedev, *Soviet Science*, 89–90.

69. Ibid., 92–100; Vucinich, *Empire of Knowledge*, 361–63; and Kneen, *Soviet Scientists and the State*, 83–84. Sakharov recalls in his *Memoirs* some of his attempts to persuade Krushchev in 1961 (215–19). On Sakharov, see also Graham, *Science in Russia and the Soviet Union*, 168–72.

70. Medvedev, *Soviet Science*, 101–2.

71. Shlapentokh, *Soviet Intellectuals and Political Power*, 85.

72. Medvedev, *Soviet Science*, 106–8; Shatz, *Soviet Dissent in Historical Perspective*, 117–37.

73. Medvedev, *Soviet Science*, 131; Shlapentokh, *Soviet Intellectuals and Political Power*, 145. Sakharov's own recounting of his decision to sign a petition in 1966 is in his *Memoirs*, 270–71. A helpful analysis of Sakharov's path to dissidence and of his political views is Dornan, "Andrei Sakharov: The Conscience of a Liberal Scientist." In the same volume, there is a useful analysis of the socioeconomic significance of Soviet dissent by Walter D. Connor, "Differentiation, Integration, and Political Dissent in the USSR." 139–57.

74. Medevedev, *Soviet Science*, 132–34.

75. Shatz, *Soviet Dissent in Historical Perspective*, 158–67.

76. Shlapentokh, *Soviet Intellectuals and Political Power*, 150–71.

77. Shatz, *Soviet Dissent in Historical Perspective*, chap. 4.

78. One is tempted to explain this on the basis of the fundamental nature of the questions that theoretical physicists deal with and of the peculiar temperament they are reputed to have. In many ways, theoretical scientists are the most ideological standard bearers of science's ideals. On these characteristics, see McCain and Segal, *The Game of Science*, 139–45; and Traweek, *Beamtimes and Lifetimes: The World of High Energy Physics*.

Selected Bibliography

Full information on materials translated in the FBIS China Daily Report, the JPRS China translations series, and the PRC English-language weekly *Beijing Review* is provided in the notes in which they are cited.

Ai Ying. "Lun zhexue dui kexue de 'zhidao' zuoyong" [On philosophy's "guidance" of science]. *Zhexue yanjiu*, 1986, no. 12: 21–26.

Barnett, A. Doak. "Ten Years after Mao." *Foreign Affairs*, vol. 65, no. 1 (Fall 1986): 37–65.

Baylis, Thomas. *The Technical Intelligentsia and the East German Elite: Legitimacy and Social Change in Mature Communism*. Berkeley: University of California Press, 1974.

Ben-David, Joseph. *The Scientist's Role in Society: A Comparative Study*. Chicago: University of Chicago Press, 1984.

Bendix, Reinhard. *Max Weber: An Intellectual Portrait*. New York: Doubleday and Co., 1960.

Berger, Peter, and Thomas Luckmann. *The Social Construction of Reality: A Treatise on the Sociology of Knowledge*. New York: Anchor Books, 1966.

Bergere, Marie-Claire. "The Chinese Bourgeoisie, 1911–1937." In *Cambridge History of China*, vol. 12: *Republican China 1912–1949*, part 1, edited by John King Fairbank, 721–825. New York: Cambridge University Press, 1983.

———. *The Golden Age of the Chinese Bourgeoisie, 1911–1937*. New York: Cambridge University Press, 1986.

Bodman, Richard W., and Pin P. Wang, trans. *Deathsong of the River: A Reader's Guide to the Chinese TV Series "Heshang."* Ithaca: Cornell University Press, 1991.

Bohm, David. *Quantum Theory*. Englewood Cliffs, N.J.: Prentice-Hall, 1951.

Bonnin, Michel, and Yves Chevrier. "The Intellectual and the State: Social Dynamics of Intellectual Autonomy During the Post-Mao Era." *China Quarterly*, no. 127 (September 1991): 569–93.

Boorman, Howard I., ed. *Biographic Dictionary of Republican China*. 5 vols. New York: Columbia University Press, 1967.

Braybrooke, George. "Recent Developments in Chinese Social Science, 1977–79." *China Quarterly*, no. 79 (September 1979): 593–607.

Brugger, Bill, and David Kelly. *Chinese Marxism in the Post-Mao Era*. Stanford: Stanford University Press, 1990.

Buck, Peter S. *American Science and Modern China*. New York: Cambridge University Press, 1980.

Buckley, Christopher. "Science as Politics and Politics as Science: Fang Lizhi and Chinese Intellectuals' Uncertain Road to Dissent." *Australian Journal of Chinese Affairs*, no. 25 (January 1991): 1–36.

CCP Central Committee Documents Research Office (Zhonggong Zhongyang Wenxian Yanjiushi). *Sanzhong Quanhui yilai zhongyao wenxian xuanbian* [Selected important documents since the Third Plenum]. Changchun: Renmin Chubanshe, 1982. Taipei reprint, 1983.

———. *Guanyu jianguo yilai dang de ruogan lishi wenti de jueyi zhushiben* [Annotations on the resolution concerning some questions in the Party's history since the founding of the country], rev. ed. (*xiuding*). Beijing: Renmin Chubanshe, 1985.

CCP Central Committee Organization Department and Documents Research Office. *Zhishifenzi wenti wenxian xuanbian* [Selected documents on the problem of intellectuals]. Beijing: Renmin Chubanshe, 1983.

Cheek, Timothy. "From Priests to Professionals: Intellectuals and the State under the CCP." In *Popular Protest in Modern China: Learning from 1989*, edited by Jeffery Wasserstrom and Elizabeth Perry, 124–45. Boulder: Westview Press, 1992.

Chen Chengbin and Yao Sha, eds. *Ziran bianzhengfa yuanli* [Principles of natural dialectics]. Changsha: Hunan Jiaoyu Chubanshe, 1984.

Chen Chengde and Guo Fengsheng. "Shijian—zhenli—kexue yujian" [Practice, truth, and scientific prediction]. *Guangming ribao*, 18 April 1983, 3. (Trans. in *JPRS China Report: Political, Social, and Military*, 31 May 1983, 82–86.)

Cheng, Chu-yuan. *Scientific and Engineering Manpower in Communist China, 1949–1963*. National Science Foundation study NSF-65-14. Washington, D.C.: U.S. Government Printing Office, 1965.

———. *Behind the Tiananmen Massacre: Social, Political, and Economic Ferment in China*. Boulder: Westview Press, 1990.

Cheng, Li, and Lynn White III. "Elite Transformation and Modern Change in Mainland China and Taiwan: Empirical Data and the Theory of Technocracy." *China Quarterly,* no. 121 (March 1990): 1–35.

Chinese Academy of Social Sciences. "Mao Zhuxi de jiaodao he guanhuai yongyuan guwu women qianjin" [Chairman Mao's guidance and concern will forever inspire our advance]. *Guangming ribao,* 22 September 1977, 1, 2.

———. *Zhongguo shehui kexue yuan* [The Chinese Academy of Social Sciences]. Beijing: 1983. (Trans. in *JPRS China Report: Economic Affairs,* 19 February 1985.)

Chinese Academy of Social Sciences Institute of Philosophy, ed. *Zhongguo zhexue nianjian 1983* [1983 yearbook in Chinese philosophy]. Shanghai: Zhongguo Dabaikequanshu Chubanshe, 1983.

———. *Zhongguo zhexue nianjian 1984* [1984 yearbook in Chinese philosophy]. Shanghai: Zhongguo Dabaikequanshu Chubanshe, 1984.

Chow, Tse-tsung. *The May Fourth Movement: Intellectual Revolution in Modern China* (Cambridge: Harvard University Press, 1960).

Clark, Donald W., and Anne B. Klein. *Biographic Dictionary of Chinese Communism: 1921–1965.* 2 vols. Cambridge: Harvard University Press, 1971.

Close, Frank. *Too Hot to Handle: The Race for Cold Fusion.* Princeton: Princeton University Press, 1991.

Cohen, I. Bernard, ed. *Puritanism and the Rise of Modern Science: The Merton Thesis.* New Brunswick: Rutgers University Press, 1990.

Cohen, Paul A. *Discovering History in China: American Historical Writing on the Recent Chinese Past.* New York: Columbia University Press, 1984.

Connor, Walter D. "Differentiation, Integration, and Political Dissent in the USSR." In *Dissent in the USSR: Politics, Ideology, and People,* edited by Rudolf L. Tokes, 139–57. Baltimore: Johns Hopkins University Press, 1975.

Coughland, G. D., and J. E. Dodd. *The Ideas of Particle Physics: An Introduction for Scientists.* 2nd ed. New York: Cambridge University Press, 1991.

Davies, Paul, ed. *The New Physics.* New York: Cambridge University Press, 1989.

Deng Weizhi. "Makesizhuyi yanjiu de 'tupo' " ["Breakthroughs" in the study of Marxism]. *Renmin ribao.* 14 March 1986, 5. (Trans. [erroneously attrib. to "Deng Weizhong"] in FBIS-China, 25 March 1986, K27–29.)

Deng Xiaoping. *Fundamental Issues in Present-Day China.* Beijing: Foreign Languages Press, 1987.

———. *Selected Works of Deng Xiaoping (1975–1982)*. Translated and edited by the CCP Bureau for the Compilation and Translation of the Works of Marx, Engels, Lenin, and Stalin. Beijing: Foreign Languages Press, 1984.

D'Espagnat, Bernard. *Conceptual Foundations of Quantum Mechanics*. 2nd ed. New York: Addison-Wesley, 1989.

———. *Reality and the Physicist: Knowledge, Duration, and the Quantum World*. New York: Cambridge University Press, 1989.

Dittmer, Lowell. "The Tiananmen Massacre." *Problems of Communism*, vol. 38, no. 5 (September–October 1989): 2–15.

Dong Guangbi. "Zhongguo Ziran Bianzhengfa Yanjiuhui shoujie xueshu nianhui gaikuang" [A general report on the first annual meeting of the Chinese Natural Dialectics Research Society]. *Ziran bianzhengfa tongxun*, 1982, no. 1: 73–75.

———. "Dingyu yinbian lilun jiqi shiyan jianyan de lishi he zhexue de tao-lun" [A discussion of the history and philosophy of local "hidden variables" theories and their experimental tests]. *Ziran bianzhengfa tongxun*, 1984, no. 2: 25–30.

———. "EPR shiyan he wuli shizaiguan" [The EPR experiment and physics' view of reality]. *Guangming ribao*, 28 April 1986, 3.

———. "Jiujing shenma shi ziran bianzhengfa?" [Just what is natural dia-lectics?]. *Ziran bianzhengfa yanjiu*, 1986, no. 4: 56–61.

———. "Mahe de kexue zhexue yu Makesizhuyi" [Mach's philosophy of science and Marxism]. *Ziran bianzhengfa yanjiu*, 1988, no. 6, 12–17; and 1989, no. 1: 19–27.

———. "EPR shiyan—Shizailun he shizhenglun de lunzheng" [The EPR ex-periment—A dispute between realism and positivism]. *Ziran bian-zhengfa yanjiu*, 1989, no. 4: 31–37.

———, Han Zenglu, and Jin Wulun. "Zhexue yao wei kexue bianhu" [Phi-losophy must defend science]. *Guangming ribao*, 20 October 1986, 3.

Dornan, Peter. "Andrei Sakharov: The Conscience of a Liberal Scientist." In *Dissent in the USSR: Politics, Ideology, and People*, edited by Rudolf L. Tokes, 354–417. Baltimore: Johns Hopkins University Press, 1975.

Duan, Ruofei, "Makesizhuyi shi wanzheng de kexue shijieguan" [Marxism is a complete scientific worldview]. *Hongqi*, 1987, no. 3: 10–16. (Trans. in *JPRS China Report: Red Flag*, 28 August 1986, 48–49.)

Fainsod, Merle. *How Russia Is Ruled*. Rev. ed. Cambridge: Harvard University Press, 1965.

Fairbank, John K., Edwin O. Reischauer, and Albert M. Craig. *A History of East Asian Civilization*. Vol. 2, *East Asia: The Modern Transformation*. Boston: Houghton Mifflin Co., 1965.

Fan Dainian. "Guanyu Zhongguo Kexueyuan fazhan zhanlue yanjiu de ruogan wenti de chubu tantao" [An initial exploration into several problems concerning developmental research in the CAS]. *Ziran bianzhengfa tongxun*, 1986, no. 1: 21–30.

———. " 'Sishier ren gongkaixin' qianshuzhe jianjie" [A brief introduction to the signers of the "Open Letter of 42"]. *Jiushi niandai* [The nineties], 1989, no. 4: 26–28.

Fan Hongye and Li Zhen. "Kexuejia dui Wu Si Xinwenhua yundong de gongxian" [The contribution of scientists to the May Fourth New Culture movement]. *Ziran bianzhengfa tongxun*, 1989, no. 3, 41–49. (Slightly modified version in Liu Qingfeng, ed., *Lishi de fanxiang*, 192–212.)

Fang Lizhi, "Cong 'Wanwu yuanyu shui' dao 'shikong shi wuzhi zunzai de xingshi' " [From "water is the origin of all things" to "space-time is the form of material existence"]. *Zhexue yanjiu*, 1982, no. 6: 18–20. (Trans. in Williams, "The Expanding Universe of Fang Lizhi," 40–42.)

———. " 'Diyi tuidong' jinxitan" [On "primordial motion," past and present]. *Ziran bianzhengfa tongxun*, 1984, no. 4: 41–47. (Trans. in Williams, "The Expanding Universe of Fang Lizhi," 45–54.)

———. "Zhexue he wuli" [Philosophy and physics]. *Ziran bianzhengfa yanjiu*, 1986, no. 5: 28–30. (Trans. in Fang, *Bringing Down the Wall*, 24–29.)

———. *Minzhu bushi ciyu de* [Democracy is not bestowed from above]. Hong Kong: Dadi Chubanshe, 1987.

———. "China's Despair and China's Hope." *New York Review of Books*. 2 February 1989: 3–4.

———. *Bringing Down the Great Wall: Writings on Science, Culture, and Democracy in China*. Edited and translated by James H. Williams. New York: Alfred A. Knopf, 1991.

——— and Yin Dengxiang. "Weiraozhe xiandai yuzhouxue de yichang kexue yu jiakexue de lunzheng" [The controversy between science and pseudoscience over modern cosmology]. *Zhexue yanjiu*, 1978, no. 1–2: 79–87. (Trans. in Williams, "The Expanding Universe of Fang Lizhi," 14–26.)

Feynman, Richard P. *"What Do You Care What Other People Think?"—Further Adventures of a Curious Character.* New York: W. W. Norton and Company, 1988.

———, Robert B. Leighton, and Matthew Sands. *The Feynman Lectures on Physics.* Vol. 3, *Quantum Mechanics.* Reading, Mass.: Addison-Wesley, 1966.

Fortescu, Stephen. *The Communist Party and Soviet Science.* Baltimore: Johns Hopkins University Press, 1986.

Friedman, Edward. "Einstein and Mao: Metaphors of Revolution." *China Quarterly*, no. 93 (March 1983): 51–75.

Furth, Charlotte. *Ting Wen-chiang: Science and China's New Culture.* Cambridge: Harvard University Press, 1970.

———. "May Fourth in History." In *Reflections on the May Fourth Movement: A Symposium*, edited by Benjamin I. Schwartz, 59–68. Cambridge: Harvard University Press, 1971.

———. "Culture and Politics in Modern Chinese Conservatism." In *The Limits of Change: Essays on Conservative Alternatives in Republican China*, edited by Charlotte Furth, 22–53. Cambridge: Harvard University Press, 1977.

———. "Intellectual Change: From the Reform Movement to the May Fourth Movement, 1895–1920." In *Cambridge History of China*, vol. 12: *Republican China 1912–1949*, part 1 edited by John King Fairbank, 322–405. New York: Cambridge University Press, 1983.

Gan Yang. "Ziyou de linian: Wusi chuantong chih queshimian" (The concept of freedom: The erroneousness of the May Fourth tradition). In *Lishi de fanxiang* (Echoes of history), edited by Liu Qingfeng, 135–53. Hong Kong: Sanlian Shudian, 1990.

———. "Yangchi 'minzhu yu kexue' dianding 'ziyou yu zhixu'" [Casting "science and democracy" aside and establishing "freedom and order"]. *Ershiyi shiji*, no. 3 (February 1991): 7–10.

———, ed. *Zhongguo dangdai wenhua yishi* [Cultural consciousness in contemporary China]. Hong Kong: Sanlian Shudian, 1989.

Ge Yuehua. "Several Problems Encountered in the Reform of Research Institutes." *Kexuexue yu kexue jishu guanli* (The science of science and the management of science and technology), 1987, no. 2: 10–11 (trans. in *JPRS China Report: Science and Technology*, 7 July 1987: 36–40).

Goldman, Merle. *Literary Dissent in Communist China.* New York: Atheneum, 1971.

———. *China's Intellectuals: Advise and Dissent.* Cambridge, Mass.: Harvard University Press, 1981.

———. "Hu Yaobang's Intellectual Network and the Theory Conference of 1979." *China Quarterly,* no. 126 (June 1991): 219–42.

———. *Sowing the Seeds of Democracy in China: Political Reform in the Deng Xiaoping Era.* Cambridge, Mass.: Harvard University Press, 1994.

———, and Timothy Cheek. "Uncertain Change." In *China's Intellectuals and the State: In Search of a New Relationship,* edited by Merle Goldman, Timothy Cheek, and Carol Hamrin, 1–20. Cambridge: Harvard University Press, 1987.

Goldman, Rene. "The Rectification Campaign at Peking University: May–June 1957." *China Quarterly,* no. 12 (October–December 1962): 138–53.

Gong Yuzhi and Sun Xiaoli. "Ziran bianzhengfa de lishi fazhan he zhuyao neirong" [The historical development of natural dialectics and its principal content]. *Ziran bianzhengfa yanjiu,* 1987, no. 3: 1–6.

Graham, Loren. *Science and Philosophy in the Soviet Union.* New York: Alfred A. Knopf, 1972.

———. *Science, Philosophy, and Human Behavior in the Soviet Union.* New York: Columbia University Press, 1987.

———. *Science in Russia and the Soviet Union.* New York: Cambridge University Press, 1993.

Grieder, Jerome. *Hu Shih and the Chinese Renaissance: Liberalism and the Chinese Revolution, 1917–1937.* Cambridge: Harvard University Press, 1970.

———. *Intellectuals and the State in Modern China: A Narrative History.* New York: The Free Press, 1981.

Griffiths, David. *Introduction to Elementary Particles.* New York: Harper and Row, 1987.

Gu Xin. "Weikexuezhuyi yu Zhongguo jinxiandai zhishifenzi" [Scientism and modern and contemporary Chinese intellectuals]. *Ziran bianzhengfa tongxun,* 1990, no. 3, 28–35.

Gu Yang. "Zhenli—biran—gongchanzhuyi xinnian: Yu Chen Chengde, Guo Fengsheng tongzhi shangque" [Truth, necessity, communist faith—A discussion with Comrades Chen Chengde and Guo Fengsheng].

Guangming ribao, 4 July 1983, 3. (Trans. in *JPRS China Report: Political, Social, and Military,* 25 August 1983, 60–64.)

Gu Zuxue. "Shilun renshi zhutixing de sange cengci" [A tentative discussion of the three levels of cognitive subjectivity]. *Zhongguo shehui kexue,* 1990, no. 6: 85–93.

Guan Hong. "Guanyu 'yueliang zai mei ren kan ta shi shifou cunzai?' de wenti" [On the problem of "Does the moon exist if no one is gazing at it?"]. *Ziran bianzhengfa yanjiu,* 1991, no. 3: 39–45.

Guan Shixu and Chen Changshu. "Kexue jishu de fazhan yaoqiu women zuo xie shenma?" [What does the development of science and technology demand that we do?]. *Ziran bianzhengfa tongxun,* 1980, no. 1: 15–17.

Hagstrom, Warren O. *The Scientific Community.* New York: Basic Books, 1965.

Hahn, Werner. *Postwar Soviet Politics: The Fall of Zhdanov and the Defeat of Moderation, 1946–1953.* Ithaca: Cornell University Press, 1982.

Halperin, Nina. "Scientific Decisionmaking: The Organization of Expert Advice in Post-Mao China." In *Science and Technology in Post-Mao China,* edited by Denis Fred Simon and Merle Goldman, 157–74. Cambridge: Harvard University Press, 1989.

Hamrin, Carol Lee. *China and the Challenge of the Future: Changing Political Patterns.* Boulder: Westview Press, 1990.

Han Zenglu. "Ping Zha Ruqiang tongzhi de 'dabian'—Jian lun youji xibao he xibao xueshuo de kexue faxian" [Criticizing Comrade Zha Ruqiang's "rebuttal"—Also discussing the scientific discovery of organic cells and cell theory]. *Ziran bianzhengfa tongxun,* 1987, no. 6: 64–71.

Hao Mengbi and Duan Haoran. *Zhongguo Gongchandang liushinian* [Sixty years of the Chinese Communist Party]. Beijing: Jiefangjun Chubanshe, 1984.

Haraszti, Miklos. *The Velvet Prison: Artists under State Socialism* New York: Basic Books, 1987.

Harding, Harry. *China's Second Revolution.* Washington, D.C.: Brookings Institution, 1987.

Hawking, Stephen W. *A Brief History of Time* (New York: Cambridge University Press, 1988.

He Xiangtao, Shen Xiaofeng, and Chen Haoyuan. "Liangzi lixue de jige xuepai" [The various schools of quantum theory]. *Ziran bianzhengfa tongxun,* 1980, no. 6: 31–37.

He Zuoxiu. "Chang yeshi 'yi fen wei er' de" [Fields also manifest "one divides into two"]. *Ziran bianzhengfa tongxun*, 1979, no. 1: 87–92.

———. "Cengzi, qingzi yeshi buke qiongjin de" [Stratons and leptons also are inexhaustible]. *Zhexue yanjiu*, 1982, no. 6: 17–18.

———. "You guan yuzhoulun de zhexue wenti" [On the philosophical problems of cosmology]. *Zhongguo shehui kexue*, 1987, no. 2: 65–72; and *Hongqi*, 1987, no. 5: 10–17.

———. "Zhiyi ' "Yi fen wei er" zhiyi' " [Doubting "Doubting 'one divides into two' "]. *Ziran bianzhengfa tongxun*, 1987, no. 2: 69–71.

———. "Wuzhi, yundong, shijian, kongjian" [Matter, motion, space, and time]. *Zhexue yanjiu*, 1987, no. 11: 3–9, 80; and no. 12: 18–23, 42.

———. "Dui 'wuzhi wuxian kefen lun' de zai tantao" [A second look at the "infinite divisibility of matter theory"]. *Ziran bianzhengfa yanjiu*, 1987, no. 6: 1–5.

———. " ' 'Youxian er wubian' shifou jiu 'buke chaoyue' " [Isn't "infinite but unbounded" just "nonsupersedable"?]. *Ziran bianzhengfa tongxun*, 1988, no. 2: 78–79.

———. "Liangzi lixuezhong de celiang guocheng shibushi bixu you 'zhuguan jieru'?" [Does the measurement process in quantum theory necessarily require "subjective intervention"?]. *Ziran bianzhengfa yanjiu*, 1989, no. 1: 8–18; and 1989, no. 2: 1–12, 75.

———. "Ping 'Liangzi lixue de "xingzhiguan" he "shizaiguan" ' " [Criticizing "The views of 'property' and 'reality' in quantum theory"]. *Zhexue yanjiu*, 1990, no. 2: 69–73.

———. "Xiandai wulixue neng wei 'renshi de zhutilun' tigong kexue jichu ma?" [Can modern physics provide a scientific basis for the "theory of cognitive subjectivity"?]. *Zhongguo shehui kexue*, 1990, no. 2: 69–83. (Trans. in *Social Sciences in China*, 1991, no. 1: 165–82.)

———. "Fenqi zai nali—Jiu 'renshi de zhutilun' da Wen Xingwu, Gu Zuxue, Liu Shuzi tongzhi" [Where is the divergence?—Responding to Comrades Wen Xingwu, Gu Zuxue, and Liu Shuzi on the "theory of cognitive subjectivity"]. *Zhongguo shehui kexue*, 1991, no. 2: 57–72.

———. "EPR 'yangmiu' ji youguan de zhexue wenti" [The EPR 'fallacy' and related philosophical problems]. *Ziran bianzhengfa yanjiu*, 1991, no. 3: 28–38.

Hoffmann, Erik P., and Robbin F. Laird. *Technocratic Socialism: The Soviet*

Union in the Advanced Industrial Era. Durham: Duke University Press, 1985.

Hu Qiaomu. "Guanyu rendaozhuyi he yihua wenti" [On the problem of humanism and alienation]. *Renmin ribao*, 27 January 1984, 1, 4. (Trans. in FBIS-China, 7 February 1984, K1-32.)

Huan Xiang. "Xinjishu geming yu woguo duice" [The new technological revolution and our country's countermeasures]. *Zhongguo shehui kexue*, 1984, no. 4: 3-12. (Trans. in *Social Sciences in China*, English ed., 1985, no. 1.)

Huan Xuewen. "Jiu 'Ershi shiji Zhongguo kexuezhuyi de liangci xingqi' yu zuozhe shangque" (A discussion with the author of 'The two flourishings of Chinese scientism in the twentieth century'). *Ershiyi shiji* [Twenty-first century], 1991, no. 7; 142-45.

Jammer, Max. *The Philosophy of Quantum Mechanics: The Interpretations of Quantum Mechanics in Historical Perspective*. New York: John Wiley and Sons, 1974.

Jin Guantao. *Wo de zhexue tansuo* (My philosophical explorations). Shanghai: Shanghai Renmin Chubanshe, 1988.

———. "Wo shi zenmayang pandeng sixiang jieti de?" [How did I climb the ladder of thought?]. *Mingbao yuekan* (Mingbao monthly), 1988, no. 3: 54-61; and 1988, no. 4: 56-62.

———, Fan Hongye, and Liu Qingfeng. "Lishishang de kexue jishu jiegou— Shilun shiqi shiji zhi hou Zhongguo kexue jishu luohou yu Xifang de yuanyin" [The structure of science and technology in history— A tentative discussion of the reasons China's science and technology lagged behind the West's after the seventeenth century]. *Ziran bianzhengfa tongxun*, 1985, no. 5: 7-23.

Jin Wulun. "Wuzhi kefenxing de liangzhong jianjie he weiguan keti de bianzhengfa" [Two views on the divisibility of matter and the dialectics of micro-objects]. *Zhexue yanjiu*, 1985, no. 12: 26-33.

———. "Xin wuzhi jiegouguan de dansheng" [The birth of a new view of the structure of matter]. *Tianjin shehui kexue* [Tianjin social sciences], 1986, no. 1: 37-40.

———. "Laibunici de danzilun zhexue he dangdai weizi wulixue" [Leibniz' theory of monads and contemporary particle physics]. *Ziran bianzhengfa yanjiu*, 1986, no. 1: 27-32.

———. "Dui 'wuzhi wuxian kefen lun' de zairenshi" [Another understanding of the "infinite divisibility of matter theory"]. *Guangming ribao*, 6 December 1986, 3.

————. "Yunyong yanyifa neng tuichu 'wuzhi jiegou wuxian kefen' ma?— Yu Zha Ruqiang tongzhi bianxi" [Can one infer "infinite divisibility of matter" by applying the deductive method?]. *Guangming ribao*, 20 July 1987, 3.

————. " 'Wuzhi wuxian kefen lun' shi xingershangxue xinnian, bushi bian-zhengfa" [The "theory of the infinite divisibility of matter" is a meta-physical belief, not dialectics—Responding to Comrade He Zuoxiu]. *Ziran bianzhengfa yanjiu*, 1988, no. 3: 49–55.

————. *Wuzhi kefenxing xinlun* [A new theory of the divisibility of matter]. Beijing: Zhongguo Shehui Kexue Chubanshe, 1988.

———— and Li Xi. "Wuzhi wuxian fenhua lun he xin de kexue shishi de maodun" [The theory of the infinite divisibility of matter and contra-dictions with the new facts of science]. *Ziran bianzhengfa yanjiu*, 1987, no. 2: 71–72.

Jin Zhong. "Lilun de daotui" [A retrogression in theory]. *Lilun yuekan* [Theory monthly], 1987, no. 12: 47–50.

Jingji ribao Editorial Board. *Zhongguo dangdai jingjixuejia zhuanlue* [Biog-raphies of contemporary Chinese economists]. Shenyang: Liaoning Chubanshe, 1986.

Joravsky, David. *Soviet Marxism and Natural Science*. London: Routledge and Kegan Paul, 1961.

————. "Bosses and Scientists." *Problems of Communism*, vol. 16, no. 1 (Janu-ary–February 1967): 72–75.

————. *The Lysenko Affair*. Cambridge: Harvard University Press, 1970.

Jowitt, Kenneth. "Soviet Neotraditionalism: The Political Corruption of a Leninist Regime." *Soviet Studies*, vol. 35, no. 3 (July 1983): 275–97.

"Juyou zhongyao yiyi de tansuo—Ji Zhongguo Jindai Kexue Jishu Luohou Yuanyin Xueshu Taolunhui" [An exploration of great significance— Notes on the Academic Conference on the Causes of the Backward-ness of China's Science and Technology in the Early Modern Period]. *Ziran bianzhengfa tongxun*, 1983, no. 1: 32–34.

Kelly, David A. "Controversies over the Guiding Role of Philosophy Over Science." *Australian Journal of Chinese Affairs*, no. 14 (July 1985): 21–35.

————. "The Emergence of Humanism: Wang Ruoshui and the Critique of Socialist Alienation." In *China's Intellectuals and the State: Toward a New*

Relationship, edited by Merle Goldman, Timothy Cheek, and Carol Lee Hamrin, 159–82. Cambridge: Harvard University Press, 1987.

———. "Chinese Intellectuals in the 1989 Democracy Movement." In *The Broken Mirror: China after Tiananmen,* edited by George Hicks, 24–51. Chicago: St. James Press, 1990.

———, and He Baogang. "Emergent Civil Society and the Intellectuals in China." In *The Development of Civil Society in Communist System,* edited by Robert F. Miller, 24–161. North Sydney: Allen and Unwin, 1992.

Kexue tongbao [Scientia] editorial. "Raise Vigilance, Eliminate All Hidden Counterrevolutionaries within the Ranks of Scientific Circles." *Kexue tongbao,* September 1956. (Trans. in u.s. Hong Kong Consulate General, *Extracts from China Mainland Magazines,* no. 18 [12 December 1955]: 48–51.)

Kirby, William C. "Technocratic Organization and Technological Development in China: The Nationalist Experience and Legacy, 1928–1953." In *Science and Technology in Post-Mao China,* edited by Denis Fred Simon and Merle Goldman, 23–43. Cambridge: Harvard University Press, 1989.

Kneen, Peter. *Soviet Scientists and the State.* Albany: State University of New York Press, 1984.

Kolakowski, Leszek. *Main Currents of Marxism.* 3 vols. New York: Oxford University Press, 1982.

Kong Xiang. "Manhaimu de zhishi shehuixue he Modun de kexue shehuixue pingjia" [A critical evaluation of Mannheim's sociology of knowledge and Merton's sociology of science]. *Zhexue yanjiu,* 1988, no. 4: 55–61.

Kraus, Richard C. "The Lament of Astrophysicist Fang Lizhi: China's Intellectuals in a Global Context." In *Marxism and the Chinese Experience,* edited by Arif Dirlik and Maurice Meisner, 294–315. Armonk, N.Y.: M. E. Sharpe, 1989.

Kwok, Danny W. Y. *Scientism in Chinese Thought, 1900–1950.* New Haven: Yale University Press, 1965.

Lang Lang. "Daibiao yizhong daoyi de husheng—Fangwen "Sishisan Ren Gongkaixin' faqiren zhi yi Dai Qing" [Representing a call for morality and justice—A visit with Dai Qing, one of the originators of the "Open Letter of 43"]. *Jiushi niandai* [The nineties], 1989, no. 4: 24–25.

Latour, Bruno, and Stephen Woolgar. *Laboratory Life: The Construction of Scientific Facts.* Princeton: Princeton University Press, 1986.

Lee, Hong Yung. *From Revolutionary Cadres to Party Technocrats in Socialist China*. Berkeley: University of California Press, 1991.

Lee, Leo Ou-fan. "The Crisis of Culture." In *China Briefing, 1990*, edited by Anthony J. Kane, 83–105. Boulder: Westview Press, 1990.

Li Honglin. *Lilun fengyun* (Storms of theory). Beijing: Sanlian Shudian, 1985.

Li Keming. "Shidai dui Makesizhuyi zhexue de yaoqiu" [The demands of the times on Marxist philosophy]. *Renmin ribao*, 17 November 1986, 5. (Trans. in FBIS-China, 20 November 1986, K13–15.)

Li Xingmin. "Huaiyi, pingquan, duoyuan—Guanyu fazhan Makesizhuyi zhexue de sikao" [Doubt, equality, pluralism—Thoughts on developing Marxist philosophy]. *Guangming ribao*, 25 January 1988, 3. (Excerpts trans. in FBIS-China, 12 April 1988, 2–3.)

———. "Zai zhexue yu kexue zhi jian" [Between philosophy and science]. *Guangming ribao*, 26 December 1988, 3.

———. "Luelun Mahe de 'siwei jingji' yuanli" [A brief discussion of Mach's "economy of thought"]. *Ziran bianzhengfa yanjiu*, 1988, no. 3: 56–63.

———. "Guanyu *Weiwuzhuyi he jingyan pipanzhuyi* diwuzhang de yixie sikao" [Some thoughts on chapter 5 of *Materialism and empiriocriticism*]. *Guangming ribao*, 27 June 1988, 3.

———. "Guanyu kexue yu jiazhi de jige wenti" [On several issues concerning science and values]. *Zhongguo shehui kexue*, 1990, no. 5: 43–60.

Liao Gailong. *Zhongguo Gongchandang de guanghui qishinian* [Seventy glorious years of the Chinese Communist Party]. Beijing: Xinhua Chubanshe, 1991.

Lin, Min. "The Search for Modernity: Chinese Intellectual Discourse and Society, 1978–1988—The Case of Li Zehou." *China Quarterly*, no. 132 (December 1992): 969–98.

Lin, Tongqi. "A Search for China's Soul." *Daedelus*, vol. 122, no. 2 (Spring 1993), 171–88.

Lindbeck, John M. H. "The Organization and Development of Science." *China Quarterly*, no. 6 (October–December 1961): 98–132.

Link, Perry. "The Thought and Spirit of Fang Lizhi." In *The Broken Mirror: China after Tiananmen*, edited by George Hicks, 100–14. London: St. James Press, 1990.

Liu Bing. "Dui ' "Youxian er wubian" shifou jiu "buke chaoyue"?' yiwen de zhiyi" [Doubts concerning the article "Isn't 'infinite but unbounded' just 'nonsupersedable'?"]. *Ziran bianzhengfa tongxun*, 1988, no. 6: 71–72.

————, Wang Zuoyue, Xiong Wei, Chen Hengliu, and Zhong Weiguang. "Dui Zha Ruqiang tongzhi liangpian wenzhangzhong yixie ziran kexue wenti de shangque" [A discussion of some natural science problems in Comrade Zha Ruqiang's two articles]. *Zhongguo shehui kexue*, 1986, no. 3: 20–24.

Liu Binyan. *A Higher Kind of Loyalty.* New York: Alfred A. Knopf, 1990.

Liu Dixiu. "Jiu Feng Nuoyiman de celiang lilun yu He Zuoxiu xiansheng shangque" [A discussion with Mr. He Zuoxiu on Franz Neumann's theory of measurement]. *Ziran bianzhengfa yanjiu*, 1990, no. 2: 67–68.

Liu Junjun. "Guanyu 'wuxing xueyuan' " [On the "invisible college"]. *Ziran bianzhengfa yanjiu*, 1987, no. 2: 33–41.

Liu Qingfeng, ed. *Lishi de fanxiang* (Echoes of history). Hong Kong: Sanlian Shudian, 1990.

————. "Ershi shiji Zhongguo kexuezhuyi de liangci xingqi" (The two flourishings of Chinese scientism in the twentieth century). *Ershiyi shiji* (Twenty-first century), 1991, no. 4, 32–47.

Liu Shaoqi. "Political Report to the 8th National Congress of the CPC [CCP]." In *Eighth National Congress of the Communist Party of China.* Vol. 1, *Documents*, 13–111. Beijing: Foreign Languages Press, 1956.

Liu Shuzi. "Xiandai wulixue yu renshi de zhutixing" [Modern physics and the subjectivity of cognition]. *Zhongguo shehui kexue*, 1991, no. 1: 99–108.

————. "Shiyong hongguan gainian lai miaoshu weiguan keti de bixuxing he juxianxing—Jian da Guan Hong tongzhi" [The necessity and limitations of using macroscopic concepts to describe microscopic objects—A response to Comrade Guan Hong]. *Ziran bianzhengfa tongxun*, 1991, no. 5: 17–24.

Lowenthal, Richard. "The Ruling Party in a Mature Society." In *The Social Consequences of Modernization in Communist Societies,* edited by Mark G. Field, 81–118. Baltimore: Johns Hopkins University Press, 1976.

————. "The Post-Revolutionary Phase in China and Russia." *Studies in Comparative Communism,* vol. 13, no. 3 (Autumn 1983): 191–201.

Lu Dingyi. " 'Baihua qifang, baijia zhengming' de lishi huigu" [A look back on the history of 'a hundred flowers blooming and a hundred schools contending']. *Guangming ribao,* 7 May 1986, 1.

Luo Rongxing, Zhu Huaxin, and Cao Huanrong. "Zhongguo gaige de lishi diwei" [The historical position of China's reform]. *Renmin ribao*, 6 October 1988, 1 and 3; and 7 October 1988, 1 and 3. (Trans. in JPRS *China Report*, 9 November 1987, 7–20.)

Ma Ding. "Dangdai woguo jingjixue yanjiu de shi da zhuanbian" [Ten great changes in the contemporary study of economics in our country]. *Gongren ribao* [Workers daily]. 2 November 1985, 6. (Trans. in *Beijing Review*, 9 December 1985, 17–20; and FBIS-China, 26 May 1986, K3–10.)

Ma Junqi. "Gongchanzhuyi zhidu de shijian jiqi dui gongchanzhuyi lilun de jianyan" [The practice of the communist system and the test it provides of communist theory]. *Zhexue yanjiu*, 1983, no. 2: 4–8. (Trans. in JPRS *China Report: Political, Social, and Military*, 6 May 1983, 66–73.)

MacFarquhar, Roderick. *The Hundred Flowers Campaign and the Chinese Intellectuals*. New York: Frederick A. Praeger, 1960.

———. *The Origins of the Cultural Revolution*. Vol. 1, *Contradictions among the People, 1956–1957*. London: Royal Institute of International Affairs, 1974.

Mann, Susan. *Local Merchants and the Chinese Bureaucracy, 1750–1950*. Stanford: Stanford University Press, 1987.

Mao Tse-tung (Mao Zedong). *Selected Works of Mao Tse-tung*. Vol. 5. Beijing: Foreign Languages Press, 1977.

McCain, Garvin, and Erwin M. Segal. *The Game of Science*. 5th ed. Pacific Grove: Brooks-Cole Publishing, 1988.

Medvedev, Zhores. *Soviet Science*. Oxford: Oxford University Press, 1979.

Merton, Robert. *The Sociology of Science: Theoretical and Empirical Investigations*. Chicago: University of Chicago Press, 1973.

Misner, Charles W., Kip S. Thorne, and John A. Wheeler. *Gravitation*. San Francisco: W. H. Freeman and Company, 1973.

Morrison, Michael. *Understanding Quantum Physics: A User's Manual*. Englewood Cliffs: Prentice-Hall, 1990.

Nanjing Daxue xuebao Editorial Board. "Xiqu jiaoxun, banhao xuebao" [Absorb the lesson, run the journal well]. *Nanjing Daxue xuebao (zhexue-shehui kexue)* (Nanjing University journal [philosophy and social sciences]), 1981, no. 4: 1.

Nathan, Andrew. *Chinese Democracy*. New York: Alfred A. Knopf, 1985.

Nie, Rongzhen. *Inside the Red Star: The Memoirs of Marshal Nie Rongzhen*. Beijing: New World Press, 1988.

Ohanian, Hans C. *Gravitation and Spacetime.* New York: W. W. Norton, 1976.

Park, David. *Introduction to the Quantum Theory.* 3rd ed. New York: McGraw-Hill, 1992.

Parrott, Bruce. *Politics and Technology in the Soviet Union.* Cambridge: MIT Press, 1983.

Pepper, Suzanne. *Civil War in China: The Political Struggle, 1945–1949.* Berkeley: University of California Press, 1978.

Perkins, Donald B. *Introduction to High Energy Physics.* 3rd ed. Reading, Mass.: Addison-Wesley, 1987.

Perry, Elizabeth J., and Ellen V. Fuller. "China's Long March to Democracy." *World Policy Journal,* vol. 8, no. 4 (Fall 1991): 663–85.

Popper, Karl R. *The Open Society and Its Enemies.* Princeton: Princeton University Press, 1950.

Powers, Jonathan. *Philosophy and the New Physics.* New York: Methuen, 1982.

Qian Xuesen. "Ziran bianzhengfa yao yu kexue jishu tongbu fazhan" [Natural dialectics and science and technology must develop in step]. *Lilun yuekan* [Theory monthly], 1988, no. 1: 1–5.

———. "Jichu kexue yanjiu yinggai jieshou Makesizhuyi zhexue de zhidao" [Research in the basic sciences should accept the guidance of Marxist philosophy]. *Zhexue yanjiu,* 1989, no. 10: 3–8.

Rabkin, Yakov M. "The Study of Science." *Survey,* no. 102 (Winter 1977–78): 134–45.

Rankin, Mary. *Elite Activism and Political Transformation in China.* Stanford: Stanford University Press, 1986.

Reardon-Anderson, James. *The Study of Change: Chemistry in China, 1840–1949.* New York: Cambridge University Press, 1991.

———. "Science in Wartime China." In *China's Bitter Victory: The War With Japan, 1937–1945,* edited by James C. Hsiung and Steven I. Levine, 213–34. (Armonk, N.Y.: M.E. Sharpe, 1992).

Richards, Stewart. *The Philosophy and Sociology of Science: An Introduction.* London: Basil Blackwell, 1987.

Rowe, William T. *Hankow: Commerce and Society in a Chinese City, 1796–1889.* Stanford: Stanford University Press, 1984.

———. "Approaches to Modern Chinese Social History." In *Reliving the Past: The Worlds of Social History,* edited by Olivier Zunz, 236–96. Chapel Hill: University of North Carolina Press, 1985.

————. *Hankow: Conflict and Community in a Chinese City, 1796–1895*. Stanford: Stanford University Press, 1989.

————. "The Public Sphere in Modern China." *Modern China*, vol. 16, no. 3 (July 1990): 309–29.

————. "Modern Chinese Social History in Comparative Perspective." In *The Heritage of China: Contemporary Perspectives on Chinese Civilization*, edited by Paul S. Ropp, 242–62. Berkeley: University of California Press, 1990.

Saich, Tony. *China's Science Policy in the 80s*. Atlantic Highlands, N.J.: Humanities Press, 1989.

————. "Reform of China's Science and Technology Organizational System." In *Science and Technology in Post-Mao China*, edited by Denis Fred Simon and Merle Goldman, 69–88. Cambridge: Harvard University Press, 1989.

Sakharov, Andrei. *Memoirs*. New York: Alfred A. Knopf, 1990.

Scanlan, James P. *Marxism in the USSR: A Critical Survey of Current Soviet Thought*. Ithaca: Cornell University Press, 1985.

Schell, Orville. *Discos and Democracy*. New York: Pantheon Books, 1988.

Schneider, Laurence, ed. "Lysenkoism in China: Proceedings of the 1956 Qingdao Genetics Symposium." Special issue of *Chinese Law and Government*, vol. 19, no. 2 (Summer 1986).

————. "Learning from Russia: Lysenkoism and the Fate of Genetics in China, 1950–1986." In *Science and Technology in Post-Mao China*, edited by Denis Fred Simon and Merle Goldman, eds., 45–65. Cambridge: Harvard University Press, 1989.

Schram, Stuart R. *Chairman Mao Talks to the People*. New York: Pantheon Books, 1974.

————. *Ideology and Policy in China since the Third Plenum, 1978–94*. London: Contemporary China Institute, School of Oriental and African Studies, University of London, 1984.

Schwarcz, Vera. *The Chinese Enlightenment: Intellectuals and the Legacy of the May Fourth Movement of 1919*. Berkeley: University of California Press.

Shatz, Marshall S. *Soviet Dissent in Historical Perspective*. Cambridge: Cambridge University Press, 1980.

Shen, Tong. *Almost a Revolution*. Boston: Houghton Mifflin, 1990.

Shen Xiaofeng and Chen Haoyuan. "Aiyinsitan yu Gebenhagen xuepai—

Chi Sirenbang de 'huxiang gongjie' lun" [Einstein and the Copenhagen school—Castigating the Gang of Four's "mutual muckraking"]. *Zhexue yanjiu*, 1979, no. 5: 59–65.

Shen Xiaofeng and He Xiangtao. "Yuzhou chidu de zaitupo" [Another breakthrough in the scale of the universe]. *Ziran bianzhengfa tongxun*, 1983, no. 1: 57–61.

Sheng Ping, ed. *Zhongguo Gongchandang lishi dacidian, 1921–1991* [Dictionary of Chinese Communist Party history, 1921–1991]. Beijing: Zhongguo Guoji Guangbo Chubanshe, 1991.

Shi Hua. "Kexuejia lianming fabiao zhengjian shiwuqianli—Fangwen 'Sishier Ren Gongkaixin' faqiren Xu Liangying" [The unprecedented joint expression of political views by scientists—A visit with the originator of the "Open Letter of 42," Xu Liangying]. *Jiushi niandai* [The nineties], 1989, no. 4: 21–23.

Shi Zhaoyu. "Mao Zedong yu Bada dui woguo shehui zhuyi zhuyao maodun lijie de yitong" [Similarities and differences in the explication by Mao Zedong and the Eighth Congress of the primary contradiction in socialism in our country]. *Zhongguo shehui kexue*, 1991, no. 6: 91–104.

Shimony, Abner. "Conceptual Foundations of Quantum Mechanics." In *The New Physics*, edited by Paul Davies, 373–95. New York: Cambridge University Press, 1989.

Shlapentokh, Vladimir. *Soviet Intellectuals and Political Power*. Princeton: Princeton University Press, 1990.

Silk, Joseph. *The Big Bang*. Rev. ed. New York: W. H. Freeman and Co., 1989.

Song Huaishi. "Kexue gongtongti zai kexue huodongzhong de zuoyong" [The role of the scientific community in the activities of science]. *Ziran bianzhengfa yanjiu*, 1985, no. 4: 12–16, 11.

State Education Commission Ideology and Political Work Bureau (Guojia Jiaoyu Weiyuanhui Sixiang Zhengzhi Gongzuo Si). *Jingxin dongpo de wushiliu tian—Yijiubajiunian siyue shiwuri zhi liuyue jiuri meiri jishi* [Fifty-six days that alarmed the soul—A daily record from 15 April to 9 June 1989]. *Neibu* (internal circulation) ed. Beijing: Dadi Chubanshe, 1989.

Storer, Norman W. *The Social System of Science*. New York: Holt, Reinhart and Winston, 1966.

Strand, David. *Rickshaw Beijing: City People and Politics in the 1920s*. Berkeley: University of California Press, 1989.

————. "Protest in Beijing: Civil Society and Public Sphere in China." *Problems of Communism*, vol. 39, no. 3 (May–June 1990): 1–19.

Su Shaozhi. "Shekeyuan Maliesuo shinian zangsang" [The CASS Institute of Marxism-Leninism's turbulent decade]. Unpublished ms. (Trans. in *China Quarterly*, no. 134 (June 1993): 335–51.)

————. "The Structure of the Chinese Academy of Social Sciences (CASS) and the Two Decisions to Abolish Its Marxism-Leninism Institute." In *Deng's China: Dynamics of the Decision Process*, edited by Carol Hamrin and Zhao Suisheng, 111–17. Armonk, N.Y.: M.E. Sharpe, 1995.

———— and Wang Yizhon. "1989 nien zhishi women" [The year 1989 instructs us]. *Zhongguo qingnian* (China youth), 1989, no. 1: 2–3.

Su Xiaokang and Wang Luxiang, eds. *Heshang* (River elegy). Hong Kong: Sanlian Shuju, 1988.

Sudbery, Anthony. *Quantum Mechanics and the Particles of Nature: An Outline for Mathematicians*. New York: Cambridge University Press, 1986.

Suttmeier, Richard P. "Party Views of Science: The Record from the First Decade." *China Quarterly*, no. 44 (September–October 1970): 154.

————. *Research and Revolution: Science Policy and Change in China*. Lexington, Mass.: Lexington Books, 1974.

————. "Science Policy Shifts, Organizational Change and China's Development." *China Quarterly*, no. 62 (June 1975): 207–41.

————. *Science, Technology, and China's Drive for Modernization*. Stanford: Hoover Institution Press, 1980.

————. "Politics, Modernization, and Science in China," *Problems of Communism*, vol. 30, no. 1 (January–February 1981): 22–36.

————. "Reform, Modernization, and the Changing Constitution of Science in China." *Asian Survey*, vol. 29, no. 10 (October 1989): 999–1015.

Teiwes, Frederick. "Establishment and Consolidation of the New Regime." In *The Cambridge History of China*, edited by Roderick C. MacFarquhar and John King Fairbank, vol. 14, *The People's Republic*, part 1, *The Emergence of Revolutionary China*, 122–33. New York: Cambridge University Press, 1987.

Thurston, Anne F. *Enemies of the People*. New York: Alfred A. Knopf, 1987.

Tong, James. "Party Documents on Anti-Bourgeois Liberalization and Hu Yaobang's Resignation, 1987." *Chinese Law and Government*, vol. 21, no. 1 (Spring 1988): 85–86.

Traweek, Sharon. *Beamtimes and Lifetimes: The World of High Energy Physics.* Cambridge: Harvard University Press, 1988.

Tsou, Tang. *The Cultural Revolution and Post-Mao Reforms.* Chicago: University of Chicago Press, 1986.

Vucinich, Alexander. *Empire of Knowledge: The Academy of Sciences of the USSR (1917–1970).* Berkeley: University of California Press, 1984.

Walder, Andrew. "The Political Sociology of the Beijing Upheaval of 1989." *Problems of Communism,* vol. 38, no. 5 (September–October 1989): 30–40.

Wang Gancai. "Qingyi fouding 'wuzhi wuxian kefen' nan yi fu ren—Yu Jin Wulun tongzhi shangque" [Lightly negating the "infinite divisibility of matter theory" will not easily persuade people—A discussion with Comrade Jin Wulun]. *Guangming ribao,* 8 December 1986, 3.

Wang Guozheng, "Heidong wuli de fazhan jiqi yiyi" [The development of black hole physics and its significance]. *Ziran bianzhengfa tongxun,* 1981, no. 6: 21–29.

Wang, Y. C. *Chinese Intellectuals and the West, 1872–1949.* Chapel Hill: University of North Carolina Press, 1966.

Wang Yubei. "Liangzi lixue de 'xingzhiguan' he 'shizaiguan' " [The views of "property" and "reality" in quantum theory]. *Zhexue yanjiu,* 1989, no. 11: 62–67.

Weber, Max. *Economy and Society: An Outline of Interpretive Sociology.* 2 vols. Edited by Guenther Roth and Claus Wittich. Berkeley: University of California Press, 1978).

Weinberg, Steven. *Gravitation and Cosmology: Principles and Applications of the General Theory of Relativity.* New York: John Wiley and Sons, 1972.

Wen Xingwu. " 'Bo wei er'xiangxing shi ziranjie de yige jiben maodun' ma?" [Is it true that 'wave-particle duality is a fundamental contradiction in nature'?]. *Zhongguo shehui kexue,* 1987, no. 3: 34.

———. "Xiangduilun shikong lilun jiqi pingjia zaitantao" [Relativity's theory of space-time and a critical reappraisal of it]. *Zhexue yanjiu,* 1989, no. 12: 33–40.

———. "Xiangduilun shikong lilun zairenshi" [Another understanding of the theory of space-time in relativity]. *Zhongguo shehui kexue,* 1990, no. 5: 29–42.

Williams, James H., ed. and trans. "The Expanding Universe of Fang Lizhi:

Astrophysics and Ideology in People's China." Special issue of *Chinese Studies in Philosophy*, vol. 19, no. 4 (Summer 1988).

———. "Fang Lizhi's Expanding Universe." *China Quarterly*, no. 123 (September 1990): 459–84.

Wu Guosheng. "Fang Lizhi—Gongheguo xuyao zheyang de xuezhe" [Fang Lizhi—The republic needs this kind of scholar]. *Ziran bianzhengfa tongxun*, 1986, no. 6, 51–62. (Trans. in Williams, "The Expanding Universe of Fang Lizhi," 88–108.)

———. "Bawo yuzhou de liangzhong guifan de zheng" [Grasping the contention over the two models of the universe]. *Zhexue yanjiu*, 1986, no. 12: 15–20.

———. "Zhexue nengfou zhidao kexue" [Can philosophy guide science?]. *Guangming ribao*, 19 January 1987, 3.

———. "Yuzhou shi wuxian de ma?" [Is the universe infinite?]. *Ziran bianzhengfa yanjiu*, 1987, no. 1: 50–55.

———. "Wuzhi shi wuxian kefen de ma?" [Is matter infinitely divisible?]. *Ziran bianzhengfa tongxun*, 1987, no. 4: 68–73.

———. "Yuzhoulun de lishi yu zhexue" [Philosophy and the history of cosmology]. *Ziran bianzhengfa yanjiu*, 1990, no. 6: 1–8.

———. "Bashi niandai ziran bianzhengfa jie zhenglun beiwanglu" [Memorandum on the debates in natural dialectics circles in the eighties]. Paper presented at the History of Contemporary Chinese Science and Third Young Natural Dialectics Researchers Societies Conference, Hangzhou, 28 October–2 November 1991.

Wu Peng. "Guanyu 'wuxian yuzhou' de xin tantao" [A new exploration concerning the "infinite universe"]. *Xuexi yu tansuo* [Studies and explorations], 1987, no. 3: 21–25.

Wu Zhong. "Houqi Modun de kexue gongtongti shehuixue" [The sociology of the scientific community of the later Merton]. *Ziran bianzhengfa yanjiu*, 1986, no. 6: 9–16.

———. "Modun de poshi lunwen: Jiben sixiang he yanjiu fangfa pinglun" [Merton's doctoral thesis: An evaluation of its basic ideas and research methods]. *Ziran bianzhengfa tongxun*, 1986, no. 4: 32–37.

Xie Xin. "Kexue shehuizhuyi, haishi nongye shehuizhuyi?" [Is it scientific socialism, or is it agrarian socialism?]. *Zhongguo shehui kexue*, 1981, no. 5: 25–39.

"Xin de changshi" [A new attempt]. *Ziran bianzhengfa tongxun,* 1979, no. 1: 10–13.

Xing Bensi. "Dui dangqian sixiang jiefang yundong de yixie kanfa" [Some opinions concerning the present movement to liberate thought]. *Renmin ribao,* 10 October 1980, 5.

Xinhua News Agency. "Zhexue shehui kexue yao wei shixian Sige Xindaihua fuwu" [Philosophy and social sciences must serve the Four Modernizations." *Guangming ribao,* 4 November 1978, 1.

Xinwen gongzuo shouce Editorial Committee and Editorial Board. *Xinwen gongzuo shouce* [Handbook of news work]. Beijing: Xinhua Chubanshe, 1985.

Xu Liangying. "Shilun kexue yu minzhu de shehui gongneng" [On the social functions of science and democracy]. *Ziran bianzhengfa tongxun,* 1981, no. 1: 3–6.

———. "Lishi lixinglun de kexue shiguan chuyi" [A proposal for a rational realist view of the history of science]. *Ziran bianzhengfa tongxun,* 1986, no. 3: 43–48.

———. "Zhenglun cong he er lai? Fenqi he zai?—Da Zha Ruqiang tongzhi, bing dui 'lishi lixing lun' zuo yidian buchong shuoming he liangchu wenzi gengzheng" [From whence comes the debate? Where is the divergence?—Replying to Comrade Zha Ruqiang, and also adding a little supplementary explanation to "Discussing historical rationalism" and correcting words in a couple of places]. *Ziran bianzhengfa tongxun,* 1987, no. 5: 61–65.

———. "Enshi Wang Ganchang xiansheng dui wo de qidi he aihu" [The gracious teacher Mr. Wang Ganchang's enlightening and caring support of me]. In *Wang Ganchang he ta de kexue gongxian* [Wang Ganchang and his contributions to science], edited by Hu Jimin, Xu Liangying, Wang Rong, and Fan Dainian, 208–22. Beijing: Kexue Chubanshe, 1987.

———. "Guanyu Aluo bukenengxing dingli he minzhu lilun guanxi de lijie" [An understanding of Arrow's impossibility theorem and democratic theory]. *Zhengzhixue yanjiu* (Studies in political science), 1988, no. 6: 56–59.

———. "Guanyu kexue jishu fazhan guilu de sikao" [Thoughts on the laws of development of science and technology]. *Ziran bianzhengfa tongxun,* 1989, no. 1: 40–46.

———. "Minzhu shi anding tuanjie de weiyi kekao baozheng" [Democracy is the only reliable guarantee for stability and unity]. *Shijie jingji dao-bao* [World economic herald], 8 May 1989, 13. (Trans. in JPRS *China Report*, 3 July 1992, 51–53.)

———. "Reform Cannot Possibly Succeed without Political Democracy." *Weilai yu fazhan* [The future and development], 1992, no. 5: 5–7 (trans. in FBIS-China, 4 January 1993, 28–30; and 8 January 1993, 19–20).

———. "Wei kexue zhengming—Dui suowei 'weikexuezhuyi' bianzhe" (To rectify the name of science—Rebutting so-called 'scientism'). *Ziran bianzhengfa tongxun*, 1992, no. 4, 33–39.

——— and Fan Dainian. *Science and Socialist Construction in China.* Edited by Pierre Perrolle, translated by John C. S. Hsu. Armonk, N.Y.: M. E. Sharpe, 1982.

——— and Qu Jingcheng. "Guanyu woguo Wenhua Dageming shiqi pipan Aiyinsitan he xiangduilun yundong de chubu kaocha" [An initial investigation into the movement to criticize Einstein and the theory of relativity during the Cultural Revolution period in our country]. *Ziran bianzhengfa tongxun*, 1984, no. 6: 32–41; and 1985, no. 1: 36–42.

Yan Jian and Shih Yiwu. *Shiyijie Sanzhong Quanhui dao Shi'erjie Sanzhong Quanhui dashiji* [A chronicle of events from the Eleventh Central Committee Third Plenum to the Twelfth Central Committee Third Plenum]. Shanghai: Zhishi Chubanshe, 1986.

Yan Jiaqi. "Zongjiao, lixing, shijian—Fangwen sange shidai guanyu zhenli wenti de sange 'fating'" [Religion, reason, and practice—A visit to three "courts" of the problem of truth in three eras]. *Guangming ribao*, 14 September 1978, 3–4.

———. *Wo de sixiang zizhuan* [My intellectual autobiography]. Hong Kong: Sanlian Shudian, 1988.

———. "Jinri Zhongguo—Yan Jiaqi tan De xiansheng, Sai xiansheng, Le xiansheng" [China today—Yan Jiaqi discusses Mr. Democracy, Mr. Science, and Mr. Law]. *Zhongguo qingnian* [China youth], 1989, no. 2: 2–4.

———. *Toward a Democratic China: The Intellectual Autiobiography of Yan Jiaqi.* Translated by David S. K. Hong and Denis C. Mair. Honolulu: University of Hawaii Press, 1989.

———. "The Nature of Chinese Authoritarianism." In *Decision-Making in Deng's China: Perspectives from Insiders,* edited by Carol Lee Hamrin and Suisheng Zhao, 3–14. Armonk, N.Y.: M. E. Sharpe, 1995.

Yan Kangnian. "N. Bohr zai Zhongguo" [N[iels] Bohr in China]. *Ziran bian-zhengfa tongxun*, 1981, no. 4: 77–79.

Yan Ling. "Woguo nongye shehuizhuyi gaizao de biyaoxing, kenengxing jiqi shixian" [The necessity for, possibility of, and actuality of the socialist transformation of agriculture in our country]. *Zhongguo shehui kexue*, 1981, no. 6: 21–40.

Yang Changgui. "Bianzheng weiwuzhuyi de wuzhiguan yu ziran kexue de wuzhi guannian" [Dialectical materialism's view of matter and the natural sciences' concept of matter]. *Zhexue yanjiu*, 1982, no. 8: 65–67.

Yin Dengxiang. "Xiandai yuzhouxue fengfule bianzheng weiwuzhuyi de ziranguan" [Modern cosmology has enriched dialectical material-ism's view of nature]. *Zhexue yanjiu*, 1982, no. 7: 48–51.

———. "Dabaozha yuzhouxue yu zhexue xiandaihua" [Big bang cosmology and the modernization of philosophy]. *Guangming ribao*, 22 July 1985, 3.

Ying Xueli and Sun Hui. "Guanyu shehuizhuyi gaizao houqi de jige lilun wenti" [On several theoretical issues in the latter period of our coun-try's socialist transformation]. *Nanjing Daxue xuebao (zhexue-shehui kexue)* [Nanjing University journal (philosophy and social sciences)], 1980, no. 4: 98–104. (Partial trans. in JPRS *China Report: Political, Social, and Military*, 25 September 1981, 21–30.)

Yu Guangyuan. "Zai yijiuwuliunian Qingdao Yichuanxue Huishang de jianghua" [Speech at the 1956 Qingdao Conference on Genetics]. *Ziran bianzhengfa tongxun*, 1980, no. 5: 5–13.

———. "Yao lingxue, haishi ziran bianzhengfa" [Parapsychology or natural dialectics?]. *Ziran bianzhengfa tongxun*, 1982, no. 1: 8–15.

———. "PSI yu ta de bianzhong—Renti teyi gongneng" [PSI and its vari-ant—The paranormal functions of the human body]. *Zhongguo shehui kexue*, 1982, no. 2: 31–45.

———. "Wei *Ziran bianzhengfa* xin yiben chuban jiang jijuhua" [A few words on behalf of a new edition of *The dialectics of nature*]. *Ziran bianzhengfa tongxun*, 1985, no. 3: 1–2.

———. "Shehuizhuyi chuji jieduan de jingji" [The economy in the initial stage of socialism]. *Zhongguo shehui kexue*, 1987, no. 3: 73–88. (Trans. in FBIS-China, 1 July 1987, K19–36.)

Yu Haocheng. *Minzhi fazhi shehuizhuyi* [Democracy, the rule of law, and socialism]. Beijing: Qunzhong Chubanshe, 1985.

Zeilik, Michael, Stephen A. Gregory, and Elske V. P. Smith. *Introductory Astronomy and Astrophysics*. New York: Saunders, 1992.

Zha Ruqiang. "Kexue shi yuelai yuezhongyao de shengchanli" [Science is an increasingly important force of production]. *Zhexue yanjiu*, 1978, no. 10: 42–46.

———. "Jianping xifang 'kexue zhexue' zhong guanyu kexue renshi fazhan de jizhong xueshuo" [A brief criticism of several theories in Western "philosophy of science" on the development of scientific knowledge]. *Zhexue yanjiu*, 1979, no. 11: 56–64.

———. "Ershi shiji ziran kexue si dachengjiu fengfule bianzheng ziranguan" [The four great achievements of twentieth-century science have enriched the dialectical view of nature]. *Zhongguo shehui kexue*, 1982, no. 4: 9–30.

———. "Ershi shiji ziran kexue de si dafaxian" [The four great discoveries of twentieth-century natural science]. *Zhexue yanjiu*, 1982, no. 6: 20–21.

———. "Makesi he ziran bianzhengfa" [Marx and natural dialectics]. *Ziran bianzhengfa tongxun*, 1983, no. 4: 4–10.

———. "Gongchanzhuyi yujian de zhenlixing he shijian biaozhun de weiyixing" [The truthfulness of communist prediction and the singularity of the practice criterion]. *Guangming ribao*, 24 October 1983, 3.

———. "Shilun chanye geming" [A tentative discussion of industrial revolutions]. *Zhongguo shehui kexue*, 1984, no. 6: 1–16. (Trans. in *Social Sciences in China*, 1985, no. 2: 75–91.)

———. "Ziranjie bianzhengfa fanchou tixi shexiang" [A proposal for a system of categories of dialectics in nature]. *Zhongguo shehui kexue*, 1985, no. 5: 33–58.

———. "Shilun xinxi shehui" [A tentative discussion of information societies]. *Zhexue yanjiu*, 1986, no. 3: 32–37, 46.

———. "Dui Liu Bing deng wu tongzhi 'shangque' de dabian" [Replying to the "discussion" of Liu Bing and the four other comrades]. *Zhongguo shehui kexue*, 1986, no. 5, 163–74.

———. "Kou maozi, fei'er polai" [Putting on hats and fair play]. *Ziran bianzhengfa tongxun*, 1986, no. 5: 69–71.

———. "Shi fazhan haishi quxiao ziran bianzhengfa?—Da Zhong Weiguang tongzhi" [Is it developing natural dialectics or abolishing it?—Responding to Comrade Zhong Weiguang]. *Zhexue yanjiu*, 1986, no. 6: 57–63.

———. "Weiwuzhuyi de yunyong yanyifa he weixinzhuyi de 'cong yuanze chufa'" [Materialism's use of the deductive method and idealism's "proceeding from principle"]. *Guangming ribao*, 8 December 1986, 3.

———. "Ziran bianzhengfa shi yige kexue tixi" [Natural dialectics is a scientific system]. *Ziran bianzhengfa yanjiu*, 1987, no. 1: 28–32.

———. "Zhengque de bianhu he shishiqiushi de fansi" [Reflections on correctly defending and seeking truth from facts]. *Guangming ribao*, 2 March 1987, 3.

———. "Ping 'Yuzhou shi yu wu'" [Criticizing "the universe began from nothing"]. *Zhongguo shehui kexue*, 1987, no. 3: 55–67.

———. "Ping 'Zhexue he wuli' ji qita" [Criticizing "Philosophy and physics" and others]. *Ziran bianzhengfa yanjiu*, 1987, no. 3: 61–76.

———. "Wuzhi jiegou cengci wuxian lun de zaizhengshi—Yu Jin Wulun tongzhi shangque" [Reaffirming the theory of the infinite levels of the structure of matter—A discussion with Comrade Jin Wulun]. *Ziran bianzhengfa yanjiu*, 1987, no. 5: 64–68.

———. "Kexue jingshen wei he wu—Zai da Xu Liangying tongzhi" [What sort of thing is the scientific spirit?—Again replying to Comrade Xu Liangying]. *Ziran bianzhengfa tongxun*, 1988, no. 3: 78, 77.

Zhexue yanjiu Commentator article. "Jiji fazhan bianzheng weiwuzhuyi ziranguan de yanjiu" [Actively develop research in dialectical materialism's view of nature]. *Zhexue yanjiu*, 1982, no. 4: 3–5.

Zhong Ku. "Woguo nongye hezuohua shi kexue shehuizhuyi de huida shengli" [The cooperativization of agriculture in our country was a great victory of scientific socialism]. *Nanjing Daxue xuebao (zhexue-shehui kexue)*, 1981, no. 4: 2–7.

Zhong Weiguang. "Shi ziran bianzhengfa, haishi Heige'ershi de ziran zhexue?" [Is it natural dialectics, or is it Hegelian natural philosophy?]. *Ziran bianzhengfa tongxun*, 1986, no. 3: 70–76.

Zhong Xuefu. "Zhexue bushi 'xintiao' erhshi kexue" [Philosophy is not "dogma" but science]. *Guangming ribao*, 19 January 1987, 3.

———. "Zhexue he wulixue guanxi de ruogan wenti" [Some problems concerning the relationship of philosophy and physics]. *Ziran bianzhengfa yanjiu*, 1987, no. 4: 1–6.

Zhongguo renming dacidian Editorial Board. *Who's Who In China: Current Leaders.* Beijing: Foreign Languages Press, 1989.

Zhou Chengkui. "Revamping Science and Technology System." *Beijing Review,* 1986, no. 24 (16 June): 21–27.

Zhou Hua. "Shehui jiegouzhong de kexue—Modun kexue shehuixue lilin de yige moshi" [Science in the structure of society—A model from Merton's sociological theory of science]. *Ziran bianzhengfa tongxun,* 1985, no. 3: 20–30.

Zhou Xun. "Zhonggong shehui kexue yanjiu de xianzhuang ji qianjing" [The present situation and prospects of Chinese Communist social science research]. *Qishiniandai* [The seventies], no. 107 (1978, no. 12): 42–50.

Zhou Yang. "Zhexue shehui kexue de fazhan guihua he baihua qifang, baijia zhengming de fangzhen" [The development plan for philosophy and the social sciences and the orientation of letting a hundred flowers bloom and a hundred schools contend]. *Zhexue yanjiu,* 1978, no. 10: 2–11.

Zhu Hongyuan and Du Dongsheng, "J/psi weizi de tiaozhan" [The challenge of the J/psi particle]. *Ziran bianzhengfa tongxun,* 1979, no. 1: 82–86.

Zi Zhongyun. "The Relationship of Chinese Traditional Culture to the Modernization of China: An Introduction to the Current Discussion." *Asian Survey,* vol. 27, no. 4 (April 1987): 442–58.

Ziman, John. *Public Knowledge.* Cambridge: Cambridge University Press, 1984.

———. *An Introduction to Science Studies: The Philosophical and Social Aspects of Science and Technology.* New York: Cambridge University Press, 1984.

Index

Academy of Sciences. *See* Chinese
Academy of Sciences
Academy of Social Sciences. *See* Chinese
Academy of Social Sciences
Ai Ying, criticized by Zha Ruqiang, 64

Bao Zunxin, signing of 1989 open letter,
15, 235, 268
Ben-David, Joseph, 261
Berlin, Isaiah, 270
Bohr, Niels, Copenhagen interpretation
of quantum theory pioneered by,
136; China toured by, 205
"Bourgeois liberalization," criticism of:
in 1981, 54; in 1987, 15, 43, 54, 132,
154
Brezhnev, Leonid I., 274, 277
Bulletin of Natural Dialectics (Ziran bianzhengfa tongxun), founding and
editorial supervision of, 130

Chen Bin, 83
Chen Boda, 208
Chen Duxiu: 1919 debate with Hu Shi,
243; views on politics and culture,
244; scientism of, 257, 261
Chen Xitong, condemnation of Tiananmen protests, 234
Chen Yi, 91, 104
Chen Yong, criticism of literary theorist
Liu Zaifu, 154
Chen Yun, 34, 228; expression of concern for intellectuals (1980), 85
Chinese Academy of Sciences (CAS): in
Cultural Revolution, 70; purge of
leftists, 87–88; post-Mao reconstitu-
tion of, 88–90; shift from Party ideology system, 91, 96–97, 103; Party
control over, 91–94; Party cadre obstruction of scientist leadership in,
93–94; reorientation of mission, 94–
96; impact of 1985 science reform
decision on, 114, 116; impact of
1987–88 "one academy, two systems"
reform on, 120–21, 122; restoration

of traditional governing procedures
in, 124
Chinese Academy of Social Sciences
(CASS): 1977 split from CAS, 96–97;
post-Mao institutional development
of, 98–102; Party supervision over,
102–3; integration into Party policy
processes, 103–6; impact of science
reforms on, 123
Chinese Association of Science and
Technology (CAST), post-Mao
resumption of activities of, 106
Chinese Communist Party (CCP): crisis
of confidence in, 10, 42–46; challenge
to legitimacy by science's norms,
18–19, 20–22; post-Mao revision of
Marxist-Leninist and Maoist doctrines, 33, 34–36, 38–42, 48, 125–26;
policy line of Eighth Party Congress
(1956), 34, 41, 49; and 1985 science
reform decision, 108, 112–14; 1984
economic reform decision of, 110
"Culture fever" (*wenhua re*), 11, 19, 246;
following CCP critique of Mao's
errors, 18, 193–94; and foreign ideas,
194–95; challenge to rationalism,
195–96

Dai Qing, signing of 1989 open letter, 14
Daniel, Yuli, 279
Deleuze, Gilles, 270
Democracy Wall movement (1978–
79), 53
Deng Liqun, 93; named CASS vice president, 97, 103; criticism of Fang Lizhi
and others, 227
Deng Weizhi, liberal view of revising
Marxism-Leninism, 65
Deng Xiaoping, 3, 31, 87; revision
of Marxist-Leninist and Maoist
doctrine, 5, 33, 34–36, 38–42, 48;
encouragement of technocratic
transformation of CCP, 10; utilitarian views of science, 17–18, 25, 62,
184, 273; and May Fourth legacy,